US SPECIAL OPERATIONS FORCES
IN ACTION

US SPECIAL OPERATIONS FORCES IN ACTION

The Challenge of Unconventional Warfare

THOMAS K. ADAMS

FRANK CASS
LONDON • PORTLAND, OR

First Published in 1998 in Great Britain by
FRANK CASS PUBLISHERS
Newbury House, 900 Eastern Avenue
London, IG2 7HH

and in the United States of America by
FRANK CASS PUBLISHERS
c/o ISBS, 5804 N.E. Hassalo Street
Portland, Oregon, 97213-3644

Reprinted in 2001
Website http://www.frankcass.com

British Library Cataloguing in Publication Data

Adams, Thomas K.
US Special Operations Forces in action : the challenge of
unconventional warfare
1. United States. Army. Special Forces – History
I. Title
356.1'67'0973

ISBN 0-7146-4795-0 (cloth)
ISBN 0-7146-4350-5 (paper)

Library of Congress Cataloging-in-Publication Data

Adams, Thomas K.
US Special Operations Forces in action : the challenge of
unconventional warfare / Thomas K. Adams.
p. cm.
Includes bibliographical references and index.
ISBN 0-7146-4795-0 (cloth). — ISBN 0-7146-4350-5 (pbk.)
1. Special forces (Military science)—United States. 2. United
States—History, Military. I. Title.
UA34.S64A33 1998
355.3'43'0973—dc21 97-29160
CIP

Typeset by Vitaset, Paddock Wood, Kent
Printed in Great Britain by
Bookcraft (Bath) Ltd., Midsomer Norton, Somerset

To ODA 502, 5th Special Forces Group, Republic of Vietnam and the grunts of A Co, 1st Battalion, 502nd Infantry, 101st Airborne Division (Air Mobile) 1965–66, none of whom thought they were anything special but all of whom were.

Contents

Acknowledgements

The author wishes to offer his profound thanks to the following persons, without whom this book would not have been possible. These individuals kindly and generously agreed to review the following sections, and provided many useful comments and insights. However, this is not meant to imply that they have any responsibility for the specific content of these sections. Any errors, omissions or oversights remain the sole responsibility of the author. Likewise, the opinions expressed and conclusions reached, except as otherwise noted, are solely those of the author.

General Content – Colonel Steven C. Hightower, US Army Special Forces, US Army War College, Carlisle Barracks, PA, 1995–97. Colonel Mark D. Boyatt, Deputy Chief of Staff for Operations, US Army, Special Operations Command, FT Bragg, North Carolina, 1996–97. Colonel Marland J. Burckhardt, Special Forces Intelligence Officer, Vietnam and JSOC; G2 XVIII Airborne Corps, Desert Shield/Storm.

Special Forces in Vietnam and the 1970s – Colonel Rod Paschall, Commander, SFOD-Delta, 1980–82; 3rd Battalion, 5th Special Forces Group, 1975–77; aide to the Commander, Special Warfare Center, 1963–64.

The Phoenix Program – Colonel Stuart Herrington, Province and District Advisor, Phoenix Program, South Vietnam, 1971 and 1972.

USSOCOM – General James Lindsay, Commander, US Special Operations Command, McDill Air Force Base, Florida, 1987–90.

Operation Provide Comfort – Brigadier General Richard Potter, Commander Task Force Alpha, Operation Provide Comfort, April–July 1991. LTC Dan Wakeman, Commander, C Co, 1st Bn 10th SFG, Operation Provide Comfort.

The Gulf War – General Bernard E. Trainor, USMC. LTC Michael B. Sternfeld, Advisor, Kuwaiti Task Force, 352nd Civil Affairs Command, January–May 1991. LTC Dan Wakeman, Commander, C Co, 1st Bn 10th SFG, Operation Proven Force, January–April 1991.

Somalia – Lieutenant Colonel Samuel J. Butler, Director of Planning, for both Headquarters UNOSOM II and US Forces, Somalia, April 1993–March 1994.

Panama – Lieutenant Colonel John Fishell (USAR), Chief, Policy and Strategy, J5 US Southern Command, August 1988–December 1989; also Military Support Group Panama, January–June 1990.

Haiti – Professor Ronald Schulz, strategist and Caribbean area specialist, US Army War College, Carlisle Barracks, PA. Brigadier General Richard Potter, Commander Joint Special Operations Task Force, Operation Uphold Democracy, September–October 1994.

Particular thanks are due to Colonel Daniel J. Kaufman, USMA, without whom this book would never have been begun, and to Dr Graham H. Turbiville of the US Army Foreign Military Studies Office, who encouraged this project and agreed to act as informal editor, and without whose support it would never have been completed.

List of illustrations

Glossary of acronyms

AFSOC	Air Force Special Operations Command
AH	Attack Helicopter
AID	Agency for International Development (also USAID)
ARCENT	US Army, Central Command
ARSOC	Army Special Operations Command
ARSOTF	Army Special Operations Task Force
ARVN	Army of the Republic of South Vietnam
AWC	Army War College
BG	Brigadier General
BN	Battalion
CA	Civil Affairs
CD	Counterdrug
CENTCOM	Central Command
CIA	Central Intelligence Agency
CIDG	Civilian Irregular Defense Group(s)
CINCCENT	Commander in Chief, Central Command
CINCPAC	Commander in Chief, Pacific Command
CM	Countermine
CMOC	Civil Military Operations Center
CORDS	Civilian Operations and Revolutionary Development Support
CP	Counterproliferation
CSAR	Combat Search and Rescue
CSOA	Combined Special Operations Area
CST	Coalition Support Team
CT	Combating Terrorism, also Counterterrorism
DA	Department of the Army, also Direct Action
DART	Disaster Assistance Response Team
DFT	Deployment for Training
DOD	Department of Defense
FAd'H	Force Armée du Haiti
FID	Foreign Internal Defense
GVN	Government of (South) Vietnam

HA	Humanitarian Assistance
HACC	Humanitarian Assistance Coordination Center
HNP	Haitian National Police
IDAD	Internal Defense and Development
IPSF	Interim Public Security Force
JCS	Joint Chiefs of Staff (US)
JGS	Joint General Staff (S. Vietnam)
JSOC	Joint Special Operations Command
JSOTF	Joint Special Operations Task Force
JTF	Joint Task Force
LEA	Law Enforcement Agency
LOC	Line of Communications
LTG	Lieutenant General
MACV	Military Assistance Command, Vietnam
MACV-SOG	Military Assistance Command, Vietnam Studies and Observation Group
MIST	Military Information Support Team
MNF	Multinational Force
MOOTW	Military Operations Other Than War
MRC	Major Regional Contingency
MRE	Meal, Ready to Eat
MTT	Mobile Training Team
NGO	Nongovernmental Organization
NLF	National Liberation Front (of South Vietnam)
NSAM	National Security Action Memorandum
NSC	National Security Council
NVA	North Vietnamese Army
OCPW	Office of the Chief of Psychological Warfare
ODA	Operational Detachment Alpha
ODB	Operational Detachment Bravo
OFDA	Office of Foreign Disaster Assistance
OSD	Office of the Secretary of Defense
OSS	Office of Strategic Services
PF	Popular Forces (formerly Self Defense Corps)
POG	Psychological Operations Group
POTF	Psychological Operations Task Force
Psyops	Psychological Operations
QRF	Quick Reaction Force
RF	Regional Forces (formerly Civil Guard)
RPG	Rocket-Propelled Grenade
SAS	Special Air Service (British)
SBS	Special Boat Squadron (Navy)

SBU	Special Boat Unit (Navy)
SEAL	Sea, Air and Land Forces (Navy)
SF	Special Forces (Army)
SFG	Special Forces Group (Army)
SFOD	Special Forces Operational Detachment (Army)
SMU	Special Mission Unit
SNA	Somali National Alliance
SOAR	Special Operations Aviation Regiment (Army)
SOC	Special Operations Command
SOCCENT	Special Operations Command, Central
SOF	Special Operations Forces
SOG	Special Operations Group
SORO	Special Operations Research Office
SOS	Special Operations Squadron (Air Force)
SOW	Special Operations Wing (Air Force)
SR	Strategic Reconnaissance, also Special Reconnaissance
SWC	Special Warfare Center (same as USAJFK)
TDT	Tactical Dissemination Team
TF	Task Force
TMD	Theater Missile Defense
TRADOC	Training and Doctrine Command (Army)
UH	Utility Helicopter
UNITAF	United Task Force
UNMIH	United Nations Mission in Haiti
UNOSOM	United Nations Operation in Somalia
USAID	US Agency for International Development
USAJFKIMA	US Army John F. Kennedy Institute for Military Assistance
USAJFKSWCS	US Army John F. Kennedy Special Warfare Center and School
USASOC	US Army Special Operations Command
USC	US Congress, also United Somali Congress
USCENTCOM	US Central Command
USDOD	US Department of Defense
USMA	US Military Academy (at West Point, NY)
USSOCOM	US Special Operations Command
UW	Unconventional Warfare
VC	Viet Cong
VCI	Viet Cong Infrastructure

Glossary of terms

Except as otherwise noted, these definitions are edited from '1997 Joint Posture Statement – United States Special Operations Forces' United States Special Operations Command, 1997.

aiding and assisting host-nation military – foreign internal defense activity involving operations to train host-nation individuals and military units in basic infantry and maritime skills; provide advice and assistance to host-nation military leaders; provide training host-nation military forces on tactics, techniques, and procedures required to protect a host nation from subversion, lawlessness, and insurgency; and develop indigenous leadership, organizational, and individual skills.

amphibious warfare – direct action operations launched from the sea by naval and landing forces against a hostile, or potentially hostile, shore. Amphibious warfare operations include pre-assault cover and diversionary operations, naval gunfire support, initial/terminal guidance for landing craft, surf observation, obstacle clearance, and other advance force operations.

anti-surface warfare – direct action operations conducted against enemy surface targets, including combatants.

antiterrorism (AT) – defensive measures, including intelligence and counterintelligence support, to reduce the vulnerability of individuals and property to terrorist acts, to include limited response and containment by local military forces. It includes that part of security concerned with physical measures designed to safeguard personnel; to prevent unauthorized access to equipment, installations, material, and documents; and to safeguard them against espionage, sabotage, damage, and theft. It also includes personal protective services that consist primarily of executive protection and training efforts in terrorist threat awareness.

armed reconnaissance – a special reconnaissance activity involving locating and attacking targets of opportunity, i.e. enemy materiel, personnel, and facilities, in assigned general areas or along assigned

US Special Operations Forces in Action

ground communication routes. Armed reconnaissance is not conducted for the purpose of attacking specific identified targets.

campaign plan – a plan for a series of related military operations aimed at accompanying a strategic or operational objective within a given time and space.

civil-administrative operations – establishment of an administration by the US National Command Authorities in (1) friendly territory, under agreement with the government of the area concerned, to exercise certain authority, normally the function of the local government or in (2) hostile territory, occupied by US or coalition forces, where the US military exercise executive, legislative, and judicial authority until an indigenous civil government can be established. Civil administration also consists of administrative assistance to legitimate host-nation governments.

Civil Affairs (CA) – a SOF principal mission involving advising and assisting commanders in establishing, maintaining, influencing, or exploiting relations between military forces and civil authorities, both governmental and nongovernmental, and the civilian population in a friendly, neutral, or hostile area of operation in order to facilitate military operations and consolidate operational objectives. CA operations include providing advice and assistance in population and resource control measures; civic action and civil assistance; organization of auxiliaries; political warfare; identification, location, and acquisition of local resources and facilities; arranging for host-nation support for deployed US forces; actions to minimize civilian interference with military operations; managing dislocated civilian populations; and, in the post-hostilities phase, CA forces assist in the effort to restore the civilian infrastructure and the transition from military to civilian control.

civil–military operations – a program of planned activities in support of military operations which enhance the relationship between military forces and civilian authorities and populations. These operations promote the development of favorable emotions, attitudes, or behavior in neutral, friendly, or hostile groups. Specific activities may include population and resources control, foreign nation support, humanitarian assistance, military civic action, and civil defense.

civil–military operations center (CMOC) – an on-the-ground 'nerve center' for civil–military operations designed to provide interface with all non DOD and other US government agency counterparts and counterparts in private, volunteer, nongovernmental, and international organizations. A CMOC may be established by the joint force commander to integrate and harmonize the various political, humanitarian, and military aspects of a mission.

clandestine operations – activities sponsored or conducted by governmental departments or agencies in such a way as to assure secrecy or concealment. Clandestine operations differ from covert operations in that emphasis is placed on concealment of the operations rather than on concealment of the identity of the sponsor. In special operations, an activity may be both covert and clandestine, and may focus equally on operational considerations and intelligence-related activities.

coalition support – a SOF collateral activity to improve the inter-action of coalition partners and US military forces. It includes training coalition partners on tactics and techniques, providing communications to integrate them into the coalition command and intelligence structure, and establishing liaison to coordinate combat support and combat service support.

coastal patrol and interdiction – a special reconnaissance activity involving area denial, interdiction, support, and intelligence operations in coastal regions. Its objective is to halt or limit the enemy's warfighting capability by denying movement of vital resources over coastal and riverine lines of communication. Seaward perimeter, harbor security, and escort duties are typical support operations. Coastal patrol and interdiction may be a stand-alone mission or may support other fleet and joint efforts, such as riverine, amphibious assault, blockade, and counterdrug operations.

combat search and rescue (CSAR) – a specific task performed by rescue forces to effect the recovery of distressed personnel during wartime or contingency operations. In accordance with joint doctrine, each service and USSOCOM are responsible for perform-ing CSAR for their respective forces; therefore, CSAR is a SOF collateral activity.

combating terrorism (CBT) – a SOF principal mission involving actions, including antiterrorism (defensive measures taken to reduce vulnerability, to terrorist acts) and counterterrorism (offensive measures taken to prevent, deter, and respond to terrorism), taken to oppose terrorism throughout the entire threat spectrum.

command and control warfare (C2W) – as a subset of information warfare, C2W is the integrated use of operations security (OPSEC), joint military deception, Psychological Operations (Psyops), elec-tronic warfare (EW), and physical destruction, mutually supported by intelligence, to deny information to, influence, degrade, or destroy adversary command and control capabilities while protecting friendly command and control capabilities against such actions.

contingency – an event involving military forces caused by natural disaster, terrorists, subversives, or required military operations. Owing to the uncertainty of the situation, contingencies require plans, rapid response, and special procedures to ensure the safety and readiness of personnel, installations, and equipment.

conventional war – author's definition. Direct military combat or the threat of such combat between the organized professional military establishments of states. It normally involves large-scale sustained combat operations to achieve national interests, objectives, or to protect national interests.

counterdrug (CD) activities – those active measures taken to detect, monitor, and counter production, trafficking, and use of illegal drugs; a SOF collateral activity.

countermine (CM) activities – a SOF collateral activity to attempt to reduce or eliminate the threat to noncombatants and friendly military forces posed by mines, booby-traps, and other explosive devices. Demining and mine awares comprise CM activities.

counterproliferation (CP) – a SOF principal mission which refers to the activities of the Department of Defense across the full range of US government efforts to combat proliferation of weapons of mass destruction (WMD), including application of military power to protect US forces and interests; intelligence collection and analysis; and support of diplomacy, arms control, export controls. As appropriate, accomplishment of these activities may require coordination with other US government agencies.

counterterrorism (CT) – offensive measures to prevent, deter, and respond to terrorism. Counterterrorism missions may include hostage rescue, recovery of sensitive material from terrorist organizations, and attack of terrorist infrastructure.

covert operations – operations which are planned and executed to conceal the identity of, or permit plausible denial by, the sponsor. A covert operation differs from a clandestine operation in that emphasis is placed on the concealment of the identity of the sponsor rather than on concealment of the operation.

deployment – the movement of forces and materiel to desired areas of operation from origin or home station through destination, specifically including intra-continental USA, inter-theater, and intra-theater movement legs, staging, and holding areas.

direct action (DA) – a SOF principal mission involving short-duration strikes and other small-scale offensive actions by SOF to seize, destroy, capture, recover, or inflict damage on designated personnel or materiel. In the conduct of these operations, SOF may employ raid, ambush, or direct-assault tactics; emplace mines and other munitions; conduct stand-off attacks by fire from air, ground, or maritime platforms; provide terminal guidance for precision-guided munitions; conduct independent sabotage; and conduct anti-ship operations.

dry deck shelter (DDS) – a shelter module that attaches to the hull of a specially configured submarine to provide the submarine with the capability to launch and recover special operations personnel, vehicles, and equipment while submerged. The dry deck shelter provides a working environment at one atmosphere for the special operations element during transit and has structural integrity to the collapse depth of the host submarine.

employment – the strategic, operational, or tactical use of forces and materiel in an area or theater of operations.

environmental reconnaissance – a special reconnaissance activity involving operations to collect and report critical hydrographic, geological, and meteorological information.

force multiplier – a capability that, when added to and employed by a combat force, significantly increases the combat potential of that force and thus enhances the probability of successful mission accomplishment.

foreign internal defense (FID) – a principal SOF mission involving participation by civilian and military agencies of a government in any of the action programs taken by another government to free and protect its society from subversion, lawlessness, and insurgency.

guerrilla warfare – an unconventional warfare activity involving military and paramilitary operations conducted by irregular, predominately indigenous forces in enemy-held or hostile territory. Guerrilla forces primarily employ raid and ambush tactics against enemy vulnerabilities.

host nation – a nation which receives the forces, supplies, and/or services of allied nations to be located on, operate in, or transit through its territory.

humanitarian assistance (HA) – programs conducted to relieve or reduce the results of natural or manmade disasters or other endemic conditions, such as human pain, disease, hunger, or privation, that might present a serious threat to life or that can result in great damage to or loss of property; a SOF collateral activity requiring significant interagency coordination.

infiltration – the movement through or into an area or territory occupied by either friendly or enemy troops or organizations. The movement is made, either by small groups or by individuals, at extended or irregular intervals. When used in connection with the enemy, it implies that contact is avoided.

information superiority – the degree of dominance in the information domain, which permits the conduct of operations without effective opposition.

information systems – the entire infrastructure, organization, personnel, and components that collect, process, store, transmit, display, disseminate, and act on information.

information warfare (IW) – a principal SOF mission involving actions taken to achieve information superiority by affecting adversary information, information-based processes, information systems, and computer-based networks, when defending one's own information, information based processes, information systems, and computer-based networks.

insurgency – an organized movement aimed at the overthrow of a constituted government through the use of subversion and armed conflict

joint civil–military operations task force (JCMOTF) – a JCMOTF is composed of civil–military operations units from more than one Service or other US agency, formed to carry out Civil Affairs in support of a joint force commander's campaign or other contingencies.

joint force commander (JFC) – a general term applied to a commander authorized to exercise combatant command (command authority) or operational control over a joint force.

joint psychological operations task force (JPOTF) – a JPOTF is composed of Psychological Operations (Psyop) units from more than one Service, formed to carry out Psyop in support of a joint force commander's campaign or other contingencies.

joint special operations air component commander (JSOACC) – the JSOACC is the aviation component commander under a joint force special operations component commander or a joint force commander responsible for planning and executing joint special operations aviation missions. The JSOACC is an integration element which may be used for operational command and control of SOF.

joint special operations task force (JSOTF) – joint task force composed of special operations fits from more than one Service, formed to carry out a specific special operation or prosecute special operations in support of a joint force commander's campaign or other operations. The JSOTF may have conventional or other non-special operations units signed or attached to support specific missions.

joint task force (JTF) – a force composed of assigned or attached elements of the Army, Navy (or the Marine Corps), and Air Force (two or more of these Services), which is constituted and so designated by the Secretary of Defense or by the commander of a unified command, a specified command, or an existing joint task force.

low-intensity conflict (LIC) – political-military confrontation between contending states or groups below conventional war and above the routine, peaceful competition among states. It frequently involves protracted struggles of competing principles and ideologies. Low-intensity conflict ranges from subversion to the use of armed force. It is waged by combination of means employing political, economic, informational, and military instruments. Low-intensity conflicts are often localized but contain regional and global security implications.

Major Force Program (MFP) 11 – one of the programs in the Future Years Defense Program. FP 11 resources the day-to-day training and operations of special operations forces. Additionally, FP 11 resources SOF-peculiar research, development, testing, and evaluation; procurement; and military construction.

military information support team (MIST) – MIST provides the capability to plan and implement information campaigns aimed at selected target audiences to educate and gain acceptance of, and support for, a sponsor's policy initiatives and/or operational activities. MISTs normally comprise military and civilian personnel from the Army's active Psychological Operations group. The individuals assigned to this unit are highly skilled in communication techniques applicable to particular countries or regions of the world and generally have area expertise, in-country experience, and linguistic ability. They are trained and equipped to operate in austere field conditions.

Military Operations Other Than War (MOOTW) – operations conducted to deter war, resolve conflict, promote peace and support civil authorities. It seeks to prevent, preempt or limit potential hostilities. Political considerations permeate all levels of MOOTW and the military may not be the primary agency involved. Types of MOOTW include arms control, combating terrorism, humanitarian assistance, insurgency and counterinsurgency, noncombatant evacuation, counterdrug operations, shows of force, nation assistance, ensuring freedom of air and sea navigation, peace operations, support to civil authorities, disaster assistance, recovery operations, strikes and raids, insurgency and counterinsurgency. (Per JP 3-07, *Military Operations Other Than War*, US DOD, 1995, vii, ix.)

mine warfare – a direct action mission activity involving the strategic and operational use of mines and their countermeasures. Mine warfare operations include offensive and defensive mine laying, detection of enemy minefields, and detection and neutralization of very-shallow water mines.

National Command Authorities (NCA) – the President and the Secretary of Defense or their duly deputized alternates or successors. The term signifies constitutional authority to direct the Armed Forces in their execution of military action.

naval special warfare (NSW) – a specific term describing a designated naval warfare specialty and covering operations generally accepted as being unconventional in nature and, in many cases, covert or clandestine in character. These operations include using specially trained forces assigned to conduct unconventional warfare, psychological operations, beach and coastal reconnaissance, operational deception operations, counterinsurgency operations, coastal and river interdiction, and certain special tactical intelligence collection operations that are in addition to those intelligence functions normally required for planning and conducting special operations in a hostile environment.

naval special warfare group (NSWG) – a permanent Navy echelon III major command to which most naval special warfare forces are assigned for some operational and all administrative purposes. It consists of a group headquarters with command and control, communications, and support staff; sea–air–land teams; and sea–air–land delivery vehicle teams. The group is the source of all deployed naval special warfare forces and administratively supports the naval special warfare units assigned to the theater combatant commanders. The group staff provides general operational direction and coordinates the activities of its subordinate units. A NSWG is capable of task organizing to meet a wide variety of requirements.

naval special warfare unit (NSWU) – a permanent Navy organization forward based to control and support attached naval special warfare forces.

overt operations – an operation conducted openly without concealment.

paramilitary forces – forces or groups which are distinct from the regular armed forces of any country but resembling them in organization, equipment, training, or mission.

peace operations – the umbrella term which encompasses peacekeeping, peace enforcement, and any other military, paramilitary, or nonmilitary action taken in support of a diplomatic peace-making process.

poststrike reconnaissance – special reconnaissance missions undertaken for the purpose of gathering information used to measure results of a strike.

precision destruction operations – a direct action mission activity involving operations against targets where minimal collateral damage is acceptable, requiring highly sophisticated and/or timed detonation of specific amounts of explosives emplaced in exact locations to accomplish mission objectives. Precision destruction operations are conducted against targets where precision-guided munitions cannot guarantee first-strike success or when the contents of the facility must be destroyed without damage to the facility.

providing population security – a foreign internal defense activity involving the supervision of tactical operations conducted by host-nation military units to neutralize and destroy insurgency threats, isolate insurgents from the civil population, and protect the civil population. Designated SOF units may also train select host-nation forces to conduct counterterrorist missions.

Psychological Operations (Psyops) – a SOF principal mission involving planned operations to convey selected information and indicators to foreign audiences to influence their emotions, motives, objective reasoning, and ultimately the behavior of foreign governments, organizations, groups, and individuals. The purpose of Psyops is to induce or reinforce foreign attitudes and behaviors favorable to the originator's objectives.

raids, ambushes, and direct assaults – direct action operations designed to achieve specific, well-defined, and often time-sensitive results of strategic or operational significance. They frequently occur beyond the reach of tactical weapon systems and selective strike capabilities of conventional forces. Such operations typically involve an attack on critical targets, such as the interdiction of lines of communication or other target systems; the location, capture, or recovery of designated personnel or materiel; or the seizure, destruction, or neutralization of enemy facilities in support of conventional forces or in advance of their arrival.

Rangers – rapidly deployable, airborne light infantry personnel organized and trained to conduct highly complex, joint, direct-action operations in coordination with, or in support of other special operations units of all Services. Rangers can also execute direct-action operations in support of conventional, nonspecial operations missions conducted by a combatant commander and can operate as conventional light infantry when properly augmented with other elements of combined arms.

recovery operations – direct action operations to locate, recover, and restore personnel or materiel held captive, isolated, or threatened in sensitive, denied, or contested areas to friendly control. Special operations recovery missions are often characterized by detailed planning, rehearsal, and thorough intelligence analysis. These operations employ unconventional tactics, techniques, clandestine search, indigenous assistance, and the frequent use of ground-combat elements.

sabotage – an unconventional warfare activity involving an act(s) intended to injure, interfere with, or obstruct the national defense of a country by willfully injuring or destroying, or attempting to injure or destroy, any national defense or war materiel, premises, or utilities, including human and natural resources. Sabotage selectively disrupts, destroys, or neutralizes hostile capabilities with a minimum expenditure of manpower and materiel.

sea–air–land (SEAL) delivery vehicle – wet submersibles designed to conduct clandestine reconnaissance, direct-action, and passenger-delivery missions in maritime environments.

SEAL team – a naval force specially organized, trained, and equipped to conduct special operations in maritime, littoral, and riverine environments.

security assistance (SA) – a group of programs authorized by the Foreign Assistance Act of 1961, as amended, and the Arms Export Control Act of 1976, as amended, or related statutes by which the United States provides defense articles, military training, and other defense-related services by grant, loan, credit, or cash sales in furtherance of national policies and objectives. As a SOF collateral activity, SOF's role in SA is primarily to provide mobile training teams and other forms of training assistance.

special activities – actions conducted abroad in support of national foreign-policy objectives that are planned and executed so that the role of the US government is not apparent or acknowledged publicly. SOF may perform any of their primary missions during special activities, subject to limitations imposed by Executive Order 12333. The conduct of special activities requires a Presidential finding and congressional oversight.

special boat units (SBU) – those naval special warfare forces organized, trained, and equipped to conduct or support naval special warfare, riverine warfare, coastal patrol and interdiction, and joint special operations with patrol boats or other combatant craft designed primarily for special operations support.

Special Forces (SF) – US Army forces organized, trained, and equipped specifically to conduct special operations in the full range of SOF principal mission areas less Civil Affairs and Psychological Operations.

Special Forces Group (SFG) – a combat arms organization capable of planning, conducting, and supporting special operations activities in all operational environments in peace, conflict, and war. It consists of a group headquarters and headquarters company, a support company, and Special Forces battalions. The group can operate as a single unit, but normally the battalions plan and conduct operations from widely separated locations. The group provides general operational direction and synchronizes the activities of subordinate battalions. Although principally structured for unconventional warfare, SFG units are capable of task organizing to meet specific requirements.

special operations (SO) – operations conducted by specially organized, trained, and equipped military and paramilitary forces to achieve military, political, economic, or psychological objectives by unconventional military means in hostile, denied, or politically sensitive areas. These operations are conducted during war and operations other than war, independently or in coordination with operations of conventional or other non-special operations forces. Political-military considerations frequently shape special operations, requiring clandestine, covert, or low-visibility techniques and oversight at the national level. Special operations differ from conventional operations in degree of physical and political risk, operational techniques, mode of employment, independence from friendly support, and dependence on detailed operational intelligence and indigenous assets.

special operations command (SOC) – a subordinate unified or other joint command established by a joint force commander to plan, coordinate, conduct, and support joint special operations within the joint force commander's assigned area of responsibility/joint operations area (draft definition).

special operations forces (SOF) – those active and reserve component forces of the Military Services designated by the Secretary of Defense and specifically organized, trained, and equipped to conduct and support special operations.

special operations group (SOG) – a flexible, administrative, and tactical Air Force Special Operations Forces unit composed of two or more squadrons.

special operations-peculiar – a term that refers to equipment, materiel, supplies, and services required for special operations mission support for which there is no broad conventional force requirement. This includes standard items used by other DOD forces but modified for SOF; items initially designed for, or used by, SOF until adapted for use as Service-common by other DOD forces; and items approved by USCINCSOC as critically urgent for the immediate accomplishment of a special operations mission but not normally procured by USSOCOM. It often includes nondevelopmental or special category items incorporating evolving technology but may include stocks of obsolete weapons and equipment designed to support indigenous personnel who do not possess sophisticated operational capabilities (draft definition).

special operations squadron (SOS) – an Air Force Special Operations Forces organization consisting of two or more flights of aircraft, normally of the same type; a basic administrative aviation unit.

special operations wing (SOW) – an Air Force Special Operations Forces unit composed normally of one primary mission group and the necessary supporting organizations, i.e. organizations to render supply, maintenance, hospitalization, and other services required by the primary mission group(s).

special reconnaissance (SR) – a SOF principal mission involving reconnaissance and surveillance actions conducted by SOF to obtain or verify, by visual observation or other collection methods, information concerning the capabilities, intentions, and activities of an actual or potential enemy or to secure data concerning the meteorological, hydrographic, or geographic characteristics of a particular area. It includes target acquisition, area assessment, and poststrike reconnaissance.

special tactics teams – an Air Force team composed primarily of special operations combat control and pararescue personnel. The team supports joint special operations by selecting, surveying, and establishing assault zones; providing assault zone terminal guidance and air traffic control; conducting direct action missions; providing medical care and evacuation; and coordinating, planning, and conducting air, ground, and naval fire-support operations.

stand-off attacks – direct action attacks by weapon systems. Stand-off attacks can be conducted by air, maritime, or ground platforms or units. When the target can be sufficiently damaged or destroyed without the commitment of close-combat forces, these attacks can be performed as independent actions.

sub-unified command – a subordinate command, composed of forces from two or more Military Departments, assigned specific military responsibilities within a unified command's area of operation by the authority establishing the subordinate command.

subversion – an unconventional warfare activity designed to undermine the military, economic, psychological, or political strength or morale of a regime or nation. The nature of subversion dictates that the underground elements perform clandestinely the bulk of the activity.

support to escape and evasion networks – an unconventional warfare activity that assists military personnel and other selected persons in moving from an enemy-held, hostile, or sensitive area to areas under friendly control; avoid capture if unable to return to an area of friendly control; and, once captured, escape.

target and threat assessment – a special reconnaissance activity involving operations conducted to detect, identify, locate, and assess a target to permit effective employment of weapons or the survey of a target to measure the results of a conventional or nuclear, biological, or chemical strike.

terminal guidance operations – direct action operations conducted by SOF to direct munitions at designated targets.

unconventional warfare (UW) – US DOD definition. A SOF principal mission involving a broad spectrum of military and paramilitary operations, normally of long duration, predominately conducted by indigenous or surrogate forces who are organized, trained, *source.* supported, and directed, in varying degrees, by *er as the* *sive, low-* UW includes guerrilla warfare and o*th* *indirect* visibility, covert, or clandestine activities of subversion, sabotage, intelligence activities, and evasion and escape.

unconventional warfare (UW) – author's definition. Those military activities conducted within a conflict environment that are not directed toward or directly supporting conventional warfare. It includes humanitarian operations, complex emergencies, insurgency and counterinsurgency, support to civil authority, nation-building and some forms of subversion, sabotage and similar activities. Intelligence gathering is an incidental function in most forms of UW. It is distinguished from conventional warfare chiefly by the fact that UW does not seek to defeat or destroy enemy military forces in combat.

unified command – a command with broad continuing missions under a single commander, composed of forces from two or more Military Departments, and established by the President, through the Secretary of Defense, with the advice and assistance of the Chairman of the Joint Chiefs of Staff.

weapons of mass destruction (WMD) – in arms-control usage, weapons that are capable of a high order of destruction and/or of being used in such a manner as to destroy large numbers of people. Can be nuclear, chemical, biological, and radiological weapons, but excludes the means of transporting or propelling the weapon where such means is a separable and divisible part of the weapon (draft definition).

1 What are special operations all about?

The US armed forces, like the militaries of all modern major powers, are trained, structured and equipped for World War II-like clashes of maneuver warfare – massive tank battles surging across the countryside, accompanied by apocalyptic doses of artillery and airpower. This is called 'conventional warfare', meaning that it follows the established conventions for the conduct of military combat. The problem is that this kind of bruising conventional mechanized combat has happened to the USA's military forces exactly once in the past 50 years: this was the Iraqi war of 1991, and it lasted not quite six days. The rest of the time, the armed forces have been doing something else.

During that same 50 years, tens of thousands of US service personnel, including some women, have died in armed clashes; not only in the slogging infantry combat of Korea and the endless bloodletting of Vietnam, but also in a mind-boggling variety of ambiguous, smaller-scale conflicts. During the same period, a particular capability was developed to deal with this array of lesser, but messy, politically charged situations that often straddled the tenuous boundary between an uneasy peace and something that was not quite war – Somalia, Haiti, Rwanda, El Salvador and Nicaragua to name a few. Generically, these ill-defined, constantly shifting forms of conflict can be termed 'unconventional warfare' (UW) because they do not follow the conventions of military conflict. They are not usually waged by the professional armed forces of a state, warring forces do not usually attempt to seize and hold terrain, and sometimes they are not even waged for a specific reason.

Unconventional warfare (UW) – US DOD (Department of Defense) definition. An SOF (Special Operations Forces) principal mission involving a broad spectrum of military and paramilitary operations, normally of long duration, predominately conducted by indigenous or surrogate forces who are organized, trained, equipped, supported and directed, in varying degrees, by an external source. UW includes guerrilla warfare and other direct offensive, low-visibility, covert or clandestine operations, as well as the indirect activities of subversion, sabotage, intelligence activities, and evasion and escape.

Unconventional warfare (UW) – author's definition. Those military activities conducted within a conflict environment that are not directed toward or directly supporting conventional warfare, including humanitarian operations, complex emergencies, insurgency and counterinsurgency, some forms of subversion, sabotage and similar activities. Intelligence gathering is an incidental function in most forms of UW. UW is distinguished from conventional warfare chiefly by the fact that it does not seek to defeat or destroy enemy military forces in combat.

There is a wide variety of unconventional threats available, many lumped together by the US Department of Defense as MOOTW (Military Operations Other Than War), now (1998) being referred to as Stability and Support Operations (SASO). These include, but are not limited to, humanitarian assistance, insurgency and counterinsurgency, noncombatant evacuation, counterdrug operations, shows of force, nation assistance, ensuring freedom of air and sea navigation, peace operations, disaster assistance, recovery operations, strikes and raids, and more (JCS, Joint Pub 3-07, *Military Operations Other Than War*, 1995, ix).

Many of these tasks, for example, freedom of navigation missions or strikes and raids, can easily be conducted by conventional forces. However, some situations involve complex combinations of missions such as humanitarian or disaster assistance, nation assistance and perhaps even counterinsurgency, all occurring at once in the same area. The Haiti intervention of 1994 is an example of such a mission.[1]

This book argues that, for the most part, the conventional warfighting forces of the USA are not the best military forces for such missions. These situations are characterized by lack of a defined enemy, the need for persuasion, negotiation and even community leadership, but also by the presence of significant elements ready and perhaps eager to resort to deadly force. The component of the US military best prepared for these conflicts is the Special Operations Forces.

WHAT DO WE MEAN BY SPECIAL OPERATIONS FORCES?

The conventional military forces of the US Department of Defense are commonly referred to as 'General Purpose Forces'. The term 'Special Operations Forces' has come to include a wide variety of military organizations, often with very different missions. This book argues that a number of these organizations perform essentially the same missions as conventional (non-SOF) forces. The Army Ranger Battalions, Army special operations aviation forces and nearly all Navy and Air Force SOF fall into this category. Others, such as the Army's Special Forces Operational Detachment Delta, perform very narrow, specialized functions. Still others, notably Army Special Forces, actually perform functions that make them well suited for unconventional warfare of the kind described here.

The best known of the US special operating units is the Army Special Forces (SF), better known as the 'Green Berets'. First brought to prominence during the Vietnam War, Army SF acquired an image as deadly, commando-style, jungle fighters, which has not diminished over the years. In addition, the US Navy and Air Force have created their own special operations units, on a much smaller scale than the Army. The Air Force units, in particular, function chiefly to support Army SOF by providing transportation, medical evacuation and fire support.

The principal SOF organizations within each service are:

Army

About 30,000 active and reserve soldiers are assigned to the US Army Special Operations Command (USASOC). Except for the 1st, 5th and 10th SF Groups and reserve units, most are located at Fort Bragg, North Carolina. The principal elements of USASOC are :

1. *Special Forces* (SF): SF are organized in five more-or-less geographically oriented, active-duty Special Forces Groups – the 1st, 3rd, 5th, 7th and 10th. Two other groups, the 19th and 20th, are in the National Guard. Each group has a headquarters, a support company, three battalions and an intelligence unit. Each battalion has three companies and a support company. Companies are also referred to as operational detachments bravo, or 'ODBs'. Each company has a headquarters and six operational detachments alpha, or 'A Teams', of 12 personnel. The team members are a commander (captain), a technician, who functions as a deputy (warrant officer), and ten noncommissioned officers (sergeants), specializing respectively in operations, intelligence, light and heavy weapons, medicine, communications, engineering and demolitions. Each team member is 'cross-trained' in at least two specialties other than their primary one. The members of these groups receive language training and

cultural orientation appropriate to their anticipated area of operations. Their basic function is to organize and train foreign military and paramilitary personnel. However, the Groups are assigned a wide variety of missions, including strategic reconnaissance and direct action (raids and the like). These are the most flexible of all special operations organizations.

2. *Rangers*: Also known as the 75th Infantry Regiment (Ranger). These units are elite, airborne (i.e. parachute) light infantry. The regiment has three battalions, all stationed at separate installations. Each battalion has a headquarters company, support elements and three rifle companies. Each company is composed of three rifle platoons and a weapons platoon with machine guns and mortars. Rangers perform a full spectrum of infantry tasks at a very high level of proficiency. Their special function is to seize and hold enemy airfields or other installations by parachute or helicopter assault.

3. *Special Operations Aviation* (SOA): The principal unit is the 160th Special Operations Aviation Regiment (SOAR), although separate Special Aviation Squadrons also exist, one of which is permanently stationed in Panama. These are helicopter units including observation, transportation and attack aircraft. Principal aircraft types are the MH-6, AH-6J, MH-60K and MH-47E. Some units are organized with a single aircraft type, while others are mixed. SOA provides aviation support to Army SOF through insertion/extraction, attack, medical evacuation, electronic warfare and other functions.

4. *Special Support Units*: The 528th Special Operations Support Battalion and the 112th Special Operations Signal Battalion both at Fort Bragg, North Carolina, provide general support for Army SOF. Other specialized support units provide services and support to specific Army SOF including Special Mission Units.

5. *Psychological Operations* (Psyops): There is one active duty Psyops unit, the 4th Psychological Operations Group, with five battalions, totaling about 1,300 personnel. There are two reserve Groups. Psyops units assess the information environment, and develop, produce and disseminate media products, including leaflets, posters, newspapers, radio and TV broadcasts and other items. Tactical loudspeaker teams provide another means for military commanders to communicate with the civil population in the area of operations. Psyop forward-liaison detachments are located in Europe, Hawaii and Panama.

6. *Civil Affairs* (CA): There is one active duty CA unit, the 96th Civil Affairs Bn, with about 300 personnel. This is a general purpose unit. The remaining 97 percent of the US armed forces CA capacity, or 24 battalions, is in the Army reserve. CA units assist local governments at all levels, supporting military operations by establishing relationships between military forces and local civil authorities. In the absence of local government, they may assist in its restoration. CA skills include disaster assessment and coordination with relief and disaster assistance organizations. CA reserve skills include the full range of governmental functions including administration, safety, public health, education, agricultural and other forms of assistance.

Navy

About 5,500 active and reserve sailors are assigned to the Naval Special Warfare Command (NAVSPECWARCOM). The principal operational commands of NAVSPECWARCOM are Naval Special Warfare Group One at Coronado, California and Naval Special Warfare Group Two at Little Creek, Virginia. A Development Group is responsible for developing requirements and testing new equipment, techniques and procedure. The Atlantic and Pacific Fleets also operate eight nuclear submarines capable of clandestine insertion and extraction of SOF. The principal elements of the command are:

1. *Sea–Air–Land Teams* (SEALs): There are six SEAL teams. Generally, a team consists of 230 persons configured as a headquarters, support departments, and 8 platoons of about 16 men each. Each platoon can operate as a platoon, two squads or four elements. About 40 personnel are assigned to the departments which include communications, intelligence, diving, air operations and similar command, control and support functions. All SEALs are highly qualified with light weapons and explosives, and as swimmers, divers and parachutists. They perform a variety of functions, including maritime interdiction, reconnaissance and raiding, often operating from aircraft, surface craft and submarines. SEALs are generally agreed to be the most physically fit of all special operations units.

2. *Special Boat Units* (SBUs): There are two Special Boat Squadron Headquarters and five SBUs. These are surface-warfare units designed to support SOF (especially SEALs) with transportation, infiltration, fire support and supply. Organization varies among the

SBUs. Generally, they are composed of a headquarters and some number of combatant craft detachments. Types of craft include the 31-foot River Patrol Boats, the 82-foot, high-speed Mark V Special Operations Craft, the 30-foot Rigid Inflatable Boat and others. The Naval Special Warfare Groups also operate a total of 13 seagoing, Cyclone Class, Patrol Coastal (PC) ships (170 foot).

3. *SEAL delivery vehicle teams*: There are two SDV (Swimmer Delivery Vehicle) Teams. These are specialized teams that provide and maintain four-man mini-submarines used for SEAL infiltration. Each team has a logistic element, four SDV platoons and two submarine Dry Deck Shelter platoons. Beginning in 1998, these are to be replaced with the similar Advanced SEAL Delivery System (ASDS).

Air Force

About 10,000 airmen and 130 aircraft are assigned to the Air Force Special Operations Command (AFSOC). The Air Force operates the 16th Special Operations Wing (SOW) at Hurlburt Field, Florida and a Special Tactics Group. The SOW includes two Special Operations Group Headquarters with nine active-duty fixed-wing SO (Special Operations) Squadrons and five rotary-wing SO Squadrons. There are three fixed-wing squadrons in the reserve components. These units operate a variety of fixed-wing aircraft and helicopters. Most are advanced variations on the C-130 turboprop transport, the UH-60 general-purpose helicopter, and the H-53 long-range helicopter. C-130 variants include attack, penetration, air-to-air refueling and psychological-operations versions. There is one reserve SOW and one Air National Guard Special Operations Squadron. Special Tactics Group provides combat-control teams and search-and-rescue teams. The combat control teams (CCT) often operate with other special operations units to guide and direct supporting Air Force aircraft.

Special Mission Units (SMUs)

These are more narrowly focused organizations equipped and trained for counterterrorism, strategic reconnaissance and other missions that are usually highly classified. Public statements 'by General Carl W. Stiner … identify the Army's Delta Force and [Navy] SEAL Team 6 as permanently assigned Special Mission Units'. They can 'accomplish surgical strikes against sensitive targets' for hostage rescue, capture of enemy leaders or recovery of classified materiel. Rangers and the SOAR augment SMUs as required and selected Air Force crews regularly train with them (J. Collins, 1994, 70, 174).

Theater Special Operations Commands (SOCs)[2]

Each theater of operations has a small Special Operations Command, or SOC, that exercises operational control over SOF (except Psyops and Civil Affairs) in that geographic region controlled by the theater headquarters. There are five Theater SOCs, each commanded by a Brigadier General and including representatives of all the various special-operations elements of all three services.

SOF Missions

Most SOF and all Army SF, Rangers and Navy SEALs are qualified parachutists. Numerous individuals in all SOF units are qualified as light-weapons and explosives experts, divers and receive specific training for extreme environments such as deserts and the arctic. Infiltration techniques such as high-altitude parachuting, small-boat use and underwater approaches are standard among most SOF units. The exceptions to this are Army Civil Affairs and Psyops units. This fact is sometimes used to argue that these units are not 'real' SOF.[3]

The question of exactly what special operations forces do is less straightforward than it might seem from the preceding descriptions. Special operations, or special ops, as they are often referred to, are not well defined. The US Special Operations Command (USSOCOM) offers the following definition of special operations:

> Special operations encompass the use of small units in direct or indirect military actions that are focused on strategic or operational objectives. They require units with combinations of specialized personnel, equipment, training or tactics that exceed the routine capabilities of conventional military forces. (USSOCOM, 1996, 1–2)

The Army Special Forces Command (USASOC) basic manual on special operations forces states that these are 'specially organized, trained and equipped military and paramilitary forces that conduct special operations to achieve military, political, economic or informational objectives by generally unconventional means in hostile, denied or politically sensitive areas' (DA, 1996, 2–1).

These two definitions differ in an important way. Although they both combine the same elements, the USSOCOM version emphasizes one view of SOF, while the USASOC version stresses another. USSOCOM's definition indicates that SOF are special because they have unique equipment and perform tasks that 'exceed the routine capabilities of conventional forces'. The tasks and methods themselves are, by implication, conventional.

The stress in the USASOC definition is on the use of these forces for 'political, economic or informational objectives' beyond ordinary military ones and employing something called 'unconventional means'. This reflects a real difference in military views of what is 'special' about special operations. Are these essentially conventional soldiers with a very high level of proficiency? Or are they something else, dedicated to purposes and functions that are different and using methods that are outside the conventional mold of most military forces, that is, 'unconventional'?

This disagreement is reflected in a division of opinion within the special-ops community as to whether they ought to be 'shooters or social workers'. In the real world the result is an uneasy division between the two extremes, with SOF units dedicated to both sort of missions and numerous variations. The argument is perhaps most pointed when applied to the numbered Army Special Forces Groups who conduct unconventional warfare. Most other SOF (especially Air Force, Navy and the SOAR) are doing the same as their conventional counterparts, and are 'special' only because of their high degree of proficiency and because they have some equipment and training not available to conventional forces.

This tension between the definitions is a consistent theme running through the history of special operations forces at least since World War II. It is not mere semantics, but reflects a real divergence of opinion among military leaders, planners and ordinary soldiers about the nature, purpose, functions and methods of special operations forces.

THE SPECIAL OPERATIONS BUREAUCRACY

Following a low point after the Vietnam War, when SOF were drastically reduced, US Special Operations Forces have risen to new heights. An entire major joint command, US Special Operations Command, under a four-star Army general, has been created with multi-million dollar facilities at Tampa's McDill Air Force Base to oversee special-ops elements of the Army, Navy and Air Force. Within the Army another new headquarters has risen at Fort Bragg,

North Carolina, called the Army Special Operations Command (USASOC). It has also been provided with new, high-tech facilities that enable it to control that service's special operators including a tailored Special Operations Aviation Regiment, the Ranger Regiment and a variety of dedicated support elements, including intelligence, communications and logistics. It even has two subordinate headquarters of its own, a Special Forces Command to control the five Army Special Forces Groups, and a Civil Affairs and Psychological Operations Command responsible for the Psychological Operations Group and the Civil Affairs Battalion. Each of the other services has established a similar, although much smaller, command structure for their own special operations units.

In addition to USSOCOM, another multi-service headquarters, the Joint Special Operations Command (JSOC) at Fort Bragg, has been created to oversee the super-secret missions of the Army's Delta Force commandos, the Navy's SEAL Team Six and the elements that provide intelligence, transportation and support for them (Collins, 1994, 69–70).

Nevertheless, most SOF are part of the Army. As of 1998 there are about 12,500 Army active-duty SOF personnel compared with 5,800 Air Force and 2,700 Navy. These organizations, from all services, together with their headquarters, staff and their counterparts in the civilian defense bureaucracy, constitute the 'special operations community'.

Altogether, this is probably a tenfold increase in special-ops strength since the post-Vietnam low point of the 1970s. The price of this expansion has been high. To a dangerous extent it has been brought about by making special operations forces more like the rest of the armed forces, albeit performing at a higher level of proficiency.

The focus of this book is on Army Special Operations Forces, principally US Army Special Forces, Civil Affairs and Psychological Operations, since these constitute the original, largest, most active group of special operators and are arguably the 'center of gravity' for all special operations.

IT IS NOT EASY BEING SPECIAL

Despite a distinguished history, Army Special Forces has not had an easy time. The US military, particularly the Army, has long distrusted the whole of idea of elite units on the general principle that such organizations have no place in the armed forces of a democracy. The specific arguments against elite units in general, and US Army Special Forces in particular, are well known to anyone who has served in, with or around any of these organizations – that they have limited utility, require a disproportionate amount of support, take the best personnel from other units, gain undeserved public attention, thus damaging the morale of other units, have a tendency toward individualism, exhibit truculence and resist traditional discipline. None of these arguments is completely correct, but over the years there has been an uncomfortable amount of truth in them. In the wake of the Vietnam War, these and other accusations nearly resulted in the disappearance of Special Forces and special operators in all the services. By the time the Iran hostage rescue became a spectacular failure, in 1980, these forces were at their lowest ebb ever.

Beginning in the 1980s those most concerned in the Army special-operations community deliberately set out to preserve the Special Forces concept by attacking these arguments at their roots, and by making special-operations forces a part of the conventional Army. A major effort was launched to give SF the image of 'the Quiet Professionals'. To a large degree, they have succeeded.

By 1997, even the beloved 'Green Beret' headgear had often been relegated to photo opportunities and ceremonial occasions. One Special Forces general could say with pride that SF liaison elements were becoming a permanent part of every conventional Army corps headquarters where they would 'wear the corps patch, wear the corps headgear'.

In 1992, *Army Magazine* published an interview with Lt General Wayne J. Downing, then commander of the US Army Special Operations Command. As illustrated in the excerpt below, this article was little short of a celebration of the triumph of the conventional model.

> In past decades, special operations forces were cast in the light of 'unconventional warfare' which often carried with it the view that they were outside the mainstream Army. It is true that special operations forces have unconventional capabilities in the sense that they possess specialties, equipment and mission areas not allocated to other units; however, as special operations forces have become doctrinally established, their roles have become conventional in the sense that this is the way the Army fights today. Drawing from the lessons of Desert Storm, special operations forces in the near future

will become firmly linked to each of the Army's corps with coordination teams assigned to that level of command. (Steele, 1992, 24–33)

In the same article, the General declared,

> I guess the message I have for the rest of the Army and for the rest of the armed forces is that we have very capable special operations forces that are partners – work together – with other elements of the armed forces to accomplish the mission. (p. 32)

Becoming an integral part of the conventional armed forces was seen by special operations leaders as the way to preserve and enhance an important military capability. But, in so doing, something vital may have been lost. While the SOF were becoming more conventional, conflict was becoming less so. There was a rise in insurgency and irredentist movements, often wrongly characterized as terrorists. Rickety governments in Haiti, Liberia, Somalia and Cambodia collapsed and required foreign intervention. Even large-scale drug trafficking became a threat, and the doctrines of state-to-state conflict had new competition as non-state actors became more important sponsors of violent conflict.

BRIEFLY LOOKING BACK

First organized to raise and train partisans in the event of Soviet invasion of western Europe, the Special Forces had, from the outset, a very close relationship with the field of psychological operations. During the Vietnam War, the long-neglected field of Civil Affairs enjoyed a resurgence and after the war became a part of Army SOF. By combining SF, CA and psychological-operations capabilities, Army SOF became, almost by accident, a unique politico-military instrument, capable of operating in the vague gray area between political conflict and open war.

In the past, the most notable arena of this gray area conflict has been insurgency and counterinsurgency. But after the demise of the Soviet Union and the coming of the world security environment, often clichéd as the 'New World Dis-Order', there has been an increase in the number of 'unconventional' conflicts, in which there is no clear a priori dominance of the military but in which military forces are still significantly involved. The recent phenomenon of 'failed states' offers a venue for politico-military involvement that cannot be ignored. This suggests a greater need than ever for military-political competency in these unconventional conflicts.

Largely by historical accident, the tactical fighting skill of the 'Green Berets' became organizationally allied with Civil Affairs and Psychological Operations units in a single command – the US Army Special Operations Command. Together they combine the types of skill that ought to be useful in 'gray-area' warfare. But at the same time, the US forces most likely to conduct these conflicts successfully have shown a tendency to neglect this field in favor of purely military competencies. Indeed, for many years the Special Forces (SF) sought to end their association with Civil Affairs and Psychological Operations because these units were thought to detract from the commando image desired by many SF troopers and leaders.

This is a strange and troubling outcome and the process by which it came about is worth considering. It is remarkable and interesting not least for the fact that there are no real villains in this piece, no mischief-working spies, no mustache-twirling cads out to destroy the special operations forces. For the most part it has been a story of people who, in seeking to do what they thought best, may have severally handicapped the USA's ability to survive and prosper in the disorder of the late twentieth and early twenty-first centuries.

DECIDING WHAT SOF DO AND HOW

However, intertwined with this is another story also worth considering. It is not enough simply to decide to create a force for some vague class of conflicts called 'unconventional warfare'. There must be some basic idea of what is to done and how this is to be accomplished before such a force can be organized, trained and employed. First of all, exactly what is the force to accomplish? Secondly, what is its operational method? For the conventional Army these questions are, in principle, easy to answer. The purpose of the conventional force is to render the military force of an enemy state incapable of preventing the USA from working its will. This is accomplished by force and violence, in a technique loosely known as 'combat'. From these basic answers stem the answers to a host of other questions. What specialties should such a military force include? What sort of equipment should it possess? How large should it be? Should it expect to operate in all geographic areas? And, of course, many more.

Unfortunately, the purpose of a US unconventional warfare force is not so easily defined. Certainly, it would serve the national interests of the US, but beyond that, what? There is no direct object so easily defined as the 'destruction of the enemy army' and no method so easily specified as 'the direct application of violent force'. Combat is not the only way to apply military power but it is certainly the least confusing. Because basic questions about unconventional war have never been answered in an organized way, the UW capability that grew up did so largely by accident and improvisation.

Doctrine: figuring out what to do and how to do it

> The development of doctrine is the cornerstone upon which a special operations capability can be erected ... our failure ... to develop doctrine has prevented special operations in the Army from gaining permanence and acceptability within the ranks of the military. (Secretary of the Army John O. Marsh Jr, 1983, in S. Cook, 1996, 37)

Doctrine is the way the US Defense Department answers questions about military forces and applies the answers in action. Generally, doctrine is a set of principles or techniques accepted as correct by practitioners in a field of endeavor, in this case the military. In the US Department of Defense version, doctrine consists of 'Fundamental principles by which the military forces or elements thereof guide their actions in support of national objectives. It is authoritative but requires judgment in application' (JCS, 1987, 118; see also DA, 1969, 26). Army doctrine, then, is a set of principles for the conduct of ground combat. Unconventional warfare, although often including violent conflict, is not principally about combat and this creates great difficulty in devising military doctrine.

The Army, and other military institutions, have long struggled with the problem of violent conflict that does not seem to be 'war' in the usual sense. Until fairly recently, the response has been to take refuge in the conventional model of war and label all these other deadly quarrels as aberrations, unique special cases that are not the proper business of soldiers. It is no surprise that specific, concrete solutions have not arisen. Given the well-known military attachment to the tried and proven, and the skepticism for vague, new-fangled ideas, it is surprising that so much official attention has been paid to this question. Attention, however, does not equal clarity.

During the 1980s and 1990s military strategists and planners adopted at least three successive formulations to characterize this environment: Low-Intensity Conflict, Military Operations Other than War and, most recently, the 1996 version, *Stability and Support Operations* (DA, FM100-20 [Draft] 1996). None of these proved satisfactory. In 1997, still another title was being sought for this category of activity. The Army's capstone manual on operations simply refers to these situations as 'conflicts'. All this seems a bit vague to help guide the young soldier in Mogadishu when the streets are filled with Somali gunmen and rocket-propelled grenades (RPGs) begin impacting on the Bakra market.

The general frustration with these forms of conflict arises from the fact that this is indeed a complex and difficult area. In both academic and military circles characterizations ranging from 'confusing and unsettled' (Hunt, 1996, 58) to 'intellectual muddle' (Olson, 1986, 3) are commonly applied to these definitional issues. In the words of the editor of *Military Review*, 'There is no shortage of thoughts on the subject. At the same time, there seems to be very little coherence, a lot of frustration, and very limited agreement' (Timmerman, 1986, I).

SOF Missions

For all the foregoing reasons the missions assigned SOF tend to be something of a hodge-podge, a collection of mismatched activities stemming from a variety of sources including congressional legislation, the desires of the services, initiatives by the special-operations community and historical precedents. Some of these, notably Civil Affairs and Psychological Operations, are capabilities, rather than 'missions' in the same sense as Direct Action or Special Reconnaissance.

As defined by USSOCOM, SOF accomplish the following missions and collateral tasks or activities (the definitions that follow have been edited from USSOCOM statements):

Missions

Direct Action (DA): Rapid, small-scale strikes and raids to seize or destroy enemy personnel or materiel.
Special Reconnaissance (SR): Reconnaissance of especially difficult objectives, often in denied areas.
Foreign Internal Defense (FID): Assistance to foreign governments threatened by lawlessness, subversion or insurgency.
Unconventional Warfare (UW): Support to long-duration military

or paramilitary operations by indigenous or surrogate forces. Includes guerrilla warfare and other forms of low-visibility military activity.

Combatting Terrorism (CT): Offensive measures to prevent, deter or respond to terrorism.

Counterproliferation (CP): Actions taken to seize, destroy, capture or recover weapons of mass destruction (i.e. nuclear, bological or chemical weapons).

Civil Affairs (CA): Activities concerning the relations between military forces and civil authorities and civilian populations to facilitate military operations.

Psychological Operations (Psyops): Operations to convey information to foreign audiences to induce or reinforce attitudes favorable to the originator's objectives.

Information Warfare (IW): Actions taken to achieve information superiority by affecting adversary information systems while protecting friendly information and information systems.

Collateral Activities

Coalition Support: Communication, coordination, training and liaison to integrate foreign forces into coalition command and intelligence stuctures.

Combat Search and Rescue (CSAR): Recovery of distressed personnel during wartime or contingency operations.

Counterdrug Activities (CD): Detection, monitoring and countering the production, trafficking and use of illegal drugs.

Countermine Activities (CM): Activities to reduce or eliminate the threat of mines, booby-traps and other explosive devices, including the threat to noncombatants.

Humanitarian Assistance (HA): Programs to relieve suffering from natural or manmade disasters or endemic conditions such as hunger or disease.

Security Assistance (SA): Programs that provide defense articles, military training, or other defense related services to foreign governments in furtherance of US national policies.

Special Activities: Actions abroad in support of US policies that are planned and executed so that the role of the US government is not apparent or acknowledged publicly. A Presidential finding and Congressional oversight is required for such actions (taken from USSOCOM Fact Sheet, undated, courtesy of USSOCOM, December 1996).

SOF Units and Missions

The various types of SOF units and their primary missions under current doctrine are:

Army
Special Forces	UW, FID, DA, SR, CT
Rangers	DA, CT
SO Aviation	DA, SR and Support all operations
Psyop	Support all operations
Civil Affairs	FID, UW, IW*

Navy
SEALS	DA, SR, CT, FID, UW**
SBU	Support all operations
SDVT	Support all operations

Air Force	Support all operations
Special Mission Units	DA, SR, CT, FID, UW

---

* IW could be practiced by most military units, conventional or otherwise.
** UW, as practiced by the US Navy, is closer to Direct Action than UW as defined by Army doctrine.

THE INTERNATIONAL ENVIRONMENT, WAR AND THE ROLE OF SOLDIERS

Unfairly, some commentators like to accuse the Army of discouraging thinking. This is simply untrue, as you cannot move huge organizations around the world at short notice without having devoted much constructive thought to the subject. The Army has many intelligent people, who think constructively, deeply and well. However, they are practical thinkers for the most part, engineers as opposed to, say, theoretical physicists.

The Army has never been a comfortable home for theoreticians at any great level of abstraction. The attitude has been that 'war' really means deadly combat, and combat is no place for airy theorizing. Col. Harry P. Ball notes proudly in his history of the Army War College:

> No matter the pressures, the War College has never deviated from its belief that its primary, overriding obligation was to the United

> States Army ... This helps explain why the army War College has
> produced few if any noted military theoreticians ... [The Army's
> need] has not been for theoreticians but for capable practitioners.
> (Ball, 1983, 491)

Nevertheless, principles do not spring full-blown from a vacuum;
they come from ideas about the nature of the world. For the US
Army, they spring from a particular conception of the international
environment, war and the role of soldiers. The fact that the
underlying presumptions of this vision are seldom examined makes
them all the more powerful.

The international environment

This vision is reflected in the Army's most recent characterization
of the nature of political conflict from a military point of view. In
the military view, the important actors in wars are nation-states,
usually referred to simply as 'nations'. These are nations in the
common-language sense, meaning any sovereign state with defined
territory and political autonomy. Arguably, what is really meant is
state-to-state conflict, since governing institutions (including the
armed forces) are usually referred to as the 'state' rather than a
nation, but that is a side issue.

Because the Army's version of war is a nation-against-nation
business (either singly or in groups), it must take place in the
international environment. As stipulated by DA, FM 100-5
Operations, the Army's basic manual on military operations,
relations between nations fall into three conditions or 'states of
the environment', characterized as 'peacetime', 'conflict' and 'war'.
All military activities short of war are characterized as 'military
operations other than war' or simply MOOTW (pronounced 'moo-
twa'). This includes essentially all those forms of organized violence
that occur during 'conflict' (DA, FM 100-5, 1993).

The nature of war

None of this, however, gets directly at the subject of war. What is
war, anyway? At a very general level, all conflict is a struggle between
opposing forces, each seeking to gain or maintain power. Power in
turn can be defined as the ability to compel action. Violent,
organized and protracted struggle between competing political
entities is commonly referred to as 'war'. Ordinarily, this includes

open war, but also a wide variety of less violent disagreements, confrontations or disharmony. The US Army, however, recognizes only one form of violent, organized, conflict as war.

Its capstone manual for operations defines war as: 'A state of open and declared armed hostile conflict between political units such as states or nations' (DA, FM 100-5, 1993, Glossary-9). Although the manual does not specify 'conventional' war, presumably this covers it. It is fair to say that, by this definition, the USA has had few wars. However, it has been involved in a wide variety of armed hostile conflicts that were neither open, nor declared, nor involved fighting states or nations. For example, the intervention in Somalia cost the lives of 42 US soldiers and airmen while wounding another 175 without ever qualifying as war.

The Army's notion of war accords well with the influential *realpolitik* formulation of Hans J. Morgenthau, that politics in general is a struggle for power (1985, 31). In this formulation, the threat of physical violence is 'an intrinsic element of politics'. But, the actual exercise of violence is seen as non-political, 'the abdication of political power in favor of military or pseudo-military power' (ibid., 33). The Morgenthau formula reflects a basic belief that politics and military operations are separate, largely autonomous and ought to be that way, as if they connected only at the very highest levels of strategy.

This view is often thought to be illustrated by von Clausewitz's well-known maxim that 'war is the continuation of politics by other means'. Experience in the swamp of ill-defined conflict suggests that the question of the degree of autonomy between the military and political spheres is not so easy. There is an area where the degree of interconnection, overlap, between these spheres is contentious and poorly defined: this is the area of UW.

Furthermore, for the military, there are disturbing indications that the nature of power may have changed in some way. After all, Algeria and Vietnam, two low-technology, agricultural nations managed to defeat France and the USA without fielding comparable armed forces or developing anything like comparable national economies. 'Student revolutionaries' were able to seize and hold the US embassy in Iran, and its inhabitants, and hold them for more than a year. As long ago as the mid-1970s some analysts began to argue that political power was becoming more diffuse as actors other than states became more influential. The result has been the emergence of what Seyom Brown called a 'polyarchy', meaning that subnational actors (for example, terrorist groups), transnationals (such as corporations) and special-interest communities and other entities would begin vying for advantage (Brown, 1974, 186). At the same time, the spread of modern technology, including weapons, has strengthened weak states and subnational actors, further confusing the issue of power and its application, especially in the international arena. In short, conventional military power may not always be the trump card of international relations; instead a variety of other, less well-defined, conflict forms have gained importance.

Unconventional warfare occurs in precisely this area, the gray area where violence has entered the practice of politics but the struggle has not yet reached the level of conventional warfare. This is an area where the protagonists may work diligently to prevent conventional war from occurring, because, if it does take place, they lose their advantage. It is also in this gray area that the unique capabilities and organization of SOF can have its greatest effect.

This is recognized in Army special-operations doctrine, which holds that 'the traditional dynamics of military power are inappropriate in conflict environments where – nonmilitary aspects drive the tactical conduct of military operations ... [and] no clearly defined enemy or battlefield exists' (DA, FM 100-25, 1991, 2–11). As will be shown, this lack of a clearly defined enemy or battlefield is one of the chief reasons for the 'grayness', or lack of definition, characteristic of the unconventional-warfare arena.

The role of soldiers

In conventional war the role of soldiers is very straightforward – to apply force and violence, 'to kill people and break things'. However, many forms of nonpolitical action, including interpersonal and criminal, also use force and violence as a method. The soldier is differentiated from these because he acts as an agent of a state, and has the sanction of the state in his application of violent methods. This differs from police in that the purpose of police is not to apply violence but to apprehend criminals. Soldiers do not traditionally seek to apprehend the enemy. However, unconventional warfare may find them doing exactly that.

Unlike soldiers, police do not carry weapons for the express purpose of killing those who defy their will. This is the definition of a soldier, one who acts as an authorized agent of a state, carrying out under the authority of that state, the state's monopoly on the legal use of deadly violence. Police use of armed violence is not about 'killing people and breaking things'; military violence is.

In fact, these are the central characteristics of the conventional model of warfare – it is armed violence on a large scale, engaged in by specialized agents of a state. The basic truth that war is a political phenomenon is seen as largely irrelevant. This is simply assumed in the model of conventional war. Politics is not considered to be the business of soldiers. Once a state of war is declared by competent political authority it becomes the business of the military until such time as the enemy state has lost its ability to resist.

CONVENTIONAL VS UNCONVENTIONAL WAR

For preliminary purposes, conventional war may be defined as:

> ... war fought by formally constituted armed forces of a state with the immediate purpose of bringing about the direct physical destruction or incapacitation of the formally constituted armed forces of some other state.

Admittedly, this definition is not at all original. Its elements have been repeated by philosophers from Hobbes to Hegel to Clausewitz. It amounts to little more than a slightly more formal statement of the Army's own definition of 'war'.

It should be understood that 'unconventional', as used in this book, is not the accepted US Defense Department definition. As used here it means any of the array of poorly defined conflicts that do not follow the conventional model. Usually this means that either the belligerents are not the agents of a recognized state or that they do not use military combat as their principal method. The term 'unconventional war', as commonly used in US military doctrine, does not, as one might expect, mean forms of politically sanctioned, violent conflict that are outside the definition of conventional war. Instead, the term is used as General Downing used it, to indicate techniques that are merely unusual including, 'guerrilla warfare and other direct offensive, low visibility, covert or clandestine operations as well as ... subversion, sabotage, intelligence activities, evasion and escape' (DOD, JP1-02, 1994, 399). These techniques are conventional in the sense defined above, but are simply not the common practice of the Army or the central focus of its efforts. This last point is important in understanding the real impact of General Downing's remarks. The fact that UW is not central to the Army's view of the world is basic in understanding the conventionalizing of special-operations forces. As long as UW was identified as the main function of SOF, and as long as UW was seen as a peripheral function, SOF were doomed to secondary status, the first choice to lose budget and resources. To put it another way: in order to be accepted as valuable players, SOF had to be part of the conventional armed forces.

Where did everybody go?

There is something very odd about the Army's notion of warfare, other than the fact that it is unduly restrictive. This is reflected in the descriptions of combat in military publications and especially in Field Manuals. The oddity is that the fighting seems to take place in an empty world. The discussions tend to ignore the people who presumably live in the areas where fighting occurs. Illustrations usually show tanks and troops maneuvering across an open, partially wooded landscape of low hills, broken only by the occasional lonely, shattered farmhouse for artistic contrast. Newer manuals depict forces deployed across a desert. These forces maneuver to defeat another army and seize terrain. The occupants of that terrain are not a consideration. The tankers' nirvana, the National Training Center, is situated in the midst of the unpopulated California desert.

The USASOC official history of Army SF makes the point that Civil Affairs and Psyops were excluded from the planning for the Gulf War until very late in the process. The reason for this, the history notes, was 'the Army's unfounded belief that it would operate in an environment virtually free of civilians' (USASOC, 1994, 112).

By the latest estimates, there are roughly six billion people in the world. Except for the tiny minority who serve in the military almost none appear in conventional doctrine. This is in marked contrast to the common-sense view of the world, and is one of the problems with the application of the conventional model of war. In the case of large-scale combat employing the massive firepower favored by conventional planners it might be presumed that the population will vacate the area if they can. However, this is demonstrably untrue of places like Beirut, Port-au-Prince and Mogadishu, where US soldiers found themselves surrounded by thousands of people and occasionally fighting in the midst of them. Even in South Vietnam, where incredibly fierce fighting occurred, the civil population, who were allegedly being defended, had no choice but to suffer under some of the most intense firepower ever applied in war.

This problem affects Army doctrine most strongly, first of all because the Army is the most doctrine driven of the services, and secondly, unlike the Navy and Air Force, its domain is the ground, the place where people live.

UNCONVENTIONAL WAR

Unconventional warfare, by contrast, not only recognizes the presence of a civil population; by nature, it occurs in the midst of the people. Its terrain is symbolic and lies in the minds of the population. In most cases physical terrain is not important except as a distraction to conventional thinkers. In most forms of unconventional warfare the objective is the allegiance of the people around whom, and presumably on whose behalf, the conflict is taking place. The occupation of some specific bit of ground is secondary, if it matters at all. This is where the often slighted but terribly important capabilities of the Civil Affairs and Psychological Operations components of SOF become critical. They are the leading edge in the struggle for people's minds, for their allegiance.

Civil Affairs units contain the expertise in working with the civilian population and restoring, or sometimes creating, the civic infrastructure of society. Psychological Operations (Psyops) units have the ability to perform an information function that allows a society to operate beyond the bounds of the village. They can help provide newspapers, radio and television broadcasts and even loudspeaker teams to advise and inform the population.

Both Civil Affairs and Psyops units are part of the Army's Special Operations Forces and an important reason that SOF has such a great capability for unconventional warfare.

The military-technical approach

Conventional warfare is a method designed for an empty battlefield, populated only by the professional soldiers of the contesting armies. This 'convention', about the nature of war as violent conflict between the formally constituted armed forces of states, together with beliefs about the definition and role of soldiers and the proper way of conducting war, is basic to that view of the proper conduct of warfighting termed the 'military-technical approach'. That is, when military planners set out to apply the conventional model, they use that approach.

The term 'military-technical approach' comes from a 1983 work by the social scientist Julian Lider. Lider published a comprehensive survey, *On the Nature of War*, in which he sought to categorize various approaches to understanding warfare. He used the term 'military-technical approach' (from an earlier work, 1977, v) to describe the US/Western/European view of conflict and war. This term characterized the way in that contemporary Western military professionals think about the nature of warfare, the way that warfighting should be conducted, and its relationship to other forms of political conflict (Lider, 1977, 22, 25). It is similar to what the historian Alfred Vagts called 'the military way': 'The military way is marked by a primary concentration of men and materials on winning specific objectives of power with the utmost efficiency, that is with the least expenditure of blood and treasure' (Vagts, 1937, 13).

The 'military-technical' approach is characterized by an emphasis on military organization, warfighting technology, and the actual conduct of hostilities. This is supported by the belief that the conduct of armed conflict is only loosely connected to the presumed political and economic origins of the conflict. In other words, military forces fight in very much the same way, regardless of the origins of the conflict in which they are engaged. This is the traditional attitude of Western military professionals (Lider, 1983, 22; also Janowitz, 1960). Although most modern military commentators agree that war is essentially socio-political in nature (Paret, 1986, 193), this view is not reflected very strongly in military doctrine. In US doctrine, the political aspect of conflict is kept separate from, and secondary to, the discussion of warfighting. If political analysis does occur, it is concerned only with those aspects of the situation that bear directly on the conduct of hostilities and the management of military forces, such as overflight rights, basing and the use of ports and airfields.

Lider points out that the 'military-technical' approach has had an important influence on the terms used to discuss conflict, especially war, which has had a corresponding impact upon the very concepts of conflict and war (1977, 24). Discussions of the technological means of war are the central focus of much US military analysis. This is especially true since World War II (Weigley, 1973, 407).

Unconconventional warfare is different

The military-technical approach and the conventional view of warfare do not work well outside the narrowly defined confines of conventional war. UW is different. People who do not understand that UW is different are likely to give the wrong advice at crucial times, miss opportunities, and jump when they should have stood still. Unconventional warfare is primarily about politics but with a significant violence component above the level of ordinary criminality. In theory, it is possible to adapt the entire US military structure to UW, but in so doing we might harm or even lose our ability to conduct the sort of high-stakes, intensive warfare that the conventional model covers. The traditional response has been to say that, well, the conventional army can do both: 'If you can fight the cat you can fight the kittens.' Not so. As was demonstrated in the Vietnam War, the conventionalizing impulse can sometimes make it impossible to fight the kittens.

Massive firepower may win battles, but only if the enemy is willing to fight that way. That does not mean that heavy conventional forces are not needed; they certainly are. The existence of these heavy conventional elements with their massive high-tech firepower is the principal reason conventional war is enjoying its current unpopularity; but they are no longer the only important part of the mix.

WHAT DOES SOF BRING TO THE TABLE?

Properly employed, SOF can make the difference in UW situations, but that is not the same thing as arguing that all, or even most, of the US armed forces should be replaced by special operators. When a carrier-based air strike or a column of heavy tanks is needed, they are needed badly and special ops will not suffice.

In 1991, Army Special Forces Task Force Alpha scored a major unconventional success in Operation Provide Comfort. SOF were able to save the lives of thousands of Kurds starving and freezing in the mountains of Turkey and Iraq as they fled the Iraqi Republican Guard. In so doing, the special operators not only saved lives but prevented major political problems with Turkey by returning the Iraqi Kurds safely home. But a big part of their success was due to the havoc wrought among Iraq's armed forces by the conventional air and ground forces of Operation Desert Storm. All three basic types of military forces – heavy, light and SOF – are needed; but they do not all need to do the same thing. Ideally, SOF is not just a superior form of light infantry; rather, it is a different kind of creature that can thrive and succeed in a difficult environment where other forces cannot.

Similarly, in 1994–95, SOF (chiefly Army SF, CA and Psyops) produced another unconventional-warfare triumph in Haiti. Fewer than 1,200 Army SF troopers, including support personnel, exerted *de facto* control over virtually all of Haiti except the cities of Port-au-Prince and Cap Haitien. In the absence of meaningful local authority, SF troopers, aided by Psyops and CA soldiers, assisted local magistrates in providing civil government and restoring the infrastructure. This is not a task that could have been accomplished by conventional forces. These examples suggest two things: first, that there is a real need for this capability, and secondly, that SOF, especially Army SOF, has the potential to do the job.

The kind of unified 'gray area' task force that SOF can field has arisen, mostly on an *ad hoc* basis, on several occasions over the years. In 1969, the concept originated of a force that would combine all the unconventional abilities of an SF Group with a small Civil Affairs Group, a Psyops Battalion, and other elements. This was the Special Action Force (SAF) concept, but was never fully implemented. In Panama a similar, even more *ad hoc*, organization called the Military Support Group was created to coordinate and assist reconstruction efforts following the 1989 US invasion. It lasted only a few months. Both of these examples came into being because of a recognized need for the capability and because no other organization existed that could do the job. Neither of these forces lasted long or was fully implemented because of uncertainty both in the military and in the US civilian government bureaucracy about the appropriateness of these as military tasks.

In the words of General Ronald Griffith, Vice Chief of Staff, the number two man in the US Army, the Army must 'adjust to a changed world, not one of major conflict but a myriad of requirements such as peacekeeping, limited conflict and fighting fires' (Muradian, 1996, 159). Flexibility, maturity, appropriate specialties, a high ratio of supervision, ability to function in austere conditions, high level of team and individual skill, rapid deployability, experience and not least of all, reputation, make special operations forces a most valuable element. Furthermore, individual SOF members often have uncommon leadership qualities that may be as important as training, especially when leavened by experience. But these virtues need to be applied where they are the most needed – in the dangerous, difficult, frustrating and ultimately necessary pursuit of unconventional warfare.

The following chapters will describe the evolution of US special operations forces, especially Army Special Forces, and some of the difficulties encountered during their 50-year process of development. Examples of recent SOF missions in the Gulf War, Panama, Somalia and Haiti will be offered as instances that highlight both the unique strengths and the peculiar weaknesses of these forces.

NOTES

1. The term 'Complex Humanitarian Emergency' has been coined to cover situations like Haiti and Somalia where there has been a collapse of government function combined with widespread suffering. However, as the reader will soon discover, the ambiguity of these forms of conflict is matched by the ambiguity of the terminology used to describe them.
2. For military command and control purposes, the USA divides the world into five geographic regions or theaters of operation: Atlantic (including North America), Europe (including Africa), Central (the Middle East and parts of Southwest Asia), Pacific (most of Asia) and Southern (South and Central America). Each region has a military headquarters for that region commanded by a four-star general. The commanders-in-chief of these regions are called 'the geographic CINCs'. They are America's senior war-fighters. There are also four 'functional CINCs' of which the commander, USSOCOM, is one.
3. The US Marine Corps has an organization called the Marine Expeditionary Unit (Special Operations Capable) or MEU (SOC). As a practical matter, this is a conventional Marine Corps Brigade trained to perform noncombatant evacuation operations (NEO) and similar functions. The MEU (SOC) is outside the concept of SOF as discussed here.

2 War outside the conventional model: a US history

'Seventy percent, maybe eighty will die, if ya make it home yer gonna wonder why.' Running cadence, US Army Special Forces. (Documentary Recordings, 1986, no. 560)

BEGINNINGS

When Army Special Forces soldiers first went to Laos and Vietnam in the late 1950s to practice their unconventional trade, they were to embark on a form of warfare with very old roots, but one that was not an important part of the US military thought. This seems odd in retrospect, because the US Army had been involved in warfare outside the conventional model since its inception.

The US Army's history of unconventional warfare began with continental militia in the American Revolution, who first fought their better-armed and better-trained opponents with a combination of political organization with guerrilla-style harassing tactics. But when George Washington took command of the fledgling Continental Army, he made it his first order of business to create an army that could fight in the properly accepted 'European' manner of its British opponents. In other words, he 'conventionalized' it. Only this way, it was believed, could the Continentals decisively defeat their enemies.

With minor exceptions, this change in emphasis marked the end of US use of unconventional warfare methods and techniques until the twentieth century. Even during the Civil War, when the famous southern 'guerrillas', Mosby and Quantrill, developed colorful reputations with their daring raids and ambushes, the US Army viewed them as nothing more than bandits with Southern sympathies who could expect to hang if captured (Hattaway, 1992, 19).

The Army had considerable early experience with Civil Affairs, especially military government, beginning with Andrew Jackson's administration of New Orleans after the War of 1812. Army officers also worked closely with civil government in the California Territory during the 1840s and again in Arizona and New Mexico following the Mexican War of 1846–48. By the close of the nineteenth century, US soldiers had acquired further Civil Affairs experience in Cuba, Puerto Rico and the Philippines (Dawson, 1996, 556–7). But, as with guerrilla warfare and counterinsurgency, none of this wealth of early experience ever seems to have been formalized as doctrine.

The frontier campaigns of the late nineteenth century were a vivid illustration of the Army's attachment to the conventional model despite an obviously unsuited application. 'Though frequently criticized, the standard offensive methods [of the frontier army] were never changed. Heavy columns ... locked to slow moving supply trains, continued to crawl about the vast western distances in search of an enemy who could scatter and vanish almost instantly' (Utley, 1973, 53). 'Even though the regular army found its principal sanction in the frontier, its leaders ... steadfastly refused to face up to the realities of the frontier mission. They seemed to have learned nothing from earlier experiences with eastern Indians' (Utley and Washburn, 1985, 172; Simmons, 1992, 112). Between 1865 and 1898, the frontier Army fought 943 official actions against hostile and determined western Indian tribes, with a large number of actions before that time (Weigley, 1967, 265–71). Despite this experience, no formal doctrine for Indian fighting was ever devised, apparently because the Army considered these campaigns to be aberrations, and not quite seemly (Utley, 1973, 46).

Likewise, the Boxer Rebellion of 1900 cost soldiers' lives but caused scarcely a ripple in Army Field Service Regulations. Similarly, the long, turn-of-the-century counterguerrilla campaign in the Philippines had no noticeable impact upon US military doctrine (Flint, 1980, 4 and Gates, 1973, 286). It did, however, mark the Army's first use of 'pacification' techniques for counterinsurgency – measures intended to win the loyalty of the population from the guerrillas to the government (Weigley, 1967, 307–8; Gates, 1973, especially 187–94). This 1904 model experiment in pacification was notably successful but never formalized, and Army methods and practices continued to be rigidly conventional. Every experience outside the conventional model, and they were numerous, was treated as an aberration.

As with the Indian campaigns, the little war in the remote Pacific hardly seemed to merit a special system of warfare. The same basic measures would have to be re-invented 50 years later to counter yet another guerrilla insurgency in the Philippines and, later, Vietnam. The 1908 and 1910 editions of Army Field Service Regulations included passages on the introduction of machine guns and the aeroplane, but incorporated no changes resulting from experience in China or the Philippines, much less the Indian Wars (US Army, 1908, 1910). Army manuals ignored these operations until 1911, when the *Infantry Drill Regulations* finally devoted two pages (out of 528) to 'Minor Warfare', defined as small-scale operations against either regulars or irregulars (US Army, 1918).

The last significant Army counterguerrilla campaign before World War II occurred in 1916 and 1917. Brigadier General John J. Pershing was dispatched by President Wilson to chase the Mexican revolutionary bandit, Francisco 'Pancho' Villa, Villa having been unwise enough to raid the US side of the border. Despite considerable to-ing and fro-ing, aided by the first tactical use of an aeroplane (and the last US use of horse cavalry and Indian scouts in combat), Pershing's forces never managed to apprehend the elusive bandit (Smythe, 1973). The idea that the lessons of this experience ought to affect US Army doctrine does not seem to have occurred to anyone.

WORLD WAR I

World War I saw no special operations in the modern sense and little Civil Affairs activity. The US Expeditionary Force did make notable use of psychological operations late in the war in the form of leaflets produced by their Propaganda Section. The section composed 20 surrender leaflets, millions of copies of which were distributed over German lines by aircraft. The leaflets were simple; comparing, for example, scanty German field rations with the relatively plentiful food given Allied prisoners of war. These straightforward appeals were effective against the Kaiser's war weary soldiers and were credited with numerous individual surrenders (USASOC, 1994, 16).

The equivalent of Civil Affairs, Military Government of the occupied Rhineland, was simply handled by the tactical units of the US Third Army assigned to occupation duties (Coles and Wienberger, 1964, 6–7).

WORLD WAR II

World War II was the real beginning of special operations and unconventional warfare for the US military. US armed forces, especially the Army, had extensive experience with all aspects of these endeavors, including Psyops and Civil Affairs. For the first time, the US government organized what would now be termed 'special operations' units.

This included a wild array of conventional organizations ranging from the commandos of the US–Canadian First Special Service Force (Burhans, 1947) to Navy Combat Demolition and Reconnaissance Units, Marine Raiders, the Alamo Scouts and the 5307 Composite Unit. The Army's original Ranger Battalions were conceived during the war (Macksey, 1987) and, after repeated activation and inactivation, continue to exist today (Adelman and Walton, 1966; M. King, 1985; Rottman, 1987). The Navy even became involved with guerrilla warfare through the largely forgotten Sino-American Cooperation Force in China (Miles and Hawthorne, 1967).

However, the Army's most extensive and successful stab at the art of unconventional warfare was surely the Philippine resistance to Japanese occupation.

US GUERRILLAS IN THE PHILIPPINES

After the Japanese invasion of the Philippines in 1941 and the defeat of US and Filipino resistance, a number of US soldiers took to the hills, where they organized and led resistance forces against the occupiers. This was an independent, *ad hoc* operation and completely unplanned; despite this and the initial lack of support from the regular forces of the US military, it was very successful.

Under the overall leadership of Col. Russell Volckman, US/Filipino irregular units were organized in the remote jungles and, after considerable difficulty, made contact with Douglas MacArthur's Pacific Command for resupply. Fighting as guerrillas, they harassed the Japanese, established extensive intelligence networks and, in January 1945, attacked Japanese units in support of the invading US forces (Volckman, 1954). On Mindano, Lt Col. Wendell Fertig organized guerrilla forces and succeeded in capturing most of the island by the end of the war (DA, 1946; Guerrilla Resistance Movements in the Philippines, 1946).

All in all, it was the very model of a partisan campaign, with US soldiers aiding local patriots against an occupying enemy. Although the guerrillas had no chance of expelling the Japanese occupiers, they succeeded in performing all the functions expected of guerrillas and, when the US relief force finally arrived, took the offensive. This Army endeavor in partisan warfare is remarkable, not least, because, as with Villa and the Indians, it had so little effect on what followed. In fact, it was explicitly rejected as an experiential base when today's Army Special Forces were first organized, in the 1950s.[1]

RANGERS AND THE OSS: GRANDFATHERS OF MODERN
SPECIAL OPERATIONS FORCES

Of all the World War II 'special operations'-style organizations, two, Rangers and the paramilitary Office of Strategic Services (OSS), were the clearest precursors of later US Special Operations Forces. They may also be the source of the confusion that surrounded the exact nature of the activities subsumed under the term 'special operations'. The 1990s' mix of conventional (Ranger), unconventional (Psychological Operations and Civil Affairs units) and mixed-purpose organizations (Special Forces), all under the heading of 'special operations' confuses and misleads. Ranger operations (reconnaissance in force, deep reconnaissance, and commando-style raids) fit neatly with the definition of conventional warfare. The others are something which, for purposes of this discussion, has been labeled 'unconventional warfare'.

US Army Rangers

Today's Army Rangers are often regarded as the elite infantry of the US armed forces (although the Marine Corps will dispute that title). They began early in World War II as an almost offhand experiment to benefit from the success of the British Commandos. As explained in the 1942 'Commando Organization' letter from Maj. Gen. James W. Chaney, Army Ranger units were formed to provide combat experience for US soldiers by allowing them to accompany British Commando units raiding occupied western Europe.

These men would then return to regular Army units, where their experience would be of benefit (Chaney, 1942). The first Ranger Battalion was formed in Northern Ireland on 19 June 1942 from US forces then stationed in the UK. That these men would receive commando training in order to accompany the British troops was apparently seen as largely incidental. Fifty of these Rangers took part in the raid on Dieppe on France's northern coast along with Canadian and British commandos. However, the original purpose was quickly overcome by events. The allied invasion of Africa was looming and the first complete battalion of Rangers to graduate from British commando training was assigned to the US 1st Infantry Division for the landings (USASOC, 1994, 17).

The Rangers came into existence as commando units, trained as coastal raiders on the British model. In 1990s' terms, they would be called 'Special Operations Forces'. What was special about them, however, was not so much what they did but the proficiency with which they did it. Like modern Rangers, they performed essentially ordinary infantry functions but did so to a very high standard (Vaughn, 1942, and US War Department, 1942). But these highly trained, highly motivated battalions were misused as conventional infantry, largely losing their 'special operations' capacity in favor of the increased firepower demanded by the conventional battlefield.

The 1st Ranger Battalion participated in the initial landings in Algeria, in Tunisia and in the Battle of El Guettar, receiving a Presidential Unit Citation for valor. Two more battalions, the 3rd and 4th, were created toward the end of the campaign in Tunisia. The three battalions together spearheaded the invasion of Sicily. At Salerno, fighting as conventional infantry, they repelled eight Nazi counterattacks to hold the critical Chunzi Pass for 18 days. By the time the Rangers staged their heroic defense at Anzio in 1944, the Ranger Force (Provisional) was very close to being a conventional regiment, complete with engineers and artillery (Rottman, 1987, 8–10).

The pitfalls of using such forces inappropriately were conclusively demonstrated on 30 January 1944. The Ranger Force was virtually wiped out by a vicious German counterattack with armor and infantry when the three battalions were discovered infiltrating near Cisterna. Of the 767 men in the Ranger Force, 761 were killed or captured (75th Infantry Regiment, 1996, 2).

The 2nd and 5th Ranger Battalions, activated in the USA, participated with distinction in the 6 June 1944 D-Day invasion at Omaha Beach, Normandy. The 5th went ashore with the 1st Infantry Division while 220 Rangers of the 2nd Battalion were assigned to neutralize German artillery positons atop the cliffs at Pointe Du Hoc. Thanks to faulty intelligence, they scaled the sheer face of the cliff through a firestorm of small arms, mortars and grenades only to find that the gun positions were empty and swarming with Wehrmacht infantry (75th Infantry Regiment, 1996, 3).

The 6th Battalion was formed in September 1944 in the Pacific theater under Lieutenant Colonel Henry Mace. The 6th was unique among the Ranger Battalions – it was the only one to conduct special operations as they had been organized and trained to do. By most measures it was also the most successful of the Ranger units. Their missions were usually a task force, company or platoon-size element that operated behind enemy lines, and involved long-range reconnaissance and hard-hitting long-range combat patrols. Their high point came in January 1945 when a company of the 6th made a 29-mile forced march past enemy lines in search of a Japanese prison camp at Cabanatuan, Philippines, where Allied prisoners were held. After finding the camp, they crawled almost a mile over flat, exposed terrain and attacked Japanese positions. Over 200 enemy soldiers were slain at a cost of two Rangers killed and ten wounded. More than 500 US and Allied prisoners of war were liberated (75th Infantry Regiment, 1996, 2).

Though not called Rangers, the servicemen in the 5307th Composite Unit (Provisional), better known as 'Merrill's Marauders', carried out similar missions in northern Burma from February to August 1944. The 5307th drew from seasoned combat veterans throughout the southwest Pacific to perform long-range patrols in the enemy's rear area. Their most significant mission was to clear the way for the construction of the Ledo Road to China. In doing so, they captured Myitkyina Airfield, the only all-weather landing strip in north Burma. The 2,997-man force, under the command of Brigadier General Frank D. Merrill, suffering heavy losses from exhaustion and illness, operating, without support or resupply, overcame the Japanese and seized the strip (75th Infantry Regiment, 1996, 2).

By early 1945, the Ranger units, the 'Marauders', the similarly organized US Marine Corps 'Raiders', the elite US–Canadian 'Special Service Force' and the Army Air Corps' 1st Air Commando had all been disbanded and not replaced (US Congress, House, 1983, 52). One retired Special Forces commander suggested that the World War II Ranger and Ranger-style units were dissolved, and Ranger training later converted to an individual skill in order to avoid the presence of elite units in the Army structure.

The concept of Rangers as highly trained conventional infantry did, however, remain firmly established in the Army's institutional memory, to be revived again and again. The Ranger units would become the chief competitor of Army Special Forces for the role of a special operations force.

Office of Strategic Services (OSS)

If any single organization can be identified as the direct ancestor of US unconventional war forces, especially Army Special Forces, it is the Office of Strategic Services (OSS). Often criticized during its lifetime as a cloak-and-dagger outfit, its influence was profound. The very terms 'special operations' and 'Special Forces', in the sense they are used today, are a product of the OSS.

The OSS was a civilian (or more accurately, paramilitary) agency that conducted a variety of wartime missions. Today's Special Forces were based directly on the OSS experience, especially the aid to anti-German partisans in occupied territory proffered by small 'Jedburgh' teams (named after the place they were trained) and larger 'Operational Groups' fielded by that organization. OSS operators provided advisory, liaison and logistic assistance to partisans in Burma, France, Yugoslavia, Norway and China, helping to raise and train antifascist guerrillas. In northern Burma, 300 of the OSS's Detachment 101 trained and led 32,000 Kachin tribesmen against the occupying Japanese, conducting raids and gathering intelligence. Unlike the other UW units it also enjoyed generally cordial relations with the conventional commanders in the theater who appreciated the accurate, timely information it provided on the enemy (Peers and Brelis, 1963; Smith, 1972; Mendelssohn, 1987).

There is an ironic connection here. In 1945, a small OSS detachment, code-named 'Deer', parachuted into the occupied French colony of Indochina with arms and supplies for an anti-Japanese organization of Vietnamese nationalists called the Vietminh. The OSS medical aid man, Paul Hogland, found the Vietminh leader, Ho Chi Minh, dying of malaria and dysentery. Hogland treated the ailing leader, saving his life (Karnow, 1983, 139).

In the course of these colorful missions, the OSS also gained a reputation for independence and derring-do that set conventional commanders' teeth on edge. To make matters worse, the organization began as a personal project of President Franklin D. Roosevelt – the Office of Coordinator of Information (OCI), a psychological-warfare organization established by the President in 1941 (Roosevelt, 1976, I: 9). Roosevelt personally selected William O. Donovan, a politically well-connected Wall Street lawyer and hero of World War I, to direct the new organization.

Donovan, however, had his own ideas about the proper role and function of the OCI. He conceived of its overall strategic mission as primarily psychological, favoring the term 'Psychological Operations' (Psyops) to describe this function. But his idea of Psyops covered much more than the term 'Psychological Ooperations' ordinarily implies. For Donovan, it encompassed 'the coordination and use of all means, including moral and physical by which the end is attained – other than those of recognized military operations' (Roosevelt, 1976, I: 99). In other words, anything that was not a conventional military operation belonged to Donovan. He devoted himself to selling this concept to Roosevelt, and to a large degree, succeeded.

Donovan saw Psyops as incorporating not only the overt information and persuasion functions traditionally associated with psychological warfare, but also as a variety of secret intelligence, sabotage, subversion and guerrilla activities (ibid., I: 5), the latter three being lumped together under the term 'special operations' (Ford, 1970, 108). This broad definition of Psychological Operations was not welcomed in the new Pentagon, since the generals quickly saw that it would give Donovan potential control over almost any operations that were not directly conventional military. Accordingly, a lobbying effort was mounted and, in 1942, OCI's strategic Psyops function was given to the Office of War Information.

The military and paramilitary functions Donovan titled 'special operations' went to a newly created organization, also headed by Donovan, called the Office of Strategic Services. In the begining, the OSS was loosely modeled after a British paramilitary organization, the Special Operations Executive (SOE). Like SOE, the OSS was to collect and analyze strategic intelligence, and carry out 'special services', all under the direction of the newly created Joint Chiefs of Staff. 'Special services' was similar in content to 'special operations', and included various forms of paramilitary operations and unconventional warfare such as sabotage and work with resistance groups, as well as 'propaganda' (ibid., 128). The OSS operational elements were called 'special forces', a term apparently borrowed from British usage. Overall, its functions were very similar to those later attributed to the US Central Intelligence Agency (CIA).[2]

The change in Psyops responsibility split the US psychological warfare capability into three separate and distinct capacities, each with a different organizational sponsor. The civilian Office of War Information (OWI) was the official authority in control of US propaganda. It was responsible for overt propaganda and for coordinating these efforts with the propaganda activities of the armed services (Linebarger, 1954, 93; Daughtery and Janowitz, 1958, 127).

The Army went ahead and created a Psychological Warfare Branch in 1942, but dissolved it later that year when JCS directive 155/4D made OSS responsible for military tactical Psyops. The same directive created a third class of Psyops when it made theater commanders autonomous with respect to their use of OSS and OWI resources (Linebarger, 1954, 97).

All this bureaucratic maneuvering created a certain amount of confusion and, largely by default, the various theaters (notably Eisenhower's Allied Expeditionary Force in Europe) undertook their psychological warfare in the traditional vein. This meant tactical, short-range, short-term attempts to undermine enemy morale and induce surrender through the use of loudspeaker messages, leaflets, and radio broadcasts (Psychological Warfare Division, 1945, 17–19). Despite initial suspicions, Army commanders began to respect these efforts for their tactical effect in bringing about enemy surrender (Paddock, 1982, 15).

Donovan's focus, however, was on special operations. 'In essence, OSS assumed operational responsibility in a field previously ignored and scorned by many diplomats and military professionals' (Ransom, 1958, 64). As described by a critic, it was 'the New Deal's excursion into espionage, sabotage, "black" propaganda, guerrilla warfare, and other "un-American" activities' (Smith, 1972, 1).

Donovan got more of what he wanted in December 1942, when the Joint Chiefs finally agreed to give the OSS responsibility for guerrilla warfare as 'organizers, fomenters and operational nuclei of guerrilla units' (Roosevelt, 1976, I: 223). This, in a nutshell, was the mission to be given to Army Special Forces units when they were organized ten years later.

Despite, or because of, their high-level sponsor, Donovan and the OSS were still not viewed with favor by the JCS (Joint Chiefs of Staff). 'There seemed to be a deep-seated disapproval of the organization of independent military forces on the part of the War Department' (Roosevelt, 1976, I: 223). As related by Ford, the JCS initially refused to provide personnel and supplies to the OSS and did not give the new organization operating instructions or even an enabling directive for six months (Ford, 1970, 109, 129). It was only after President Roosevelt personally intervened that the OSS was finally given an operational responsibility (ibid., 169). The organization was opposed with particular vigor by the Army Staff, especially the intelligence chief, Maj. Gen. George Strong.

Strong condemned OSS plans for guerrilla warfare as 'essentially unsound and unproductive' (Strong, 1942). If guerrilla warfare were to be carried out at all by the Allies, Strong stated, it should be conducted by conventional Army units and 'take the form of raids ... practically identical with commando operations'. The JCS was especially concerned that OSS personnel would be conducting operations in US-dominated theaters of war outside the control of the conventional theater commander.

Accordingly, in 1942, JCS placed OSS deployed elements under the control of the theater commanders in whose areas they were operating, rather than having them report directly to Headquarters,

OSS, in Washington (JIC, 1976, 4). Only the personal intervention of President Roosevelt succeeded in gaining military cooperation, however grudging, with the OSS.

The OSS and its Jedburghs went into business in German-controlled France. They began 'special operations' by fielding British-trained 'civilian' (paramilitary) three-man Jedburgh teams to aid resistance groups in harassing the occupying Germans. As a note of continuity with later developments, one William Colby jumped into occupied France as part of a Jedburgh team. The same Bill Colby later led CIA unconventional warfare missions in Vietnam during the 1960s before finally becoming Director of Central Intelligence in 1975 (Colby, 1978, 34–6).

As the organization's responsibilities increased, the OSS created 'Operational Groups' (OGs) composed of French-speaking US Army volunteers. The OGs were organized into 15-man 'sections' consisting of two officers, and 13 enlisted men: infantrymen, engineers (demolitions), signalmen (radio operators) and medical technicians.

Operating in uniform, these 'sections' parachuted behind German lines, where they joined members of the French anti-German resistance. They organized and trained the local resistance groups and led them in carrying out harassment and sabotage attacks against German installations, cutting enemy lines of communication (LOCs) and providing intelligence to the Allied commanders. By early 1945, there were 75 OG teams assisting French partisans (OSS, 1945, 'Aid to the French Resistance', 2–3; also Operations Reports, 1944).

These partisan-support operations became the enduring model for the US Army's conduct of unconventional warfare, enshrined in doctrine when the first Special Forces units were organized by OSS veterans in the 1950s. The OSS Operational Groups were the model for the Special Forces 'A Team' of today.

In 1944, the combined headquarters formed by SOE and OSS in London was renamed 'Special Forces Headquarters' (Paddock, 1982, 29). Among the visitors to the building was a young OSS officer named Aaron Bank, who had begun making a nuisance of himself with his idea that the US Army needed a permanent partisan-warfare capability. Bank would go on to become the founder of US Army Special Forces.[3]

In yet another ironic connection with the future Vietnam War, an OSS officer, Lt Col. Peter Dewey, was killed at a Vietminh roadblock in 1945, the first US soldier to die in Vietnam (Karnow, 1983, 140).[4]

The beginning of Navy and Air Force Special Operations

Unlike the Army, which was dragged into the special operations business, the Navy and the Army Air Force (AAF) managed to avoid the kind of painful experiments the Army was going through. In large part this was because, for those services, there really was no distinction between special operations and other types of mission. The only important difference was the nature of the customer they serviced, conventional or special. Both the Air Forces and the Navy recognized this and would make it a continuing argument against the organization of separate special operations forces for the next 50 years.

Despite this position, the Army Air Force found it necessary to assign specific units to the support of Allied clandestine operations. The first of these, Special Flight Squadron (in reality a medium bomber unit), was organized in Tunisia in 1943. Later renamed the 885th Bomb Squadron (Special), it supported OSS and SOE teams throughout the Mediterranean and the Balkans. In England, the Eighth Air Force designated four squadrons of heavy B-24 bombers for the same purpose in Europe. Despite some internal AAF resistance, these Eighth Air Force 'Carpetbagger' units grew until by mid-1944 they totaled 70 B-24s and C-47 transports. A group of modified B-26 medium bombers was added in 1945 for the purpose of receiving coded transmissions from the short-range radios of OSS operators in occupied Europe (USSOCOM, 1996, 2–8, 2–9).

In Asia, a special AAF unit was created to provide support to Allied long-range penetration units such as General Orin Wingate's British-led 'Chindits' and Merrill's Marauders. Called the 1st Air Commando Group, the composite unit included all manner of attack and support aircraft from gliders to P-51 fighters and C-47s to the first helicopters used for combat support, the Sikorski R-4. Although not engaged in unconventional operations, the Air Commandos pioneered the whole field of air support to ground troops, essentially inventing air assault, medical evacuation and personnel recovery. The Air Commandos were so successful that a 2nd and 3rd Air Commando Group were also activated. Almost as an afterthought, a small group of B-24 bombers in China was assigned to support OSS missions in China and southeast Asia (ibid.).

True to form, AAF Headquarters abolished the Air Commando Groups as soon as possible and in 1944 all three were absorbed by conventional Air Force units. The OSS support units did not even last as long as the OSS itself and were disbanded or absorbed in 1945.

Like the AAF, the Navy did not set out to organize an unconventional force and, with one or two tiny and soon forgotten exceptions, did not do so. But it did find that the exigencies of amphibious warfare required new skills not found in the fleet. In 1943 volunteer demolition experts were trained as swimmers and formed into the first Navy Combat Demolitions Units for the specific purpose of conducting beach reconnaissance and destroying obstacles to an amphibious landing (Fawcett, 1995, xi; USSOCOM, 1996, 2–7).

Fielded in early 1944, the units became known as UDTs, Underwater Demolitions Teams. After adding charting and surveying to their skills, the UDTs went on to lead dozens of invasions and other naval operations in the Pacific and, with their British counterparts, help prepare the beaches for the Allied landings at Normandy. By the end of World War II there were about 3,500 'frogmen', divided among 30 teams. Collectively, they had participated in every significant amphibious operation of the war after 1943. Like the other unconventional units they were disbanded at war's end and only a small number of experienced men remained in the Navy (Fawcett, 1995, xii).

The birth of military Civil Affairs

If the histories of Psychological Operations and Special Operations were interwoven from the beginning, none of that history included Civil Affairs. While President Roosevelt may have been an enthusiast of some forms of warfare he apparently did not approve of the idea of the military performing civil administrative functions and believed the State Department should handle this aspect of the war. The official US Army Special Operations Command history states that when the first School of Military Government was opened at the University of Virginia in May 1941, it was without the knowledge of the president (USASOC, 1994, 31).

After Secretary of War Henry Stimson managed to convince Roosevelt of the necessity for such a creature, the US Army Civil Affairs Division (CAD) was activated on 1 March 1943 under the command of Major General John H. Hilldring, the only commander CAD would ever have. During the war CAD provided Civil Affairs assistance to liberated friendly territory and military government for occupied enemy areas. All things considered, Civil Affairs Division had remarkable success dealing with as many as 80 million civilians, friendly and enemy. It assisted civilian populations with a wide range of needs including restoration of utilities, water purification, disposal of the dead and food distribution while also performing auxiliary tasks from recovering stolen art treasures to disarming teenage partisans (USASOC, 1994, 33).

Civil Affairs units were quickly disbanded at the end of the war and removed from the active service entirely. By 1948, only 40 Civil Affairs personnel remained in the US military structure, all within a single reserve unit, the 300 Military Government Group, at Fort Myer, Virginia.

The critics gather

For all their accomplishments, the Rangers and the OSS both continued to have more than their share of detractors. Their operations were accepted as important by the military only insofar as they supported the conventional battle. However, the fact that many special-operations missions *were* in support of the conventional battle made few friends for these units. The arguments marshaled against them were very similar to those that would be heard again and again throughout the history of special-operations forces. Little credit was given for their successes.

Both during and after World War II, senior military commanders generally felt that special operations units like the OSS and the original Rangers contributed little to the overall success of the allies. Critics charged that elite special-purpose units did nothing that could not be done equally well by 'good conventional infantry' (King, 1985, 75). In the Pacific, the lordly General Douglas MacArthur successfully refused to allow OSS operations. He also rejected their assistance in organizing the Philippine guerrillas (Paddock, 1982, 31–2). Evaluating OSS support to the French Resistance, the War Department General Staff summary (an Army product) refers to the 'so-called resistance activities in France', and grudgingly, credits 'local French ... for the end results accomplished' (DA General Staff, 1944, 1).

It is true that many OSS resistance activities were 'haphazard, poorly organized, and uncoordinated with overall operations' (Paddock, 1982, 31). It is also true that the relatively tiny OSS unconventional warfare operations in Burma, Yugoslavia, China, Norway and France tied down several German and Japanese divisions while maintaining morale and the spirit of resistance in the occupied nations and providing tangible evidence of Allied support.

Some observers felt that such specialized units (especially Rangers and the OSS) were detrimental in two respects. First, it was believed that these units were undeservedly 'glamorized', detracting from the record of standard, conventional units (Ladd, 1978, 37; Cohen, 1978; Slim, 1956, 546–9; Vandegrift, 1964). Secondly, this attitude was not mitigated by the general truculence and swagger (and sometimes outright arrogance) too often exhibited by such units (Beaumont, 1988, 5).

Another criticism was that such special organizations were actually counterproductive. Supposedly, they monopolized needed resources and the best available personnel for what were seen as purely secondary operations (Beaumont, 1974, 112; Cohen, 1978). This last complaint seems to have little merit in the case of the Rangers or the OSS, which were, by World War II standards, tiny organizations. The OSS, the larger of the two, included only 4,097 Army personnel in 1943, rising to a high of only 8,360 by May of 1945 (US War Department, 1945, 15).

The OSS also had unique problems with bureaucratic competition within the US government. Its opponents within the civilian bureaucracies included the FBI (Federal Bureau of Investigation) and the State Department. J. Edgar Hoover, the FBI Director, saw Donovan as a threat and led a personal campaign against him that lasted into the 1950s. Under Hoover's direction, the FBI fought successfully to keep its intelligence resources in South and Central America out of OSS hands (Troy, 1981).[5]

Psychological operations, both within and without the OSS, came under fire as well. There was considerable opposition to the 'civilian' nature of Psyops in personnel and function. In the words of an Army officer, 'one US medium tank has proved far more effective than all the bag of trick gadgets, which merely offend good taste and give nothing concrete where want is great ... I believe that such agencies as the OWI and OSS can profitably be eliminated in the future' (US War Department General Staff, 1942). These attitudes had serious repercussions for unconventional warfare, since it was the civilian-led, paramilitary OSS, and not the military services, that sought to capitalize on the potential for guerrilla warfare offered by partisan elements in German and Japanese occupied territory.

In early 1945, Donovan proposed that the OSS capability be preserved in the form of a 'central intelligence authority' which would retain many of the wartime OSS personnel. His memorandum to the President was leaked to the press, where it generated critical headlines and a brief public furor that convinced Roosevelt to wait for 'a more propitious moment' (Ford, 1970, 303–4). After the President's death in April that moment seemed unlikely to arrive.

Under pressure from the military, the State Department, the FBI and his personal convictions, Roosevelt's successor, Harry S. Truman, saw a 'spying and sabotage' agency in peacetime as both unnecessary and politically unwise (Ransom, 1958, 71–2; also Ford, 1970, 312). The OSS was quickly ordered disbanded on 1 October 1945, fewer than 60 days after the Japanese surrender. Research and analysis functions were assigned to the State Department and its remaining operational elements to the War Department as the Strategic Services Unit. Once under War Department control it vanished almost immediately in the postwar draw down (US War Department, 1976, vol. 2, 440–60).

Some of its members, however, were given the option of joining the regular military, where they became influential in developing US special operations during the 1950s (Colby, 1978, 61). Indeed, the experience of these OSS veterans, especially Aaron Bank, would become the definitive example of unconventional warfare in US military practice and doctrine (for example, Morris, 1979, 25). Aaron Bank, Herbert Brucker, Jack Shannon and Caesar Sivitella would become the founders of US Army Special Forces. William Colby, as noted, went on to the CIA, where he conducted paramilitary missions in southeast Asia and eventually became director of the agency. Edward Lansdale was apparently assigned to both military intelligence and the OSS after 1943, an arrangement that would continue with the CIA after World War II (Lansdale, 1984).[6]

The World War II special operations cited above were almost exclusively in support of conventional operations conducted by the regular armed forces. The Ranger units provided support by conducting special purpose raids and by acting as elite conventional units. The OSS teams conducted sabotage raids, tied down enemy regular armed forces in rear-area security chores, and kept alive the resistance in occupied countries.[7]

US planners believed that conventional concepts still obtained for these partisans, and that their efforts were simply an extension of conventional operations (Laqueur, 1976, ch. 1). Accordingly, the training received by most OSS operators was tactical military training with the addition of specialized techniques such as clandestine radio communication (Brucker, 1989; Bank, 1986, 18–41). There was also a strong tendency for national and service-level planners to see these partisans only in the context of the allied struggle against the Axis powers, and not in the context of their own domestic political environment, including even the outright revolutionaries (such as Tito in Yugoslavia and Ho Chi Minh in Indochina).

OSS operators, on the other hand, found these issues to be of great importance in planning and conducting their operations, sometimes requiring that otherwise-promising plans be canceled (Bank, 1986, 116). Bank offers a clear example of this when he reports that an OSS plan to infiltrate members of the French Army into Indochina for a raid against the Japanese was canceled because Ho Chi Minh's OSS-assisted Vietminh 'will turn from harassing the Japanese to attacking them [the French infiltrators]. They will not countenance the return of French elements' (Bank, 1986, 115–16). The relationship between OSS and War Department service staffs and theater commanders was strained because of this and similar incidents, contributing to anti-OSS feelings in the upper levels of the uniformed services.

Operating from the conventional perspective, US military planners did not regard socio-economic or political factors as important variables in these subconflicts. Seen within the context of massive world-wide conventional warfare, these subconflicts were regarded as 'sideshows' – auxiliaries to the major effort to destroy the enemy armed forces. It is important to note that, while OSS operators had a greater appreciation of cultural and political factors, they still saw their operations as an adjunct to the larger conventional effort (Peers, 1948, 12; see also OSS, 1945). Given this attitude, it is not surprising there was little attempt to institutionalize the experience or capabilities of the unconventional units before they were hurriedly disbanded.

In the end, there was no real attempt to develop a military doctrine that would incorporate the experience of the World War II special-operations units. The parallel development of doctrine for unconventional war also received little emphasis until hostilities in Vietnam and then was confined largely to counterguerrilla (rather than counterinsurgency) considerations.

THE POSTWAR LOW: THE 1940S AND 1950S

Shortly after World War II US defense policy became centered on a single overriding objective – Soviet containment, initially in response to Soviet expansionist activity in the Middle East (Campbell, 1960). From the late 1940s to the early 1990s, opposition to the Soviet Union was the central element of US national security policy. During the mid-1950s these policies led to a concentration on nuclear war to the detriment of other forms of engagement, including unconventional warfare.

As early as 1948, the Joint Chiefs of Staff backed away from supporting peacetime military involvement in unconventional warfare and from creating anything like a 'separate guerrilla warfare school and corps'. While cautiously endorsing the concept that 'the United States should provide itself with the organization and means of supporting foreign resistance movements', nothing military was done to implement it (JCS Memorandum 1807/1, 1948).

During this period, civilian agencies enjoyed what little primacy was to be gained from such involvement, notably the fledgling Central Intelligence Agency. Shortly after dissolving the OSS, President Truman established the Central Intelligence Group (CIG) to reconcile the often conflicting intelligence assessments that the White House received from various sources within the US government. On 26 July 1947, the National Security Act came into effect, replacing the CIG with a permanent national intelligence structure: a Central Intelligence Agency (CIA), directly responsible to the President, and an advisory National Security Council (NSC). Like the CIG, the new CIA had no covert operations capability, but this was not long in coming. At its first formal meeting on 10 December 1947, the newly created NSC issued directive NSC 4 'Coordination of Foreign Intelligence Measures'. This directive ordered the Secretary of State to coordinate anti-communist propaganda and, in secret annex NSC 4A, ordered the CIA to supplement this effort with covert psychological warfare. Approved by President Truman, and supported by congressional funding from the agency's general appropriation, NSC 4A put the CIA into the covert-operations business (Ranelagh, 1987, 115).[8]

On 19 June 1948, the National Security Council issued Directive NSC 10/2, 'taking cognizance of the vicious covert activities of the USSR, its satellite countries, and Communist groups' and establishing the CIA Office of Special Projects 'to plan and conduct covert operations'. Covert action included some of the ingredients of military special operations and unconventional warfare and was defined as:

> ... propaganda, economic warfare, preventive direct action, including sabotage, anti-sabotage, demolition and evacuation measures; subversion against hostile states, including assistance to underground resistance movements, guerrillas and refugee liberation groups, and support of indigenous anti-communist elements in threatened countries of the free world. Such operations shall not include armed conflict by recognized military forces, espionage, counter-espionage, and cover and deception for military operations.
> (Leary, 1984, 131–3)

The same directive also called for the CIA Special Projects Office to coordinate with the JCS for the planning and conduct of such activities during wartime (ibid.,131–4). This Directive presumed a clear distinction between peacetime and wartime, a condition that has seldom been met in US foreign policy since.

By the time of NSC 10/2 the USA's first postwar involvement in counterinsurgency was already underway. After communist guerrilla activity began in Greece in 1946, President Truman presented what became known as the Truman Doctrine (Truman, 1947, 531–3). Briefly, this doctrine held that the USA, in order to protect its own national security, must 'support free peoples, who are resisting attempted subjugation by armed minorities or by outside pressures' (ibid., 543). As a foreign-policy doctrine, it was clear, perhaps even noble, and an invitation to trouble.

The Truman Doctrine program for security assistance to Greece and Turkey established the prototype for such assistance efforts. The President asked for and received funding for 'relief assistance' and also for 'the detail of US civilian and military personnel' (ibid., 533). A US military mission was dispatched to Greece, where it assisted in rebuilding the Greek army along conventional lines. The insurgency gradually died out for various reasons, most of them unconnected with the new US-model Greek Army. However, according to Asprey, the training provided the Greek military 'was erroneously considered a primary factor in the defeat of the insurgents' (1975, 814–17). Other commentators pointed out that several other factors were more important than the new army, including the insurgents' loss of active foreign support, loss of sanctuary, a series of factional splits among them, and their mistaken attempt to adopt conventional military tactics (O'Ballance, 1966; Selton, 1965; Kousoulos, 1965).[9]

DOCTRINE FOR THE POSTWAR WORLD

The first glimmerings of an emerging doctrine for unconventional warfare (the term was then almost unknown) was the Army's attempt to write a doctrine for dealing with guerrillas. Based on its perception of the experience in Greece and the partisan support operations of World War II, the Army produced its first manual dealing with one of the forms of unconventional warfare: counterguerrilla operations. Written by Russell Volckman, the Philippine guerrilla veteran, FM 31-20 *Operations Against Guerrilla Forces* was published in 1951. It stated, as a matter of fact, that guerrilla war was 'war conducted by irregular forces in conjunction with regularly organized forces as a phase of a normal war'. The US Army's involvement in these operations was to take the form of 'detached regular forces in the enemy's rear areas'. Remarkably, in view of Volckman's three-year long, *ad hoc*, irregular Philippine campaign, the manual claimed that guerrilla operations were 'generally of short duration, conducted by detached regular forces in the enemy's rear areas' (DA, FM 31-20, 1951, 1, 2–3).[10]

The next version of the same manual, published in 1955, outlined a basic counterguerrilla doctrine based on small-unit action. While the 1951 version had at least recognized the importance of political factors, the 1955 one presented counterguerrilla operations as purely a tactical military question. The subsequent edition, in 1958, was retitled *Guerrilla Warfare and Special Forces Operations*, and continued the same basic theme: that guerrilla operations required little special (i.e. unconventional) expertise, and were merely an adjunct to and determined by conventional operations. It became a central concept in the US approach. US military perceptions of unconventional operations began with partisan irregulars fighting as guerrillas against an occupying enemy, as had the Free French of the Interior and the anti-Japanese Filipinos and ended with the successful US-backed counterguerrilla campaign in Greece. The role of the US Army was to advise, supply and help lead these patriotic elements until US and/or allied conventional armed forces could come to the rescue. This became the preferred model of 'unconventional warfare' for the US military.[11]

The awkward fact that the Greek problem had been a communist insurgency rather than a partisan resistance was not allowed to cloud the issue. The vital distinction between insurgency and guerrilla war was obscured and largely lost. This presumed near-identity between guerrilla war (a military technique) and insurgency (a political condition) became a root cause of much subsequent difficulty.

The confusion surrounding the whole idea of special-operations organizations and their missions is illustrated by the brief and abortive history of the Army's 'airborne reconnaissance' concept between 1946 and 1948 (Paddock, 1982, 69–70; Rottman, 1987, 22). Prompted by the then-Secretary of War, Robert Patterson, the Army prepared a study of the utility and feasibility of 'airborne reconnaissance units' of the 'types developed by OSS' (US War Department General Staff, 1947). First titled the 'Airborne Recon Company' and then the 'Ranger Group', the proposed organization at various times combined various commando and partisan support missions 'to organize and conduct overt and covert operations behind enemy lines, thereby assuming functions formerly performed by units of the OSS' (Army Ground Forces, 1948).

The operational concept for the unit was a mix of OSS and Ranger capabilities: tactical raids and sabotage in the enemy rear, development, training and supply of partisans (resistance groups), reconnaissance and espionage, recruitment, training and control of foreign civilian agents and captured enemy agents, counter-espionage, 'black' Psyops, and the creation of escape and evasion systems for downed aviators and escaped prisoners of war (POWs). All of these to be accomplished by a single unit with a total strength of about 115 officers and 135 enlisted soldiers (ibid., 8). In any event, the organization was never formed and the concept quietly sank beneath the weight of its own confusion.

Like the preferred model of conventional war described earlier, the preferred model of 'unconventional warfare' (irregular partisan warfare in support of the conventional battle) remained fixed in US doctrine with remarkable stability. Something of this spirit was reflected in the Lodge Bill of 1950 (US Congress, Senate, Public Law 597, 1950) which allowed aliens to be sworn in as members of the US armed forces. This was a time when many Western leaders feared a Soviet ground invasion of western Europe. The underlying notion of the Lodge Bill was that in time of war the alien members of the US Army could be returned to their native countries to conduct partisan guerrilla warfare against Soviet forces (Prados, 1986, 89). In fact, many former displaced Europeans from World War II did eventually become members of the Army's original Special Forces units, whose mission was exactly that.

ANOTHER SUCCESS IN THE PHILLIPPINES

The early 1950s did see one outstanding success in the development of unconventional warfare methods and techniques, although it was completely outside existing doctrine. In 1952, the Eisenhower administration became concerned with the communist-led People's Liberation Army (commonly known as 'Huks') in the Philippines. Former OSS officer, Edward G. Lansdale, by then an Air Force colonel and intelligence officer, had worked with the Philippine armed forces immediately after World War II. Now he returned there as a special member of the Joint US Military Advisory Group (JUSMAG).

In that capacity, he eventually became a trusted advisor to Philippines President Ramon Magsaysay in the campaign against the Huks. Lansdale did not see counterinsurgency as a wholly military proposition and distrusted any exclusive reliance on conventional military means. Instead, he combined several military and non-military programs. He termed this approach 'psywar' and thought of it as a psychological campaign aimed at exploiting Huk weaknesses and fears while creating social and economic programs to win the loyalty of the rural population (Lansdale, 1972, 69–83). The military component was a series of small-unit operations by Philippine government troops aimed at separating the Huk guerrillas from the population. The intent, however, was not to destroy the guerrillas in the field but rather to destroy the legitimacy and popular support of the political movement that underlay them. Philipine soldiers were taught to behave correctly, avoid common offenses such as theft, and show respect for the population among whom they worked. By 1953, the Huk rebellion had been defeated 'politically, and morally, as well as militarily' (ibid., 123).

Despite its successful outcome, the Philippine experience had little noticeable effect on Army doctrine, perhaps because of its political character and 'psywar' methods. Nonetheless, in January 1954, Lansdale was told to prepare for a similar assignment in the Republic of Vietnam (Lansdale, 1972, 126).

THE KOREAN WAR (1950–53)

Not surprisingly, UW and special operations in the Korean War were a sideshow. The major forces of all combatants were conventional armies operating in the same manner as those of World War II. As during World War II, unconventional efforts in the Korean conflict were intended purely to support conventional military operations (Brodie, 1973).[12]

This does not mean there were no opportunities for unconventional warfare. With the outbreak of the war in 1950, thousands of anti-communist Koreans, including South Korean soldiers, were left behind enemy lines by the rapid pace of the North Korean People's Army (NKPA) advance. The US Army and the CIA made a variety of *ad hoc* efforts to conduct a version of unconventional warfare by organizing these Korean nationals as guerrillas in the enemy rear. One of these, UNPIK, or United Nations Partisan Infantry-Korea included a number of Special Forces officers in late 1952 and early 1953.

For its part, the Army trained and directed anti-communist Koreans in partisan operations including raids, sabotage and intelligence gathering. It also became involved in supporting partisan groups and intelligence agents with supplies delivered by sea and aircraft (Vanderpool, 1983, 138–41; HQ Guerrilla Division, 1952). In the south, US military police and elements of the conventional Army divisions cooperated with South Korean military units in eliminating NKPA units attempting to fight as guerrillas behind United Nations' (UN) lines. These were not 'counterinsurgency' operations since there was no attempt to organize an insurgency. The NKPA had no evident popular support among the South Korean people and made little attempt to develop any (Day, 1989). Fighting as Ranger-style commandos, the northern soldiers were quickly hunted down and captured, or killed.

The CIA and the Army attempted to carry out their respective operations in parallel, but the chronic UW problem of poor coordination appeared again, creating a problem with overlapping organizations and missions (Vanderpool, 1983, 140). By now it was generally accepted that in such operations there was a serious difficulty in coordinating UW activities with those of conventional units. These guerrilla warfare activities were considered 'special operations' and conducted separately from psywar activities.

Civil Affairs in Korea

By the outbreak of the war, the Civil Affairs lessons of World War II had been largely forgotten and, for the most part, Civil Affairs were treated like partisan operations, a marginal business attended to mostly as an afterthought. Conventional commanders regarded CA as a form of disaster relief and, since the South Korean government functioned throughout the war, saw little scope for military government. Furthermore, the rise of nongovernmental relief organizations, such as CARE (Cooperation for American Relief Everywhere), and UN and US State Department civil-assistance agencies all contributed to the confusion, with overlapping responsibilities and unclear mandates (USASOC, 1994, 45–6).

Psychological Operations in the Korean War

Psywar or Psychological Operations activities in Korea were the province of the Army's newly created 1st Radio Broadcasting and Leaflet Group, and consisted almost entirely of tactical leaflet drops and radio and loudspeaker surrender appeals, as during World War II. Strategic Psyops was still not considered a military task by most of the conventional Army.

Of particular interest, however, was the creation in 1950 of the Army's Office of the Chief of Psychological Warfare (OCPW), headed by then-Brigadier General (later Major General) Robert McClure, who had been Eisenhower's Psychological Operations (propaganda) officer during World War II. Unlike the OSS's guerrilla operations, psychological warfare had become an accepted (if not emphasized) element of the military establishment.

In his analysis of this issue (the acceptance of psychological warfare) Paddock attributes the acceptance of Psyops to the fact that the Army developed 'formal staff sections and units ... to employ this weapon. Military men were in command and made the final decisions as to its use ... Thus psychological warfare acquired a measure of legitimacy within the Army and survived as a formal activity after the war' (Paddock, 1982, 36).

Certainly this was important, but it was not necessarily the whole answer. The Army could have as easily incorporated the OSS guerrilla-warfare concepts if indeed its only real objection was that the OSS represented a military capability outside the War Department (though under JCS direction). It may well be that Psyops represented exactly what Paddock calls it, a new 'weapon' but no more than that. As applied by the Army it was clearly an adjunct to the conventional battle, not too dissimilar to traditional calls on the enemy to surrender. Furthermore, unlike OSS operations, Psyops forces did not set out to be in any way independent of conventional commanders.

Air and naval special operations in Korea

When hostilities began in Korea, the new United States Air Force (formerly the AAF) expected to support a variety of special operations including counterinsurgency and covert missions. Three composite Wings were created, the 580th, 581st and 582nd, all loosely based on the successful World War II Air Commando Groups. In the event, however, air special operations were generally restricted to supporting CIA and Army clandestine insertions throughout the Korean peninsula. These were accomplished with ordinary C-47 and C-119 transports, leaving little scope for the new composite Wings. Only the 580th was actually deployed to Korea and all three were deactivated with the war's end in 1953.

With only one major amphibious operation during the war, the landing at Inchon, the Navy's UDTs did not play a major role. Still, a few teams were created and the range of their activities was considerably increased. The original World War II 'frogmen' had not even received weapons training, but, given the lack of necessary beach reconnaissance, the Korean War UDTs began to conduct seaborne raids behind enemy lines. These new missions proved very successful as the teams attacked and destroyed enemy ships, harbor facilities, shore installations and later bridges and other targets well removed from the sea. The UDTs even became involved with clandestine operations, assisting CIA and Army supported partisan units. Quietly and without any special fanfare, the Navy UDTs had made a permanent transition from beach reconnaissance specialists to full-fledged commandos (Fawcett, 1995, xii).

Rangers in Korea

The Army's tendency to conventionalize special operations units was demonstrated with the next generation of Ranger units, recreated for the Korean War. In the fall of 1950, four companies of Rangers were formed from volunteers in Korea. The initial units received no school training but a Ranger Training Center was created at Fort Benning, Georgia. Ranger students at Fort Benning received a six-week program training them as infiltrators, specializing in raids, sabotage and demolitions with the intention that these units would strike at objectives well in the enemy rear (Ranger Company, 1950). The 1st, 2nd, 3rd and 4th Ranger companies finished the first cycle on 13 November 1950. The 3rd company remained at Fort Benning to train the remaining 5th, 6th, 7th and 8th companies. The 2nd Ranger company was made up entirely of black volunteers, who were experienced troopers from the 555th Infantry Regiment (Airborne).

A total of 17 Ranger companies were eventually operational in Korea. The Ranger units tended to become nomads, attached to varying infantry regiments for various periods of time, during which they were usually employed as shock troops in the most dangerous parts of the front lines. They were often used for patrols well in front of friendly lines but performed other dangerous tasks as well, including raids and ambushes. The 1st Ranger Infantry Company (Airborne), for example, infiltrated nine miles behind enemy lines to destroy the headquarters of the 12th North Korean Division. Two North Korean Regiments fled from the area as a result (Payne, 1996).

Unfortunately, most conventional commanders saw little use for the special capabilities of these units, too often using them to spearhead assaults, and as counterattack forces to restore lost positions. Even though the highly motivated Rangers were effective in these roles, they tended to be attributed out of action by their high casualty rate (up to 90 percent for some units). All Ranger companies in Korea were disbanded on 1 August 1951. The personnel were transferred to conventional infantry units and the 'troop spaces' (i.e. personnel authorizations) were awarded to the newly established Special Forces the following year (Bank, 1989; Payne, 1996).

On 22 October 1951, the Chief of Army Field Forces changed the emphasis of Fort Benning's Ranger program from training airborne companies to teaching individuals. The Ranger Training Command at Fort Benning was replaced by a Ranger Department in the Infantry School there. But, since there were no Ranger units remaining in the Army, the mission of the department was to provide rigorous but conventional infantry training to junior officers and NCOs and then return them to their units. The Ranger concept had now come full circle back to its original intent of 1942.

The most direct connection among elite light-infantry units, unconventional operations and US Special Operations Forces was not, as might be expected, through the development of Ranger-style units, but instead through Brigadier General Robert McClure, holder of the little noticed title, Office of the Chief of Psychological Warfare (OCPW). McClure's influence and that of Colonel Aaron Bank led to the formation of the USA's first dedicated peacetime special-operations unit.

NOTES

1. For an account of Blackburn's operations in the occupied Philippines see Philip Hawkins, *Blackburn's Headhunters* (1955).
2. 'Black' propaganda is that which purports to originate from a source other than its actual one. For example, Allied broadcasts to German troops would sometimes falsely identify themselves as being official German military broadcasts. 'White' propaganda attributes itself to its actual source, while 'gray' material is not attributed to any source.
3. The definitive, or at least most detailed history, of the OSS is the US War Department History Project, Strategic Services Unit, War Reports of the OSS (Washington, DC: GPO, 1976), 2 vols., originally compiled for JCS use in 1947–48. This was published commercially in 1976 by Walker and Company, New York. For a critical appraisal see R. Harris Smith (1972).
    There is a wealth of literature on the SOE and British UW operations in World War II. A brief popular account is Patrick Howarth's *Undercover* (1980). The

authoritative source, however, is Hinsely's (2 vols.) *British Intelligence in the Second World War* (1979).

4. For an account of OSS activity in Indochina see Archimedes L. Patti's *Why Vietnam?* (1980). Patti was head of the OSS Indochina Desk in Washington during 1944. In August 1945 he became OSS chief of station in Hanoi, until October when he left at French insistence.

5. For a (pro-CIA) account of the internecine conflict between OSS (and later CIA) and the Army/FBI see Thomas F. Troy's *Donovan and the CIA: A History of the Establishment of the Central Intelligence Agency* (1981).

6. William Colby is presumably familiar to the reader. Edward G. Lansdale, an Air Force Intelligence Officer assigned to the CIA, conducted unconventional warfare operations in the Philippines and Vietnam during the 1950s. Other OSS veterans went to the CIA including Kermit Roosevelt and Harry Rositzke (*Bibliography of Intelligence Literature*, no author listed, Defense Intelligence College, Washington, DC, 1985).

7. That Ranger Battalions were constantly employed as conventional infantry is clearly indicated in the World War II After Action Reports of these units now on file at the Washington National Records Center in Suitland, Maryland. See, for example, 1st Ranger Bn After Action Report, 9 April 1943, microfilm INBN 72-37, roll 1, frame 221; 3rd Ranger Bn After Action Report, 31 July 1943, microfilm INBN 72-37, roll 4, frames 2–4; 4th Ranger Bn After Action Report, 5 October 1943, microfilm INBN 72-37 roll 4, frames 124–6; 5th Ranger Bn After Action Report, 22 July 1944, microfilm INBN 72-37 roll 5, frames 2–5; 5th Ranger Bn After Action Report, 10 March 1945, microfilm INBN 72-37, roll 5, frames 365–73.

8. The contemporary debate over this establishment is summarized in 'Memorandum Respecting Section 202 (Central Intelligence Agency) of the Bill to Provide for a National Defense Establishment', 25 April 1947; see Allen Dulles (1947, 526).

9. This policy was formalized by the Mutual Defense Assistance Act of 1949 (PL 329), which provided for the establishment of Military Assistance Advisory Groups (MAAGs) in friendly nations requesting such assistance.

10. A copy of Volkman's original manuscript is located in the Archives of the Special Warfare Center, Fort Bragg, North Carolina.

11. The remainder of the scant military literature on guerrilla warfare during the 1950s consisted of: Virgil Ney, *Guerrilla Warfare in the Philippines* (1953); Robert M. Kennedy, DA Pamphlet 20-243, *German Anti-Guerrilla Operations in the Balkans (1941–1944)* (1954); Fred H. Barton, *Salient Operational Aspects of Paramilitary Warfare in Three Asian Areas* (1954); Gene F. Hanrahan, *Japanese Operations Against Guerrilla Forces* (1954); Edgar M. Howell, DA Pamphlet 20-244, *The Soviet Partisan Movement, 1941–1944* (1956).

12. Colonel Volckman was one of those involved in organizing the Army's guerrilla warfare units in Korea (Vanderpool, 1983, 86). For a general account of US-Army sponsored guerrilla operations in Korea, see Day (1989). For an account of US Special Operations in Korea see Rod Paschall (1975).

3 The creation of Army Special Forces

General McClure's interpretation of his 'psychological warfare' mandate went far beyond the notion of distributing surrender leaflets. Like Donovan's version of the term, his included commando raids, partisan support, covert and clandestine activities. In 1951, McClure organized a 'Special Operations Division' within OCPW and recruited Col. Aaron Bank (an OSS veteran) as operations officer. Apparently under Bank's influence, the name was soon changed from 'Special Operations Division' to 'Special Forces Division' (DA, OCPW, 1951).

Col. Bank was then released from the OCPW and on 19 June 1952 became the first commander of the newly authorized 10th Special Forces Group (SFG) (Airborne) at Fort Bragg, North Carolina. It was the first formal Army peacetime unit ever dedicated to special operations. The unit's wartime mission was to develop, organize, train, equip and direct anti-Soviet resistance forces in eastern Europe in the event of war with the USSR. Authorized 400 soldiers, its strength upon activation was a grand total of ten. But, the 10th Group grew quickly, reaching its expected limit of 932 men (Bank 1986, 187). It drew volunteers from among former Rangers, regular Army paratroopers, OSS veterans, a number of Lodge Bill émigrés (largely from eastern Europe), and others. This was an unlikely and fortuitous combination.[1]

As leaders of a very small, all-volunteer organization, Bank and his officers could be very selective in choosing personnel. The 10th consisted almost entirely of long-service veterans with no first-term enlistees or extremely junior soldiers. Most of the members had seen combat service and most of those had been members of elite units. In particular, the OSS vets brought to the 10th a degree of expertise in denied-area operations that was unique. These former OSS operators took a leading role in forming the SF organization, consciously modeling it on their experience with partisans in World War II (Bank, 1986, 187). The newly created group became at once the most multi-talented organization in the US armed forces and probably the world.[2]

The Lodge Bill émigrés also brought something unique to the mix. They were for the most part well-educated men, often with advanced degrees, in a period when a high-school diploma was the only educational requirement for a commission in the US Army. The émigrés formed an important part of the noncommissioned officer corps of the Special Forces. English was a second language for these men but they possessed native fluency in a wide variety of European languages from Russian and Polish to Hungarian and Greek, adding depth to the French- and German-language skills of the OSS members. In one or two instances SF team medics actually held medical degrees from European universities and trained other medical personnel from the 10th in advanced techniques well beyond the skills of ordinary medical aidmen. This began a tradition of training SF medics as paraphysicians rather than simple first-aid providers.

The early connection between SF and Psyops was continued when the Psychological Warfare Center was created at Fort Bragg at the same time to provide formal instruction in psychological warfare for Army personnel (US Secretary of Defense, 1952, 73). Operating on McClure's broad definition of 'psychological operations', the Center also had responsibility for the newly created Special Forces.

Once established as part of the Psychological Warfare Center, the new unit was placed in a set of abandoned World War II wooden barracks on a back corner of the fort called Smoke Bomb Hill. The 10th saw itself as clandestine and covert from the beginning, as evidenced by Bank's training and by General McClure's strong negative reaction to a single-sentence mention of the new unit in *Newsweek* magazine (ibid., 193–4). Until the Vietnam War period the Special Forces remained almost unknown to the public and were often regarded with skepticism by the military establishment.

Army Special Forces soon showed a tendency to evolve into conventional commando/Ranger-type raiding units, with a corresponding loss of unconventional capability (Vanderpool, 1983, 141, 146–8; Paddock, 1982, 101–9). This continued the important and lasting trend first noted in the Ranger case in World War II: units organized to conduct unconventional warfare and/or special operations tend to devolve toward the preferred conventional model (Guerrilla, TOE, 1952; also HQ Guerrilla Division, 1952).

Bureaucratic competition with the CIA and the resulting desire for a military unconventional-warfare capability, combined with the bitter example of the Ranger units, reinforced Banks and McClure's tendency to focus the Special Forces on partisan support operations similar to those of the OSS Operations Groups in World War II. Acting on their model of war as an autonomous activity, military officers, in particular McClure, resented civilian CIA operations within what the Army considered its exclusive province, the battlefield. Unconventional activities might not be exactly 'military' but they were not considered civilian, at least not by McClure and those around him. Others, including Army Secretary Frank Pace might not be enthusiastic about unconventional warfare but they were even less enthusiastic about surrendering turf (McClure, 1953).

Two prominent and influential OSS veterans, aside from Colonel Bank, were Major Jack Shannon (Executive Officer and assistant to Bank) and Major Herbert Bruckner, training officer (interview Bruckner, 1989; Mahan, 1989). In personal correspondence with the author, Colonel Bank stated of this formative period: 'I applied all my OSS background to our training, doctrine, concepts, planning, standards, and goals. The OSS legacy was our bible' (Bank, 1989). This is most obvious in the formation of the 'A-team' (initially called the 'FA-team') as the basic Special Forces operational element. This was the basic organizational element of the Army SF and originally was designed as a 15-man detachment, purposefully similar in organization and concept to the 15-man Operational Group section deployed by the OSS (Brucker, 1989; Operational Groups, 1944).

Bank was adamant that 'the Philippine experience played no role. It was the European accomplishments of the Jeds [Jedburgh Teams] and the Operational Groups of OSS in Europe that was the basis for all our efforts.' He added that no Ranger doctrine of any kind was incorporated in the original organization or operational concept of Special Forces (Bank, 1989).

Bruckner agreed that Volckman's experience, 'all that jungle stuff', had no application to the purely European-oriented Special Forces. Certainly, the focus of SF training was exclusively European, concentrating on the establishment of 'stay-behind' teams expected to hide from advancing Russian forces and emerge in the enemy rear area to organize partisan resistance (interview, Bruckner, 1989; also Simpson, 1983, 19–27, and Bank, 1986, 150–1).

Despite this Eurocentric attitude, and undeterred by the example of Ranger misuse, Special Forces-trained officers were placed under the conventional Army command structure in Korea. While a few assisted the 8th Army's *ad hoc* and largely disorganized guerrilla-warfare efforts, most were assigned as replacements in regular Army divisions, where they had no noticeable impact on the war. An additional group of SF officers and men was apparently also dispatched to Korea as a team 'but their mission was unknown' (Cleaver *et al.*, 1956, 73, 156–7).

In any case, according to Bank, no SF officer who had served in the Korean War guerrilla effort 'taught any doctrine or concepts connected therewith' upon return to Special Forces (Bank, 1989). After the end of the Korean War, some number of Army officers were detailed to the CIA 'on loan'. Some of these in turn were apparently recruited by the Agency but also retained their status as active duty Army personnel. Apparently, a few of these became Special Forces officers and both gave and received training at the Psychological Warfare Center, once again underlining the connection between Special Forces operations and the sort of covert and clandestine activities normally associated with the CIA (Perry, 1989, 89). CIA interest in the fledgling SF was marked by occasional visits to the SWC and consultations with Bruckner and others on their operational experience in Europe (Bruckner, 1989).

In 1953, the bulk of the new 10th Special Forces Group was transferred to Bad Toelz, West Germany, to prepare for resistance operations in Soviet-occupied Europe in the event of war. The SF soldiers remaining at Fort Bragg were reorganized into a new unit, the 77th Special Forces Group (Simpson, 1983, 41–2). A few of the SF troopers at Fort Bragg were dispatched as advisors and trainers to assist the Army of South Vietnam against a growing guerrilla insurgency. That same year Special Forces Capt. Harry Cramer was killed in a training accident, becoming the second US soldier to die in Vietnam (Stanton, 1985b, 35).

The psychological-warfare component of military operations entered a period of de-emphasis while increasing stress was placed on the purely military aspects of Special Forces operations. This was reflected by a name change on 10 December 1956, when the Psychological Warfare Center was renamed and divided into a headquarters, the US Army Special Warfare Center, and a school – the US Army Special Warfare School. The changes reflected the increasingly combat-related emphasis of their activities (USASOC, 1994, 52).[3] The change was welcomed in the 10th whose SF soldiers were not anxious to associate themselves with Psychological Operations, as indicated by Colonel Volkman:

Those of us who had worked on these programs ... were very opposed to have [sic] Special Forces associated with or under the Psychological

Warfare Center ... there was in general a stigma connected with psychological warfare, especially among combat men and we didn't care to have it 'rub off' on Special Forces ... Behind the lines operations and the 'dirty tricks game' had enough opposition among conventional military minds. (Paddock, 1982, 151)

Doctrine for Special Forces and unconventional warfare was notable chiefly by its absence. In 1957, the US Strategic Operations Force, Far East (Provisional), a planning organization, issued a classified report concluding that the USA needed a doctrine which would enable the Army to conduct unconventional warfare (defined as operations against a guerrilla insurgency). What little doctrine existed was almost purely tactical (US Strategic Operations Force, 1957). The report had no apparent impact and no expanded doctrine was forthcoming. The Army's concern remained firmly fixed on conventional warfare.

Rising communist influence in Asia did concern Army planners, and in April 1956 a classified organization called the 14th Special Forces Operational Detachment (Area) (Airborne) was activated at Fort Bragg under the cover designation of the 8251st Army Unit. This 16-man detachment was targeted against the Pacific with the mission of leading local resistance against any Soviet or Chinese military thrust in Asia. Three other clandestine SF detachments were activated in Japan with similar missions and given the deliberately unremarkable name of the 8231st Army Unit (USASOC, 1994, 53).

On 24 June 1957, the 1st Special Forces Group was activated at Camp Drake, Japan under the command of Colonel Frank Mills, another OSS veteran. The 1st SFG took control of the secret units and was immediately transferred to the island of Okinawa, where it organized Mobile Training Teams to instruct Asian allies in 'unconventional warfare tactics'. Okinawa was at that time also the home of the CIA's paramilitary support base located at Camp Chinen under Army cover. As reported by Edward Lansdale in a 1961 memo to Maxwell Taylor, 'it comprises a self-contained base ... with facilities of all types necessary to the storage, testing packaging, procurement and delivery of all types of supplies – ranging from weapons and explosives to medical and clothing' (Sheehan, 1971, 137–8).

In 1960 a small Army Special Forces Detachment under the command of Colonel George Morton began carrying out a number of training functions in Vietnam including instruction for CIA-controlled operations (Morton, 1976). As described by the US Army Special Operations Command's official history, Army Special Forces soldiers in the Republic of Vietnam taught Ranger-style courses while other SF advisors trained South Vietnamese members of 'clandestine, paramilitary and special unit programs' (USASOC, 1994, 53).

DOCTRINE FOR GUERRILLAS AND OTHERS LIKE THEM

If Special Forces units and individuals were to teach 'unconventional warfare' and similar subjects, exactly what would these lessons be based on? Army doctrine and experience in these areas was by now shallow, to say the least. Little had been preserved from the Korean War experience and even less from the guerrilla operations in World War II. In fact, the lessons taken from the Korean experience were mostly conventional and best described as 'low-key'. Studies by the Army ignored the guerrilla efforts and concluded that its conventional war doctrine was correct: 'the mass of material from Korea ... reaffirms the soundness of US doctrine, tactics, techniques, organization and equipment' (Army Field Forces, 1951; see also Infantry School, 1954).

Army capstone doctrine continued to treat guerrillas much as Clausewitz had in 1830, as irregular auxiliaries to the conventional main force. This was true of the 1944, 1954, 1956 and 1958 versions of the basic manual for military operations, first titled *Field Service Regulations, Operations* and later retitled Field Manual (FM) 100-5 *Operations*. The only manual to treat guerrillas or unconventional war at all seriously was the purely tactical 1951 manual *Operations Against Guerrilla Forces*, mentioned earlier.

The next attempt to formalize doctrine for guerrilla operations was FM 31-15 *Operations Against Airborne Attack, Guerrilla Action and Infiltration* (published in 1953). This suffered from confused purposes, stemming from the attempt to group dissimilar threats because all were marginal military endeavors and ancillary to the main effort, which was, of course, the direct, decisive clash of major ground-force elements.

A somewhat more comprehensive approach emerged in 1955 with the publication of DA FM 31-21, *Guerrilla Warfare*, which continued to treat guerrillas as friendly auxiliaries but also offered advice to conventional commanders on how to conduct counter-guerrilla warfare. In all these cases guerrilla action was seen purely as a question of operational technique.

Guerrilla warfare equals conventional warfare

This is a crucial point: as was seen in the Greek example, there arose a tendency to view guerrilla war, first of all, as an exclusively conventional form of warfare, ignoring its political and social context and, secondly, seeing it as important only insofar as it supported and enhanced the conventional combat capacity of regular armed forces. Guerrilla warfare was not seen as an important method of warfare in its own right. This carried a significant implied message: as practitioners of an indecisive form of war, guerrillas could not prevail against professional, conventional armed forces. Therefore, there was no need for any highly specialized counter-guerrilla doctrine.

Carried further, since guerrilla war divorced from political context is merely a specialized application of conventional warfare methods, there was even less reason for a great deal of specialized doctrine, organization, or training to conduct guerrilla war. For Special Forces, the conclusion was that to be committed to such a peripheral area of concern, meant they certainly did not need or deserve a great deal of attention or support.

As reported by General Maxwell Taylor, the assumption of the 1950s was that 'if the armed forces were prepared to cope with nuclear war, they could take care of lesser contingencies' (Taylor, 1972, 174). This implied that guerrillas are not a serious threat to the existence of an advanced industrial state. Even if this was correct, it did not necessarily follow that such forces are not a serious threat to the interests of such a state outside its national borders, especially if national interest is defined in terms other than those of simple survival.

THE EISENHOWER ERA AND 'MASSIVE RETALIATION'

By 1950 US national security policy had become fixed with remarkable constancy on the Soviet Union. In military terms this meant that US forces needed to be able to meet and defeat the armored tank legions of the USSR on the plains of western Europe. The need to counter Soviet and Warsaw Pact forces in western Europe served as both the justification for a large standing armed force and the principal mission requirement driving military structure and core doctrine (Kennan, 1947; H. Brown, 1983; Garthoff, 1985; and Luttwak, 1986).

But, in a curious way, this fixation on Soviet communist expansionism led the US military into the netherworld of unconventional war. It soon became clear that the USA and its European NATO (North Atlantic Treaty Organization) allies were unlikely to pay for the kind of standing peacetime armies that could confidently meet the 100-plus divisions of the Soviet Union and the Warsaw Pact. Unlike the Soviet autocracy, with its command economy, the democratic states of the West had to look for a cheaper solution.

Under the Eisenhower administration the availability of nuclear weapons and the desire to provide maximum security at minimal dollar cost led to a policy of nuclear deterrence. President Eisenhower termed this 'massive retaliation' in his State of The Union Speech of 7 January 1954.

As President, Eisenhower expressed his preference for the conventional model of military operations, disdaining the messy business of small, unconventional conflicts. 'I saw no sense in wasting manpower in costly small wars that could not achieve decisive results under the political and military circumstances then existing' (1963, 454; see also Gaddis, 1972, 164). The idea that anything other than large-scale conventional combat could ultimately be decisive never seems to have crossed Ike's thoroughly conventional mind.

Two Army Chiefs of Staff who served in the Eisenhower administration, Generals Matthew B. Ridgeway and Maxwell D. Taylor, opposed Eisenhower's defense policies on two grounds. First, they felt that the nuclear option was largely a bluff – the US would never use nuclear arms for any purpose short of national survival. Secondly, they believed that, given the first consideration, the USA's national interest could only be served by strong conventional forces (Perry, 1989, 62–5).

Obviously, a national defense based largely on nuclear retaliation was not congenial to Army planners. As Chief of Staff, Gen. Taylor proposed a 1955 'National Military Program' based on his belief that US interests would be threatened by a series of 'limited wars', and Soviet-backed insurgencies in Third World nations (Perry, 1989, 66–7). The general intent was to improve the Army's capability to fight small wars in non-European environments (Cocklin, 1959, 1–3). For Army strategists 'limited war' was the Army's means of survival in a policy environment oriented toward nuclear war. 'Limited war' meant small-scale conventional war well below the nuclear threshold.

Taylor became the leading spokesman of this school. In his

analysis, Eisenhower's proposed reductions in conventional Army forces would have left the country without the necessary range of responses for any situation short of general nuclear war. Although not a fan of Special Forces nor an advocate of unconventional operations, Taylor continued to maintain that the exclusive reliance on nuclear retaliation was a recipe for disaster (Taylor 1959a, 38–42).

The Army called together its senior operational commanders during 1959 for the first World Wide Combat Arms Conference. As a measure of the Army's lack of concern with special operations, counterinsurgency and UW, none of these topics was raised in any form at the conference (USCONARC, 1959).[4]

Even so, members of the 77th SFG were deployed to Laos in 1959 under civilian cover to assist French UW forces training the Laotian Army. The French withdrew their support that December, leaving the SF to carry on alone. The Army's Deputy Chief of Staff for Operations seems to have selected the still unproven Special Forces for a clandestine training mission in Laos simply because they were the only Army unit with both military skills and a language capability (French) suitable for the training of Laotian military units. Thanks to the OSS veterans and the Lodge Bill soldiers, significant numbers of SF were fluent in French, the principal European language of Southeast Asia. According to at least one source, their specialized training as partisans/guerrillas apparently played little role in the decision (Mountel, 1989). This tasking, however, gave the SF new credibility as practitioners of guerrilla warfare and counterinsurgency.

After retiring from the Army in 1959, Taylor wrote *The Uncertain Trumpet*, in which he reiterated his belief that Soviet nuclear arms, the rise of mutual deterrence, and a Soviet mood of aggressiveness made armed conflict short of nuclear war likely, necessitating flexible 'limited war' forces (Taylor, 1959b, 60–4). As might be expected, this was in no way an unconventional program or one which included Special Operations Forces.

General Taylor's intention was simply to enhance US conventional combat and logistic abilities so US policymakers would not be forced to use nuclear weapons for any issue short of national survival (ibid., 158–61). Although his immediate impact on doctrine and policy was small, Taylor did come to the attention of Sen. John F. Kennedy, the Democratic nominee for President. Impressed with Taylor's book, Kennedy used the General's arguments in criticizing Eisenhower's defense policies during the 1960 presidential campaign.[5]

Special Forces persevere

Meanwhile, thanks to the efforts of a few true believers, SF continued to exist in small units overseas and in its obscure corner of Fort Bragg. The confusion around the role of SF is illustrated by the Army's 1960 decision to assign an official 'lineage' to the Special Forces, a sort of military pedigree. It is interesting that this official lineage consisted entirely of various elite special-purpose, conventional units including Rogers' Rangers of French and Indian War fame (*c*. 1756) and extending through the World War II Ranger battalions and the Canadian–US 1st Special Service Force (DA Directive, 1960). The OSS, not being an Army organization, was not included.

Colonel Bank called this lineage, 'The sorriest dis or misinformation I've run across yet. The only precursor of the USASF [US Army Special Forces] is the OSS.' The phrase 'blatant nonsense' is crossed out in Bank's letter (Bank, 1989). Nevertheless, the official lineage of Army Special Forces, as established by the Department of the Army, consisted of conventional special-purpose infantry organizations. This persisted until 1986, when the Ranger elements were removed and made part of the lineage of the newly recreated Army Ranger Battalions.

Although not part of the official lineage, Special Forces also 'adopted' as an ancestor the 5307th Composite Unit (Provisional) (Merrill's Marauders), a conventional unit created for long-range penetration missions in the China–Burma–India Theater of World War II (USJFKIMA, 1960). Considering these curious facts, Paddock suggests that, lacking any clear heritage of unconventional-warfare organizations, the Army simply took the next best option and 'borrowed the lineage of some well-known "elite" special purpose units of WWII fame' (Paddock, 1982, 24). This is probably correct as far as it goes, but fails to consider the effect of claiming as precursors, organizations that have no more in common than a superficial similarity in method and, in the case of Merrill's Marauders, not even that.

THE HIGH POINT OF UNCONVENTIONAL WARFARE: THE 1960S
AND THE KENNEDY YEARS

The Vietnam War period is vital to understanding the development of Special Operations Forces, concepts of unconventional warfare and the organizational responses that led to present-day special operations. The Vietnam case will be examined in detail in the following chapters; for the present it is only necessary to outline briefly some early developments of the period.

As noted earlier, during the late 1950s and early 1960s, some US military and civilian planners became disturbed by the increasing incidence of communist (USSR)-sponsored subversion and insurgency in less developed nations, and were alarmed by the victory of avowedly communist elements in China and Indochina (for example, Pye, 1962, and Trinquier, 1964). The recognition continued to grow that these forms of warfare were more common than the conventional type. Furthermore, not all of them could safely be ignored. A few thinkers sought to counter the methods of these movements by proposing military forces which would be 'concerned with the full range of military–political–economic affairs' (Spore, 1960, 128). Still, it was hard to get anyone in the Army to listen except for a handful of eccentrics on Smoke Bomb Hill in Fort Bragg.

The election of John F. Kennedy as President in 1960 marked a distinct change in White House military thinking. Kennedy had long been concerned about the threat of communist-supported insurgencies (Sorenson, 1965, 654; Hilsman, 1967, 423), and was especially concerned by a speech Soviet Premier Nikita Khrushchev made in 1961 entitled 'For New Victories of the World Communist Movement'. In it, Khrushchev pledged to support 'just wars of national liberation' with the clear implication that this was an important step in the collapse of the West (US President, 1961, 418, 461, 624; Khrushchev, 1961; see also US Congress, Senate, 1961, 7). Kennedy distributed copies of the Khrushchev speech at the first meeting of his National Security Council and directed Robert McNamara, his Secretary of Defense, to begin developing a counterguerrilla capability (Blaufarb, 1977, 52).

A year later Secretary McNamara responded to what he termed 'the communist design for world conquest':

> The force of world communism operates in the twilight zone between subversion and quasi-military action ... In all four services we are training fighters who can, in turn, teach the people of the free nations how to fight for their freedom. (McNamara, 1962, 298)

In remarks addressed to the Army, McNamara added 'To deal with the Communist guerilla threat requires some shift in our military thinking. We have been used to developing big weapons and mounting large forces. Here we must work with companies and squads, individual soldiers' (McNamara, 1962). It is important to note that the emphasis here was on scale (the size of units involved) rather than changes in the essential function of these forces. It is also interesting to note that this came from the man who would shortly preside over and support the introduction of massive amounts of 'big weapons and large forces' into the Vietnam War.

A longtime critic of massive retaliation and an admirer of the 'flexible response' theories of Maxwell Taylor, the new President called on the retired general to chair the Cuba Study Group investigating the USA's first major unconventional-warfare disaster, the CIA's failed Bay of Pigs invasion. Taylor was critical of the JCS performance in advising Kennedy on the military aspects of the CIA-run invasion and blamed the old special operations bugaboo – poor planning and lack of coordination with the conventional forces. The Study Group report called for closer planning and coordination at the national command and interagency levels and more attention to 'paramilitary' operations (Memorandum No. 4, 1961).[6]

Taylor's recommendation was to form a new organization at the undersecretary level to act as a Cold War staff for the President. While this recommendation was not implemented, the President did approve an organization titled the Special Group (Counter-insurgency). The Special Group (Counterinsurgency) was formally constituted in January, 1962 and chaired by Taylor, who wrote the group's charter: 'to insure proper recognition throughout the US Government that subversive insurgency ("wars of national liberation") is a major form of politico–military conflict equal in importance to conventional warfare' (National Security Action Memorandum 124, 1962). To state this was one thing, to come to grips with it was another. None of the members had any notable expertise in counterinsurgency nor any particular interest in it, either personal or organizational. In acting as the President's oversight group for counterinsurgency matters, the influence of the Special Group was both limited and of short duration. When Taylor left in October 1962 to take the post of JCS chairman, the Special Group lost whatever influence it had. In 1966 it was quietly absorbed by the National Security Council (ibid., 36).[7]

Although Kennedy apparently saw General Taylor as a champion of new military thinking, there is a real question as to Taylor's commitment to the whole notion of counterinsurgency. Interviewed in 1982, the General recalled feeling that counterinsurgency was 'just a form of small war' (Krepinevich, 1986, 37). Unconventional warfare and elite forces were still not part of his equation for national defense.

On freedom's frontier

Unfortunately, the real world would not wait for doctrinal adjustments and bureaucratic reorganization from Washington. By the late 1950s the USA had found itself in a peculiar kind of twilight war against communist revolutionary movements around the world, especially in the Philippines and Southeast Asia. Initially, unconventional warfare activities in Southeast Asia, including Laos and Vietnam, had been largely the responsibility of the CIA although a small number of Special Forces soldiers were assigned to the US Military Advisory Group in Vietnam during the 1950s.[8]

In neighboring Laos, Special Forces personnel had participated in Project White Star since 1959. By 1961, 300 of them were part of a joint DOD–CIA project to enable the Laotian Army to counter insurgent activity by Pathet Lao guerrillas operating with massive assistance from the self-styled North Vietnamese Army (NVA). Since the departure of the French, the SF soldiers had became active combat advisors as well as trainers.

Although the Vietnam unit had been generally successful in a low-key way, the unit in Laos experienced considerable difficulty. For one thing, there was notable friction between the US trainers and their Laotian government counterparts. However, the SF had been very successful in creating what they called the 'Armee Clandestine' by recruiting from disaffected minorities who had suffered from both the Laotians and the North Vietnamese. Although the tribesmen proved to be excellent guerrillas, their loyalty to the US-supported Royal Lao government was nonexistent (Blaufarb, 1977, 134-41).

To some observers it seemed as if the CIA–SF operation in Laos was actually producing a culturally alienated force of Lao mercenaries, loyal and responsive mostly to their US advisors. This was the practical result of creating a military force devoid of political context. Understandably, there was great difficulty in persuading the Laotian government or its military leaders to support this military training effort (US Army Special Warfare Center, 1961).

From the viewpoint of the Special Warfare Center and the 77th SFG, the Laos mission had provided a chance actually to test their methods, weapons and communications in combat. It gave them their first large-scale success, new credibility and a wealth of experience plus visibility at the decision-making level in Washington (meaning the White House). To their eventual detriment, it also affirmed the SF–CIA connection to a degree that made the Army leadership understandably nervous.[9]

In addition to their popularity with the White House and the CIA, US Army Special Forces continued to attract attention both publicly and inside the Army, but in a manner that would later prove problematic. Kennedy was concerned about communist encroachment in the Third World. The continuing insurgency in Laos and later in Vietnam worried him greatly and he was convinced that the struggle in Southeast Asia was an example of Soviet-sponsored subversive insurgency (Schlesinger, 1965, 539–41).

President Kennedy and his brother Robert quickly found that Special Forces, thanks to their organization as small, flexible, self-sufficient teams, was the only available tool which allowed them to quickly influence events in Laos and Vietnam (Paschall, 1989). The Kennedys' opinion was confirmed when the President visited Fort Bragg in 1961 to see the SF soldiers in action. He met and was much impressed with Colonel William Yarborough, the commander of the Special Warfare Center (SWC) and with his troopers.

Yarborough pulled out all the stops and his soldiers gave the President a show worthy of a military Disneyland. In addition to their genuine bedrock skills, they also displayed a high degree of showmanship. Using all their collective experience, the SWC crew demonstrated combat skills, weapons from bows to exotic rifles and hand-to-hand combat abilities that were impressive (if only distantly related to their military mission). The Lodge Bill soldiers demonstrated their multi-lingual fluency (creating the impression that all SF troopers were equally fluent). It was all topped off by a finale that featured a soldier flying past the grandstand with a futuristic rocketbelt. The rocket get-up was not part of the SF's inventory and had been borrowed for the occasion, but it made an impressive finish.

Whatever he thought of the rocketbelt, Kennedy was struck by the dash and daring of the elite soldiers and equally struck by the fact that they had been trained to fight as guerrillas. Their individual and collective excellence appealed to him, and he saw in these unique soldiers a remedy for the troublesome problem of insurgency (Kennedy, Msg., 1961).

The President also noted the SF soldiers wore their distinctive, though nonregulation, green-beret headgear. During this period SF personnel had been forbidden on pain of court-martial to wear their green berets. This order originated with Gen. Paul D. Adams, then commander of 18th Airborne Corps (the senior command at Fort Bragg). Reportedly, Adams had awakened one morning during a field exercise to find a line of Mercurochrome drawn across his throat and a sign on his chest announcing his assassination by SF troopers. At least among the SF members, the no-beret order was viewed as an act of jealousy and petty revenge (Rheault, interview, 30 June 1989). Yarborough, at considerable personal risk, ordered his troops to wear their berets for the President's visit and managed to obtain Kennedy's approval for the headgear. This helped endear Yarborough to the soldiers, but did nothing to enhance the image of Special Forces at Army command levels (Rheault, interview, 13 April 1989).

As had been the case with the OSS and Roosevelt, the Special Forces owed their success to the sponsorship of the President. But, as with Roosevelt's OSS sponsorship, Kennedy's adoption of unconventional warfare as a technique (however vaguely defined) and of Special Forces as an instrument of that technique met with considerable resistance from within the military establishment (Stillwell, 1961; Rifkin, 1962).

Nevertheless, Kennedy's relationship with SF grew so close that he insisted on personal contact with Yarborough. Unfortunately the President also tended to treat Special Forces as a separate service. As described by Paschall, Robert Kennedy on more than one occasion greeted a meeting of the Special Group (Counterinsurgency) by saying words to the effect of, 'I see the Army, Navy and Air Force here, why isn't there anyone from the Special Forces?'. Yarborough had been promoted from Colonel to General at Kennedy's insistence, and then again to Major General in order to represent Special Forces at the interservice level.

This personal access gave the SWC both visibility and influence but made it less than welcome at the JCS level, where it seemed to compete with the established services. Special Forces commanders, through Yarborough, acquired the ability to make material and other support requests directly to the national command level, where they would often be endorsed by Robert Kennedy directly to Defense Secretary McNamara, bypassing the parent service and the JCS. This back-door relationship, however useful it may have seemed at the time, was 'a bad error in the long run' (Paschall, 1989).

The situation was not improved by National Security Action Memorandum (NSAM) 162, published in 1962, assigning more Special Forces personnel 'to support CIA covert paramilitary operations'.

Matters were made even worse when the same memorandum tasked the DOD to 'increase its capability to fund, support and conduct wholly or partly covert paramilitary operations' in cooperation with the CIA (Pentagon Papers, Vol. II, 1971, 683). Not only was the Pentagon losing control of its elite soldiery, it was being told to pay the CIA's bills.

Within the Army it was felt that Special Forces, a subcomponent of the Army (and a relatively junior one), should be treated as one more asset of the conventional army and not as if it were a unique force in its own right. Accordingly, the command levels of the Army began to adopt a two-pronged approach to dealing with SF. As would be the case in later years, a policy of superficial compliance was coupled with one of long range diminishment. Although the funding requests were usually filled promptly, and the materiel requests more slowly, personnel requests were often not met at all. Paschall sees this as a long-term bureaucratic strategy. In 1963, SWC submitted a list of about 30 Army officers, mostly OSS veterans, for transfer to Special Forces. Despite several efforts, none of these was ever transferred and the 'talent received was almost invariably inferior' (Paschall, 1989).[10]

A program of action: Kennedy responds to insurgency

Kennedy began his anti-communist efforts in South Vietnam by demanding a wide ranging review of US activities there. In May 1961 an interdepartmental task force conducted a massive review of US policy and operations in Vietnam and produced 'A Program of Action for South Vietnam', including the objectives cited below:

1. Unconventional Warfare: Expand present operations of the First Observation Battalion in guerrilla areas of South Vietnam under joint MAAG–CIA sponsorship and direction. This should be in full operational collaboration with the Vietnamese, using Vietnamese civilians, recruited with CIA aid.
2. In Laos, infiltrate teams under light civilian cover to southeast Laos to locate and attack Vietnamese communist bases and lines of communications. These teams should be supported by assault units of 100–150 Vietnamese for use on targets beyond capability of teams. Training of teams could be a combined operation by CIA and US Army Special Forces.
3. In North Vietnam, using the foundation established by intelligence operations, form networks of resistance, covert bases and

teams for sabotage and light harassment. A capability should be created by the MAAG in the South Vietnamese Army to conduct Ranger raids and similar military actions in North Vietnam as might prove necessary or appropriate. Such actions should try to avoid any outbreak of resistance or insurrection which could not be supported to the extent necessary to stave off repression.

4. Conduct overflights for dropping of leaflets to harass the Communists and to maintain morale of the North Vietnamese population, and increase gray broadcasts to North Vietnam for the same purposes (Yarborough, 1987, 1–2).

This program of action was very significant because, when later issued as a National Security Action Memorandum, it would remain the blueprint for much unconventional warfare and special operations activity throughout the Vietnam War. In particular, paragraph one resulted in the creation in Vietnam, first of the CIA Combined Studies Division for UW (precursor of MACV-SOG), and later the introduction of the Fifth Special Forces Group. Paragraph two led to the expansion of the White Star project in Laos and then in 1962, to its replacement by the CIA's Project 404 (for details of the CIA operations in Laos, see Parker, 1995). Paragraph three was especially significant because it imposed self-created limits on special operations and unconventional warfare activity in North Vietnam, leading to the creation of 'notional' (i.e. nonexistent) guerrilla resistance as a deception measure. These operations and those in paragraph four would become the responsibility of the Combined Studies Division and later MACV-SOG. These issues will be dealt with in greater detail in following chapters.

The Army responds by running very fast while standing still

President Kennedy called for 'a wholly new kind of strategy; a wholly different kind of force and therefore a new and different kind of military training' (US President, 1961, 2). What he got was business as usual but with UW trimmings: regardless of the wrapper, the contents of the package remained conventional warfare. Describing the Army's reaction to Kennedy's program, Maxwell Taylor remembered feeling that 'all this dust coming out of the White House really isn't necessary'. It was 'something we have to satisfy, but not much heart went into [the] work'. He sounded a long-standing theme when he added that he felt the Special Forces were not doing anything that 'any well-trained unit' couldn't do (Krepinevich, 1986).

The US Army War College reacted by beginning its first Senior Officer Counterinsurgency Course in May 1962. The overwhelmingly conventional content was explicitly criticized in a report by the class members (US Army War College, 31 May 1962, 18). The same class also recommended that conventional doctrine be combined with the specialized requirements of counterinsurgency to provide doctrine usable by the entire Army and not merely by specialized elements (ibid., 33–4; see also Ball, 1983, 355). The impact of all this can be judged by the fact that Colonel Harry Ball's official history of the curriculum of the Command and General Staff College devotes exactly one paragraph to Vietnam-era counterinsurgency training, in a volume of 534 pages (Ball, 1983). For most of its training and doctrine, the addition of 'civic action' to otherwise conventional doctrine was the only notable change in the Army's approach to counterinsurgency (Summary Report, 1962, 8).

Also in 1961, President Kennedy continued to press the military establishment when he ordered DOD's research and development (R&D) arm, the Advanced Research Projects Agency (ARPA), to create an office for Special Warfare research. As recorded in the personal papers of Colonel Donald Blackburn, Deputy Director of Development for Special Warfare, the emphasis of this new office was operational, technological and conventional. In fact over half of the 1961 development budget (21 million dollars) was devoted to a single general purpose item, night vision devices (12 million dollars). According to Blackburn, 'small "limited war" programs got lost' in the big budget, conventional R&D process (Blackburn, 1983, 316–17).[11]

In July 1961, the Kennedy administration launched the Limited War Task Force, composed of civilian scientists and retired military officers. As might be expected, this group placed most of its attention on military technical issues (ibid., 316–17).

Within the Army, another new research office was created, the Special Warfare Directorate. Their approach, however, was highly abstract and sought to develop and apply general principles of revolution, rather than being devoted specifically to Vietnam, Indochina or even Southeast Asia. The Directorate in turn created a Special Operations Research Office (SORO) at American University (ibid., 310). The major product of the SORO was a 'Casebook' on Insurgency and Revolutionary Warfare (Jureidini *et al.*, 1962) analyzing 23 contemporary revolutions and insurgencies. Remarkably little attention was paid in the Directorate's work or that of the SORO to Vietnam *per se*, as a culture, as a unique nation, or even as a state.[12]

The flurry of organizing continued in 1962 when the Department of the Army commissioned the Special Warfare Board, at the SWC in Fort Bragg. Its only significant product was an extensive report reviewing all special-warfare forces and all operations, including counterinsurgency (Special Warfare Board, 1962, 219–22). The board report did emphasize that counterinsurgency should involve all elements of the Army and not simply Special Forces (ibid., 43). It concluded that all eight active Army divisions (in other words, most combat soldiers) should be 'indoctrinated' and trained in counterinsurgency, as should all Army officers of the rank of Colonel and above. The board also recommended that the strength of Army Special Forces should be raised from its then-current level of 2,300 to 4,600 (ibid., 100–5). It also specified a general doctrinal problem, in that:

> Until very recently, US Army actions in the Special Warfare field have been entirely within the hot war concept. Doctrine, organization, training and operational planning have been directed towards guerrilla operations, escape and evasion and psychological warfare, and all considerations have been restricted to an overt war or post-war atmosphere ... Army doctrine and in fact national policy have inhibited Army actions in the politico-economic and psychological fields. (ibid., 4–5)

Similar conclusions were drawn by a Continental Army Command (CONARC) board convened on the same topic in March 1962 (USCONARC, March, 1962). Focusing on the topic of counter-insurgency, the report noted, 'we are having some difficulty in the terminology area in defining exactly what we mean by counterinsurgency and how it fits into the spectrum of the military arts' (ibid., A-3-1). CONARC was at that time the proponent of doctrinal development in the Army.

President Kennedy tried again in a letter to the Army dated 11 April 1962. The letter noted that the Marxist challenge of insurgency and guerrilla warfare had 'various facets' such as 'guerrilla warfare', 'wars of subversion, covert aggression and, in broad professional terms, special warfare or unconventional warfare'. The key to his approach was to be security assistance by military forces, including tactical, logistical and communications training. In addition, there was to be a political and economic dimension:

> Pure military skill is not enough. A full spectrum of military, paramilitary and civil action must be combined to produce success.

> The enemy uses economic and political warfare, propaganda and naked military aggression in an endless combination ... Our officers and men must understand and combine the political, economic and civil actions with skilled military efforts ... (Kennedy letter, as reproduced in DA Office of the Chief of Information, 1962, 3)

The military reaction to this direction was yet another flurry of activity, presenting at least the appearance of compliance. The second World Wide Combat Arms Conference, held in June 1962, featured 'special warfare', 'counterinsurgency', 'guerrilla operations', and 'Cold War operations', as major topics (USCONARC, 'Report on the World Wide Combat Arms Conference II', 1962).

The JCS established a Special Assistant to the Chairman for Counterinsurgency and Special Activities. At least partially because of presidential insistence, Army Special Forces was given the counterinsurgency mission. The Navy organized SEAL Teams from existing Underwater Demolition Teams (US Congress, House, 1983, 57), as its counterinsurgency element, creating yet another elite commando-style raiding force, similar in concept to the Army Rangers. Likewise, the Air Force rechristened some of its transport squadrons as 'Air Commando' units without making any substantial change.

What Kennedy sought was a reorganization of conventional military thinking to meet the demands of counterinsurgency warfare (Blaufarb, 1977, 82). What occurred was an attempt to fit the existing military structure to the counterinsurgency problem. In the words of Major General Louis Truman, the principal deputy chief of staff at CONARC, 'The proper balance must be given to counterinsurgency training along with conventional type of warfare ... Counterinsurgency is an additional mission that we are taking on' (USCONARC, March 1962, A-16-1). The viewpoint that counterinsurgency was essentially a mission for conventional light infantry was also reflected in the last of the 'pre-Vietnam' field manuals on counterguerrilla warfare, DA FM 31-16 *Counterguerrilla Operations*, issued in 1963.

In the end, much of the training that ordinary service members received in counterinsurgency/unconventional warfare (during that period the terms were often used interchangeably), consisted of no more than a 45-minute, DOD-produced film on counterinsurgency titled, 'The Third Challenge – Unconventional Warfare' (AFIF 123, 1962).

Of course, Special Forces was not neglected in the burst of activity around counterinsurgency. A group of 400 Special Forces soldiers and 100 non-military advisors was dispatched to Vietnam in 1961 on the direct orders of the President in addition to the SF trainers already there (Simpson, 1983, 69). Also, since 1960, a limited number of Special Forces personnel had been under the operational control of the CIA in Vietnam, a situation which continued until 1963. In 1961, the Fifth Special Forces Group (5SFG) was created at Fort Bragg, North Carolina, with specific responsibility for the Republic of Vietnam (USAJFKSWC, 1988, 7).

Furthermore, when the Army's first formal counterinsurgency school opened in 1962 on Okinawa it was under the auspices of the First Special Forces Group. Not surprisingly, Richard D. Bishop, an instructor at the school, recalls that although the training included 'a few psyops and civil affairs classes' it was organized essentially as a light infantry tactical course along Ranger lines, using Ranger training materials (Bishop, 1989).[13]

The selection of the Army's Special Forces as the instrument of Kennedy's policy of anti-communist engagement in southeast Asia is generally portrayed as the result of their military skills (Kelly, 1973, 7) and self-proclaimed elite status, all of which appealed to the President's own values. But at least as important in the choice of SF was the type of flexible soldier it produced (or attracted), and the unit's emphasis on foreign-language ability. Little attention was paid to the organization's intensive area orientation, an OSS technique formalized in SF doctrine as the 'area study'. This technique amounted to an in-depth study of the geographic area in which the SF unit was to be employed. This was not simply a weather and terrain analysis of the type made by conventional units, but a cultural (socio-political) analysis of the area of operations. More importantly, it was an attempt to understand the political context and motivations of the struggle. These elements quickly became obscured and lost in favor of the image of the Special Forces soldier as a deadly and resourceful fighter on the mythical model of the American frontiersman.[14]

Years later, historian Alexander S. Cochran, Jr conducted a detailed survey of US military planning for operations in Vietnam during this period, and found that the counterinsurgency emphasis of the President and his advisers was no more than 'a superficial distraction to the military' (Cochran, 1984, 65; Krepinevich, 1986). Operational military planning was directed toward conventional operations, including the establishment in 1962 of the Military Assistance Command, Vietnam (MACV) as a command and control element in Vietnam (Krepinevich, 1986, 65).

In a personal letter written in 1963, Major General Harold K. Johnson, then acting Army Deputy Chief of Staff for Military Operations, said:

> When this administration [Kennedy] came into office they were searching for ideas that could be pursued with 'vigor'. One of the fallouts of course was the Special Forces activity. They put on a good show and have a certain appeal about them. The Army agreed that this was a good idea and agreed that the function probably belonged to the Army, but sort of yawned in backing it up. (Johnson, 1963)

Regardless of the Army leadership's apparent lack of enthusiasm, the men of the Special Forces along with their Psyops and Civil Affairs brethren, were soon deeply embroiled in the Vietnam conflict; a long, costly and frustrating struggle that would shape the future not only of Special Operations Forces but of the entire US military.

NOTES

1. Colonel Bank served in an OSS Operational Group and as a Jedburgh team leader in France (Bank, 1989).
2. Including Volckman. Volckman was also an associate of Lansdale and had worked with Vanderpool, another CIA operator, in the Philippines (Vanderpool indicates his CIA association in a personal letter dated December 1980). Vanderpool papers, MHI.
3. See Murrey Dyer's *The Weapon on the Wall: Rethinking Psychological Warfare* for an account of the general decline of attention to psychological warfare during the Eisenhower years (1959).
4. Examples of the professional debate of this period concerning the Army and limited war include: Maxwell Taylor, 'On Limiting War' (1958); Col. Francis X. Bradley, 'The Fallacy of a Dual Capability' (1959), pp. 18–22 (Bradley takes the position that only a nuclear capability is required) and Lt Col. H. P. Rank, 'A United States Counter-Aggression Force' (1959).
5. It is sometimes suggested that Maxwell Taylor resigned as Army Chief of Staff in protest over these strategy and policy disagreements. Kinnard, however, reports that Taylor stated, in an interview by Kinnard, that his resignation occurred simply because he had served his full four years in the Chief's position and retired on schedule (Kinnard, 1988, 24).
   In the last months of Taylor's tenure as Army Chief of Staff (1955–59) he undertook a review of Army training programs to determine their suitability for special operations and, in particular, counterinsurgency. However, in view of Taylor's own comments (1972, 200–1) the review seems to have had no impact on Army planning, operations or training. Perry (1989, 85–91, 357) discusses this review as evidence of Taylor's early interest in guerrilla warfare and counterinsurgency.
6. Kinnard, a retired Army Brigadier General, refers to these recommendations for paramilitary capability as 'a counterinsurgency model' (Kinnard, 1988, 15). In fact,

the word 'counterinsurgency' does not appear in the memorandum, which illustrates the confusion around issues of definition in unconventional warfare.

Bank, for example, contends that 'paramilitary' and 'guerrilla' are 'synonymous terms'. Adopting a Maoist model, the only distinction he makes is that in the final phase of the war, guerrilla bands join together to become paramilitary 'conventional' formations (Bank, 1989).

7. The principal membership was: Robert Kennedy (the President's informal chief of staff and formal Attorney General), U. Alexis Johnson (Undersecretary of State), Roswell Gilpatrick (Undersecretary of Defense), Gen. Lyman Lemnitzer (Chair of the JCS), John McCone (director of the CIA), McGeorge Bundy and Edward R. Murrow (USIA).

8. In 1959, the Special Forces were formally given 'assistance to friendly governments' as an additional mission. This had little impact on either training or doctrine.

9. Gen. Richard G. Stillwell's report 'Report on Counter-Insurgency Operations Course and Related Matters' (dated 6 October 1961) emphasized that 'Special Forces be considered as an ancillary, rather than a primary, source for meeting world-wide counterinsurgency/counterguerrilla training and operational assistance' (CONARC, 1962,101–2).

10. It is perhaps significant that there were 30 former OSS operators still in the Army and holding field grade rank at this point (1962-3). The presence of these OSS veterans throughout the Army might account for the general acceptance of the Special Force's self-defined function of unconventional warfare defined as partisan support.

    A further example of the post-World War II distaste for elite units was a measure forbidding airborne (parachute infantry) units from wearing distinctive insignia (Rheault interview, 13 April 1989).

11. A 'Limited War Laboratory' was opened at Aberdeen Proving Grounds, Maryland in 1962. Like unconventional warfare units, the lab lost its less conventional identity and was later renamed the US Army Land Warfare Laboratory. The organization closed in 1972 when its functions were taken over by the Army's engineering and development laboratory at Natick, Massachusetts.

12. SORO also produced a lengthy study of the Cuban Revolution (1953–59) in September 1963. In November another study was published titled 'Undergrounds in Insurgent, Revolutionary and Resistance Warfare'. The last major publication of the SORO was a 1965 volume, entitled 'Human Factors Considerations of Undergrounds in Insurgencies'.

    In part there was a problem of limited expertise about Vietnam. The Association for Asian Studies reported 1,552 members in 1960, of whom 202 claimed to be students of Southeast Asia (all fields). None of these was a Vietnam specialist *per se* (Hu Chen, Charles O., *The Association For Asian Studies: An Interpretive History*, 1973).

    In 1970, the *New York Times* (NYT) reported that scholarly expertise on Vietnam was nearly nonexistent and that specialists on North Vietnam were nonexistent. The *Times* found no specialist in any aspect of Vietnam with a tenured professorship at any US university. Only 30 American students were found studying the Vietnamese language (NYT, 8 June 1970, 1: 7). Academics and university officials interviewed defended this state of affairs, saying that they were 'fed up' with Vietnam and that they were rejecting government-sponsored 'pseudo-scholarship' (ibid. and NYT, 21 June 1970, sec. 4, 17: 2). John K. Fairbank reports that Harvard proposed a professorship in Vietnamese history in 1966. The position was not actually established until 1975, the only such position in the country (*Chinabound*, 1982, 392–3).

13. Bishop also alleges that the basic program of instruction for the school was a CIA

product influenced by Walter W. Rostow, national security advisor to President Kennedy (Bishop, 1989). Rostow denies that he had any direct role in formulating this program of instruction (personal correspondence with the author, dated 9 November 1989).

14. Brian Jenkins confirms this from his own recollection as SF officer in Vietnam during the mid-1960s when the organization had begun to attract those drawn to the 'killer image' (interview, April 1988). Kent Anderson's treatment of his own experiences as a 5th SF NCO leaves the impression that SF had no real function other than efficient killing (Anderson, 1987).

4 Special Forces in Vietnam – Part I

> to show you their military defeat, I go back to their political defeat,
> which is at the heart of everything. (Vo Nguyen Giap, North
> Vietnamese Minister of Defense, 1969; Fallaci, 1976, 80)

US Special Operations Forces were still new when the war in Vietnam
began to widen after 1960. It was here that the US armed forces
encountered an enemy who made up for military inferiority with
political sophistication – and worse, applied that sophistication to
the battlefield. Army Special Forces became involved in two separate
parts of the war – the well-known, overt counterinsurgency effort
and the small, covert and clandestine 'special operations' war.

IN THE OPEN – OVERT OPERATIONS

As noted earlier, the Kennedy administration was worried about
communist expansionism and saw the insurgency in Vietnam as a
test of US ability and resolve. Needing a means to influence the course
of the war, official attention naturally turned to the administration's
favorite military organization, Army Special Forces. In the words of
Kennedy advisor Walt Rostow, 'we aren't saving them for the junior
prom' (Rostow Memorandum, cited in Kahin, 1986, 131). Furthermore, the administration wanted to avoid the public introduction
of combat troops and SF offered a possible means of doing this
quietly with a minimum of public attention.

For the SF troopers, the problem in South Vietnam was not a
trivial one. Guerrilla insurgency might not be decisive in conventional terms but it had its peculiar charms and its unique strengths.
The US-backed government of President Ngo Dinh Diem lacked
popular support and its army, the Army of the Republic of Vietnam
(or ARVN), was largely ineffective. The Communist Party in South
Vietnam (Lao Dong or Workers' Party), closely tied with its brother
organization that ruled the North, took full advantage of the political
strengths of insurgency while being supported by the conventional
combat forces of the North Vietnamese Army.

These forces had begun infiltrating into South Vietnam along a 1,000-kilometer infiltration route that snaked from North Vietnam west through Laotian mountains and jungle back into South Vietnam. Called the 'Ho Chi Minh Trail', in honor of North Vietnam's revolutionary leader, construction and repair of this complex road and trail network would be continuous for the next ten years. Eventually it would extend far south into Cambodia, creating a 20,000-kilometer spiderweb of roads and trails branching into South Vietnam at several places. This extensive infiltration route was perceived by US strategists as the key to the war and became the target of much of the special operations activity during the Vietnam War.

KNOWING THE ENEMY: THE COMMUNIST PROGRAM IN
SOUTH VIETNAM

During 1959 and 1960 the tempo of dissident political activity increased in South Vietnam, especially recruiting and 'proselytizing' by the Lao Dong party among key sectors of the population. It was a broad-based program and they emphasized gaining the 'active support' of critical elements in South Vietnam, especially teachers, students, local officials and the military, but did not neglect less likely candidates such as merchants and landlords. Material support and military cadres from the North also began slipping south along the trail (Spector 1985, 327, 330; see also VDD, 1979). During 1960, the Lao Dong allied with other political dissident groups to form a united front organization called the National Liberation Front of South Vietnam, commonly referred to as the NLF, funded and controlled from North Vietnam. Although presented as a united front of opponents of the Diem regime, it was thoroughly dominated by the Lao Dong (Pike, 1966, 76).

The NLF campaign in South Vietnam was similar to Lansdale's successful Philippine campaign. The NLF might not consist of political masterminds, but they clearly understood their priorities in this situation. Military defeat of the enemy was not in the cards after the USA entered the war and would not be possible until they left. In the meantime, victory lay in organizing politically and avoiding defeat. The communists began with a genuine understanding of the Vietnamese culture, both nationally and regionally, and combined that understanding with a willingness to exploit whatever aspects best suited their purposes. The communist movement therefore emphasized only those aspects of its program most likely to have wide appeal among the South Vietnamese. Their cadres combined nationalist and nativist appeals, playing on traditional Vietnamese xenophobia with skillful exploitation of the short-comings of the South Vietnamese Government (GVN) to build political legitimacy for itself (NLF documents in Porter, 1979, 119–20; also Pike, 1966, 92–8).

Profiting from the errors of their war against the French, the NLF did not emphasize its Marxist revolutionary ideology; nor did it present a radical social program. Instead, it offered itself as a conservative, indeed traditionalist, nationalist force wholly compatible with the traditional, village centered life of the rural population (Giap, 1966, 5–36). Demonstrating a sophisticated grasp of Vietnamese fears and values, the NLF sought to appear as a popular defense against Diem's exploitative central government and foreign (i.e. US)-sponsored modernization, never missing a chance to compare the 'depravity' of life under Diem to 'the wholesome life' of the 'liberated zones' (i.e. NLF-controlled areas) (Nguyen and Danh, 1966, 179; also Troung-Son, 1966).

The NLF also understood the importance of organized, targeted violence and established a military arm for their political movement. While armed violence was strictly an enabling tool for the NLF political movement, it was this aspect of the revolution that captured and held the attention of Saigon's military advisors. At first, this 'violence program' consisted of a series of small 'armed missions' that served as a nucleus for local guerrilla forces, incorporating experienced veterans of the war against the French whenever possible. These elements grew into the organization the Americans christened the 'Viet Cong' (VC). The armed nuclei gathered support and recruits, while conducting a campaign of terrorism and intimidation in those areas where popular support was reluctant or missing, especially at the village level. At the same time a series of carefully targeted Viet Cong terrorist operations kidnapped, killed and terrorized low-level government representatives such as school teachers and policemen. This demonstrated the inability of the Saigon regime to defend either its territory or its loyalists. At no time, however, did purely military logic override political priorities:

> The two to five hundred 'guerrilla incidents' per week that went on in Vietnam, week after week for five years had no purpose in themselves – indeed when viewed in themselves often made no sense – except to serve the political struggle movement. Thus the primary purpose of the violence program was to make possible the political struggle movement. (Pike, 1966, 99)

THE SAIGON GOVERNMENT REACTION

By 1961, the Saigon government was well aware of this political activity, at least in general terms. However, thanks to poor intelligence collection outside the principal cities, combined with a corrupt and inefficient police system, there was little useable information on which to plan a comprehensive response. Furthermore, most of Saigon's attention (and that of its US advisors) was focused on North Vietnam. The few internal intelligence resources outside the major cities were fixated on the Viet Cong. The lack of intelligence information on the unconventional warfare activities of the NLF and its political structure would remain problems throughout the war as intelligence collection continued to focus on the conventional threat posed by the North Vietnamese Army and Viet Cong military units. Although the unconventional (terrorist) operations of the NLF/Viet Cong quickly became obvious, the Saigon government's corrupt and inept police and clandestine services were helpless to deal with them in any very useful way.

The communist idea of organizing the population was neither original nor secret and the government of South Vietnam (GVN) quickly began its own program to organize the countryside. There were two basic solutions, one was to relocate the threatened population and concentrate it in protected areas or protect the villagers where they were. Both options had one basic purpose: to prevent or reverse NLF influence among the rural, village-dwelling farmers who made up the bulk of the South Vietnamese population.

The GVN opted for the first solution with a US-supported, Diem-sponsored initiative called the 'agroville' program. This was the first of several schemes for large-scale resettlement of the rural population. Two types of 'agglomeration' centers were established, both more similar to refugee camps than to traditional villages.

One was for 'Viet Cong families', vaguely defined as those suspected of being sympathetic to, or especially vulnerable to, the NLF appeals. In practice, these persons were simply whomever the local officials designated. They were arbitrarily transferred to the camps and placed under heavy government surveillance in their new location. The other type of center was for those villagers known to be loyal to the GVN but living in remote or inaccessible areas away from GVN control. Essentially, the scheme amounted to a consolidation of hamlet inhabitants into a newly constructed central village or 'agroville'. Most of the labor-intensive relocation and construction work was done by the relocated peasants without compensation (Zasloff, undated, apparently *c*. 1963, 2–5).

As described by Maj. Pham Ngoc Thao, a key official in the program, it was a military scheme designed to improve security, but ignoring the economic and social implications of relocation. According to Zasloff, 'it was clear at the outset that the peasant disliked the program', upsetting as it did the traditional way of life. Furthermore, the agrovilles were constructed by what amounted to forced labor, and were operated on a standardized plan with no allowance for varying local conditions. Finally, there was a serious economic disadvantage, since the relocated peasant still worked the same land, now located at a greater distance from his dwelling. Although militarily useful, the system was hated by virtually all that it displaced and nothing was done to regain their loyalty. It did, however, accomplish its purpose of severely handicapping NLF organization in the affected areas (Zasloff, *c*. 1963, 7).

Because of the threat to their own program, and to exploit peasant dissatisfaction, NLF reaction was bitter and relentless. Viet Cong guerrillas harassed, sacked and burned the agrovilles whenever possible. Officials active in agroville work were threatened and sometimes assassinated, especially those who were unpopular or particularly corrupt. An equally relentless NLF propaganda campaign was conducted to further exploit peasant dissatisfaction and threaten any villagers who cooperated. Pointedly ignoring their own foreign support, communist cadres in the south made a special point of identifying Diem with the Americans as co-sponsors of the resettlement effort (Chinh, 1960).

This last was a continuing theme of NLF propaganda as they sought to establish themselves in the minds of villagers as a bulwark against the fearsome foreigners, as ethnic defenders and protectors of traditional Vietnamese life. The NLF gained credibility and support by demonstrating that they would fight the agrovilles. The assassination of corrupt local GVN officials, supported the Viet Cong claim to be peasant defenders (Zasloff, *c*. 1963, 27).

SPECIAL FORCES TAKE A HAND: PACIFICATION AND THE
CIVILIAN IRREGULAR DEFENSE GROUP

By 1961 the situation in some rural areas was very bad for the Saigon government. Under pressure from the NLF, the GVN was unable to exercise any meaningful sovereignty over its highland frontiers or its remote lowland districts in the Mekong Delta. This was especially true of those areas where non-Vietnamese ethnic and religious minority groups were established, since these largely disenfranchised minorities were always regarded as no more then sources of labor and tax revenue making them very susceptible to NLF appeals. This created a sort of 'safe zone' for the NLF while depriving the government of revenue, intelligence and any real estimate of the extensive Viet Cong military activities, including supply bases, training camps and the like. The communists, on the other hand, continued to exploit their freedom of movement in these areas by supplying themselves from the local economy while actively recruiting in the government controlled zones (Kelly, 1973, 19).

The US Embassy persuaded the Diem government to drop the agroville concept in favor of a CIA plan to create support among the peasants and cut off that same population as a source of support for the Viet Cong. This was the Civilian Irregular Defense Group (CIDG) program, the centerpiece of the US-sponsored 'internal development' effort in Vietnam.

As with agrovilles, the basic concept of the program was to deny the Viet Cong access to the rural population of Vietnam. In reality, propaganda aside, the peasant farmers benefitted not at all from the NLF program, since it imposed draft, taxation and labor demands at least as onerous of those of the Saigon government at its worst. Moreover, it was strongly inclined toward coercion and violence where propaganda failed. For these reasons, US analysts were certain that there was an opportunity to return these people to loyalty or at least willing acquiescence to the GVN.

However, rather than forced relocation to protected areas, under this scheme movement would be minimized and the population armed and trained to act in its own defense. Once the areas were secure and the population organized for self-defense, the program would be turned over to the Vietnamese, who would solidify the loyalty of the area to the government. The expectation was that the villagers would welcome the opportunity to resist Viet Cong coercion and ally themselves with the government. In return, the participating villages and hamlets would receive various benefits such as public health and medical care, education and farming assistance, and the like. Seeing these concrete benefits, they would become active supporters of the Diem government and reject the communist blandishments. Other villages, emboldened by the example, would also join the program, gradually spreading the areas of government control throughout the countryside.

US Special Operations Forces in Action

Much of the CIDG development effort (although by no means all) was devoted to the forested central highlands region of the II Corps Tactical Zone (CTZ). This area had been identified by the GVN's US military advisors as vulnerable to communist encroachment with the object of dividing South Vietnam into two vulnerable sections, north and south. The highlands were occupied by ethnic minorities practicing primitive slash-and-burn agriculture and living in scattered tribal villages. Many of these were non-Vietnamese Montagnards of the Rhade, Meo (or Hmong) and other tribes.

Even though some Meo lived in Vietnam, their principal tribes were located in the mountain areas of northeast and central Laos. Like their counterparts in Laos, most of them had a lengthy history of misuse, abuse and exploitation at the hands of both the communists and the national government. Accordingly, many of them nursed a burning hatred for the ethnic Vietnamese regardless of political distinction. The Vietnamese returned the favor and referred to the Montagnards as 'moi', or 'animal'.

The CIDG militia units were the essential element of the program, since without military protection, the Viet Cong would simply seize control. These self-defense groups were to be established at the village level where they would 'pacify' the immediate area, meaning they would keep Viet Cong elements out of the village, patrol the local area and defeat or expel any Viet Cong units encountered. The 'pacified' areas surrounding CIDG 'area development' camps were to be integrated into the already existing national strategic hamlet program.

THE SPECIAL FORCES ROLE

Although planned and funded by the CIA, the CIDG program was executed entirely by Army Special Forces. In November 1961, the first of 26 'A' teams arrived to execute the program. The major responsibility of US Special Forces was to create the CIDG camps and train and assist the self-defense units (Kelly, 1973, 35). In these early days, most SF in Vietnam spoke only English and French. This allowed them to communicate with the village chiefs in most cases, but not necessarily with the ordinary people of the villages. Unlike other foreign troops, however, the SF made it a point to pick up at least a little Montagnard or Vietnamese as they went along. The unique aspect was that these SF soldiers lived in the villages and took an interest in the villagers while assisting with self-defense, providing help with development projects and participating in combat operations.

In the Central Highlands, each 12-man Special Forces 'A' Team was expected to establish an area development center at the district (county) level and train a little over a thousand tribespeople as village self-defense militia. In addition, each development center was to have a CIDG Company or Camp Strike Force of 300–400 full-time CIDG soldiers as a reaction force against Viet Cong attacks in the area. As part of this process the SF also constructed standard base camps with packed earthen walls, trenches and various defensive fortifications. These were built in the form of a star. This had been a standard pattern for defensive works since the eighteenth century and provided a practical defense against infantry attacks and enemy infiltration. However, the static camps seemed antiquated and absurd to conventional officers raised on the concept of mobile warfare.

Originally, the focus of SF participation was firmly on the development of the village defense forces and organizing district-level quick response units to support them. Their limited offensive activity was mostly confined to the vicinity of the village where they kept VC units off-balance through intensive patrolling and destruction of enemy rice caches. They also established the first grass-root intelligence system to collect detailed, systematic information on the NLF and the VC. The SF teams simultaneously conducted numerous simple civil affairs programs to improve sanitation, water production, and agriculture. Team medics gave basic medical aid. They were assisted by the USAID (US Agency for International Development), which provided at least a minimum of funding and supplies. An elementary form of Psyops was conducted by GVN officials who made appeals for the villagers to support the government.

The US soldiers liked the rugged, self-sufficient Montagnards whom they often compared to American Indians and found they quickly developed into effective, resourceful soldiers. Although the Rhade were the most easily trained and effective fighters, other Montagnard tribes and other minority ethnic and religious groups in the III and IV Corps areas were also trained as CIDG. The Montagnards responded to the fair treatment and respect accorded them by developing deep and lasting ties of loyalty to the Special Forces men who lived and worked among them, following local customs, and often risked, sometimes losing, their lives in defense of the villages.

By late 1962, the military piece of the CIDG program was

considered an unqualified success. The program involved several hundred villages, including a number that had been under Viet Cong control. Several hundred square miles of Vietnam, home to about 300,000 Rhade, Meo and other tribespeople, were secured from Viet Cong infiltration or control by 33,000 local militia troops in units organized under CIDG (Kelly, 1973, 37). Pleased to have a genuine, demonstrable success, the CIA's Saigon station began requesting more Special Forces soldiers for an expanded program.

TOO MUCH OF A GOOD THING

The Army responded with skepticism. The Pentagon was not pleased by the prospect of so many soldiers working on a military program, but controlled by a civilian agency in a war zone. The SF community was already too cozy with the CIA for military comfort. Several senior Army officers visited the CIDG program during early 1962 but their evaluation did not mirror the CIA's enthusiasm. Most were not thrilled with the SF approach to begin with and felt that, since support for the program was largely military, it ought to be under military control. Lieutenant General Harold K. Johnson, Army Deputy Chief of Staff for Operations (later Chief of Staff) summarized the feelings of the Army leadership this way:

> I was not very happy with their approach to the problem. Here was a mobile force that was supposed to be training guerrillas. That's what the Special Forces talent was supposed to be, and what they did was build fortifications out of the Middle Ages ... simply building little enclaves in each tribal area ... (Krepinevich, 1984, 74)

The existence of large, trained CIDG forces, tied down in village defense, was just too tempting. Both MACV (the US Military Assistance Command–Vietnam) and the conventionally minded ARVN commanders saw better uses for them. The SF troopers' training and leadership had produced some of the best light infantry in Vietnam, in many instances better trained and motivated than their ARVN equivalent. Thus began a theme that would be repeated over and over again. The SF would repeatedly train village-defense forces, only to see them marched off for conventional combat or diverted to other purposes.

There was another problem. When the time came, the GVN civil authorities were not overly anxious to spend money on social programs for the CIDG villages. By late 1962, only one 'developed area' was considered ready for transition, the Buon Enao village complex. The villages in this area were gradually turned over from US SF to the GVN between November 1962 and June 1963. The GVN promptly transferred the local CIDG troops (who had been recruited to protect their hamlets and villages) to other parts of the province, failed to pay health workers, and removed some of the facilities to other locations. When Vietnamese officials proved both unable and unwilling to support the area either financially or logistically the project began to fall apart. According to a 5th SF report on the CIDG program, the Buon Enao complex quickly became disorganized and ineffective (Operations Report, 5th SFG, 31 October 1967, 17).

If the return to Vietnamese civil administration was a failure, the military aspects of the program were, if anything, too great a success. There was building sentiment for getting the SF and their CIDG soldiers out of the village-defense business and into the jungles chasing VC, and DOD actively sought to do just that. After consultations in Washington, CIA and the State Department agreed in July, 1962 to 'Operation Switchback', a plan to turn the program over to the Defense Department (Stanton, 1985b, 51). Two weeks later, MACV headquarters received a cable from the Pentagon with new orders for the SF to be used 'in conjunction with active, offensive operations, as opposed to static training activities' (Krepinevich, 1984, 72).

MACV TAKES OVER

By early 1963, the nature of the CIDG program changed noticeably as MACV (with Pentagon approval) tried to put the Special Forces and the units they trained to better use. With the death of President Kennedy in November of that year, Special Forces lost their most important patron, allowing other influences to come into play. The most significant of these was the Pentagon's desire to find a more 'useful' conventional role for the special operators. The original village-defense units began to receive more weapons and equipment along with offensive training. They also began to fight as conventional infantry, seeking out enemy units for attack (Operations Report, 5th SFG, 1963). Blaufarb, commenting on these developments, sees this as a change from counterinsurgency (village defense) to 'unconventional warfare' (offensive operations) (1977, 107). In terms of the present discussion, it was a change from unconventional warfare (denying the enemy access to the population) to conventional warfare (operations intended to destroy the enemy armed force).

Despite the success of the CIDG as a self-defense and military training system, by June 1963 it was apparent that the Vietnamese military aspect of the program was not going well. The US Special Forces had done their end, but the transition to Vietnamese hands was to prove problematic. To accomplish the turn-over to Vietnamese authorities, the US Special Forces were partnered with their Vietnamese Army equivalent called the Luc Luong Dac Biet (Airborne Special Forces) (LLDB). In US military communications the LLDB was commonly referred to as VNSF, or Vietnamese Special Forces, since these were the soldiers who were to take over the US SF role. Unfortunately, the VNSF/LLDB included a high number of persons with money or personal influence who had joined as a way to avoid combat duty with the ARVN and consequently had turned LLDB into a sort of palace guard. The association with the generous and well-supplied Americans also made the LLDB assignments a fertile ground for corruption of all sorts.

Although there were undeniably some brave and effective VNSF, too many of them had no use for field service, avoided combat, disliked the peasant minorities in the CIDG and had no great regard for the Americans (Stanton, 1985b, 60–1). After a few months' experience trying to win them over, US Green Berets became frustrated, viewing their LLDB 'counterparts' as corrupt, lazy, untrustworthy and prone to theft. In American parlance, 'LLDB' came to stand for 'Lying, Little Dirty Bastards'.

SEALING THE BORDER

Given the ineffectiveness of GVN support and the overall inability or unwillingness of the VNSF to assume their responsibilities, it seemed a criminal waste of military capability not to use the CIDG where it 'really counted', in the conventional battle. MACV was eyeing the CIDG units as a source of soldiers for surveillance of South Vietnam's porous borders and especially the Americans' long-standing fixation, the Ho Chi Mhin Trail. As soon as it gained the authority to do so, MACV gave the CIDGs responsibility for border reconnaissance as a major mission. This responsibility called for 'active patrolling by screening forces, which often operated from forward operating bases when the CIDG campsite was some distance from the border' (Kelly, 1973, 47).

The assumption of border responsibilities shifted the SF training program to the production of 'strike forces'. The village militias had reached a total strength of about 38,000 in late 1963 (Clarke, 1988, 71), but were gradually reduced over the next two years in favor of the CIDG 'strike force' companies. These grew in strength from about 13,000 in 1963 to about 22,000 in 1965 (Kelly, 1973, 82). This also meant the loss or reduction of civic-action programs carried out in the villages. The original misuse of the CIDG had been to employ them away from their home villages and tribal farming areas, but at least it kept them in or near their original districts or provinces. The new mission moved the camps even farther away, into remote and often inaccessible border sites where they could be supported only by aircraft.

Special Forces Command in Vietnam, aware of the serious negative impact of these moves, protested to both MACV and Washington. MACV turned a deaf ear and continued the transition of SF personnel and village defense forces to conventional strike forces. The task of these conventionalized CIDG elements was, as articulated by MACV's commander General William Westmoreland, to seal the Lao–Viet border (Henry, 1989). This was a necessary mission, but the difficult terrain and the distances to be covered placed it utterly outside the ability of irregular units organized for village defense, even with Special Forces assistance and support.

By July 1963, MACV decided that enough training had been accomplished and the SF was to phase completely out of village defense and into action against the enemy. After November 1963, very few hamlet militia were trained under CIDG, 'almost none' after April 1964 (ibid., 49). By mid-1964, 18 Special Forces Detachments (approximately 250–300 men in total), were operating 25 border camps or 'border projects' involving 11,250 CIDG 'strike force' troops (Kelly, 1973, 47). Meanwhile, away from the CIDG areas, GVN relocation of villagers in VC-influenced zones continued. Another program was begun to fill the village-defense vacuum by creating another local defense militia called Regional Forces/Popular Forces, universally referred to as 'Ruff Puffs'.

During this period the bonds between the US Special Forces soldiers and the tribespeople continued to grow, distancing the CIDG from both the civil and the military elements of the GVN. This trend was encouraged by the continued weakness of VNSF leadership combined with endemic GVN corruption and blatant racial prejudice against the ethnic minorities.[1]

One effect of arming a disaffected minority like the Montagnards was to raise the possibility of independence or at least autonomy. One of the products of SF intelligence collection was information about the rise of a widespread Montagnard separatist movement. The trends listed above and their history of abuse by the GVN apparently contributed to the rise of an armed Montagnard independence movement *Front unifé de la lutte des races opprimées* (FULRO) or 'United front of the oppressed races' (USMACV Command History, Annex A 1965, 347–52, and Annex B, 1966, 697–706; MHD, 1969). CIDG began to look like a FULRO army.

An abortive FULRO uprising in 1964 included several of the CIDG camps and resulted in several Vietnamese deaths. Although the rebellion was ended through the intervention of US SF advisors, FULRO and Montagnard independence ambitions remained alive. The incident solidified ARVN/GVN distrust of both the CIDG and Special Forces, and did little to endear them to MACV.

RELOCATION AND CONVERSION

To a large degree, both MACV and Washington understood that they were dealing with a traditional culture in Vietnam. What they did not understand is why that made a difference. In a nutshell, the relevant difference was that people in an industrial society, especially the government bureaucracy and the military, are accustomed to moving, physically changing their residence and work location several times over a lifetime; traditional societies are not. For them, these kinds of changes are wrenching and normally occur only under great stress.

To understand the basic error made by MACV and others, it is important to recall that the CIDG units had been developed as home-defense militia or 'territorials'. Territorial forces are militia units whose membership is drawn largely from some specified political subdivision (or territory). They are intended principally for the defense of their home district, village or hamlet. CIDG and their successors as village militia, the Regional Forces/Popular Forces (RF/PF) – all originated as territorial forces. But as each was created they were quickly transformed into general-purpose, regular military formations and used well away from their local areas. All of these territorial forces quickly lost much of their effectiveness by losing the advantage of local knowledge and the motivation of defending their homes.

This was especially true of the extremely family- and village-centered traditional cultures in rural Vietnam, in particular the Montagnards. CIDG recruiting became a problem after the transition to conventional offensive operations and border surveillance: 'consequently several of our camps were manned with CIDG people the Vietnamese Corps commander had graciously provided to us from jails and military prisons. I got suspicious at Ashau during an inspection when I noticed Claymore mines facing toward the camp' (Henry, 1989). There was, as usual, continuing dissatisfaction with the performance of the Vietnamese SF, and in particular their stubborn unwillingness to work with the ethnic minorities who made up the bulk of these units (Stanton, 1985, 10).

In 1965, conventionalization proceeded further when SF advisors took on the additional responsibility of training scout units from each CIDG camp. Headquarters, MACV authorized creation of five new battalions of minority ethnic (principally non-Vietnamese) volunteers. Given the usual racial and ethnic prejudice among VNSF, ARVN and local GVN officials, the US SF were left to organize, train and lead the new battalions (Kelly, 1973, 8, 9).

By now the original, unconventional warfare, concept of CIDG, had been virtually abandoned, leaving many villages unprotected. Remaining CIDG units not transferred to the border camps came under operational control of ARVN corps commanders. These commanders continued to treat the CIDG as conventional forces, employing them in joint combat operations with ARVN units.

By the end of 1965, the conversion of the remaining CIDG village-defense units to light conventional infantry was about complete (Operations Reports, 31 December 1965, 41–2). The change was underpinned by the creation of a new, conventional table of organization for these units complete with crew-served weapons (TOE 1-66, 1966). Despite the continuing efforts of SF commanders to return the program back its original purposes, there was no support from either MACV or the Defense Department and the village defense aspects of the program quietly withered over time.[2]

THE CONVENTIONAL ARMY IN COMMAND

The year 1965 was also when US ground forces (Army and Marine Corps) entered the war in large numbers. As divisions of soldiers and Marines arrived in the jungles and highlands, their adaptation to the ongoing Vietnam conflict was interesting in that neither formal doctrine nor conventional military orientation were modified in any comprehensive fashion. Although both services continued to conduct operations within the preferred (conventional) model, they did develop and institutionalize changes at the tactical level that made those operations more efficient (Henry, 1964; West,1967; Kelly, 1973, 165; Ewell and Hunt, 1974). 'An operational doctrine based on "search and destroy" was nothing more than a validation of conventional operational level thinking, cast in a high technology mold' (K. Sheehan, 1988, ch. 7, 5). There was little change in doctrine, because few generalizable tactical or operational lessons were identified. The official US Army 'Lessons Learned' for 1965 recommended that additional emphasis be placed on training in 'basic infantry techniques and small unit tactics' (USCONARC, 1965, Appendix 1, 1). This was also borne out by an Army postwar study covering technological innovations and refinements of conventional infantry tactics (Ewell and Hunt, 1974, esp. 106–47).

The role of the ARVN in defending its own country was quickly eclipsed by the larger, better-equipped US combat units. As an operational headquarters, MACV placed most of its emphasis on the US divisions and brigades, relegating the ARVN to the secondary role of local security. Generally, the US units had no great faith in their Vietnamese allies as fighting men. In the words of Col. (then Major) David Hackworth of the US 101st Airborne Division, 'never ... give a Vietnamese unit a role that was critical to any operation, and never ... trust a Viet. And on both counts I never did, over the entire four years I spent in Vietnam' (Hackworth, 1989, 531).

During 1965–66 the US Agency for International Development (USAID) began to build up a province pacification program, which pursued a variety of efforts such as road and school building, well-digging, agricultural assistance, refugee relief, and so forth.[3] This program was of limited value for three reasons: (1) the pervasive corruption of the South Vietnamese government; (2) the non-integration of USAID efforts with parallel military advisory efforts in the provinces, despite much 'liaison' (Hall, 1986, 125; Vann, Memorandum, 1966) and, most important (3) without CIDG, the Viet Cong could deny effective access to the population in many of the rural areas where the bulk of the population resided (DTIC, 1967; also DTIC, 1968).

In areas where the pacification program was successful it was often because of the personal intervention of the SF and MACV advisors, who took care to insure that USAID supplies reached the villagers for whom they were intended, rather than becoming 'lost' in the system (i.e. stolen) (Hall, letter, 1988). Headquarters, 5th Special Forces, went so far as to publish instructions (complete with a diagram) on the 'Dual Channel Concept', under which advisors were to 'follow your counterpart's requests with information through your advisory channels, informing the next higher headquarters about the request and asking them to insure appropriate action is taken' ('A' Detachment Handbook, 1966, 120–1).

By the mid-1960s, the CIA was still funding portions of the CIDG program despite its change in orientation away from unconventional warfare. The CIA–SF funding channel had become formalized, with congressional appropriations being made to the DOD, which transferred the funds to the CIA, which in turn transferred them to the 5th SFG and MACV's Studies and Observation Group (MACV-SOG) (Colby interview, 1988).

The original intention was to avoid GVN interference, but it also had the effect of fragmenting the US effort and further alienating it from the government it was intended to support. It also gave Headquarters MACV another reason to distrust the 5th Group and assert that they were, yet again, out of control.[4]

By 1968, corruption among VNSF commanders had become so pervasive that the 5th SFG resumed control of all pay for CIDG members (Operations Reporter, 31 January 1969, 78). The following year a Military Police captain was assigned to Headquarters 5th SFG to command a 'graft and corruption section' aimed at least at reducing the problem to manageable proportions (Senior Officer Debriefing, 1969).

The original SF 'area development' program continued to sputter as the emphasis on conventional military operations grew. In 1966, Headquarters 5th SFG underlined this emphasis by advising subordinate SF commanders that the 'SF counterinsurgency program' had three objectives: 'destroy the Viet Cong', 'establish firm governmental control over the population', and 'enlist the population's active and willing support of, and participation in, the government's programs'. These objectives were to be accomplished while executing the SF/CIDGs 'assigned missions': 'Border surveillance and control, operations against infiltration routes, and operations against VC war zones and bases' ('A' Detachment Handbook, 1966, 6). If the lack of coordination between largely political objectives and wholly military missions was noted, it was not remarked upon.

Efforts at improving government control outside the cities were also hampered by the increasingly military nature of the South Vietnamese government. By 1966, ARVN Corps commanders had gained significant control in the civilian government, becoming more and more involved in the administrative functions of the civilian Province Chiefs. John Paul Vann (formerly a MACV advisor to ARVN, then a USAID Province advisor) observed during this period that the Vietnamese military was interfering widely with police operations and using payoffs to place their allies in local GVN positions. He also complained of continuing ARVN mistreatment of civilians (Vann, 1965).

As evaluated by the 5th SFG, this reduced the strength of ties between the national government and the provinces, resulting in military officers and the various GVN agencies responding more directly to their own chain of command with little effective overall direction or coordination ('A' Detachment Handbook, 1966, 111). Surveys of the civilian population during this period indicated the growth of a gradual disaffection with the GVN (Attitude Report, 1967). This disaffection was encouraged by the generally urban, elite character of the GVN administration in the rural areas. The GVN administrators, including province and district chiefs, were drawn from what a MACV 'Working Paper' described as 'a small, alienated, urban class' in charge of the government and the military (MACV Working Paper, 1967).

Despite the growing military character of government, the GVN rural presence was often ineffectual. In a letter to Daniel Ellsberg, Vann complained that the VC had general freedom of movement in much of the II Corps (central highlands) area, including so-called 'secure areas' under GVN control. According to Vann, local VC elements were conducting assassinations of GVN police and officials while larger (company-size) VC units were capable of attacks on both US and ARVN positions (Vann, 30 March 1965). Because of the threat, many government appointed village chiefs did not even spend the night in their village but retired to the nearest ARVN compound by sunset.

John Vann became the figure most associated with this kind of criticism. As a USAID Province Advisor, he believed that there was a larger reason for Viet Cong success in influencing the population: they had succeeded in harnessing 'the anger and the aspirations of poor Vietnamese' to the cause of social revolution which they were leading in the South (N. Sheehan, 1988, 34) In September 1965, Vann had circulated in Saigon and Washington a ten-page proposal titled 'Harnessing the Revolution in South Vietnam'. The essential notion of this proposal was that the Saigon government needed to concentrate less on the military defeat of the Viet Cong and gain the support of the peasants, thus capturing the social revolution from the communists. Vann was alarmed by the continued US and South Vietnamese military policy of relocation, removing the rural population into 'protected' or 'strategic' 'hamlets', and refugee camps around the district towns (ibid., 38).

The relocation policy was, however, perfectly in accord with the conventional model of war, which sees civilians as impediments in the 'combat zone'. In fact, the very concept of a 'combat zone' supports the conventional view of warfighting as something that occurs apart from the general population. They are seen as impediments to be removed both for their own safety and for the promotion of efficient and effective military operations. In Vietnam it appeared that the quicker and surer method was simply to empty the countryside. In 1968 Ambassador Taylor reported that 'the total population under secure Government of Vietnam control has increased from 6.6 million in mid-1965 to 10.8 million in mid-1967', the majority of that achieved through relocation and the movement of refugees to the district towns or major cities (Schell, 1968, 71).

The policy of population control (or 'security') by relocation was defended by its adherents as an effective unconventional warfare technique which, if pursued, would separate the communist guerrillas from the population (Hall, 1988). General Westmoreland received a copy of the Vann proposal, but was unpersuaded. His intention was to restore the country to government control as US forces gradually destroyed the VC and North Vietnamese Army units. The role of the South Vietnamese army (ARVN) was to act as an adjunct to the US offensive.

The population would be protected by resettlement or whatever local militia could be spared, but the emphasis was on the military defeat of the enemy, and the quicker the better. This led to an insatiable demand for soldiers and, in turn, the conventionalization of the Regional and Popular Forces (RF/PF). Just as the CIDG had been, the Ruff Puff units were to be 'upgraded' from a widely scattered, village-based irregular light infantry to 213 regular infantry companies including mechanized (armored-car) and river-patrol units (COMUSMACV, 'Role of RF/PF in Pacification', 1967, 1742–51).

In addition to the 'relocated' villagers, the increasing tempo of the war and the application of technology in the form of greatly increased firepower created thousands of refugees (Vann, 1965). Bernard Fall commented during this period that the French had used less bomb tonnage during the entire 56-day battle at Dien Bien Phu than the USA was employing on any given day (1967, 231). Massive sweeps by conventional units (for example Operation Cedar Falls in January 1967) were intended to destroy guerrilla strongholds but often succeeded in creating even greater numbers of refugees, while failing to come to decisive grips with the enemy (ibid.; also Operations Reports, 5th SFG, 14 November 1967).

In 1967, MACV launched a series of four massive division-scale conventional operations in Binh Dhin Province, a long time communist stronghold. Major Vernon Gillespie of the 1st Battalion, 9th Cavalry, participated in those operations:

> This was the third time we'd run up against the NVA 22d regiment. Every time we'd run up against them, we'd tear them up and they'd fade back into the mountains. Six months later they'd come back, completely refurbished. (Gillespie, 1985)

This policy of conventional engagement through massive firepower generated huge numbers of refugees, disrupting the social order. Combined with the pacification practice of relocation, these policies did nothing to solidify Vietnamese society in the South. Instead, it uprooted that society and tore at its integrity. Air and artillery attacks on suspect Viet Cong movement and 'occupied' areas during 1967 killed about 24,000 civilians. The total US and South Vietnamese military deaths for the same period were about 19,000. The war imposed a terrible burden on soldiers and civilians alike.

VIETNAMIZATION II: THE SECOND ATTEMPT, 1968–73

The attempt at pacification entered its final stage in 1967 when US support to the South Vietnamese was unified under the control of MACV. In March, President Lyndon Johnson and his senior advisors on Vietnam (including General Westmoreland) met on Guam with the leadership of the GVN. It was agreed that more emphasis on Vietnamese self-help was required and a three part structure was adopted to accommodate this. Westmoreland would remain overall US commander, Gen. Creighton Abrams would take charge of upgrading the ARVN and a new post would be created to handle pacification among the civil population. The new position, Deputy COMUSMACV for Civil Operations and Revolutionary Development

Support (CORDS), was created to integrate the various US military and civilian programs aimed at reasserting GVN control over the countryside (Westmoreland, 1990; also 1989, 213–14).

In May, Johnson dispatched Robert Komer to become General Westmoreland's deputy for pacification. CORDS was an 'ad hoc instrument' intended to 'provide a non-military and primarily political function' (Colby, 1988). In the event, CORDS quickly developed a strongly military character that it retained throughout the war. The concept was to create unified inter-agency province teams composed of military advisors to the RF/PF and the various civilian advisors in each province. These teams reported to a deputy commander for pacification in each corps region, who in turn was directly subordinate to Komer. At its height, the CORDS program consisted of 5,000 US military personnel and about 1,000 civilians (Colby, 1988), illustrating the overwhelmingly military character of the program. It is revealing that, after 13 years of involvement with the Diem regime and the GVN, 11 years after Lansdale's development programs, the internal development effort in South Vietnam was still 'ad hoc'. It is even more revealing that this *ad hoc* organization, however poorly coordinated, was an advance on earlier, even more fragmented efforts.

Pacification proceeded, but the disaffection between US and Vietnamese officials continued to be a problem, as evidenced by the US official quoted by Roger Hilsman (Assistant Secretary of State for Southeast Asia) in 1967: 'The improvement here is real but it is 100 percent due to US effort, and not one-tenth of one percent due to the Vietnamese effort' (Hilsman, 1968, 426).

Still, things seemed to be looking brighter and General Westmoreland told the National Press Club that 'the war had reached an important point when the end begins to come into view'.

TET 1968 – HOW TO WIN THROUGH LOSING

Pacification took a serious blow on 31 January 1968, during Tet, the Vietnamese lunar new year celebration. Under cover of a truce they themselves had declared, Viet Cong and NVA struck at every major city in South Vietnam, numerous district capitals and several minor cities, along with the majority of military installations. Ten provincial capitals and Hue, the old imperial capital, were occupied and in Saigon guerrillas penetrated the US Embassy itself. ARVN and the Americans counterattacked and in three days of heavy fighting recovered most of the enemy gains. Fighting was protracted only in Saigon and Hue, which were cleared of enemy by 25 February.

Both ARVN and the village militias fought well. It was a serious blow to the communists, who lost about 45,000 killed, more than half the attacking force, and another 7,000 captured. US and ARVN losses were less than 10 percent of that. It was a military disaster of the first order for the NLF, but it was also a political and psychological victory, a fact that was received with resentment and incomprehension at MACV.

Prior to Tet 1968, many villages considered 'secure' had been reluctant to commit themselves to the GVN. For these ordinary Vietnamese, the Tet offensive demonstrated that the USA and the GVN had failed to establish any truly secure areas, even within the US Embassy itself. In the USA, moreover, the effect of the Tet Offensive was profound. Influential members of the news media, certain public opinion leaders and some segments of the public became convinced that the war was unwinnable. In retrospect, Westmoreland's earlier optimistic attitude seemed to many Americans to stem from either cynicism or deceit.

Even if the VC main force units were driven off, as was usually the case, especially after 1968, the NLF political infrastructure usually remained. Even the security and GVN control of hamlets surrounding Saigon was in doubt (Komer, message, 21 July 1968). The vexing problem of rooting out this infrastructure gave rise to the Phoenix Program (discussed later). According to Hilsman, writing in 1968: 'They have the capacity to strike back almost anywhere ... There is no convincing evidence that the recent offensive was a "desperate last gasp" or that the Viet Cong and North Vietnam could not continue to take the present rate of casualties for years' (Hilsman, 1968, 425). Nevertheless, the MACV position remained that pacification progress was no more than a matter of the availability of resources (MACV message, 1968, 35).

The Tet 1968 attacks were followed by two smaller offensives including 'heavy ground attacks' at seven US SF camps in August and September (Senior Officer Debriefing, 1969). Despite the comments of Hilsman and others, there was a feeling both at MACV and in 5th SF Headquarters that Tet had been 'a desperate last gasp', and that the 'military phase' of the war was over and 'political phase' was about to begin. The late-summer attacks were characterized as the failure of 'a rather feeble attempt at a third offensive' (Operations Report, 31 October 1968, 3).

Perhaps Tet 1968 was not a classic Napoleonic battle of annihilation, but at least from MACV's perspective, it would do. The
enemy had apparently been destroyed in combat at least to the extent
of being regressed to the level of a guerrilla force and, after all, that
was the object of the exercise. At the US Military Academy at West
Point, Lt Col. Dave R. Palmer wrote, 'It is possible to speak of the
war in Vietnam in past tense ... The war ended in August of 1968,
when sorely battered Communist troops were unable to engage the
allied war machine' (Palmer, 1969, 45, 110). The fighting might go
on, but the war was over.[5]

That same year General Westmoreland returned to the USA to
become Chief of Staff of the Army and was replaced as Commander,
MACV by his deputy, Gen. Creighton W. Abrams.

The role of province advisor, the most influential advisory
position, was turned over to MACV during 1968, relegating the SF
advisors to the less significant sector and subsector positions
(Operations Reports, 1969, 32). By the end of 1968 the Special
Forces missions had become stabilized as:

1. advise and assist Vietnamese SF and support CIDG
2. act as sector/subsector advisors under MACV
3. provide intelligence to MACV
4. conduct special operations
5. conduct the MACV Recondo School
6. organize, train, equip, and command Mobile Strike Force
   Commands ('Mike' Forces).
   (Operations Reports, 1968, 1969; Senior Officer Debriefing, 1969, 2)

These missions remained constant until the SF was withdrawn from
RVN. Item 6, the Mobile Strike Force, was removed from the list
in 1970 and the last Strike Force unit converted to ARVN in
December 1970 (Operations Report, November 1970, 1, 17–18).

CIDG BECOMES A 'SECOND ARVN'

During the period 1968–70 the Special Forces gradually turned over
the CIDG troops to complete Vietnamese Army control. Under
ARVN, they were retitled 'Vietnam Army Rangers', and fully
absorbed as regular government soldiers (CORDS, message, July
1968; Kelly, 1973, 151–2). In July 1968, CORDS was still faced
with the never-satisfied need for village-defense forces. Returning

to the original concept of the RF/PF, CORDS began to emphasize their development as territorial security forces (for example for village defense) (CORDS, message, July 1968).

In particular, Komer, as CORDS chief, opposed what he saw as 'an increasing trend' to convert the RF/PF 'into a second ARVN' (Komer, memorandum 27 October 1968). Komer's attitude was not entirely welcome at MACV where General Abrams complained that an average of 40–45 percent of District RF/PF units were employed country-wide in local security chores. On 29 October 1968, Abrams ordered that US advisors 'and their ARVN counterparts ... free up additional forces' for offensive action, adding 'make sure this happens' (Abrams, message, 1968). But, despite three years of large-scale US and Vietnamese conventional operations, local security was a problem that simply refused to go away.

In December, CORDS authorized the organization of 278 new Regional Force companies (CORDS, message, December 1968) and quickly followed this, in January 1969, with an authorization for additional companies (CORDS, message, January 1969).

THE SPECIAL ACTION FORCE

In 1969 the Army Special Warfare Center at Fort Bragg began promoting the concept of a military organization that would combine all the unconventional abilities of an SF Group with a small Civil Affairs Group, a Psyops Battalion, an Engineer Detachment, a Medical Detachment, an Army Security Agency unit capable of classified communications and such other specialist elements as might be required. This was the Special Action Force (SAF) concept, and in some versions even included Intelligence and Military Police Detachments (Simpson, 1983, 69) Four SAFs were eventually created, at least on paper. However, only one, the SAFASIA, built around the 1st SF Group on Okinawa, ever came close to being actually manned in the form envisioned. Although SAF elements performed various piecemeal missions, especially in Asia and Latin America, none were ever deployed as a unit (1st SFG, 1971, 3–5). Eventually, the concept faded away.

This was for a simple reason – all of their functions except the commando role were already the province of other US Agencies operating in the countries where a SAF might be deployed. Agencies such as US Military Assistance Group, Agency for International Development (USAID), the CIA, the US Information Service and others did not welcome what they could only view as competition from such an organization. Since the SAF would have to be invited in by a host country through the US ambassador, the opposition of such agencies operating out of the US Embassy made it very unlikely such an invitation would be forthcoming; none ever was (Simpson, 1983, 70–1, 197).

Sadly, this kind of competition was not limited to the SAF or even US agencies. By 1970, continuing friction between GVN representatives and US agencies, and among the agencies themselves, reached the point that local negotiation became impossible and both sides 'relied heavily on Washington for arbitration of disputes'. This friction, combined with the 'fragmentation in the US community' had obvious implications for US policy and operations in the field (OSD, 1971, vol. 2, 4.1–5.1). The US effort in Vietnam became a replica of the bureaucratic struggles characteristic of US domestic government.

THE US WITHDRAWAL BEGINS

Beginning in 1969 the atmosphere surrounding US involvement changed as the US government moved toward a unilateral withdrawal from the war. Events acquired a new complexion as it became clear that President Nixon, newly elected on a pledge to end the war, was determined to extricate the USA from its involvement.

In a White House speech delivered over national radio and television on 14 May 1969, Nixon abandoned his earlier insistence on an NVA withdrawal prior to any US departure, and called for phased simultaneous withdrawals (US President, 14 May 1969, 484). The following month President Nixon met with President Thieu on Midway Island, where the US leader set forth a new policy aimed at releasing the USA from Vietnam: US troop withdrawals justified by Vietnamization and pacification.

The NVA threat was to be neutralized through negotiation. This policy was quickly made concrete in the form of a new mission statement for General Abrams and MACV. They were to give first priority to Vietnamization, support pacification, and to do what they could to impede the flow of supplies to the VC and the NVA in the South. In the words of Henry Kissinger, Nixon's national security advisor, 'We were clearly on our way out of Vietnam by negotiation if possible, by unilateral withdrawal if necessary' (Kissinger, 1979, 272). The negotiations and the general philosophy of withdrawal by whatever means had a serious impact on the attitudes of all participants, on both sides. In Hanoi, Vo Nguyen Giap, North Vietnamese Minister of Defense, declared that the Americans had suffered 'a political defeat' (Fallaci, 1976, 80).

In February and March, the NVA and Viet Cong conducted 'widespread coordinated attacks-by-fire and ground probes on population centers and military installations throughout Vietnam'. The attacks 'sputtered on and off for the next two months' (Senior Officer Debriefing, 1969, 9). At the same time, Headquarters 5th SFG looked toward the 'scaling down of forces' with the 'cessation of hostilities possibly imminent' (ibid., 4).

Meanwhile, the upgrading of the ARVN had its own problems. Dispirited ARVN conscripts, too often bedeviled by poor leadership and worse training, also understood the Americans were leaving. As recalled by Bobby Muller, a MACV advisor: 'Every, every, every, every firefight that we got into, the ARVN broke, the ARVN … ran. I was with three different battalions and the story never changed' (Muller, 1990, 409).

The political struggle continued into 1969 as military-intelligence officials reported continuing signs that the NLF was pursuing its strategy of exerting as much control as possible over the rural population while attacking small US and GVN military outposts, and vulnerable cities (codename SPHINX, based on captured documents and prisoner interrogations; see also NYT, 26 June 1969, 3:1). That same year the NLF announced the formation of a Provisional Revolutionary Government for South Vietnam (ibid., 11 June 1969, 1: 6). This was actually little more than a redesignation of the existing NLF 'shadow government' infrastructure in the South, but it did have the psychological effect of implying that the NLF was consolidating its hold over the rural population. MACV-CORDS response to the difficult security situation in the countryside was to consolidate RF companies into conventional battalions (CORDS, message, 4 July 1969) and provide police training (CORDS, message, 15 June 1969).

By January 1970, 80,000 US soldiers had been withdrawn from Vietnam. US policymakers in Washington and planners in Saigon began to turn with a sense of relief to planning for 'postwar' Vietnam (JCS, L. to COMUSMACV, 2 February 1970). In February 1970, the US Senate Foreign Relations Committee heard testimony that the NLF infrastructure remained largely intact and that the Viet Cong had resumed terrorism against GVN village officials.

Nevertheless, on 20 April, President Nixon announced that

'progress in training and equipping South Vietnamese forces has substantially exceeded our original expectations'. Accordingly, he stated, an accelerated rate of withdrawal was justified which would bring the total US withdrawal to approximately 265,000 by December 1970, 'based solely on the progress of our Vietnamization program' (US President, 1970, 373–7).

The emphasis then went to the creation of conditions that would make the withdrawal possible. This included emphasis on the MACV advisory effort. The problem here was that the MACV effort was founded on the conventional notion that almost any good soldier could perform such a role. Nevertheless, the negative perceptions mentioned earlier about advisory duty tended to reduce the quality of the personnel involved. The Human Measurement and Research Office (HUMMRO), the Pentagon's 'human factors' research group, found in 1970 that only 24 percent of those serving as advisors had requested the assignment.

According to the HUMMRO study of 605 US advisors during 1969–70, only 37 were graduates of the Special Warfare Counter-insurgency Course, only 55 had completed the Military Assistance Programmer Course, and only 194 had even completed the basic Military Advisor's training course (Graham and King, 1973, 89). This was not new. As early as 1967 General Westmoreland had expressed his concern about the effectiveness of the US advisors in a message to General Harold K. Johnson, US Army Chief of Staff (Westmoreland to Johnson, 28 May 1967). Warrant Officer Frederick Leppin, an advisor during this period, complained that his advisory team had no specialized training, little to contribute, and too often felt nothing but 'dislike and contempt' for the Vietnamese (Leppin, 1976, 19). Needless to say, none of this concern with the quality and success of the conventional advisory effort led MACV or the Pentagon to conclude that perhaps the Special Forces were, after all, something special.[6]

On 31 August 1970, the GVN announced that 92.8 percent of South Vietnam was under government control (*New York Times*, 22 September 1970, 8: 1). This contrasted starkly with evidence not only of RF incompetence but lack of support from the population whom they were supposedly guarding (MACV Report, 5 January 1970).[7]

Several reports from late 1969 and early 1970 indicated that the VC retained their ability to attack US and Vietnamese units, and implied that the NLF infrastructure remained substantially intact in various regions of the country (MACV, messages, 28 December

1969, 2 February 1970, 6 February 1970, and 7 February 1970). A DOD Intelligence report in March stated flatly that enemy morale remained good and the infrastructure active in the 4th CTZ while reporting that US and ARVN Psyops efforts were 'generally ineffective' (DOD, 1970, 10). Later that year, 5th Special Forces Group Operations Reports depicted persistent low-level activity (chiefly rocket and mortar attacks) against lightly defended military installations, province capitals, and district towns (Operations Reports, November 1970).

The year 1970 also saw increasing militarization of formerly non-military assistance programs as the Nixon administration continued to shift US social and economic programs in RVN to military control. Other programs were left to operate independently or were administered jointly between the US and GVN agency or department involved, and the CIA (*New York Times*, 10 June 1970, 1: 2). Testifying before the Senate Foreign Relations Committee, Ambassador William Colby remarked on the lack of coordination among the various US agencies, but promised that the situation would soon be improved (Colby, statement, 1970).

On 26 July 1970, the 5th SFG was formally ordered to 'phase out' all remaining CIDG camps to ARVN control by March 1971, the conversion to be followed by the 'phase out' of US Army Special Forces from Vietnam (Operations Report, November 1970, 19). On 1 March 1971 the 5th Special Forces Group began its redeployment from Vietnam to the USA (Kelly, 1973, 179).

During the same period (1970) a POLitical WARfare (POLWAR) program was initiated by MACV and the 5th SFG. But, as indicated by the Operations Reports for 1970, this was 'an internal affair', a propaganda campaign 'tuned to effecting a smooth transition of the CIDG' as it became integrated into the Army of the Republic of Vietnam (Operations Report, November 1970, 41).

CREATING A SUCCESS: OPERATION LAM SON 719

Operation Lam Son 719 seems in retrospect to have been a tailored response to MACV's new mission statement. It was intended to bolster ARVN confidence, provide evidence of the success of Vietnamization, and impede the flow of enemy supplies to the South. It failed in all three objectives.

An ARVN attack with US support on VC/NVA supply bases in Laos, Lam Son 719, was regarded by US military planners as proof of the soundness of conventional methods and their application to Vietnam. It would also show the results of MACV's advisory programs to turn the war over to the ARVN. In December 1970 both military intelligence and supporting sources indicated an unusually heavy enemy stockpiling of supplies in Base Area 604 in Laos, near the Laotian village of Tchepone, about 70 kilometers across the border from the US/ARVN base at Khe Sanh. An upcoming NVA attack on the two northernmost provinces of South Vietnam seemed to be indicated. Lam Son 719 was to attack across the border in force, disrupt the NVA base areas, destroy their supplies and, hopefully, inflict significant casualties.

Although Palmer's account credits the Vietnamese, especially President Thieu, for originating the operation (Palmer, 1984, 303), Davidson asserts that Abrams and MACV 'originated, promoted, and supported' the idea (the quote is from Colonel Lung of the ARVN, provided in Davidson, 1988, 658). Several facts contribute to the tentative conclusion that Davidson is correct. First of all, there was the need to demonstrate convincingly that the ARVN could defeat the NVA if Vietnamization was to have any credibility. Secondly, according to the US after-action report, only light opposition was expected. Thirdly, such a spoiling attack, even if only partially successful, could still stave off any major NVA attack on northern RVN for at least a period of months. Although Abrams left no explanation of his reasoning, it seems at least probable that these were significant factors in his thinking.[8]

The actual operation was, though perhaps not the disaster portrayed in the US media, certainly not a decisive military victory or even a psychological success. The ARVN advance began on 8 February 1971 with a two division infantry attack, supported by armor, artillery and aircraft. Within three days the advance had halted with little accomplished, while enemy pressure built.

In an attempt to salvage at least a public-relations success, President Thieu ordered a helicopter assault into Tchepone, the original objective. On 6 March, following heavy bombardment by the US Air Force, two ARVN infantry battalions were airlifted from Khe Sanh to Tchepone by US helicopters. The troops entered the deserted village on 7 March, and the next day began to withdraw to ARVN lines. The entire ARVN task force, heavily pressed by the NVA, then began withdrawing to the Vietnamese border. The retreat, followed by a North Vietnamese counterattack across the Lao border, nearly developed into a rout, immortalized by US television coverage of frightened ARVN soldiers clutching the skids of US helicopters.[9] If Lam Son 719 was to be the proof-test of MACV's advisory effort, it had failed miserably.

On 7 April 1971, two weeks after the ARVN had been ignominiously ejected from Laos, President Nixon stated on national television that 'tonight I can report that Vietnamization has succeeded' (US President, 1972, 524). The President's speech included a pledge to withdraw US forces at 'an accelerated pace' to bring the total of troops withdrawn to about 365,000 by 1 December 1971. This amounted to two-thirds of the US strength at its height (January 1968) when 540,000 US soldiers were deployed in Vietnam (ibid., 524).

Regardless of the lack of ARVN success, conventional US commanders found much to praise in the performance of their own soldiers and the soundness of US doctrine. US ground forces had cleared the way into Laos for the ARVN units, but did not cross the border themselves. General Berry of the 101st Airborne Division (Airmobile) reported that, 'Our experience in conducting airmobile operations in support of Lam Son 719 confirms the soundness of the concept and the principles of airmobility developed by the US Army'. Berry also affirmed continuing US faith in firepower, commenting favorably on the use of 'concentrated, massive volumes of firepower', including its use against 'suspicious areas' (Berry, 1971). Maj. Gen. Talbot, Commandant of the Army's infantry training and doctrine center at Fort Benning, Georgia, found these operations to be 'amazing and gratifying' (Talbot, 1971, 1).

CONTROL OF THE POPULATION

In an important sense, the central issue of the Vietnam War, had always been one of population loyalty and control. These issues were not easily resolved, in important part owing to the difficulty of determining who (GVN or NLF) was actually in 'control' at any given time. As with the Psyops effort, population-control programs were evaluated in terms of the effort expended, rather than the results achieved.[10]

Jeffery Race's thoughtful study of the pacification war in Long An Province (Race, 1972) concluded that the US/GVN pacification measures were a failure that ended by 'driving people into the arms of the Party'. The principal factors in the failure were the relocation and persistent employment of inappropriate means of military mass violence (ibid., 266).

In the words of Advisor Bobby Muller:

> Cam Lo was a refugee village ... taken from another place. I didn't understand it then, but for Vietnamese, villagers, their rice paddy and their little ancestral burial ground defines their universe. You take it away from them as we did and you've totally disrupted what they relate to. (Muller, 1990, 408)

In June 1971 the *Washington Post* made public a 'leaked' MACV study which stated that Vietnamization in the Delta region (IV CTZ) continued to falter. As related by journalist Ward Just, between January and April 1971, 54 Regional and Popular Force bases had been overrun in IV Corps, double the loss of the previous year (*Washington Post*, 6 June 1971, 1). No really satisfactory solution to the empty village-defense role left by the conventionalization of the CIDG ever materialized. MACV and some elements of the GVN proposed that yet another local militia organization, the Combat Youth, be retained as the primary village defense with the remaining PFs 'responsible for overall village defense' (i.e. area defense). But 'Washington authorities' (not further specified) opposed this because of what they considered to be the undue proliferation of paramilitary forces (R-185, 1972, 81). The gradual conversion of CIDG elements to conventional mobile warfare rather than local defense functions was especially ironic, if (as Rheault suggests) those villages where the CIDG kept its local identity remained more secure than those where it did not. This has proven impossible to document from available materials (Rheault interview, 13 April 1989).

During 1971, MACVs continued the accelerated redeployment of US forces back to the USA (Abrams, message, 7 July 1971). The clock was running on US departure – the USA was on its way out of the war. All that remained for MACV and CORDS was to develop Vietnamese capabilities as well as they could and put the best possible face on the results. The official Army publication, *American Military History*, published in 1973, revised in 1985, treats the Vietnam War as having ended with successful Vietnamization in 1971 (Matloff, 1985, 646–7).

It might not be too strong to suggest that by 1972 and 1973 the NLF had, in some areas, become the GVN at the district level and below, both through intimidation and infiltration of members, supporters and sympathizers into civil and military positions. Americans had long felt that VC influence was strong in both the ARVN and the GVN (Henderson, 1979; Hackworth, 1989, 705–37; Rainey, 1990).[11]

In June 1972, Vann (by then director of the Second Regional Assistance Group, the senior advisor for the II Corps region) delivered an address to a group of advisors in Nha Trang. He stated that the 'social revolution' he had spoken of in 1965 had now been captured from the communists 'partly by design, but mostly by the accident of war'. In effect, Vann argued, a form of forced urbanization had occurred as many peasants were 'relocated' or fled as refugees to the district towns and cities. This urbanization had created a class of 'consumers' for the farmers (N. Sheehan, 1988, 55). Vann did not explain how this sort of mass social dislocation could possibly benefit the short term stability of Vietnamese society. Nor was it clear how this disaffected mass could fail to be a fertile ground for NLF recruitment.[12]

That summer American sentiment against involvement in Indochina continued to mount as the US Congress debated a series of narrowly defeated end-the-war resolutions.[13] In the words of Sen. Mike Mansfield, 'I am only rigid and inflexible on getting the hell out of Indochina and staying out' (CQ, 1972, 462). The long US role in the struggle finally ended on 27 January 1973, when representatives of the US, South Vietnam, and North Vietnam signed a ceasefire agreement, including provisions for the withdrawal of US combat elements, while leaving the Viet Cong and North Vietnamese forces in place in the South.

In an ironic postscript in 1974, MACV decided to economize on officer personnel by assigning the few remaining SF Detachment Commanders to double as Province/District Senior Advisors and to locate the handful SF detachments in the province or district capital. At last, the militia, Civil Affairs, Psyops, intelligence and other province or district-level counterinsurgency activities were unified under one US officer responsible directly to the US Senior Corps Advisor (Henry, 1989) – too little, far too late.

AN EVALUATION

Col. Charles M. Simpson III (US Army [ret.]) Deputy Commander of the 5th SFG (1966–67) evaluated the CIDG program in 1983, calling it 'an excellent example of the right way to fight an insurgent war. The program developed some well-trained offensive light infantry, but never lost sight of the real target of the effort – the people. Some 45,000 Vietnamese, who would never otherwise have been eligible to bear arms were effectively integrated into the military scheme of things in South Vietnam' (Simpson, 1983, 214). This statement is hard to credit on the record, as it has been consistently shown that, while the program may well have developed some 'well-trained offensive light infantry' (of dubious loyalty to the GVN), it determinedly lost sight of the 'real target' and never regained it. Rather than serving as a local defense force, defending its homes and loved ones, most of the CIDG, and many of the RF/PFs, became regular infantry, operating far from their homes. Instead of serving as a linking mechanism between the people and their government, they served as another step in the militarization of the South Vietnamese government, producing a government remote and divorced from the interests of its people. This is doubly ironic because, as related by Rheault, those CIDG units that did remain in their home areas proved more reliable as security forces than the RF/PF (Rheault, 1989).

There were certainly misgivings and some bitterness among the SF soldiers who had devoted so much time to the CIDG. They had overcome great difficulties, including motivating civilians who were often at odds with the GVN, advising an 'inept and disinterested LLDB', and maintaining isolated outposts along an indefensible border (Stanton, 1985b, 293). For all their problems, the SF-trained and led CIDG often outperformed their counterparts in the ARVN and, during the counterinsurgency phase of the program, secured hundreds of villages and hamlets.

None of this was very important to the conventional Army. As far as the Army was concerned, Special Forces provided 'a front behind which it could continue to develop forces for the familiar European contingency' (Krepinevich, 1986, 112). Something of this spirit may have been at work when the Army once more changed the name of the Special Warfare School, this time to the more innocuous sounding 'Institute for Military Assistance'.

CONCLUSIONS

In the Vietnam case we see the basic elements of the Army's self-concept and its view of war vividly played out. As shown by the examples of the Special Forces CIDG program, and the later Regional Forces/Popular Forces, the strong tendency was to convert popular forces to conventional military units. This misuse of the various local defense organizations (regardless of their value as village defense and disutility as regular forces) reflects the sincerely held belief that only conventional forces can be effective in battle. This is no doubt true, when the enemy is a comparably conceived conventional army.

As in World War II, those units, notably Special Forces, with unconventional functions, were seen as useful, praiseworthy, and successful only to the extent that they directly supported the conventional battle. UW functions, especially Psychological Operations, were seen as essentially peripheral and given short shrift (Chandler, 1981, 132).

The stubborn conventional belief that battle is the essential function, the defining function, of an army is reflected in the continuing attempts to bring NVA/VC forces into decisive engagement where they could be annihilated. This same focus on battle and the use of violent force is found in the massive use of firepower (despite the inevitable civilian casualties) and the attempt to relocate the civilian population away from the enemy. This ignored two central problems: these two policies (use of massive firepower and civilian relocation) acted to disrupt the fabric of Vietnamese society and place further stress on the already troubled relationship between the GVN, the ARVN and the population they were allegedly to nurture and protect.

The US Army's belief about the nature of armies and their function as organizations to do battle led to the obvious conclusion that an army that could fight, would fight. Any army might maneuver to seek advantage but in the end it could not refuse battle; to refuse for an extended period would, in the US Army's view, negate an army's entire rationale for being. Therefore, when the Viet Cong suffered severe losses during Tet 1968, and subsequently failed to renew large-scale battle, obviously it must be because they were unable to do so, and this inability was the definition of defeat. Given this interpretation, it was perfectly reasonable to believe, as General Palmer did, that the war was over. All that remained was to clean up the battlefield.

Since the US Army's theory of war assumes universal principles of conflict, it treats all conflict as fundamentally the same, differing importantly only in relative degree of violence. It is an approach that leads to the discarding of political, cultural and psychological factors which may be crucial. As Maxwell Taylor observed ruefully after the war:

> First, we didn't know ourselves. We thought we were going into another Korean War, but this was a different country. Secondly, we didn't know our South Vietnamese allies. We never understood them,

and that was another surprise. And we knew even less about North
Vietnam. Who was Ho Chi Minh? Nobody really knew. (Karnow,
1983, 50)

CIVIL AFFAIRS AND PSYCHOLOGICAL OPERATIONS

Civil Affairs and Psyops enjoyed something of a renaissance during
the Vietnam War. In theory, the 5th Group was an organization
intended to combine SF, Psyops and Civil Affairs, augmented with
intelligence personnel and military engineers at the group level. The
fielding of these resources, however, seemed to falter and it was
never actually implemented in the coordinated manner intended.

Although the 5th Group was augmented with the small 2nd Civil
Affairs Group in 1966, the use of CA was not the SF Group's top
priority. The same year, each 'A' team was also augmented with a
Psyops officer and NCO when such personnel were available. The
two Psyop members had the additional responsibility for CA at the
team level (USASOC, 1994, 71). CA was interpreted as small-scale
development projects.

The most extensive use of Psyops was separate from Special
Forces operations. The Army's 6th Psyop Battalion arrived in
Vietnam in 1965 and was absorbed on 1 January 1966 by the newly
activated 4th Psychological Operations Group (POG). The 4th POG
was later supplemented by the 7th POG and they became the
principal Psyops sources for the remainder of the war. Although the
operators tried to use all of the traditional Psyops media: radio,
loudspeakers and leaflets – the major emphasis was on the creation
and distribution of leaflets.

There had been a US/GVN Psyops program in place in South
Vietnam since the late 1950s with indifferent results. As a conse-
quence, Army Psyops had considerable competition from similar
organizations in the other services, the US Embassy and, after 1968,
the Civil Operations and Revolutionary Development Support
(CORDS) organization. This resulted in confused and overlapping
efforts.

Although Psyop efforts were directed at the Viet Cong and
included the usual surrender appeals and testimony from captured
guerrillas, much of the program was also was directed at the civilian
population. Radio, loudspeakers and leaflets were used to emphasize
a number of major themes if not always in a consistent manner.
These included appeals from defectors and captured guerrillas as

well as accounts of 'communist atrocities, land reform, village defense ... health measures and Vietnamese traditions'. The US Joint Public Affairs Office also inaugurated a TV network, operated by the Vietnamese government, that stressed similar themes such as messages from Viet Cong defectors (USASOC, 1994, 73–4). Nevertheless, all this was seen as pretty much marginal to the military effort.

As the war wound down in the early 1970s, Civil Affairs suffered the same fate as it had at the end of World War II. Units were gradually disbanded and deactivated. By the mid-1970s virtually all the Civil Affairs strength of the US armed forces was back in the Army reserve, just as in 1948. The future effect of this would be to require a lengthy and sometimes politically difficult call-up procedure whenever Civil Affairs expertise was needed for active service, as it often would be in the following decades.

RANGERS IN VIETNAM

A total of 13 American LRRP (Long Range Reconnaissance Patrol) companies were created in Vietnam from volunteers already in the country. These companies were each designated by a letter of the Army phonetic alphabet as charlie through papa companies (there was no 'J' or juliet company). Each was assigned to a conventional brigade, division or other unit to provide reconnaissance. Working in small groups, they performed as conventional scouts and raiders, relying on stealth to conduct reconnaissance, raids and ambushes throughout the war. On 1 June 1969 the LRRP companies were collectively redesignated the 75th Infantry Regiment (Ranger). Incidentally, although the unit insignia identified the LRRP companies as 'Airborne Ranger' units, many members were neither parachutists nor graduates of the Ranger training program. A number, however, were graduates of various division-run patrolling schools or LRRP training by Detachment B-52 of the 5th SFG. Following the precedent set in World War II and Korea, the LRRP/ Ranger units were disbanded as part of the US withdrawal.

NAVAL AND AIR SPECIAL OPERATIONS IN VIETNAM

Navy UDT's had progressed slowly during the 1950s, acquiring new skills (for example, parachuting) while developing new forms of underwater breathing apparatus. Their number, however, remained small and their influence nil in the larger Navy. Air Force special operations remained barely alive by supporting clandestine operations in aid of various anti-communist guerrillas. As an example, Det 2 of the 1045th Observation, Training and Evaluation Group undertook missions into Tibet for parachute insertion and resupply of CIA-trained guerrilla forces. The same unit also supported the CIA's failed attempt to invade Cuba at the Bay of Pigs in 1961. They were able to reach across the Caribbean and deep into the Himalayas thanks to a newly developed four-engine aircraft, Lockheed's turboprop C-130 'Hercules'. This airplane and its multiple modifications would become a mainstay of American special operations for the remainder of the twentieth cenutury (USSOCOM, 1996, 2–11, 2–12).

The proliferation of special operations units under the Kennedy administration affected the Navy and Air Force as well as the Army. As noted earlier, in 1962 the Navy reassigned 100 sailors and 20 officers from UDTs to form two new organizations called SEAL teams, adding the task of training indigenous personnel to their list of responsibilities. In 1961 the Air Force began redesignating existing units as 'air commandos' and training them for counter-insurgency missions using diverse aircraft including the C-130, the new UH1 'Huey' helicopter and the prop-driven A-1E 'Skyraider', a modernization of the venerable 'Thunderbolt' fighter from World War II. The first of these units, the 4400th Combat Crew Training Squadron was established at Hurlburt Field in a remote corner of the sprawling Eglin Air Force Base in Florida's panhandle (USSOCOM, 1996, 2–14. 2–15; Marquis, 1997, 32). Hurlburt Field remains the home base of US Air Force special operations today. The 4400th undertook a series of overseas training missions and by 1966 was training local aircrews in nine countries including Laos and Thailand.

In the early 1960s the Army Special Forces in Vietnam had their own mini-air force in the form of rugged twin-engined DeHaviland 'Caribou' transports flown by Army pilots. When an interservice squabble forced the Army to give its fixed-wing air cargo capacity to the Air Force, air commandos took over the support mission. By 1966, there were 6,000 men and 550 aircraft assigned to air special operations, a number that would not be reached again for more than 20 years. The year 1966 also saw the development of large fixed-wing gunships, C-47s, C-119s and C-130 transports, modified to deliver unprecedented volumes of firepower. The gunship, especially the AC-130 attack variant, became a lasting feature of special operations (Marquis, 1997, 34).

As US involvement in the Vietnam War drew to a close Air Force and Navy SOF went into steep decline. The Navy cut its SEAL/UDT elements by 50 per cent but at least sought to preserve the capability. The Air Force was unsure of what use to make of a special operations capacity that served only to support Army ground forces and occasionally the Navy. This uncertainty was reflected in a series of reductions and pointless name changes until 1978 when all remaining 'commando' aircraft were consolidated as the 1st Special Operations Wing, back at Hurlburt Field. By 1979, the air commandos were almost completely disbanded (USSOCOM, 1997, 2–16; Marquis, 1997, 35).

NOTES

1. Roger Hilsman commented: 'What we call corruption is a set of arrangements that underpin the whole structure of traditional Vietnamese life. Changing these fundamental arrangements would involve a social revolution as fundamental and violent as that being controlled by the communists' (Hilsman, 1968, 427). More-over, this is the kind of fundamental cultural difference that is very important for unconventional operators to understand and almost impossible for conventional militaries to deal with.

2. Paschall, who participated in the CIDG program, states, 'from 1962 to November 1963, we were making great inroads into VC-held territory ... that is why Hanoi made the decision to change the parameters – they began sending in battalion and later regiment-sized units in early 1964. They were actually in worse shape than we were from spring '63 to early '64' (personal correspondence, December 1996).

3. For details of USAID operations see Ch. 13 (Vietnam), Vol. 1, *Administrative History – Agency for International Developmentt* (*c*. 1969, 377–499).

4. Colby states that CIA funding was continued because the Agency could authorize the passage of funds to the SF 'A' team (village) level. MACV funding had to go through GVN channels in Saigon (1988). This had the effect of further alienating SF units from MACV's dominant conventional elements. Rheault comments that, unfortunate side-effects aside, this is the 'only way to fund UW ops' (1989).

5. A Brookings Institute staff paper of this period (1968) displays the attitude that the war is largely over and some form of negotiated settlement with North Vietnam could be expected (Haviland *et al.*, *Vietnam After the War: Peacekeeping and Rehabilitation*, 1968). Palmer went on to become a Lieutenant General and Superintendent of the US Military Academy at West Point.

6. For other indications of early concern with the effectiveness of the conventional advisors, see messages Abrams (Deputy Commander USMACV) to Johnson 15 July 1967 and Johnson to Abrams 17 July 1967, Abrams Papers, MHI.

7. One example cited by the report is that of a RF squad, asleep on duty when attacked. There were no sentries or listening posts, and most significantly, the local populace failed to warn the RF of the enemy presence. It is also of interest that the RF company tasked to support the squad did not go to their aid and apparently had not made any plan to do so.

8. Davidson points out that the expectation of light opposition was supportable on historical grounds, since the NVA had never before offered a 'resolute defense' of their base areas as evidenced by the US/ARVN invasion of Cambodia in 1970 and other operations inside RVN (1988, 658).

9. For a thoughtful and detailed account of Lam Son 719 and Dewey Canyon II (the supporting US operation) see Kieth W. Nolan, *Into Laos* (1986).

10. The NLF criteria for control were simple, based on the degree of access to the people. A village or hamlet in which the NLF could freely 'proselyte' the people and collect taxes, even if only in the hours of darkness, was said to be under 'complete control'. One in which ARVN or territorial forces prevented this was said to be under 'limited control'. No category was established for 'completely GVN controlled' (SPHINX, 1 December 1970).

    The GVN equivalent was the MACV-CORDS developed Hamlet Evaluation System (HES). Instituted in 1967, this curious system measured government activity at the hamlet level. Each hamlet was rated from 'A' (most secure) to 'E' (virtual Viet Cong control), or 'VC' (total Viet Cong Control), based on 'security factors' (defense capability) and 'development factors' (GVN programs active). Hamlet Evaluation System, DEPCORDS.

11. Lt Col. James Rainey, a member of MACV J-2 (combined intelligence) in 1972–73, states that US distrust of the Vietnamese in general, and ARVN in particular, was so profound that US intelligence simply refused to pass current information to their Vietnamese counterparts (interview, 23 January 1990).

12. Vann, a retired Army lieutenant colonel, was the only civilian ever to be appointed senior advisor for a Corps region. This was a military position otherwise occupied by a major general.

13. The best known of these was sponsored by Congressmen John S. Cooper (R-KY) and Frank Church (D-ID), the 1972 Cooper–Church Amendment to 70-S381-8.3 Foreign Military Sales Act. See also, 1972's HR 381-47 Termination of Hostilities in Indochina.

5 Special Forces in Vietnam – Part II

The previous chapter described the attempt to use Army Special Forces in an unconventional manner – to organize the rural population of South Vietnam for self-defense against insurgents and to promote popular loyalty to the government. This chapter examines three other uses of special operations forces (chiefly Army Special Forces) during the Vietnam War: MACV-SOG, the Mobile Strike Force Commands (i.e. 'Mike' Forces) and the Phoenix Program (including its action arm, the Provincial Reconnaissance Units or PRU).

The operations of MACV-SOG and the Mike Forces, although portrayed by the Army as 'unconventional' were strongly conventional affairs. The better-known and far more controversial Phoenix Program was much closer to unconventional warfare. Furthermore, Phoenix is an instructional case because in some respects it anticipates the later difficulties of unconventional operations in the post-Cold War world. Describing these programs, General Westmoreland praised MACV-SOG and the Mike Forces. However, he characterized Phoenix as 'immoral, criminal' and 'not a military function' (Westmoreland interview, 1990).

MACV-SOG: Military Assistance Command, Vietnam – Studies and Observation Group

Although the last MACV-SOG mission ended more than 25 years ago, it is an important part of the history of special operations forces and especially Army Special Forces. The experience of the SOG veterans was crucial in solidifying the preferred definition of 'special operations' as military activities (for example, reconnaissance and raids) rather than political–military activities (for example, village defense and organization or Psyops). As the OSS/Jedburghs did after World War II, the SOG veterans would shape the conception of special operations for the generation to come. Since its inception, official data on MACV-SOG in the form of messages, reports and the like was highly classified, especially with regard to specific operational detail. However, beginning in the mid-1990s, much of that information was finally declassified making a more open discussion possible.[1]

The precursor to the group was a Vietnamese Army unit organized in 1956 for covert and clandestine operations directed against the North with training assistance and other support from the CIA and Army Special Forces (SF). The Vietnamese organization operated under several names over the years, including the Clandestine Action Force and the 1st Observation Group. It carried out few operations and saw little or no success.

Although the original rationale for the Vietnamese organization was covert and clandestine reconnaissance, it took on a more conventional anti-guerrilla combat role in 1960 when the pace of Viet Cong operations began to increase. After his July 1961 inspection tour, General Edward G. Lansdale recommended to Maxwell Taylor (by then JCS Chairman) that the unit be relieved from these conventional operations in favor of 'denied area missions' (Lansdale, 1961, 6). This did not occur.

As Viet Cong and North Vietnamese Army activity in South Vietnam continued to increase during 1962 and 1963, the Military Assistance Command, Vietnam (MACV) began to act less like a logistic and advisory element and more like an operational headquarters, seeking to consolidate control of US military operations in Vietnam. One of the projects it inherited from the Central Intelligence Agency was the low-priority effort to train Vietnamese special operations units for operations in denied areas.

The Central Intelligence Agency, through its Combined Studies Directorate, continued to support and fund these activities through early 1963, when MACV took over that role under Operation Switchback. By this time much of the training was conducted by SF personnel without significant CIA participation. Consequently, its operations quickly gained a distinctly military flavor and in 1963 it was renamed the Vietnamese Special Forces Command (VNSF) or LLDB (Luc Luong Doc Biet in Vietnamese). In the past, the LLDB had been something of a palace guard, with a swaggering attitude and little interest in combat. The Vietnamese proved reluctant to act on their own and, as before, few missions were carried out, none successfully. When it was clear that the Vietnamese were not able to conduct these missions without help, pressure began to mount for greater US involvement.

Major General William B. Rosson, a long-time critic of

unconventional warfare, made a series of inspections of Vietnam operations and had recommended the redirection of SF away from hearts-and-minds village defense work toward developing a more conventional, offensive force. Later, he and General Taylor both began to push for 'a radical increase' in the number of US Special Forces teams assigned to the border surveillance mission, the training of the LLDB and 'covert offensive operations in the North as well as Laos and South Vietnam' (Pentagon Papers, Vol. II, 1976, 653). The result was Operations Plan 34A. In very general terms, the plan called for a series of activities including:

1. Expand present operations of the First Observation Battalion in guerrilla areas of South Vietnam under joint MACV–CIA sponsorship and direction. This should be in full operational collaboration with the Vietnamese, using Vietnamese civilians, recruited with CIA aid.
2. In Laos, infiltrate teams under light civilian cover to southeast Laos to locate and attack Vietnamese Communist bases and lines of communications. These teams should be supported by assault units of 100 to 150 Vietnamese for use on targets beyond the capability of teams. Training of teams could be a combined operation by CIA and US Army Special Forces.
3. In North Vietnam, using the foundation established by intelligence operations, create a capability in the South Vietnamese Army to conduct Ranger raids and similar military actions in North Vietnam as might prove necessary or appropriate. Such actions should try to avoid any outbreak of resistance or insurrection which could not be supported to the extent necessary to stave off repression.
4. Conduct overflights for dropping of leaflets to harass the Communists and to maintain morale of the North Vietnamese population, and increase gray broadcasts to North Vietnam for the same purposes.

SOG was to be the action arm for Op Plan 34A.

The plan was approved by President Lyndon Johnson in January 1964 and on 24 January Headquarters MACV issued General Order 6 creating MACV-SOG.[2] It was created as a joint unconventional warfare task force responsible for special operations in Burma, Cambodia, Laos, North and South Vietnam, and border areas of China. In short, it was to be the joint service, unconventional-war task force for Southeast Asia (in official US parlance of the time: a JUWTF (pronounced 'Joo-f')), including Army, Navy and Air Force elements. However, MACV headquarters was not overly trustful of special-operations units and was hesitant to create a separate headquarters for them. For this reason, SOG was never formally constituted as a formal JUWTF which would have given it an official sanction it never attained (Mountel interview, 20 July 1989; see also Saal, Vol. I, 79–80, 83).

Army Special Forces Colonel Clyde R. Russell was named MACV-SOG's first commander, aka 'Chief, SOG'. Colonel Russell divided the unit into a more-or-less conventional structure of personnel division, intelligence, operations and so forth. However, under MACSOG 30 (Operations and Training Division) were five branches (commonly referred to as 'Ops'). These branches were: Operation 31 (Maritime Studies Branch), Operation 32 (Air Studies Branch), Operation 33 (Psyops Branch), Operation 34 (Agent Ops) and Operation 35 (Ground Studies Branch, for US ground operations in denied areas). These names later changed (for example, Operation 34 became the Field Studies Branch) but their essential functions remained the same. Over the years additional divisions were added until, by 1971, there were 21 specialized sections.

Despite its joint-service nature, most of the 2,000 Americans and 8,000 Vietnamese assigned during SOG's history were US Army Special Forces and VNSF personnel. Except for a number of Navy SEALS and Vietnamese sailors and UDT (Underwater Demolition Team) divers, the non-Army personnel largely performed supporting roles, notably air and sea transportation. Later, Army military intelligence teams and psychological operations personnel were also added to the roster (Stanton, 1981, 251).

The CIA connection quickly became tenuous. Several CIA officers continued to perform a 'liaison' function, but were confined chiefly to the psychological operations area, where their political expertise was expected to be of value. As originally constituted, the deputy command position in SOG was to be filled by a CIA officer but none was ever appointed to the post (Blackburn, 1983, 339; Simpson, 1983, 146). In fact, coordination between SOG and the CIA apparently was poor (Blackburn, 1983, 354). There was a distinct suspicion in some quarters that the CIA wanted to keep its distance from the new organization.

The US-run SOG was a new organization under MACV, but initially outside the operational control of that headquarters. As recalled by General Donald D. Blackburn (SOG commander 1965–66), SOG was not initially responsible to MACV's staff. Rather, all missions were subject to Joint Chiefs of Staff (JCS) approval through the Special Assistant for Counterinsurgency and Special Activities, 'with White House approval' (ibid., 340). In time this would change as SOG also became a tactical and operational asset for US conventional forces in the Republic of Vietnam (RVN).

SOG was intended as a combined US–Vietnamese group and moved rapidly to acquire additional manpower, establishing training centers for indigenous personnel drawn from from the SF trained Civilian Irregular Defense Groups. Some personnel were also assigned from VNSF, ARVN and the Vietnamese Navy. During 1964 and 1965, border surveillance missions were conducted in Laos and Cambodia and a series of 'non-attributional' amphibious raids were carried out by US and indigenous forces against the North Vietnamese coast. Navy SEALs, working with Vietnamese Navy sailors, infiltrated sabotage teams ashore for attacks on infrastructure targets (Prados, 1986, 247–8).

General (then Colonel) Blackburn, an Army officer, took charge of SOG in 1965 and immediately came under pressure from Washington and MACV to do something about infiltration from the North and the Ho Chi Minh Trail. Accordingly, Blackburn states that he set out to focus SOG on anti-infiltration missions. The particular geographic focus was to be the Annamite Mountain region along the Laos–RVN border, in terrain that was considered hospitable to special operations along the Ho Chi Minh Trail (ibid., 343). 'Hospitable' in this case meant rugged. But that ruggedness also meant the same terrain was 'hospitable' for the North Vietnamese Army (NVA).

One of the early efforts was called 'Leaping Lena' and illustrated the unit's initial problems. This operation attempted to insert six-man South Vietnamese Special Forces reconnaissance teams by parachute along the Ho Chi Minh Trail in Laos. The VNSF teams proved inept and were quickly captured or killed. In the words of General Blackburn, it was a 'fiasco' (Blackburn, 1983, 343). The failure of Leaping Lena and a general lack of faith in the motivation and ability of VNSF led to the decision to field composite teams made up entirely of SOG troopers: Americans and a few trusted Vietnamese formed the leadership, but the bulk of the soldiers came from the same population base that supplied the SF-run Civilian Irregular Defense Groups (CIDG) and were often recruited from CIDG units. Most of these were Vietnamese ethnic minorities (often Montagnards). After 1964 SOG was largely a US operation, with little significant participation by majority-culture South Vietnamese.

The Ho Chi Minh Trail was a continuing target of these operations.

The North Vietnamese had been engaged in gross, systematic violations of Cambodian neutrality by developing a series of headquarters, base camps, training areas and supply dumps connected by the Trail on the Cambodian side of the Cambodia–RVN border. Although a number of MACV-SOG camps (about a half dozen) were targeted against the Trail in Laos, an extensive effort was also launched against these Viet Cong and NVA sites in Cambodia. These missions were staged from 'launch' sites (usually CIDG Camps) along the Laos and Cambodian border (Blackburn, 1983, 233). Reconnaissance teams of six to 15 men (usually two to five Americans and the remainder non-majority culture Vietnamese) would operate within a zone fairly close to the South Vietnam border.

As time went on, more US Navy and Air Force members were added to SOG but, initially, most US personnel were Special Forces soldiers, formally assigned either to 5th SFG or MACV, plus a small number of CIA 'paramilitary' officers. In 1968, this practice was formalized for the SF personnel by the creation of 'Special Operations Augmentation' (SOA), a cover organization to make it appear that personnel were assigned to 5th MSF. SOA troops were actually posted on secret orders to MACV-SOG, supposedly masking the connection with Special Forces (Stanton, 1981).[3] In fact, this made the connection between covert/clandestine direct action and SF closer than ever in the minds of both conventional planners and SF operators.

Once established, MACV-SOG retained five primary responsibilities throughout the war, generally related to Oplan 34A: (1) cross-border operations to disrupt enemy lines of communication and sanctuaries in Laos, the Demilitarized Zone and Cambodia; (2) location and rescue of captured Americans and Vietnamese as part of assisting the escape and evasion of all imprisoned personnel and downed airmen; (3) training, launch, recovery and support for various types of agents with UW missions, including the simulation of anti-government partisan movements in North Vietnam; (4) psychological operations including 'black' radio broadcasts (falsely identifying themselves as official NVA stations); and (5) various special missions such as 'dirty tricks' (for example, placing booby-trapped ammunition into enemy caches), and recovery of sensitive items.

Blackburn describes one example of a psychological warfare program called 'Paradise Island' in which North Vietnamese fishermen were picked up at sea by Vietnamese fast patrol boats and taken to a GVN-controlled island. The fishermen were told this was a liberated zone of North Vietnam and then subjected to two days of sumptuous treatment and political indoctrination, after which they were given gifts (such as transistor radios that only received certain RVN stations) and returned to the North (Blackburn, 1983, 342). This was part of a longer-term effort to create or simulate a revolutionary movement inside North Vietnam. However, there seemed to be no such thing as a resistance movement in the North and Blackburn states that 'at no time' did US personnel conduct 'resistance warfare' operations in North Vietnam (NVN). However, Vietnamese teams were inserted for harassment and intelligence gathering, but all failed to return. Most dropped out of contact immediately after parachuting into the North but a few radio operators who did contact their base in the South included duress codes in their messages. They had been captured and were transmitting under enemy orders (ibid., 340).

Suggestions were also made in SOG that, based on SF CIDG experience in the Republic of Vietnam, it might be possible to develop a 'friendly environment' for resistance operations among the Meo tribes in the North who had revolted at the same time as their counterparts in the South. Nothing was ever done to implement this possibility (ibid., 342).

There was never any serious intention of creating an actual insurgency in NVN or in bringing about the collapse or overthrow of the northern government. Rather, as Paschall states, the intention was to harass and intimidate that government by creating the illusion of an internal resistance movement (Paschall interview, 7 March 1989).

A similar proposal was made to open a Guerrilla Warfare Operational Area in the Laotian panhandle by creating a resistance movement among the Montagnard tribesmen there. It met an equally cool reception (Blackburn, 1983, 349). Commenting on the possibility of resistance operations on the World War II–OSS model in NVN, Blackburn pointed out that US policy always looked toward a ceasefire and a negotiated settlement. After such a ceasefire, 'where would these teams of resistance personnel find themselves?' (ibid., 341). This raises a basic issue, since this question must be asked of any insurgent support operation. Unless total victory (as in World War II) is the only acceptable end, the question of the fate of the resistance movement must always be considered.

In any event, permission was finally granted for SOG to create a 'notional' guerrilla-warfare area in North Vietnam with the object of convincing the North Vietnamese government that a guerrilla insurgency existed in their own country. This was a very interesting experiment since it created several problems with few corresponding advantages. First of all, the intent was to support the conventional battle in the South by forcing Hanoi to dedicate resources against the 'notional' guerrillas, resources which would otherwise be used to support the war in the South. It is questionable how successful this effort was in convincing the Hanoi government that such a threat existed. As noted, the 'operators' infiltrated into the North tended to disappear quickly and with disturbing regularity. This led to the obvious conclusion that there was little effective anti-government sentiment in the North and later to the belief that some of SOGs operations were compromised from the start. Secondly, such an effort would presumably be based on the ethnic minorities in North Vietnam. If the northern government did become convinced there was such an insurgent threat, its security forces would obviously retaliate against the innocent minorities.

In general, SOG's missions were difficult, dangerous, clandestine and sometimes covert activities, which required an exceedingly high level of dedication and training but were not unusually specialized in the military or technological sense. Although commonly referred to as 'unconventional warfare' missions, the missions were 'unconventional' only in the sense of being unusual. This became increasingly true as the war went on. Even the apparently unconventional efforts to simulate an indigenous resistance in North Vietnam (as 20 years later in Nicaragua) faltered for lack of a supporting political context and the apparent lack of interest or ability on the part of MACV/VNSF or the CIA to create one.

Although these efforts continued (along with the Psyops), as time passed they became less important. Instead SOG was ordered to concentrate on a more conventional but extraordinarily difficult part of their overall mission, reconnaissance in denied areas. The bulk of SOG efforts were directed toward reconnaissance and strike missions in support of MACV's conventional forces, commonly in 'denied areas' (that is, enemy occupied or controlled) outside South Vietnam, chiefly in Laos and Cambodia. In 1967, after many attempts, MACV commander General William Westmoreland finally received permission to penetrate deeper into Laos, extending their zone to 20 kilometers from the border. The primary mission of the SOG units was reconnaissance for massive USAF B-52 bomber strikes against Laos and Cambodia as part of the continuing effort to disrupt North Vietnamese supply routes, support bases and headquarters there (US Congress, Senate, 1973, 231–5).

SOG's accomplished this dangerous and difficult effort with four basic tactical elements: 'Spike' RTs (Recon Teams), SLAM

Companies (Search-Location and Annihilation Mission), 'Hatchet Forces' (several SLAM Companies used as reaction/exploitation elements) and 'Bright Light' Teams (originally designed for prisoner-release raids, then used as cross-border rescue/reaction teams). All of these missions were hazardous and some were extremely so. For example, one operation placed an SF 'A' team and a company-sized indigenous force along the Trail in southern Laos as bait to draw an enemy regiment of several battalions into the open. Having succeeded, the troopers then called in waiting air strikes to decimate the enemy while fighting for their own lives at odds of more than 100 to one. To add further to the extraordinary danger of these operations, Hanoi took the position that the SOG reconnaissance personnel were spies and not protected by the Geneva convention. Anyone captured could expect to be interrogated under torture and summarily executed.

As a note of historical detail, beginning in 1967 the actual cross-border operations were controlled by intermediate headquarters designated 'Command and Control' North (located in DaNang and responsible for operations in Laos), South (located in Ban-Me-Thout and responsible for operations in Cambodia), and Central (located in Kontum, established in 1969, with responsibility for the Laos–Cambodia border area) (US Congress, Senate, 1973, 233–4).

Likely targets would be identified by aerial photography and then evaluated on the ground by SOG reconnaissance teams (ibid., 354). This reliance on aerial photography for target identification led to a significant problem, since it was necessary for a 'recon' team to enter the area in order to confirm the nature and suitability of the target. These teams would then call for either air strikes or attacks by SOG's follow-up strike forces (ground-assault units), usually of platoon size. The assault teams were needed since not all targets could be usefully struck by air. However, this meant that the team was entering an area where the enemy had often been alerted by the activity of the reconnaissance elements.

> The visible effect on the North Vietnamese who were there was the same as taking a beehive … and poking it with a stick! If their effectiveness was in any way altered it certainly did not appear to be to our good. (ibid., 239)

As soon as the SOG recon elements demonstrated a consistent ability to locate high-payoff targets and direct strikes against them (usually employing aircraft), MACV began a continuing effort to integrate the organization further into its command structure. This was apparently motivated both by the perceived need for greater control of this asset and by the desire to take advantage of its capability (ibid., 360, 239). By 1967, American and South Vietnamese success had increased pressure on enemy units and routed the VC from about 2,000 square miles of their former territory in South Vietnam. Hanoi responded by seizing more territory around its sanctuaries in Cambodia and expelling local officials. This area became the focus of many SOG operations.

Beginning in 1967, a number of conventional (that is, non-Special Forces) officers were placed in charge of some MACV-SOG operations. This may also have been motivated by a desire to bring MACV-SOG and the SF personnel under conventional discipline. One example was Col. Jonathan Ladd, a SF officer with SOG, who was both public and vocal in his criticism of the way MACV was fighting the war. Although Ladd was certainly well intentioned (and in many respects correct), this only reinforced the belief of conventional officers that SOG was another example of the tendency of special operators to get out of control.

After the Tet Offensive in 1968, the focus of these operations changed somewhat as US commanders sought to have theater reconnaissance assets placed in more direct support of US and ARVN units (ibid., 238). MACV redirected much of the SOG activity toward direct support of conventional commanders in South Vietnam in order to 'help kind of tidy up the situation' (ibid., 236, 244). Some of this reorientation meant conducting reconnaissance in the Corps Tactical Zones. MACV's subordinate commanders in the US tactical units showed great enthusiasm for SOG's ability to provide tactical intelligence which could be immediately exploited. This conventionalization of SOG continued to the point at which some elements of MACV recommended the creation of battalion-size strike forces. By 1969 SOG was, in some respects, largely a theater and Corps reconnaissance and strike asset for the conventional forces.

At the same time, MACV continued its interest in cross-border operations, chiefly by airpower – namely B-52 bombings. The center of interest for the bombings was COSVN (Central Office South Vietnam), the coordinating headquarters for North Vietnamese and Viet Cong military activity in Central and South Vietnam. Former MACV intelligence chief, Lt. Gen. Philip Davidson, stated that COSVN was believed to be directly subordinate to the NVN Politburo, making it the crucial link between North Vietnam and operations in the South (1988, 814). The B-52 missions were directed against COSVN's suspected location in Cambodia about five miles from the Vietnamese border (ibid., 594). It was the SOG troopers who were called on to make a series of very risky forays into Cambodia to assess the results of the MACV-directed bombing raids. Although a great deal of damage was done to enemy assets, COSVN remained elusive and MACV continued a strenuous but ultimately fruitless effort to locate and destroy it.

Cross-border reconnaissance operations continued at the same time and the early success of these target-finding missions led to the creation of larger teams (13–25 men) providing strike data for massive B-52 'arc-light' raids (ibid., 235, 240). This was another set of extraordinarily hazardous operations taking place as they did in areas 'swarming with North Vietnamese troops'.[4] The inserted team's only contact with its base was a tenuous radio relay maintained through a light Army aircraft, flying a 'racetrack' near the border (ibid., 235).

These teams also had a permanent secondary mission to capture enemy soldiers if at all possible. Experience had shown that even NVA officers were often unenthusiastic about their mission and, given good treatment, could became information sources of great value. In addition to intelligence collection, operators also routinely conducted ambushes, placed sensors in enemy areas, placed mines and booby-traps, tapped field communications lines and sought downed aviators.

It was also about this time that the SOG operators began to work with a new and very effective fire-support system called 'Spectre'. These were cargo aircraft, originally World War II-era C-47s, converted to hold fast-firing General Electric miniguns capable of firing thousands of rounds a minute. Homing in on targets identified by the SOG teams, the heavily armed planes would circle in a tight orbit over the target, pouring out a waterfall of 7.62 or 20mm rounds that could devastate a football-field-sized area in seconds. These missions were a great success, destroying thousands of enemy vehicles and disrupting traffic along sections of the Ho Chi Minh Trail. Later versions of the system featured newer C-130 turboprop cargo planes with infra-red and night-vision devices as well as 105mm cannon. Up through the 1990s these gunships, in ever-improved models, would become the staple of special-operations fire support.

SOG continued in this role, locating targets, gathering intelligence and directing air strikes until 1971. On 11 October, Sergeant First Class Audley Mills was killed. SFC Mills was on his third combat tour when he became SOG's final casualty. In December, the last

SOG recon mission penetrated the Ashau Valley, placed air strikes on enemy positions and withdrew unharmed (Plaster, 1997, 338). In anticipation of the US withdrawal, SOG was replaced by a Vietnamese organization, the Strategic Technical Directorate (STD), manned by VNSF and assisted by a cadre of 155 SF soldiers who made up STD Advisory Team 158 (Saal, 1990, Vol. 1, 360–1). The Montagnard veterans who had served so long and so well with the Americans refused to be a part of the Vietnamese-run STD and were also replaced by VNSF. The STD struggled to perform SOG's missions, but when the last SF troopers left in March 1973 the organization collapsed. On 12 March 1973, STD ceased operations and was disbanded (ibid., 368).

Within Special Forces, MACV-SOG was regarded as an elite assignment and was much sought after. For individual soldiers, these were the 'big leagues' or 'running with the big dogs'. For conventional planners and commanders, these were supportable, understandable, productive missions suitable for an elite force. SOG activities, such as ambushes and directing of air strikes, offered a short-term payoff that was welcomed by the supported conventional commanders.

The legacy of MACV-SOG came down in many forms. Colonel Roger Pezzle, a MACV-SOG veteran, praised the conduct of SOG's deep reconnaissance operations and, in a prophetic observation, suggested that this success provided a basis for giving special forces the strategic reconnaissance mission in planning for future conflicts (Pezzle, 1984, 141). Colonel Pezzle was also influential in the revival of SOF after the low point of the early 1980s. The use of 'Spectre' gunships as a special-operations fire-support asset was pioneered by SOG, as were a variety of exotic infiltration and extraction techniques. When SFOD-Delta was formed, two SOG veterans, Walter Schumate and Dick Meadows, were instrumental in organizing the unit. General Jack Singlaub, a former SOG commander, influenced the creation of the Special Operations Command. According to SOG veteran John L. Plaster, when special operations 'Bright Light' teams were organized in the Gulf War to rescue downed pilots, their concept and organizational procedures were an outgrowth of those created by the Vietnam-era 'Bright Light' teams (Plaster, 1997, 340).

For a unit of its size, MACV-SOG had an unequaled combat record. At least seven Medals of Honor were awarded to SOG troopers as well as uncounted Silver and Bronze Stars. In addition to providing invaluable intelligence unobtainable elsewhere, SOG's operations tied down thousands of NVA troops, by some estimates as much as a battalion per SF soldier.[5] At the height of SOG activity, in 1969, the unit's kill ratio was estimated at 150 to one. But SOG's missions were expensive – more than 300 Americans and at least three times that many 'strikers' were lost. Of the 300, about 57 were MIA, of those perhaps 15 were taken alive (ibid.). None ever returned.

The Mobile Strike Forces (Mike Forces)

As described in the previous chapter, units designed for offensive operations against the National Liberation Front (NLF) had been a part of the CIDG program since 1963, and contributed to conventionalization by directing 5th Group's attention away from the frustrations of unconventional ops and toward the main force battle with the North Vietnamese Army.

In 1964, MACV undertook a logical extension of this capability and ordered the 5th Group to organize Project Delta, a long-range reconnaissance unit responsible to Headquarters MACV for in-country missions. The 5th in turn created Detachment B-52 as the core of the new unit with the remainder made up of select Vietnamese and CIDG members. Delta was a huge success as the group managed to perform a wide variety of difficult jobs. Delta entered long-denied VC sanctuaries, directed air strikes against formerly inaccessible areas, recovered prisoners, rescued downed aircraft crews, conducted deception operations, wiretapped NVA/VC communications, performed photo reconnaissance and developed reams of intelligence not otherwise obtainable (Stanton, 1985b, 194–5).

Pleased with this demonstration of capability, in 1965, MACV directed SF advisors from Delta to take on the additional responsibility of training scout units from each CIDG camp. In June, HQ MACV authorized creation of five new battalions of minority ethnic (i.e. ethnically non-Vietnamese) volunteers. This took the form of 150–200 man, US-led 'strike forces'. These battalions were originally created to act as reinforcement and reaction forces to defend the CIDG camps. In effect, they were a sort of mobile reserve for the 5th SFG with the principal mission of relieving CIDG camps under siege. This gave the Commander, 5th SFG, a force under his own control which could be used to influence the course of battle, without begging or borrowing conventional forces on a catch-as-catch-can, emergency basis.

The Mike Forces, however, quickly suffered the same fate as every other SF-trained element – since they were better trained (and occasionally better equipped) than the average ARVN unit they were in demand for other roles besides 'passive' village defense and quick reaction. Instead, the mission quickly expanded to include direct assistance to the conventional forces. By the end of 1965, a Mike Force had been established in each of the four corps tactical zones and a fifth at HQ 5th SFG (the 'Hollywood' Mike Force), each led by a 5th SF 'A' team. Initially, the reaction force operating from Headquarters, 5th SFG in Nha Trang, was called the 'Mike Force'. Other similar SF organizations were generically known as 'strike forces', but the term Mike Force was loosely used to mean any SF-lead reaction force.

These were the best armed and trained of all the CIDG-derived units. Created without ARVN or VNSF cadre, these original Mike Forces were composed largely of the same ethnic minorities with whom SF had been working. The Nung mercenaries (ethnic Chinese) who had often made up the cadre of USASF-organized units in the early 1960s were, by 1965, dispersed, their numbers badly depleted by combat death and injury (Rheault, 1989).

In 1966 MACV took another step toward 'conventionalizing' the SF effort when it directed the 5th SFG to undertake 'offensive guerrilla warfare' (Operations Report, 31 October 1966, hereafter cited as OR; see also Colby, 1988), based on the success of Delta. The 5th SFG began developing its own clandestine direct action capability using CIDG soldiers to form organizations described as 'mobile guerrilla forces' (Kelly, 1973, 8; see also Kelly, 1980).

Late in 1966 the final step in this process occurred when General Westmoreland, as COMUSMACV, ordered the 5th to consolidate 'all in-country Delta type special forces assets' to provide a reconnaissance and reaction capability for US conventional commanders (OR, 31 October 1966, Inclosure 4, 1). In response, the 5th Group formed three 'Greek letter' units each organized around a SF B-team: Omega (B-50) under I Field Force to support II Corps (ibid., Inclosure 5, 1), Sigma under II Field Force to support III Corps (B-56), and Delta to support US Senior Advisors in I and IV Corps, while also providing MACV with a 'reserve capability'. In addition, Delta was to establish a long-range reconnaissance school for soldiers from the conventional US units (ibid., Inclosure 6, 1). By mid-1969, 10,502 CIDG had been consolidated into such organizations, 'in theory jointly commanded by the VNSF and the USASF, in practice by the USASF' (Senior Officer Debriefing, 1969, 3).

The direction of the 'conventionalizing' effect is clearly seen in the relative strength figures for the principal SF programs between October 1966 and October 1969:

	Oct. 1966	Oct. 1969
CIDG	34,800	28,163
RF/PF	28,000	737
MSF	3,200	10,502

Compiled from 5th SFG Operations Reports.[6]

These units were designed to conduct what 5th SFG described as 'unconventional warfare' (Blackjack, 1967, 3), although the unconventional aspect was hard to discern. Initially intended as reconnaissance units, USASF leaders recommended that these units undertake offensive operations (ibid., 7). This meant sustained 'guerrilla-style' operations inside Viet Cong 'safe' areas, where SOG units attacked supply bases, disrupted logistics, gathered intelligence, and directed air and artillery strikes. Missions like these were highly successful examples of SF ability to do light infantry things superbly well, but, like the others, they were not examples of 'unconventional warfare'. For all practical purposes, these were regulars, led and trained by US professionals and utilized as conventional soldiers. They operated from fixed military installations, were infiltrated by helicopter and small boat, resupplied by air, and conducted 'search and destroy' operations, 'night ambushes', and reconnaissance missions (ibid., 7). An example of these operations and their somewhat muddled nature is the series of 'Blackjack' operations carried out from April through July of 1967 by the 'Mobile Guerrilla Force' in I Corps (Blackjack, 1967, inclusive).[7]

Although operating inside a 'designated GWOA' or Guerrilla Warfare Operational Area (ibid., 11), the 'guerrilla' aspect of these operations was simply that these were light, mobile forces who avoided extended direct contact with large enemy forces. These operations were examples of US Special Forces doing what it did best, namely conducting light-infantry operations under difficult circumstances. They were also examples of 'guerrilla warfare' (i.e. warfare characterized by guerrilla tactics) carried out by conventional units for conventional purposes. In 1968, the 'guerrilla' designation was dropped altogether and, although their function was still described as 'mobile guerrilla warfare' (Senior Officer Debriefing, 1969), the units became known for the remainder of the war as Mobile Strike Forces.

SF conventional activity reached its high point in the creation of Special Forces Team B-36 under 5th SFG (Nha Trang) in 1967. B-36 operated the Long Hai Training Center and was responsible for the leadership and training of the all-Cambodian 3rd Mobile Strike Force Command, culminating with their participation with elements of SOG in the May 1970 invasion of Cambodia. Following the withdrawal from Cambodia, B-36 trained Cambodian recruits at Long Hai as standard conventional infantry troops and assembled them into battalions. As described by the 5th SFG's official history, at no time did B-36 perform anything other than conventional infantry missions (Organizational History, 5th SFG, 1962, 114, 121).

The last Mobile Strike Force, the Nha Trang Mike Force, responsible for local security at the 5th SFG headquarters was 'phased out' and converted to an ARVN Ranger unit in December 1970 (Bishop, 1989; also Kelly, 1973, 192).

The heritage of these units was carried on by Special Forces veterans still on active service some 20 years later. These veterans, assigned to the US Military Group in El Salvador, created Quick Reaction Forces (QRF) consciously based on the Mike Force model (Mills, 1989, 8).

DIRTY WORK: THE PHOENIX PROGRAM AND THE PRUS

If MACV-SOG was the 'good' model for special operations, the infamous Phoenix or Phung Hoang (in Vietnamese) program was the 'bad' model. Since glamorized and sensationalized as 'assassination squads – tightly run, inhumanly disciplined, viciously exacting in their retribution' (Perry, 1989, 92), Phoenix has been widely and publicly condemned as 'the quintessential evocation' of amoral or immoral US conduct in war (Galloway and Johnson, 1973, 354; Lackey, 1989, 84; quote from Beckman, 1989, 12).

In actuality, the program seems to have been both more and less than might be expected from its public image. In particular, it suffered from a sort of schizophrenia: on one hand, it was consistently attacked as a program of torture and terrorism, and at the same time accused of laxness and accommodation with the NLF. While its effectiveness was widely criticized, postwar accounts by COSVN and NLF leaders indicate that it was certainly much more effective than allowed by US critics during the war (Karnow, 1983,

602; also interview with Karnow, 1989). The Phoenix program originated as an intelligence-driven, unconventional warfare effort aimed at the political and terrorist elements of the NLF. The story of this program illustrates the difficulties of purely unconventional-warfare programs both in execution and in acceptability.

Phoenix and the PRU

As described by Stuart Herrington, an Army intelligence officer assigned to Phoenix:

> Their [VCI] presence in the village intimidated the population into silence. There were two types of VCI, those known to the villagers and those who were 'secret agents' for the Ban-an-ninh security cadre. The latter could and would squeal on anyone who got too close to the GVN. (Herrington, 1996)[8]

The notion of attacking the political legitimacy of the NLF and Viet Cong was, however, glimpsed dimly if at all. All available documentation from the period deals exclusively with tactical and security objectives. When the program actually got underway early in 1968, MACV advisors and Special Forces personnel became involved from the outset.

Prior to the initiation of Phoenix, US/GVN initiatives against the NLF 'shadow government' in the South had been sporadic and consisted of intermittent, uncoordinated police and secret service arrests of suspects, often in the wake of military 'sweep-and-clear' operations.

Typically, US infantry units would sweep through a village believed to be under NLF control in order to eliminate any Viet Cong units nearby. The Americans would then secure the village while GVN national police and ARVN intelligence personnel screened the population. At the same time US medics would treat local medical problems, and GVN propaganda teams would harangue the assembled villagers. The screening process consisted of little other than checking the GVN-issued identity cards all citizens were required to possess (MACV Directive 381-46, 1967). US soldiers referred to these scornfully as 'county fairs'. Hundreds of individuals were sometimes detained for indefinite periods after this screening with nothing that could reasonably be called due process.

The program was based in part on MACV's belief that the VC main force elements had been defeated after the Tet Offensive early in 1968. The GVN, aided and abetted by MACV, began a concerted attempt to expand security in the countryside through the expansion of the Regional and Popular Forces. The arming of the people through the People's Self Defense Program made it at least possible to regain (or, in many cases, gain for the first time) control of the rural areas from the NLF (Colby, 1970, 4). However, any serious attempt to regain political control of the contested countryside required intelligence information that just was not available. Phoenix grew out of a highly secret 1967 program in cooperation with the CIA to correct the unconventional intelligence vacuum in South Vietnam. Called ICEX (Intelligence Coordination and Exploitation), it was initiated to bring some order to the poorly coordinated GVN, ARVN and US intelligence-collection effort in the South. The Tet offensive, followed by a second series of much weaker enemy offensives in April and May, set back efforts to put the program in place until mid-1968, when it was renamed Phoenix, or 'Phung Hoang' in Vietnamese.

The origin of the name 'Phoenix' is unclear. However, an undated memorandum, located in the Phoenix File at Fort Bragg's Special Warfare Center refers to a truly obscure book called *L'Art a hue* by one L. Cadiere. Published in Hanoi at an unspecified date, the file notes it as the original source of information on 'Phung Hoang', which it defines as a mythical Vietnamese bird said to be a harbinger of peace. 'The Phung Hoang does not show itself except in times of peace and it hides at the slightest sign of trouble.' According to the memo, the name Phoenix (after the mythical bird) was chosen as the closest English-language equivalent.

Phoenix was intended to attack the political infrastructure which supported the insurgency and gave it a meaningful political context. In the words of Jeffery Race, a student of revolutionary warfare, Phoenix 'was the only recognition within the government violence program that the conflict in Vietnam differed radically from the kind of war to which existing doctrine and organization were adapted' (Race, 1972, 237).

Finally, it illustrates the uneasy relationship between the covert action demanded by insurgency (as exemplified by the CIA) and the traditional role of the military (represented by MACV). In the words of General Westmoreland, participation in Phoenix 'terribly distorted' the role of the Army. It was 'dirty work', 'improperly conducted' and, in short, 'not a military function' (Westmoreland, interview, 1990).

Those feelings, however, were retrospective. In the heat of a Saigon summer in 1967, the program was seen as a solution to a serious intelligence shortfall. When first organized after partition in 1954, the intelligence services of the GVN were directed primarily against North Vietnam with little attention paid to domestic, internal collection. The principal covert intelligence operation, the CIA-assisted 'Bureau E Liaison Service', was targeted entirely against the north.

Phoenix began as part of the new Civil Operations and Revolutionary Development Staff (CORDS) pacification program in 1968 to correct these intelligence shortcomings. The CORDS program included as one of its components a highly secret MACV-sponsored, CIA-supported project aimed at the elimination of the NLF clandestine political structure ('infrastructure') inside South Vietnam, referred to in US usage as the VCI (Viet Cong Infrastructure) (Memorandum, ASD, 1968).[9]

Each province had what was, in effect, an NLF 'shadow government' organized in traditional communist underground fashion. A central committee served as the ruling and coordinating body for roughly 11 functional organizations. The exact number varied from province to province. To the degree that MACV focused intelligence resources on the Viet Cong, it concentrated on the Province Unit, the military arm of the province committee, which carried out guerrilla warfare through attacks on ARVN, GVN and US personnel. The other functional organizations, the less obviously military ones, were generally ignored. But these other organizations were vital to the military actions of the Province Unit. They included the communist Secret Police, Military Proselytizing Unit, Medical Service and the Ban-an-ninh (Security Section). The last-named was the terrorism, espionage and assassination arm of the province committees and COSVN (Green Book, 1970, 66). Ban-an-ninh fielded an estimated 25,000 agents nationwide, making it 'one of the largest espionage organizations ... in the history of warfare' (Ranelagh, 1987, 437–8).

The VCI supported the military operations of the VC and the NVA by providing intelligence, guides, food, military supplies (including weapons and ammunition) and logistic support. The Ban-an-ninh directed and implemented a 'systemic campaign of terrorism, extortion, subversion, sabotage, abduction and murder to achieve Communist objectives ... developed, sustained, and supported by Hanoi' (Colby, 1970, 2). More importantly, the VCI provided something unmentioned in Colby's testimony: the political context and rationale for the insurgents. Lacking this context, the VC/NVA forces were no more than bandits, lacking any legitimacy.

In 1968, William Colby (on loan from the CIA) was appointed

head of CORDS. Colby had been a long-time paramilitary operator and OSS veteran and, by this time, one of the CIA's old Vietnam hands. He was also a long-time believer in SOF and immediately sought experienced Army SF and Navy SEALs for Phoenix, as well as CIA operators.

As might be expected, MACV clung determinedly to the conventional view of Phoenix as primarily military. In February 1968, a message from General Westmoreland to General Cao Van Vien, Chairman of the RVNAF Joint General Staff (JGS) announced the transfer of 'over a hundred US military personnel' to Phoenix, proposing that this would produce 'improved intelligence for offensive military operations and territorial security' (Message, COMUSMCV, 27 February 1968).

At its heart, Phoenix was no more than an information co-ordination program designed to bring together all the collection assets in South Vietnam to identify and neutralize the NLF/Viet Cong infrastructure in South Vietnam. The manner of this neutralization, however, was to become the source of controversy. The primary initial step was to place a US intelligence officer in each district to coordinate Vietnamese intelligence activities and keep organized records so that coherent data on the enemy political and military infrastructure reached his opposite number at province headquarters.

The basic purposes of Phoenix, as outlined by Stuart Herrington, were quite simple. In order, the program sought to (1) convince VCI members to defect or 'rally' to the GVN side, (2) failing that, capture or arrest them and, finally, (3) kill them when all else failed (Herrington, 1996).

At least in theory, Phoenix offered two improvements over earlier *ad hoc* efforts – it brought some order out of the chaos of intelligence collection through a coordinated program involving all available intelligence assets. In other words, records were kept and centralized at District Intelligence and Operations Coordinating Centers. Also, the program did provide a semblance of due process. It was hoped that this would avoid making enemies of formerly loyal peasants in the way the massive sweeps had. Suspects were identified by intelligence agencies and apprehended by the PRU. These cases were then subject to a quasi-judicial review by the province chief, a judge and six national police officers called the Province Security Committee. These reviews dealt only with written case files, no witness appeared and no testimony was presented. In addition, these arrests were based on intelligence information, which was often circumstantial or inferential, rather than the sort of hard evidence usually associated with a legal proceeding ('Internal Security in South Vietnam, PHOENIX', 1970, 12–15; Herrington, 1996).

Also, in theory, there was no organizational reason to involve the military in what was, essentially, a police/internal security activity. One USAID program was of special interest, the USAID Public Safety Directorate (PSD). Although the bulk of PSD programs were aimed at bolstering the faltering civilian National Police, some were cover for CIA projects to improve the police capability against the NLF's covert supporters in South Vietnam. However, the CIA and the GVN police/intelligence system lacked the resources to carry out the missions and was forced to depend on the host government for labor and MACV/SF for intelligence officers and advisors. HQ MACV, which had long favored the creation of a military-style constabulary to replace the troubled and ineffective National Police force, derisively known as 'white mice', was inclined to support the move as a necessary step forward (DA Report R-185, 1972, 261).

On 1 July 1968, President Thieu issued Decree Number 280 establishing the Phung Hoang Plan (Phoenix) with a central Phung Hoang committee at the national level. Although the program was placed under the Minister of the Interior, who was responsible for domestic police functions, the primary membership was military. This was especially noticeable at the regional or Corps level, where the program was the responsibility of the military commander of the CTZ (Memorandum, Komer, 22 July 1968).

The primary operating levels were the province headquarters and the district-intelligence and operations-coordinating centers. The Provincial Reconnaissance Units (PRUs) were to carry out the actual apprehension of the suspects. However, these suspects were members of an enemy 'government' at war with the GVN. Furthermore the suspects were themselves normally armed and often accompanied by a well-armed escort. Therefore, these 'apprehensions' had most of the aspects of a military operation rather than of a civil arrest by police. Not surprisingly, problems quickly developed in coordinating police and military efforts (Message, Komer, June 1968).

The PRU were organized, developed, and funded by the USA to conduct operations against the VCI both by capturing or killing its personnel, and by interrupting its functions (Colby, 1970, 7; Race, 1972, 237). PRU's immediate precursor, the Province Action Teams (PAT, also called Political Action Teams), had been organized by Colby as the CIA's Saigon station chief in 1965. The Ban-an-ninh had mounted an extensive and successful program to intimidate and paralyze the district and village level of the GVN through torture, assassinations and kidnapping of local officials, schoolteachers, health workers and the like. The PATs were part of a counter-terrorism initiative to halt the Ban-an-ninh's assassination program. Precise statistics for VC and NVA intentional killings of civilian noncombatants are, of course, not available. However, it was an extended and deliberate program pursued as a matter of policy. The scale and duration of the effort may be judged by the following estimates of such killings: 1958–66 approximately 12,000; 1964–9 (overlapping period) approximately 20,000; 1969 approximately 4,600 (Herman, 1970, 37–40). Lewy arrives at a total of 36,725 assassinations and 58,499 abductions from 1957 through 1972 (1978, 454).

Originally the PATs were composed chiefly of Vietnamese whose families had suffered at the hands of the Viet Cong. The teams operated in small-squad to platoon-sized units in areas of the countryside familiar to them. These two factors gave them the advantage of motivation and local knowledge resulting in early success through a careful, almost surgical, effort targeted specifically against NLF/VC leadership and key personnel. By 1966, the three operational teams had killed 150 Viet Cong and captured 200 others, including their weapons.

Despite their success, the PAT teams were not without critics. Wayne Cooper, a State Department advisor, characterized them as terrorists, using 'assassination, abuses, kidnaping, and intimidation against the Viet Cong leadership' (Marchetti and Marks, 1974, 245). As recounted by Peer de Silva (CIA station chief in Saigon), MACV felt that the PATs were competing with MACV's programs for manpower and, as essentially military operations, ought to be under military control. 'They've got to be made to look like soldiers and act like soldiers', one MACV general said, sounding the usual complaint against UW forces (de Silva, 1978, 238–9). Ambassador Maxwell Taylor supported Westmoreland in his desire to take over the program, and by November 1966 the PATs were under MACV control where they quickly evolved into PRUs, a much more 'military' title.

Under Phoenix, PRU units were reorganized less along police and secret-service lines and more along military methods. They were created by US military and civilian US advisors as platoon-sized paramilitary organizations assigned to province headquarters. By 1968, the country-wide, total PRU strength (less US advisors) was about 4,000 (Memorandum, ASD 1968). Although intended as an internal security force, these were military units operating under the authority of the GVN General Staff until April 1969. After that date they were nominally a part of the GVN national police, but with an ARVN officer as national commander (Decree 044-SL/NV, 1969). In practice, however, these units remained under military operational control with an ARVN officer assigned as the PRU Commander in each province (although technically the Province Chief was in command of the PRU) (Colby, 1970, 7; see also Memorandum, Parker, 1969).

Rather than the Viet Cong victims sought as PAT members, the PRUs recruited Viet Cong defectors. The PRUs were led by ARVN officers with the assistance of MACV, Special Forces and SEAL advisors under the general control of the CIA. Other Americans involved had intelligence and logistic duties.

The same conventionalizing effects that operated on SOG operated on the PRU as well. As the program became part of Phoenix in 1968, officers and noncommissioned officers from the ARVN were recruited to fill out the PRU ranks, especially in critical leadership roles (Memorandum, Parker, 1969). As soon as it developed that the PRUs could develop target information for the major conventional units they came into demand as target acquisition resources. There was also a tendency for the information developed by Phoenix and the PRUs to be used as the basis for large (and ineffective) sweep-and-clear operations by conventional forces (Memorandum, Parker, 1968).

These conventionalizing tendencies evolved the PRUs from the small, stealthy patrols of the PATs, to the status of strike forces in their own right, very similar in purpose, equipment and methods to units of the US military. Rather than seeking out key NLF leaders, the object became to conduct raids against Viet Cong units. As described by Chief Petty Officer Mike Boynton, USN (a Navy SEAL and PRU advisor in Ba Xuyen Province during 1969):

> the majority of the ops we ran were K-BAR ops. I would take about sixty guys broken down into ten guys per chopper (slick). Either a heavy or light fire team would be supporting the op. For my time, a light fire team was two slicks (UH1 helicopters) with door gunners. A heavy fire team was a pair of Cobra gunships. Above the whole thing would be a C&C [Command and Control] bird containing a South Vietnamese officer, usually a major or lieutenant colonel, along with a MACV Army officer of equal rank. We had air cover right on

hand. Medevacs ... for wounded and I could call in air strikes from the carrier offshore. With my people and the proper support, we could take on three or four hundred VC at a time. (Boynton, as quoted in Fawcett, 1995, 106–7)

Another example was the Cape Batagngan operation, which employed two USMC Battalion-size Landing Forces, two US Army Battalions, an ARVN Battalion, an Air Cavalry Troop, naval blocking forces, a Regional Force company 'and the full gamut of technical service assets' (Memorandum, Parker, 1968).

Many critics of the program ignored the fact that the program was grounded in Vietnamese law. The legal basis was the RVN Constitution of 1967, Article 4, which forbade 'any activity designed to publicize or carry out Communism' (Colby, 1970, 5). This provision was implemented through a series of laws against such political crimes as treason, espionage, insurgency, revolt or terrorism. As national-security-related crimes these were the province of military courts. This is not to say that trials under Phoenix were models of democratic jurisprudence. For example, under Phoenix, a procedure was created for 'administrative' (i.e. summary) sentencing of suspects for up to two years (ibid., 5–6). However, it must be recognized that these operations were conducted under wartime conditions in an atmosphere of enemy assassinations, terrorism and intimidation directed against ordinary courts and police.

In the words of Douglas Valentine, a CIA operations chief in the northern highlands, 'Sure we got involved in assassinations. That's what the PRU were set up for, assassinations. I'm sure the word never appeared in any policy directives, but what else do you call a targeted kill?' (Valentine, 1990, 319). Although General Abrams conceded the utility of a force targeted against the NLF infrastructure, the program caused concern since it involved MACV in a potentially controversial program controlled by other agencies. The possibility of abuse was clear and worrisome. Abrams was no fan of Special Forces and especially distrusted their association with covert operations. Concerned that these units were exercising their well-known tendency toward independent action, the MACV commander made it his goal to bring SF back 'under control' (Abrams, 1968; Perry, 1989, 229–30).

The risks of Phoenix seemed worthwhile when, in December 1968, the GVN announced that of an estimated 80,000 NLF political agents in South Vietnam, 15,000 had been captured or killed (*New York Times*, 6 January 1969, 7:1). But Abrams's forebodings were justified when the program began to come under public criticism.

Phoenix's gains seemed less impressive when, in June 1969, the NLF announced formation of a Provisional Revolutionary Government for South Vietnam, allegedly an alliance of nationalist elements in the South (*New York Times*, 11 June 1969, 1:6). After all, how effective could the Phoenix operations be if the NLF was forging ahead with its consolidation of anti-government factions in the South?

Next, in August, the *New York Times* reported that the Phoenix program had 'bogged down' because of 'local accommodation' by GVN officials. According to the *Times*, 80 percent of those arrested were either acquitted, allowed to escape, or received sentences of 'a few months or less'. Furthermore, the major NLF training base at Cu Chi, 20 miles from Saigon, continued to operate throughout the war, surviving both conventional sweeps and the best efforts of the Phoenix operators (Nguyen Thi Anh, 1987). Even worse, from MACV's point of view, the same *New York Times* article also publicized Special Forces' involvement in the program (19 August 1969, 12:1).

The *Times*'s statistics are less damning when understood in the political context of the period. Peace negotiations were underway in Paris, and GVN officials understood that in the event that some accommodation was reached with the NLF, the 'enemy infrastructure' might well become part of the new government. Local GVN officials could not help but be aware that, in that case, it would be well not to have seriously offended them.

Moreover, this negative publicity came at an inopportune time. A month after the *Times* article, six SF intelligence officers, unconnected with Phoenix, were accused of the assassination (with CIA complicity) of a South Vietnamese intelligence operator alleged to be a double agent (*New York Times*, 25 September 1969, 14:1). SF officers objected that those accused of the murder were, in reality, not Special Forces personnel at all, but were military-intelligence officers assigned to Headquarters 5th SFG as part of Project Gamma, a separate intelligence program targeted against VC/NVA activities in Cambodia. Using the cover of a Civil Affairs and Psychological Operations program, Gamma was regarded as highly successful until it was apparently penetrated by the Viet Cong (Stein 1992, 100-10).[10] Although the case was not connected with Phoenix, the elements of Special Forces/CIA complicity, espionage and assassination generated a deluge of sensational press coverage and added to the increasingly negative image of SF, MACV's conduct of the war and the Phoenix Program.

Understanding the potential for abuse, Colby issued a directive reminding US military personnel in Phoenix that they were 'under the same legal and moral constraints with respect to Phoenix operations as they are in regular military operations ... they are not authorized to engage in assassinations ... but they are entitled to use reasonable military force ... in rallying, capturing, or eliminating the Viet Cong Infrastructure' (Colby, Phoenix Directive, quoted in Colby and McCarger, 1989, 247–8).

Nevertheless, by the end of 1969, Phoenix had acquired a reputation as an assassination program, and a poorly run one at that, with an additional reputation for torturing suspects. After less than a year in the program, Abrams ordered his advisors not to participate directly in PRU missions and not to sanction any incidents of torture (Clarke, 1988, 379–80). At the same time, he sought to drastically reduce US military participation in the program. Abrams took special pains to break the SF–CIA connection and bring the SF soldiers back into the regular Army chain of command, 'a project he was convinced was essential if the military was to survive the Vietnam debacle' (Perry, 1989, 230). He also set out to remove the most unconventional of the SF officers and replace them with solid, regular Army men (ibid., 231).

MACV's subsequent support to Phoenix can be estimated by their assignment policy for the program. By December 1970, the MACV component of Phoenix was 192 officers short of the 392 required to man the District Intelligence and Operations Coordinating Centers that were the heart of the program, and 191 short in the critical middle grades of captain and major. In an attempt to fill the gap, 159 lieutenants were assigned to the vacant captains' positions (MACCORDS-PHX, 1970), thus putting the least-experienced officers in the most important positions.

Despite the controversy over its general effectiveness the program scored some important achievements. Even if Phoenix was not a death blow to the insurgency in the South, it did make serious inroads and severely handicapped many VCI operations. NLF leaders interviewed by Stanley Karnow after the war reported that Phoenix had been viewed as 'very dangerous'. 'We never feared a division of troops, but the infiltration of a couple of guys into our ranks created tremendous difficulties' (Mdm. Nguyen Thi Dinh in Karnow, 1983, 602). Col. Bui Tin, a Viet Cong officer, called it 'a devious and cruel' operation that cost 'thousands of our cadres' (ibid., 602; also interview with Karnow, 1989).

For their part, many SF soldiers felt that they were doing the most dangerous, difficult and often isolated duties of the war, while being constantly carped at by MACV and the Pentagon for their alleged personal failings and lack of conventional discipline. 'Special Forces personnel in remote forts felt abandoned by higher headquarters, a feeling intensified by haphazard mail delivery, slow support and a nonresponsive decorations system' (Stanton, 1985b, 187).

As noted earlier, the experience of the PRUs and the Phoenix Program illustrates the difficulties of purely unconventional-warfare programs both in execution and in acceptability. To some observers the program looked disturbingly like terrorism (Galloway and Johnson, 1973, 354), and was certainly well outside the conventional military model. The political consequences of Phoenix were significant as a step in the continuing process of the militarization of Vietnamese society, and the consequent blurring and eventual usurpation of civilian authority.

The US Army Special Operations Command official history, compiled in 1994, discusses both the CIDG program and MACV-SOG in Vietnam, but contains not a single mention of the Phoenix program or the Provincial Reconnaissance Units that supported it. The current feeling about Phoenix is perhaps best illustrated by a fellow special-operations officer who reviewed this chapter and pointed out, not unkindly, that 'it's as much as your career is worth to say anything good about Phoenix'.

If the entire struggle in Vietnam is conceived of as a fight for legitimacy in the eyes of the people of South Vietnam between and among various factions, notably the NLF, the Saigon government and the government of North Vietnam, it becomes obvious that this conflict was waged on three principal levels of violent conflict: (1) a state-to-state war between the rival Vietnamese governments; (2) a guerrilla insurgency waged against the Saigon government by the NLF; (3) a campaign of sabotage, terrorism and subversion carried out by specialized arms of the NLF. The US forces in Vietnam concentrated on the level of conflict with which it was most comfortable and familiar – the conventional war against NVA units in the South and the guerrilla units of the NLF.

This is surprising when one considers that, during the conflict, there was wide general agreement that the essential issue was the relationship of the government of South Vietnam with its people. In the words of a 1976 study by the Army's Special Warfare Center, 'nearly every analyst and political and military leader agreed that pacification was the key requirement for building a viable national government and defeating the insurgency' (Special Warfare Center, 1976, I–10).

Postwar accounts by senior officers are revealing in that few devote significant attention to the insurgent, unconventional aspects of the conflict (Drew, 1988; also Westmoreland, 1976; Summers, 1982; and Palmer, 1984). A review of this literature by Drew (1988, 3) is summarized in the statement attributed to a senior general officer who is alleged to have said in 1985 that US military planners ought not to worry about 'those kinds of wars' (referring to insurgencies) because the military can 'muddle through' (ibid., 3).

Harry Summers's influential analysis of the war sees the outcome as a failure by the US military to effectively apply conventional military methods. His analysis is exceptional insofar as it accounts for the insurgent revolutionary aspects of the struggle, dismissing them as a negligible influence confined to the very early phases of the war, prior to the massive US conventional presence (Summers, 1982). Summers is interesting because of his resolute desire to act inside the conventional model by identifying a state (North Vietnam) and its army as the enemy, and then seeking to bring it into annihilating battle by invading North Vietnam.

This kind of thinking had important consequences for the future. A basic conceptual error of this period was carried forward with grave consequences for future LIC efforts. The idea arose that President Kennedy and his advisors had identified US Army Special Forces as the basic source of unconventional expertise, based on their training in the conduct of guerrilla warfare. In retrospect, this is somewhat akin to arguing that a fire department should consist chiefly of arsonists.

Colby commented that: 'The reason we did this was that the SF was the most flexible military around – and had proved themselves effective in the early CIDG program under CIA direction. The "arsonists" did not change, their instructions did, when MACV told them to conduct "offensive guerrilla warfare"' (Colby, 1988).

Most military commentators would disagree with this analysis. 'You fight fire with fire, it takes a thief to catch a thief, you've got to be one to know one' (Henry, 1988). The flaw in this line of reasoning is that SF were never trained as insurgents; they were professional soldiers trained to fight as guerrillas. Guerrilla warfare became confused with revolutionary insurgency because such insurgents commonly employed guerrilla operations as part of their revolutionary strategy. Rheault argues, as does Kief, that Special Forces' training in guerrilla warfare did give them an understanding of the strengths and weaknesses of the guerrilla (Rheault, 1989; Kief, 1989).[11]

This is true only in the most direct, military-operational sense, which sees guerrilla war as a particular set of tactics. It provided knowledge of the tactical-military aspects of guerrilla operations while ignoring or obscuring the political elements and context which makes guerrilla insurgencies possible. This is a crucial weakness, because, unlike conventional Clausewitzian warfare, political and cultural elements predominate in such insurgencies. The fact that the military elements of insurgencies are commonly carried out through guerrilla tactics is of secondary importance. US SOF in general and Special Forces in particular were political only in the most general sense and not designed to counter political threats.

It was assumed that there was a significant carry-over between the ability to conduct guerrilla warfare and the ability to counter it. First of all, the larger question for US national policymakers was not really to counter guerrilla war, although it was sometimes misconceived that way, but was how to counter leftist (chiefly communist) revolutionary movements, regardless of the conflict method chosen by the revolutionaries. In the Vietnam case the primary objective was always to influence the actions of a state (North Vietnam). US policymakers, like the Army, came to view the insurgency as one minor element in an essentially state-to-state conflict.

US Army guerrilla-warfare doctrine of the period assumed that Special Forces units would cooperate with (if not outright co-opt) a pre-existing popular-resistance movement including at least the elements of a political infrastructure. Furthermore, this was expected to occur in the context of a formerly independent nation occupied by an aggressive foreign power. The role of the US forces was to train and lead this resistance movement, harrying and harassing the enemy and reducing its ability to resist the liberating conventional armies of the US and its allies. (This can be referenced out of any of the volumes of SF training material produced at the JFKIMA [John F. Kennedy Institute for Military Assistance], c. 1965–75.)

Little in this operational concept is useful in opposing a revolutionary insurgent force. In US military usage, 'counterinsurgency', by definition, presumes that the counterinsurgent forces are agents of a government opposed with armed violence by some portion of the population it purports to represent (JCS, 1987, 187). This is the reverse of the situation envisioned in the US concept of guerrilla/ partisan warfare previously examined. Most important, it is not simply the military reverse, with the SOF in the capital city rather than hiding in the hills; it is the political reverse. Unlike opposition to an occupying power, which is clearly legitimate, the insurgency exists only because the issue of political legitimacy is in doubt. Conceptually at least, the US SOF, by taking the side of the government, may be seen as an occupying power rather than a liberating force.

The heart of revolutionary warfare was, and is, political organization and in this area US doctrine, especially SOF operational doctrine, was weak to nonexistent. The thrust of US Army SOF doctrine became conventional and 'military-technical' in that the emphasis was almost exclusively on the tactics, techniques and technology of armed combat. Much attention was (and continues to be) devoted to details of equipment and applications of technology (Goodall, 1988). The 1960s and 70s SOF (largely composed of Army Special Forces and a small number of Navy SEALs) concentrated on that part of the business with which they were most familiar – tactical military operations. These units saw themselves as trainers, professors of individual and small-unit tactics. The other chief emphasis was on the means of logistic support for such operations, usually by means of aerial delivery from the supported conventional force (DA, FM 31-20, 1965, especially 52–81; 82–149; 167–90).

In general, the real achievements of Army Special Forces in combining military ability with political understanding were largely ignored. Elliot Cohen, an academic critic of special operations, alleges that Special Forces played only a 'small role in the war', since their operations were on the village level and confined to geographically peripheral areas (1978, 73). To the extent that this was true, it was due more to lack of opportunity than inability.

This also avoids the central issue. Adopting the conventional model uncritically as his vehicle to criticize special forces, Cohen misses the point that, as a political struggle for legitimacy, the most important part of the war was exactly that part conducted among the rural villagers who made up the bulk of the population. Perhaps the most significant, clearly 'unconventional' effort was the successful early CIDG program. The CIDG initially denied large areas of the central highlands to the NLF and the North Vietnamese. This was achieved through a deep and lasting rapport developed between the 'Montagnard' tribes people and Special Forces soldiers (Kelly 1973, 19–41; Yarborough, 1987, 6).

A central element in this success, too often unacknowledged, is that it occurred with minority peoples (primarily the Montagnards, but others as well) excluded from Vietnamese society. To some degree the Special Forces' success in organizing what amounted to an independent Montagnard army resulted from their identification with the self-determination desires of the Montagnard peoples and the Montagnards' desire to possess a capability which would counterbalance the GVN. In other words, the army the 5th SFG created was not a Vietnamese one and was in part a product of both parties' dislike for the South Vietnamese. The point here, and the lesson, is that the force became a captive of its own political context, as evidenced by the continuing problems with FULRO, the Montagnard independence movement and GVN attempts to bring it under ARVN control.

The CIDG success was built on the single important, operationalizable concept to emerge from the spate of social and behavioral counterinsurgency research: that unconventional-warfare operators must be able to operate outside their own cultural milieu. They must understand and be able to work within the value systems, the 'social consensus', the world view of the persons for whose benefit they are allegedly striving.

Much of this success, however, was built not upon formal political–military training (little of which actually occurred), but upon the simple realization of this fact by individuals and their willingness to act upon this realization. To its everlasting credit, the Army Special Forces in Vietnam was able to attract such flexible persons, place them in appropriate positions and allow them the latitude to create their own jobs in the absence of useful doctrine or national policy.

Nevertheless, the success of any unconventional-warfare effort rests first and foremost on the policies of the host government, that state being assisted by the US. The basic requirements are, first of all, for the host government to possess or at least be capable of moving toward a system of governance which will be granted wide legitimacy by the population of that nation. This may or may not be liberal democracy on the US model, but some form of reasonably open, responsive, participatory system is needed. Secondly, there must be a unified US approach based on an understanding of the peculiar historical, cultural, geographic, political and other idiosyncratic influences on the host nation's society.

Institutionally, however, the Army Special Forces did not seek to build on its Vietnam successes as a political-military actor. Instead it sought to broaden its mission 'beyond the rather narrow specialty of unconventional warfare', meaning support to indigenous soldiers (Kelly, 1973, 171). It is revealing that by this time the term 'unconventional warfare' as used by Kelly had come to mean 'guerrilla' war. It is even more interesting that Kelly apparently regarded what the 5th SFG had been doing as guerrilla war.

CONCLUSIONS

The dominance of the Army paradigm and its resulting 'puzzle solutions' (the military-technical approach and the conventional model of warfighting) had important impacts on the prosecution of the war. Once the 1965 decision was made to introduce large numbers of US troops, it was inevitable that the military effort, with its greater resources, would become the dominant influence on US policy in Vietnam. Furthermore, because of its military-technical orientation, this influence would be to enhance purely military approaches to the conflict. Finally, the apolitical, indeed politics-rejecting, nature of these approaches made it impossible to resolve the conflict.

US Army doctrine, as evidenced by the Vietnam case, did not reflect the altered state of international conflict. It was especially unsuitable to forms of violent conflict where political elements predominated. These are cases which do not follow the 'classical' dichotomous model of war as a state very distinct from that of peace.[12]

The lesson of the failure in Vietnam, however, was seen as evidence reinforcing the validity of the conventional model and especially those elements of the underlying paradigm that mandated clear separation of the military and political spheres. Military leaders believed that political cowardice, ignorance of warfare, and bureaucratic interference had prevented effective application of the conventional model (Westmoreland, 1979, 35–8). In remarks before the Army's Command and General Staff college in 1979, General Westmoreland castigated the US's political leaders of the Vietnam period: 'every practical measure designed to encourage him [the enemy, North Vietnam] to change his aggressive strategy was undercut by expressions and action reflecting a lack of resolve, a naive understanding of warfare or blissful ignorance' (ibid., 39).[13]

In an unconscious echo of Jomini, Upton and Mahan, Westmoreland concluded: 'When our political leaders commit us to war, the military voice should be given priority consideration ... "It takes the full strength of a tiger to kill a rabbit," and we should use appropriate force to bring the war to an end' (ibid., 42).

Regardless of the circumstances of the failure in Vietnam, Special Operations Forces had first risen to prominence in that war and were closely associated with it in the minds of the public and the Pentagon, as well as the civilian decision-makers.

NOTES

US personnel assigned to 5th Special Forces 1964–70:

October 1964	951 (Stanton; Opns Report not available)
October 1965	1,828 (Stanton; Opns Report not available)
October 1966	2,589 (Opns Report)
October 1967	2,726 (Stanton; Opns Report for October 67 does not give strength figures)
October 1968	3,538 (Opns Report)
October 1969	3,741 (Opns Report)
October 1970	2,521 (Opns Report) 'phasedown' begins*

* per message HQ USMACV to HQ 5TH SFGA, dated 11 October 1970, ref: Phase V Redeployment (Keystone Robin) in 5th SFG Opns Report dated 15 November 1967, Records Group 472, Box 3, MF AD514-723, WNR.

As noted, there are numerous discrepancies in these figures. For example, Co. E, 5th Group was dedicated as a 'special operations' unit and, in 1968, had 598 US personnel operating under control of MACV-SOG as part of the Prairie Fire missions in Laos. These troops are not included in the figures above (Stanton, 1981, 241).

Special Forces Commanders in Vietnam, 1962–70:

Col. George C. Morton, Sept 1962 – US Army SF Vietnam (Prov)
Col. Theodore Leonard, Nov 1963 – US Army SF Vietnam (Prov)
Col. John H. Spears, Aug 1964 – 5th SFG
Col. Wm. A. McKean, Jul 1965 – 5th SFG
Col. Francis J. Kelly, Jun 1966 – 5th SFG
Col. Jonathan F. Ladd, Jun 1967 – 5th SFG
Col. Harold A. Aaron, Jun 1968 – 5th SFG
Col. Rbt. B. Rheault, May 1969 – 5th SFG
Col. Alexander Lembres, Jul 1969 – 5th SFG
Col. Michael D. Healy, Aug 1969 – 5th SFG

Of the ten SF commanders in Vietnam, only three (Leonard, Rheault and Healy) had extensive prior experience with Special Forces. Of the eight 5th SF Group commanders only Rheault and Healy were long-time SF soldiers, and one of them (Rheault) served as the 5th's commander for only two months. McKean took command without so much as a single day's SF experience and gave rise to the policy that incoming 5th Group COs would first gain experience by commanding 1st SF Group on Okinawa.

The officer who succeeded him, Kelly, earned the nickname 'Splash' because he refused to jump on the rough coral drop zones of Okinawa during his 'orientation' assignment and would make only water landings. Another, Lembres, not only had no SF experience but, in the words of another former commander, had been 'strictly a staff wallah' until chosen by Abrams to take 5th Group. Upon arrival at Nha Trang, Group personnel discovered that Lembres not only had no SF or command experience but was not even qualified as a parachutist. Accordingly they took the new commander to a local drop zone for 'qualification' and 'had him jump until he broke his leg'. General Abrams then, allegedly, called Westmoreland (by then Army Chief of Staff) and complained that the 5th was trying to kill Lembres. According to the story, Westmoreland was not notably sympathetic and dispatched Colonel 'Iron Mike' Healy to command the Group. Healy, a long-time SF veteran (and qualified parachutist) was readily accepted and remained in command until the Group returned to the USA in 1971.

Assignment histories of 5th SF Group commanders provided by Nancy Cross, Historian, 1st Special Operations Command, Fort Bragg, NC, and Richard Bishop, Special Forces Association, Fayetteville, NC. The story of Colonel Lembres's abbreviated command tour was provided for use without attribution by a former 5th Group commander.

1. For example, the Army's official history of Special Forces in Vietnam does not so much as mention SOG. See Kelly (1973).
2. In its internal documents, SOG was often referred to as 'MACSOG.' However, here the more familiar 'MACV-SOG' is used.
3. Other former SOG personnel have stated that no such 'secret orders' were ever written. As with many aspects of the Vietnam War, this practice seems to have varied over time and among units. Early on in the US involvement, the mere existence of SOG was secret. Later in the war it became widely known thanks to newspaper publicity.
4. An estimated 100,000 North Vietnamese Army troops and an undetermined additional number of Viet Cong were operating out of these sanctuaries against US and South Vietnamese forces in South Vietnam.
5. This ratio, however, does not include the large number of indigenous 'strikers' who made up the bulk of SOG's operational manpower.
6. These figures coincide with Stanton's for the same period except for the October 1969 MSF figure, which he places at 9,326 (Stanton, 1981, 241). All strength figures for 5th SFG and its programs are approximate. There are numerous irreconcilable differences among the various official accounts. Various counting methods were used at different times, different units were sometimes included, and in some cases, aggregate figures are provided with no detailed breakdown. For example, the Army official study gives a 'peak' figure of 42,000 CIDG and 40,000 RF/PF, but does not state to which period this refers (Kelly, 1973, 172). Neither Stanton nor available operations reports agree with those figures by a factor of 8–10,000 for any period (Stanton, 1981, 241). As the Army study notes, official reports contain 'numerous irreconcilable discrepancies' as, for example, in the number of detachments assigned sector and subsector advisory missions, and the number of Regional and Popular forces advised (Kelly, 1973, 82).
7. For a first person account of one Blackjack Operation (Blackjack 34, near Quan Loi, 18 July 1967) see James G. Donahue, *No Greater Love: A Day with the Mobile Guerrilla Force in Vietnam* (1988).
8. Colonel Herrington points out that suspects were also apprehended by a variety of military, paramilitary or police agencies, including the Police Special Branch, the Regional Forces/Popular Forces and others (Herrington, 1996).
9. Infrastructure was defined as 'the political, administrative, supply, and recruitment

apparatus by which the Communists seek to impose their authority upon the people of South Vietnam' (confidential briefing statement prepared by Ambassador Colby for presentation to the Fulbright Commission, February 1970, declassified 4 January 1989, by USAMHI).

10. For an account of the complexities of this case see Jeff Stein, *Murder in Wartime* (1992).

11. SF experience in guerrilla warfare (as opposed to training in guerrilla warfare) is hard to substantiate. Insofar as can be determined through interviews and available documentation, US Army SF had no actual experience at guerrilla warfare between its organization in 1950 and the creation of the 'Mike' Forces in 1965. Paschall reports that some SF personnel did operate with guerrilla units in the Korean War; Bank has stated to the author that these men were not allowed to influence SF training or doctrine after their return in 1953.

12. Flint goes so far as to assert that 'the US Army gained nothing permanent in organization, tactics, or doctrine from the later wars in the Pacific, with the possible exception of tactical airpower using the helicopter' (Flint, 1980, 29).

13. For an examination of some of the other notable exponents of this explanation for the US defeat, see Jeffery P. Kimball, 'The Stab-in-the-Back Legend and the Vietnam War' (1988).

6 The post-Vietnam doldrums

'I'd order another helicopter.' (President Carter's reply when asked what one thing he would change about his Presidency, W. King, 1989, 103)

EMPTY SUCCESS: THE RAID ON THE SON TAY POW CAMP[1]

The last major special operation of the war, a multi-service raid to free American prisoners of war (POWs), was a spectacular example of meticulous planning, inter-service cooperation and skillful, courageous execution of a complex and dangerous mission. But despite all this it ultimately ended in frustration, driving home another important lesson of special operations that would be proven again and again in the following years. Skill, courage and flawless execution are fruitless without correct and timely intelligence on which to base the mission.

By May 1970, former MACV-SOG commander Don Blackburn was assigned as Special Assistant for Counterinsurgency and Special Projects to the Joint Chiefs of Staff. In that capacity, he received news that a group of American prisoners in North Vietnam had managed to signal US strategic reconnaissance assets from a compound near Son Tay, about 23 miles northwest of Hanoi. Blackburn ordered further reconnaissance and carried the news to the Joint Chiefs, who were intensely interested. Over 470 Americans were believed to be held prisoner in North Vietnam and the POW issue was very worrisome for all concerned. Nearly 100 attempts had been made to rescue POWs since 1966, but none in the North. Furthermore, although some South Vietnamese had been freed, not a single living American prisoner had been recovered. This isolated camp, located well away from the massive defenses of Hanoi, looked like a golden opportunity. It took until 10 July to assemble the required intelligence, conduct initial planning and convince the Joint Chiefs that the plan was feasible.

For security reasons, it was decided to assemble and prepare the rescue force in the US. After considering a variety of options, including inserting secret agents and pre-positioning the Task Force in nearby Laos, Blackburn and others planned to launch the Task Force from Thailand in a mix of C-130 transports, HH-53 (and one HH-3) helicopters and A-1 fighter bombers. The air element would place a Special Forces assault team in the compound to rescue the prisoners and extract all by helicopter. Simultaneously, Navy carrier aircraft would stage a large diversionary strike to draw the attention of North Vietnamese air-defense elements away from the raid. Instead of bombs, the planes were to drop flares in front of the heaviest active air-defense system in the world. On 8 August, Air Force Brigadier General LeRoy G. Manor, commander of USAF Special Operations at Elgin AFB FL, was finally tasked to assemble a Joint Contingency Task Force and free the prisoners. The mission was code named 'Operation Ivory Coast', the units conducting the mission were to be 'Task Force 77'.

Colonel Arthur (Bull) Simmons at Fort Bragg immediately began to select the ground-assault team from combat-proven Special Forces veterans. About 500 candidates were initially screened and told only that they were being asked to volunteer for 'a classified mission with considerable risk involved'. Simmons, a medical officer and two Special Forces sergeant majors then interviewed roughly 450 candidates before finally selecting 120 for the raid force. Meanwhile, Air Force planners began to assemble pilots and crew from special operations aviation units, including some personnel especially withdrawn from Southeast Asia for the mission.

On 20 August training began in the backwoods of Eglin AFB where the would-be raiders created a mock-up of the Son Tay compound on which they practiced assiduously. Security was so tight that the raid team was advised of the timing of Soviet reconnaissance satellites so that they could conceal their preparations during the satellites' passage overhead. Security officers monitored all telephone calls from the Air Base and from Blackburn's Washington office, at one point catching even Blackburn in a slip of the tongue about the raid. The priority of the mission was such that Blackburn and Manor could obtain almost any support they requested, from night-vision devices to custom-made machetes designed especially to cut down the doors of the prison huts in the camp. The CIA delivered a detailed model of the target, complete with accurate trees and shrubs. The national reconnaissance office dedicated both hypersonic SR-71 spyplanes and Buffalo Hunter unmanned aircraft to reconnoiter the Son Tay area and the planned route of the raid force. All this meticulous preparation took time, a fact that was seen as worrisome but necessary.

Meanwhile the aerial reconnaissance effort was handicapped by seasonal cloud cover over the target that balked the high-flying SR-71s and a disturbing North Vietnamese capacity for shooting down the reconnaissance drones. Of eight missions, seven were shot down and the eighth returned without usable photos. Nevertheless, SR-71 surveillance on 2 and 6 November did seem to show activity around the Son Tay compound and a mysterious nearby cluster of buildings dubbed 'the Secondary School'.

On 12 November, Blackburn finally received an initial go-ahead from the Pentagon and on 14 November 1970 Task Force 77 landed in Thailand. It was more than five months after the initial intelligence about Son Tay had been received. One of the CIA briefers who met them was none other than George Morton, the first Special Forces commander in Vietnam and now retired.

The force then waited four more days in Thailand, until 18 November, when President Nixon gave his personal approval to the mission. Back in Washington, Blackburn received devastating news: intelligence officers now believed the prisoners had been moved. Upon examination the intelligence seemed ambiguous and new SR-71 missions obtained infrared tracks in the compound. Someone was in there and the Task Force was chafing to go. At the same time, word arrived that 17 prisoners had died in captivity – at least some had died under torture and others had been executed. Mindful of the dead POWs, Secretary of Defense Melvin Laird gave the final go-ahead on 20 November. The mission was on.

By about 0200 hours on 21 November the Task Force had completed its aerial refueling and the lead C-130 began dropping flares and firefight simulators near the target compound. The A-1 fighter bombers took up station nearby, to be called for air support if required. Air Force F-105 fighters began attacking nearby surface-to-air missile sites and, at the same time, the Navy began its diversionary flare runs, utterly confusing the North Vietnamese air-defense system.

The first serious problem occurred when the raid support element landed by mistake 400 meters away, at the 'Secondary School'. The mysterious buildings turned out to be military barracks and the raiders were immediately taken under fire. Reacting at once, they assaulted the buildings, killing a number of North Vietnamese soldiers and a group of what seems to have been Chinese military advisors. Whoever they were, they came out shooting, and Simon's

22 men killed an estimated 100 of them. Realizing they were in the wrong location, the support element recalled their aircraft and proceeded to the correct target. But the error had enabled them to clear what would have been a major, unanticipated, threat to the success of the raid.

The loss of the support element was noted immediately, but the Task Force was so well rehearsed that the assault leader, Lieutenant Colonel Elliott Snydor, had only to order 'Execute Plan Green' and the raiders adjusted without hesitation. By this time the NVA at the prison compound were alerted and engaged the assault force at once with grenades and automatic-weapons fire. A confused running firefight developed as TF 77s assault teams cleared the buildings and security elements took up position, all the while returning fire against enemy attacks.

In the midst of all this, Captain Dick Meadows shouted through a power megaphone as prisoner-release teams began to search the compound, 'We're Americans. Keep your heads down. We're here to get you out.' There was no answer from the prisoner huts. Search teams began to report the cells were empty and Meadows checked for himself. Seconds later he notified Simons that there were no prisoners; it was a 'dry hole'. Simons immediately ordered a withdrawal and, after a total of 26 minutes on the ground, Task Force 77 lifted off. Meadows ran to an explosives-laden helicopter that had been abandoned according to plan and triggered a timing device, then boarded the last helicopter to leave the compound. Six minutes later a huge explosion destroyed the prison camp. Not a single one of the raiders had been lost and the mission had been beautifully executed, but the fact remained, the prisoners were not there.

The press lost no time in branding the mission a colossal failure and an intelligence disaster. What they overlooked was that the relevant decision-makers understood the camp could be empty but had decided the risks were worth while. Also, the raid had to be considered a tactical success. It achieved all the requirements for success in a raid – surprise, speed and skill in execution. Furthermore, it did have at least two important effects. First, it caused North Vietnam to bring all the American prisoners to Hanoi, where their treatment improved remarkably. Second, it demonstrated an amazing capacity to place a full-scale task force in the heart of an enemy country, take two well-defended enemy compounds in minutes and withdraw virtually unscathed. This was unprecedented in the history of military operations. The lack of POWs did not change the fact that the execution was little short of brilliant. In the words of William McRaven, a military theorist, 'The raid on Son Tay is the best modern-day example of a successful special operation and should be considered text book material for future missions' (McRaven, 1993, 494).

WE'LL NEVER DO THAT AGAIN

There was a palpable sense of relief among senior Army commanders that the USA was on its way out of Vietnam. With the endless agony behind them, military planners and leaders turned back to their preferred focus on the conventional battlefield and the Soviet threat in Europe as the centerpiece of military operations. Almost over-night the armed forces dropped even the appearance of concern with unconventional warfare as they strengthened their conventional posture.

> For many American military men, the Vietnam outcome confirmed their view of special units. The Green Berets became the symbol of the kind of war that was fought in Vietnam and, for many Americans, a symbol of all that was wrong with the US military policy and the military. (Sarkesian, 1986, 87)

In 1971, as US forces were withdrawing from Vietnam, President Richard Nixon spoke of the danger of 'over involvement', but at the same time of avoiding 'the deceptively smooth road of isolationism'. This 'Nixon Doctrine' represented a 'redefinition of the US's role in the world'. The USA would continue to provide a shield against any 'nuclear power' that threatened a nation 'allied with us or ... whose survival we consider vital to our security'. However, 'we will look to threatened countries and their neighbors to assume primary responsibility for their own defense, and we will provide support where our interests call for that support and where it can make a difference' (US President, 1972, 422–3; also US President, 1969, 553–4).

Nixon's announcement marked the beginning of a period, extending through the end of the Carter administration in 1980, that critics saw as marked by the desire for a unilateral US withdrawal from military, especially unconventional, involvement outside the North Atlantic community, regardless of what interests might be sacrificed (Schultz, 1989, 2; Sarkesian, 1986, introduction). However, events were to frustrate this policy, forcibly reminding the USA that superpower interests are not so easily disposed of. In this case, trouble came in the form of the same unconventional conflicts that had so worried President Kennedy.

It was also during this period that the term 'low-intensity conflict' was popularized from British military usage by Brig. Gen. Frank Kitson (Great Britain, [ret.]) in his book *Low-Intensity Operations* (Kitson, 1971).

Army doctrine for counterinsurgency was now termed International Defense and Development (IDAD), and later Foreign Internal Defense (FID). IDAD appeared with the 1974 publication of DA FM 100-20 *International Defense and Development* the precursor to 1981's DA FM 100-20 *Low-Intensity Conflict*. Continuing the tradition of generality in definitions, internal defense was defined as 'the full range of measures taken by a government and its allies to free and protect its society from subversion, lawlessness and insurgency'. Internal development was defined as those actions taken by a government 'to promote its balanced growth by building viable institutions ... that respond to the needs of its society' (DA, 1974, 1-1).

These doctrinal developments were largely moot as US policy swung strongly away from these types of involvement as indicated by Congress's passage of the Clark Amendment, legally restricting US involvement in Third World conflicts. This distaste for unconventional involvements also took the form of continuing criticism of US counterinsurgency involvement as both bad national policy and a failure of military technique (Fitzsimons, 1972, especially 123–214; also Fulbright, 1972).

Despite its wholly secondary role, psychological operations also came in for a share of the general criticism of unconventional warfare (Watson 1978). The rare work praising special operations forces was usually concerned with those elite conventional units organized on the Ranger model (e.g Darragh, 1977, 17–19).

In contrast to the scholarly enthusiasm of the early 1960s, a series of academic critiques emerged of 'low-intensity conflict' (by which the writers usually meant counterinsurgency) and special operations (meaning MACV-SOG and Phoenix-type efforts). In general, these treatments revolved around two basic criticisms. Military counterinsurgency was alleged to be ineffective and probably immoral, since it supposedly thwarted the legitimate aspirations of peoples for responsive, participatory, non-corrupt government (Ahmad, 1971, 1–2; Barkley and Garrett, 1971; Bloomfield and Leiss, 1970; Prouty, 1973, especially Ch. 19). Still other critics, usually within the military, argued soldier participation in civic action programs would 'erode the basic readiness to fight which is the lifeblood of the Army' (Bradford and Brown, 1973, 204). A complaint that continued throughout the 1990s. Military critics further charged that special operations were either of dubious value and/or likely to exceed their original intentions and result in negative political consequences (Blackstock, 1977, 1257–9; Fitzgerald, 1972; Cohen, 1978; Mantell, 1974).

Mainstream opinion in the Army held that the USA's military strong suit was the ability to field heavy armored formations supported by airpower and capable of large-scale, extended combat. This was supported by the belief that the US Army had 'won' the guerrilla portion of the Vietnam War with conventional forces and that this portion of the conflict had been the least important one. Col. Zeb B. Bradford, analyzing the Army's experience in Vietnam, observed: 'We would be wrong to redesign the Army, or a significant part of it, in an effort to compensate for assumed deficiencies in counterguerrilla capabilities, based on our Vietnam experience' (1972, 76). Bradford later co-authored (with Col. Frederick J. Brown) a widely read study, titled *The United States Army in Transition*, which restated the same beliefs (Bradford and Brown, 1973).

Doctrine for the Army's conventional combat forces during the 1970s was centered on the notion of 'active defense'. This concept was based largely on the Army's desire to focus even more strongly than before on conventional mechanized warfare and, especially, to take advantage of the lessons of the 1973 Yom Kippur War (Romjue, 1984, 5). The authoritative volume on Army doctrine for the period (DA FM 100-5, *Operations*, 1976) dealt only with conventional and nuclear conflict. Under the concept of 'active defense', the utility of Special Operations Forces was nil and the capability continued to erode. Four of the seven active duty Army Special Forces Groups were deactivated between 1969 and 1974 (US Congress, House, 1983, 8). Army Special Forces declined from a strength of 13,000 personnel in 1971 to less than 3,000 by 1974 (ibid., 8).[2]

On 28 January 1974 the Army Rangers were recreated yet again as an 'elite' conventional infantry unit when the 1st Battalion, 75th Infantry was formed at Fort Benning, Georgia, and then moved to its present home at Hunter Army Airfield in Fort Stewart, Georgia. A second 660-man Ranger battalion, the 2nd Battalion, 75th Infantry, was added in October (Rottman, 1987, 46). Meanwhile, funding for Special Operations Forces decreased rapidly from over

$1 billion at its high point in 1969, to less than $100 million in 1975 (*Defense Monitor*, 1987).

By 1977, Lawrence E. Grinter, a professor at the National War College, could flatly state 'the Army is finished with counter-insurgency' (Grinter, 1990). Douglas Blaufarb's survey of Army doctrine and operations led him to conclude 'the army has not acknowledged any degree of error in Vietnam ... and has dismantled the centers and training programs that might keep alive ... a commitment to the notion that counterinsurgency calls for some modification of the prevailing wisdom' (1977, 199). Other major peacetime contingencies (such as the Mayaguez incident) were left to the Navy/Marine Corps and the Air Force, while insurgency support was simply nonexistent. The Army did, however, maintain a minor interest in counterterrorism (discussed below).

WHAT ABOUT SPECIAL FORCES?

Not all Army Special Forces personnel viewed the reductions in SF strength and visibility as entirely bad. The rapid expansion of SF in the 1960s had, in the view of some, seriously diluted the quality of the force. Among the small number of those remaining from the early 1960s, there was a strong feeling that SF had gone seriously awry. They believed that the Vietnam expansion had allowed in too many marginally qualified members. More subtly, it was also believed that the expansion had attracted the wrong kind of people (i.e. conventionally minded), who had turned the organization toward Ranger-style raiding and reconnaissance roles and away from unconventional warfare. The likely and appropriate opportunities for Special Forces involvement seemed to them to call for a much smaller organization. These officers and NCOs favored a further reduction in overall strength and a considerable lowering of the organization's visibility to reduce the feeling that SF was somehow in competition with the remainder of the Army. One officer and former SF Group commander even advocated the end of the most visible symbol of SF, the green beret. These people were, however, a distinct minority and without significant influence. As it developed, the organizational preference would be to embrace the conventional roles, in order to give SF and special operations a secure place in conventional warfighting.

SPECIAL FORCES AS A STRATEGIC ASSET

During the mid-1970s the impact of the Nixon Doctrine, and a desire to recover from the drastic cutbacks of the post-Vietnam period, led Special Forces to seek roles in which it could support the Army (at national level) rather than theater commanders. Senior SF officers who had entered Special Forces during the Vietnam War were most familiar and comfortable with the successful and generally approved roles of SF during that war – the conventional support missions for the regular armed forces: Project Delta, MACV-SOG (in its recon and targeting role) and the Mike Forces.

This acted to continue the trend begun in Vietnam away from unconventional warfare and toward more conventional missions. Within Army special-operations circles, there was a conscious decision to 'play ball with the services' (Paschall, 1989; Kief, 1989). In practice, that meant that Special Forces would become part of the mainstream, shedding its 'independent' image in favor of being an accepted member of the 'combined arms team'. Col. Robert Mountel, a senior officer at SWC and a former SF Group commander, referred to this as almost a 'paranoia' about not being considered part of the Army (Mountel, interview, 14 July 1989).

This trend was contradicted by a growing consciousness among Congressional policymakers that the problem of unconventional threats had not gone away with the Vietnam War (US Congress, Senate Hearings, 1975). But this was the era of limited goals, as exemplified by the 'Carter Doctrine', a modest declaration that the Persian Gulf area was a vital interest of the USA. There was no taste among executive branch policymakers for anything like unconventional involvements by the military.

However, some executive policymakers, including President Carter, his national security advisor Zibignew Brezinski, and Joint Chiefs of Staff (JCS) Chairman General Jones (US Air Force) did see a need to develop a military capacity for small-scale 'classified activities', especially a counter to terrorist acts like the attack on the 1972 Olympics in West Germany. Special Forces seemed like the logical vehicle for these missions, but there was no particular urgency, and no short-term results were sought (Turner, interview, 1989). This realization apparently began the line of reasoning that would lead to the creation of the Army's Delta Force, the premier special-operations element.

Within the special operations community, the Special Warfare Center (SWC, then called the Center for Military Assistance), undertook a top-secret project in 1975 to evaluate the experience of Army special operations units in Indochina and project future roles for these units, especially Army Special Forces. The project was completed in 1976. Titled the 'Multi-Purpose Force Study: US Army Special Forces', it was more commonly referred to as the Mountel study, after its principal author, Col. Robert Mountel, by then chief operations officer of the Center. The bulk of this influential study remains classified. However, a quotation from an unclassified summary paragraph is instructive:

> ... there is a pervasive lack of understanding, interest and support of unconventional warfare and Special Forces as a valid national response option. Based on research conducted for this study, this state of mind is nearly identical to that which existed in the mid-1950s. [The role of Special Forces] is generally perceived by many to be limited to the conduct of guerrilla warfare in support of conventional forces. (SWC, 1976, 2–3)

The study went on to emphasize that Special Forces represented a broad range of capabilities, placing special emphasis on the flexibility of these units and their utility against various peacetime threats but especially in conventional war. As in the Kelly report of 1973, the Mountel report did not seek to institutionalize the hard-won SF lessons the Vietnam era, but rather sought to expand the role of SF into the conventional arena. By the end of 1976, training for 'foreign internal development' (the new term for counterinsurgency) had been virtually eliminated from Army service schools (Doughty and Smith, 1976, 6; Vought, 1977, 34; Doughty, 1979). The bottom line was that, as far as the military was concerned, counterinsurgency was a dead end and Special Operations Forces needed to prove that they were useful to the rest of the armed forces.

REALITY INTRUDES

Unfortunately the real world kept intruding. At about the same time Carter was considering 'classified missions', the Hanafi Muslim terrorist kidnappings occurred in Washington, DC, bringing home the fact that there was little capacity to deal with terrorist threats. When the Washington Metropolitan police asked for military assistance in that incident there was no unit with the skills to provide useful help. Shortly after that (1977) the West German counterterrorist unit GSFG-9 successfully stormed a terrorist-captured airliner in Mogadishu, Somalia, releasing the passengers. The West German government had also been taken aback by the terrorist hostage incident at the 1972 Olympics in Munich, and they too had been worried about a repetition. The paramilitary GSFG-9 was their answer to the problem. President Carter was impressed with the West Germans' performance and sought a similar capability for the USA (Turner, interview, 1989). Supposedly, the President sent a letter through channels to the Joint Chiefs of Staff, asking 'do we have the same capability as the West Germans?' After considerable discussion it was decided that no such capacity existed but, as one of the generals present is alleged to have stated, 'I'm not going over to the White House and tell him we don't' (Beckwith in Griswald and Giangreco, 1992, 61).

This gave added impetus to the creation of a specialized counter-terrorist unit to be called 1st Special Forces Operational Detachment Delta (better known as SFOD-Delta, or simply Delta Force), activated on 19 November 1977 (Beckwith, 1983, 118). As noted above, Army officers during the 1970s had maintained a steady, if low-key, interest in measures against terrorism, especially when terrorist acts were directed against Americans (Elliott, 1976; Collins, 1978).

Delta was initially the brainchild of Lt. Gen. Edward Meyer (at that time Army Deputy Chief of Staff), who, independently of Carter and Brezinski, had determined that the Army needed a counter-terrorist capability and managed to convince Army Chief of Staff Gen. Bernard Rogers. It was purely an Army initiative, conducted with no JCS enthusiasm or involvement (Mountel, interview, 20 July 1989).

Delta's operational concept was first conceived as a more-or-less Ranger/commando style unit by Col. Charlie Beckwith, a veteran of 5th Group in Vietnam.[3] A former Project Delta commander with the 5th in Vietnam, Beckwith also had experience with the British Special Air Service (SAS) commandos and (at CINCPAC) had monitored the activities of MACV-SOG (Beckwith, 1983, 90). He was certain that he knew what it took to deal with terrorists and that was a unit of 'shooters' – a small, highly trained team capable of executing counterterrorist missions. At the same time, another Special Forces counterterrorist reaction team code named 'Blue Light' was also created within the 5th Group as an interim measure until Delta became operational (Paschall, 1989; also Beckwith, 1983, 117, 119). The Blue Light team was organized as a more multifunction organization per the Mountel study, capable of a range of functions similar to those performed by the OSS 30 years previously. Blue Light's emphasis was on clandestine operations, including specialized reconnaissance and operations in denied areas much like the original Special Forces functions envisioned by Colonel Bank and the 10th Group 24 years earlier. Whatever the advantages of such an organization, it received little support at the upper levels of the Army.

Beckwith's straightforward concentration on hostage rescue as a mission and direct assault as a method was much more to the liking of conventional leaders. The creator of Blue Light, Col. Robert Mountel (Commander of the 5th SFG at Fort Bragg), was not viewed with favor by Delta's commander. As seen by Beckwith, 'he had to put Charlie Beckwith out of business' (Beckwith, 1983, 117). For his part, Colonel Mountel was not pleased with Beckwith's 'bullshit and gunsmoke' approach to counterterrorism. As described by Mountel:

> It [Delta] was basically a pastiche of techniques and backgrounds – some borrowed from the SAS, some borrowed from the Vietnam across-the-border operations – and all blundered into a macho whole that did not square with what I thought I knew about the requirements of counter-terror operations in the twentieth century.[4] (quoted in J. Adams, 1987, 101)

'Chargin' Charlie' Beckwith also valued autonomy and had a reputation as a bluff, independent operator rather than a team player. He believed 'if I am going to do something unique, something dangerous, then I'd better have all my own horses', by which he meant personnel, equipment, funding, and supplies (Beckwith, 1983, 79). In the opinion of some at Fort Bragg, in Beckwith's hands, Delta was emerging as the very model of a special operations unit as conceived of by its detractors – expensive, independent, arrogant, out of uniform, outside normal chains of command, and too specialized for its own good.

The parallel Delta and Blue Light programs did nothing to dispel this notion when Army Chief of Staff General Rogers (and President Carter) discovered that two separate counterterrorist units had been created where one had been authorized. The 5th Group commander received a blistering message from the Army Chief of Staff and Blue Light was instantly abandoned (Beckwith, 1983, 130–1, 154). In the Pentagon, muttering continued that the damn snake-eaters were out of control again.[5]

As far as the US DOD was concerned, there was nothing very special about special ops and no dearth of units capable of unconventional missions. DOD officials testified before Congress in 1978 that a variety of conventional military units were capable of unconventional, especially counterterrorist, operations. The list included Army Rangers and Special Forces, Marine Corps Reconnaissance Companies, Navy SEALs, and others (US Congress, Senate Hearings, 1978, 192). This point is especially pertinent because that same 1978 testimony included 'rescue of hostages' as a specific, existing capability (US Congress, Senate Hearings, 1978, 197). Yet, when the time to employ this capability came, a year later, this ability proved illusory. Maybe special ops was something special after all.

What had been presented in 1978 was a laundry list of light infantry forces, most capable of rapid response and parachute deployment. There was nothing at all deceitful in this presentation. In fact it harked back to the long-time belief in military circles that any good conventional (infantry, Ranger, Marine, etc.) unit could carry out most of these missions. All the forces listed (including the SEALs) were well-trained, rapidly deployable, light infantry units. Their training, equipment and doctrine reflected the Department of Defense concern with its basic mission: to be prepared to conduct conventional military operations against conventional enemy military units. But, with the single exception of Army Special Forces, none of these organizations proved well prepared to carry out unconventional warfare assignments, including hostage rescue. This approach of expecting conventional units to carry out unconventional tasks once again reflected the persistent notion that Special Forces are not very special and that their missions can be carried out by standard organizations (McCollum, 1976, 16–22; Beaumont, 1974, 186–7).

By the end of the 1970s, the US ability to conduct unconventional warfare was virtually nonexistent. In the words of one specialist in revolutionary conflict, US capacity in this area had 'withered into virtual uselessness' (quote from Shackley, 1983, 19; Tanham *et al.*, 1978; see also Beaumont, 1979). The suggestion that Army Special Forces were most appropriately employed as assets directly supporting conventional combat units continued to surface occasionally in the professional literature (Schlacter and Stubbs, 1978, 15).

Then, one year later, in late 1979, came the defining event in the history of modern US special operations – the Iranian hostage crisis.

Sixty-six members of the US Embassy in Tehran were taken hostage by Islamic militants and imprisoned on the embassy grounds. When the crisis occurred no US DOD organization existed which could attempt a rescue. *In extremis* rescue was not yet part of the military lexicon and President Carter's forebodings proved correct. The closest capability was that of the Army's SFOD Delta. However, that small unit was never intended for a mission of such magnitude. Furthermore, no provision had been made for the sort of support required to deliver the Delta troopers to the midst of a hostile country half-way around the world. Four months of training and the creation of a special supporting task force were required before Delta could be deployed (Beckwith, 1983, 177–216).

An *ad hoc* support force was cobbled together from Army, Navy Air Force and Marine Corps units with the purpose of placing the as yet unblooded SFOD Delta in position to rescue the hostages and then return rescuers and rescued to the USA. A fleet of C-141s carried the 120-man force to Masirah Island, off the coast of Oman, where they transferred to three MC-130s accompanied by three fuel-bearing EC-130s. They landed 200 miles southeast of Tehran at night on a remote desert airstrip and waited for the arrival of eight Navy RH-53D Sea Stallion helicopters from the aircraft carrier *Nimitz*. In addition to the Delta troopers, the mission included a 12-man road watch team, composed primarily of Rangers, to secure the site while the helicopters refueled. The mission, Operation Eagle Claw, ended in disaster when mechanical problems compelled the rescue force to abort their mission at the covert airstrip before even arriving at the embassy. Then, as the force was in the midst of a nighttime withdrawal, a large RH-53 helicopter collided on the ground with a fuel and ammo-laden C-130 transport. The resulting explosion and fire killed eight Americans, injured several others, and forced the would-be rescuers to abandon the bodies of the dead, five helicopters, much of their equipment and a number of secret documents.[6]

The abandoned helicopters were later destroyed by Navy fighters but the mutilated bodies and the wreckage of the burned-out aircraft abandoned in the Iranian desert remained an image that haunted US special operators. In the minds of some it became an indelible symbol of the weakness of US Special Operations Forces. For them, overcoming this image became a powerful motivator.

In order to avoid a possible Congressional investigation of the mission, a JCS commission was convened to report on the rescue mission failure (Ryan, 1985, 107). The Carter administration

1. *US Special Operations Forces on a Scud-hunting mission during Operation Desert Storm.*

2. *Joint Special Operations Forces hunting Scuds in the Iraqi desert during Operation Desert Storm.*

3. *The Mark V Special Operations Craft.*

4. *The SEAL delivery vehicle, similar to a miniature submarine.*

5. The USS *Cyclone* [left], a USSOCOM *Patrol Coastal Ship*, and the *Bellatrix* [right], a Dominican patrol boat, enforcing the embargo of Haiti in 1994.

6. *A special tactics airman heads for shore after dropping from a helicopter.*

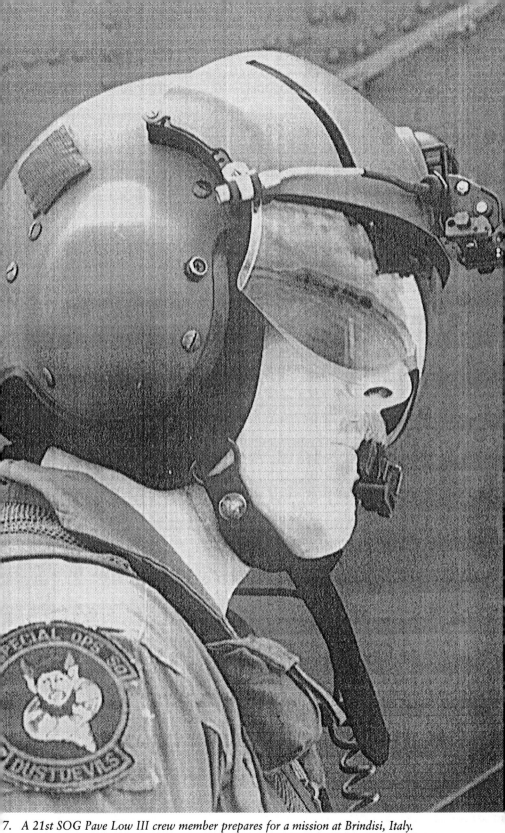

7. A 21st SOG Pave Low III crew member prepares for a mission at Brindisi, Italy.

8. *A parachutist during a joint combined training exercise in Venezuela.*

9. *A Psyop loudspeaker team making public announcements and telling Haitians in the streets to remain calm.*

10. *A Ranger on night patrol in Les Cayes, Haiti.*

11 Under fire from Marxist guerillas, USSOCOMM-trained Colombian police spray defoliant from a government plane over opium poppy fields

apparently was wary because the President had not consulted with Congress in advance of the operation, nor did he inform them until after the mission had been aborted. This was defended on the grounds that the rescue was not primarily a hostile action against Iran. Administration officials added that, had the mission proceeded past the initial stage, Congress would have been consulted. Congressional leaders were unanimous that the administration had not complied with the War Powers Resolution, but were disinclined to pursue the issue any further. The JCS's so-called 'Holloway Investigation', named after its chairman, Adm. James L. Holloway III, was limited in its authority as a 'review group' to examining only the military-operational aspects of the rescue mission. The unclassified version of the Holloway report did not deal with national command-level issues involving the president, the Secretary of Defense or the Joint Chief of Staff. As of 1997, the classified version of the report had not been made public. In the public version of its report the commission blamed '*ad hoc* organization' combined with excess secrecy for the failure. It reported that

> the Joint Chiefs of Staff had to start, literally from the beginning ... find a commander, create an organization, provide a staff, develop a plan, select the units, and train the force before the first mission capability could be obtained. (US JCS, 1980, vi)

The Iranian hostage crisis and the disastrous failure of the US rescue effort marked what is perhaps the lowest ebb of both US special-operations capability and attention to those forms of violent conflict outside conventional warfare. The rescue mission was portrayed in the press as a 'pathetic disaster' in which 'elite US commando forces staggered around like suicidal versions of the Three Stooges' (Mandell, 1989, 739). Despite intense criticism of both the Defense Department and the Carter administration for the rescue failure (US DOD, 1980; Fialka, 1980; Fine, 1980; Gabriel, 1980–81; Scott, 1980; Webbe, 1980), no significant moves were made to alter or improve this capability. Because of the association between special operations and the mission failure, SOF as a concept lost even more credibility with the upper echelons of the conventional military (Mountel, interview, 20 July 1989).

Within the Army forces, Gen. Meyer sought to correct both real and perceived deficiencies through a proposed 'Strategic Services Command', a joint command that would provide a co-ordinated, multi-service approach to problems such as terrorism and insurgency. Seeing this as an Army attempt to gain control of Navy and Marine Corps special-operations resources, the latter two services combined to block the proposal (Meyer, 1990).

Various 'lessons' of the Desert One tragedy were proposed and counterproposed but one of special interest is the contention that a unified special-operations command would have prevented the failure by providing greater coordination among elements and avoiding the excess security compartmentalization blamed by both Ryan and the Holloway commission (among others). This was the old special-ops bugaboo of poor command and control and lack of coordination. This view is borne out by the narrow tactical-operational focus of the Holloway report, but even that document makes specific criticism of what the commission saw as excess security and poor coordination within the armed services (US DOD, 'Holloway Report', 1980, 13–14, 17, 57–8).

In this interpretation the problem was not a failure of command and control but rather bad luck exacerbated by tactical-operational problems (an unexpected sandstorm, the sudden appearance of Iranian civilians at the remote landing site, mechanical failure, poor selection of pilots, an overly complex plan and so forth). Certainly, the mission had more than its share of bad luck, but much of this would have been mitigated by better planning and coordination at all levels, coordinated planning that was hindered by the diffuse, compartmentalized nature of the operation (Gabriel, 1980–81, 6; T. Adams, 1987, 105–6).

One permanent gain from the mission was the use of Army Rangers as the force of choice to support Delta's larger operations by providing security, reaction forces and the like. The combination of Delta and the Rangers would appear over and over in future special operations. This practice also gave rise to the idea of the Special Mission Unit (SMU) and set the pattern for SMU operations. In the future, SMU organized around Delta and/or its Navy equivalent (SEAL Team Six) and supplemented by Rangers and Air Force assets would become the elite of the SOF community, selected for the 'most sensitive and difficult reconnaissance and direct action missions' (Collins, 1994, 133). Another, but unspoken, lesson of the Eagle Claw disaster was that such missions are not only inherently dangerous, but they carry serious risks of failure. As the Carter administration and other observers quickly learned, those failures can have important political consequences. Within special-operations circles, especially in the CIA, there was a growing consensus that the risks were not worth the potential rewards.

This lessened bureaucratic resistance toward allowing the Army to develop such a capacity (Turner, interview, 1989).

In the midst of the Iran Hostage Crisis, the foreign-policy concerns of a great power were made immediate when the USSR invaded Afghanistan. Dissatisfied with a symbolic boycott of the Moscow Olympics and a largely ineffective grain embargo, the Carter administration was forced to rely on covert, unconventional means. This took the form of support to the Afghan resistance (ibid., 1989).

The perceived importance of these operations was illustrated by the subsequent Annual Report of the Secretary of Defense to Congress which devoted only a single two-sentence paragraph to the rescue failure and none to the Afghan resistance (US DOD, Annual Report, 1981, iii). Of the entire 317-page document, only ten pages were devoted to 'Non-NATO' contingencies (ibid., 81–9; see also Brown 1983).

One immediate result of the Iran failure was the realization that special operations needed something other than *ad hoc* aviation support. The realization was given immediacy by Pesident Carter's order that, despite the failure of Eagle Claw, rescue planning would continue. Shortly afterwards the Army gave the special-operations aviation mission to a helicopter support unit of the 101st Airborne Division at Fort Campbell, Kentucky, the Army's only heli-borne division. The unit immediately began an intensive training program in low-level, night operations. Designated the 160th Aviation Battalion, on 16 October 1981, the unit became known as Task Force 160 because of the constant attachment and detachment of units to prepare for a wide variety of missions. The battalion's continual series of night training operations resulted in the nickname 'Night Stalkers' (History, 1996, 1).

CONTINUING FOCUS ON THE SOVIET THREAT

The overwhelming concern for conventional operations was reflected in the Army's efforts to develop better 'operational concepts' for mechanized war in Europe as the centerpiece of US military doctrine (Starry, 1978, 10–11). Like so many doctrinal developments, this did not bode well for Special Operations Forces. What appeared was an operational concept called 'AirLand Battle Doctrine' (DA FM 100-5, *Operations*, 1982). Like all US Army conventional war doctrine, 'AirLand Battle' was apolitical in the sense that it took place outside any political context. Its only objective was the physical destruction of the enemy force. The specific location where battle occurred was important only insofar as its physical character impeded or advanced this end. The political, cultural, economic or other characteristics of the populations normally residing in the battle areas were irrelevant to the conduct of combat. As a doctrine clearly intended for conflict in Europe, the only apparent political context was the broad ideological one of East versus West (USSR and its allies vs the USA and its allies). It was quite insensitive to the idea that various independent nation-states were involved on both sides, some of which were likely to reject the implied notion that their primary value was to provide a location for the battle.

'AirLand Battle' was formally presented as official doctrine in DA FM 100-5 Operations published in August 1982. The AirLand Battle scheme was based on conventional concepts of warfare and the Army's traditional commitment to the importance of the offensive in warfare (DA FM 100-5, 1982, 11-1 through 11-8). Its most unique feature was an emphasis on 'Deep Attack' operations targeted against Warsaw Pact 'follow-on' forces synchronized with maneuver and attack at the line of contact (TRADOC, 1981). This was a highly technological doctrine, dependent on sophisticated sensors and surveillance systems to locate the deep targets, rapid communications and data processing systems, and weapons systems (including tactical nuclear weapons) with the range and accuracy to strike targets at ranges of more than 100 kilometers (DA FM 100-5, 1982). It was also a 'tailored' doctrine in the sense that it was explicitly designed to counter the threat posed by the USSR and its Warsaw Pact allies in Europe. AirLand Battle was created as a solution to the problem of the Warsaw Pact's preponderance of conventional forces (Starry, 1978, 2). However, it was presented as 'the Army's basic operational concept' (DA FM 100-5, 1982, 2-1).[7]

Making an explicit connection with Napoleonic concepts and 'principles of war', the Army Training and Doctrine Command publication introducing AirLand Battle Doctrine began with a quote attributed to Napoleon, Maxim No. 10:

> With an Army inferior in numbers, in cavalry, and in artillery, a commander must avoid a general action. He must make up the deficiency in numbers by rapidity of movements; want of artillery by the nature of his maneuvers; inferiority of cavalry by the choice of positions. In such circumstances the morale of the soldier is a great factor. (TRADOC, 1982, 2)

Within the Army, the cultural emphasis on decisive battle created some difficulty in fully accepting this doctrine on the grounds that it carried concepts of maneuver warfare to an extreme, depriving combat commanders of needed strength at the preferred point of contact with the enemy – the direct contact battle. Army field commanders were concerned that 'you can't win deep' (London, 1984, 27).[8]

Under AirLand Battle Doctrine the role of Special Operations Forces was either reduced to that of raiding and deep reconnaissance for the large conventional formations (Hadley, 1985, 73–83), or to supporting the conventional efforts indirectly by supplying, training and leading partisans in the enemy rear in order to 'disrupt the enemy's ability to prosecute the main battle' (DA FM 100-5, 1982, 7–23). Unconventional warfare was reduced to its traditional military meaning of support to partisans operating as guerrillas.

CONCLUSION

The end of the Vietnam War saw the USA disillusioned with military intervention and especially the type of internal conflicts that had led into the 'Vietnam quagmire'. The decade of the 1970s was a period of de-emphasis on special operations and a severe reduction of Special Operations Forces. However, as always, the real world declined to accommodate itself to doctrine and events such as the growth of international terrorism demanded a response. The creation of Delta was one response to this threat, but the usual *ad hoc* approach to special operations led to the spectacular operational failure of these forces in the Iranian hostage-rescue mission.

Given the need for and utility of military force as an essential ingredient for national survival in the anarchic society of nation-states, it is not surprising that the USA continued to seek a doctrine for the useful application of these forces to further its national security interests in the new international environment. In his analysis of US strategic imperatives for the 1980s, Samuel P. Huntington identified 'local conflicts and instability' threats to US interests as coups, insurrections, insurgencies and limited conventional war directed against governments friendly to the USA. He asserted that 'the United States needs a strategy and the capabilities to deal with threats to its interests that arise from these types of conflicts' (1982, 4).

This is similar to the rationale set forth in the Draft Manual on Low-Intensity Conflict prepared by the Army–Air Force Center for Low-Intensity Conflict, which concluded: 'the United States now faces challenges to its global interests from the lower end of the conflict spectrum that are far more troubling and complex than it faced at the beginning of World War Two' (DA FM 100-20, 1987, 1). This was an interesting remark, since it alleges that the situation in the late 1980s of nuclear stalemate, revolutionary warfare and 'Third World developments' (ibid., 2) was 'far more troubling and complex' than the threat posed in 1941 by two globe-spanning, militarily superior fascist powers engaged in open warfare against the USA and its allies. Perhaps it was so 'troubling' because the situation was not only more complex but also less amenable to traditional, conventional solutions.

Meanwhile Special Operations Forces faced a troubling situation of their own – a bureaucratic war over the future of special ops that was as fierce and deadly in its own bloodless way as any jungle firefight.

NOTES

1. This account of the Son Tay Raid is compiled from Benjamin F. Schemmer, *The Raid* (New York: Harper & Row, 1976); General Blackburn's Oral History file at the Military History Institute, Carlisle Barracks, PA; and Richard F. Brauer, 'Case Study: The Son Tay Raid', USAWC, 1984.
2. Nelson Kief, a former DOD staffer, comments that 'the cuts would have been deeper, but the Army wanted to hold slots for its surplus of Lieutenant Colonels/Colonels' (Kief, personal correspondence of the author, 9 June 1989).
3. The basic idea for a elite special-mission force within Army Special Forces had been repeatedly proposed in various forms by Colonel Beckwith since 1963 (Beckwith, 1983, 51–3).
4. Colonel Mountel (US Army, [ret.]) states that this quote is an accurate statement of his sentiments but is not his own words (telephone interview, 14 July 1989; personal interview, 20 July 1989).
5. Admiral Turner reports that, in 1986, Helmut Schmidt, former Chancellor of West Germany, told him that the West Germans had rejected their own military as a hostage-rescue force on the grounds that military organizations were 'too rigid and hierarchical for the type of imaginative ... operations ... needed' (Turner, personal papers, courtesy of Stansfield Turner).
6. There are several accounts of the hostage crisis and rescue mission. The most detailed is *The Iran Hostage Crisis – A Chronology of Daily Developments*, report prepared for the Committee on Foreign Affairs, US House of Representatives by the Foreign Affairs and National Defense Division, Congressional Research Service, Library of Congress, March 1981. Colonel Beckwith's own account is given in *Delta Force* (1983). (For a brief description, see J. Adams, 1987.)
7. Prior to this period, the term 'AirLand Battle' simply meant close coordination between ground forces and supporting aircraft (DA FM 100-5, 1976, 8-1, 8-3). A

full account of the genesis and development of the AirLand Battle concept can be found in Britt Lynn Edwards's 'Reforming the Army: The Formulation and Implementation of AirLand Battle 2000' (1985).

8. Within the Army's conventional model of war there is a longstanding debate between advocates of 'attrition' warfare and those of 'maneuver' warfare. In essence these are both conventional approaches oriented toward the defeat in the field of the enemy army and differ only in regard to most effective ratio of maneuver to sustained combat (see, for example, DuPuy, 1987, 165–82).

7 Special ops in the bureaucratic jungle

THE REAGAN DOCTRINE AND THE REVIVAL OF SPECIAL OPERATIONS

In 1980 the total strength of all Army Special Forces combined was no more than 3,000, an incredible decline from its peak strength of 13,000 in 1969. In other words, there were fewer soldiers in all of Army SF in 1980 than had been in the 5th Group alone during the Vietnam War. The number of special operators in the other services was negligible, except in the US Marine Corps, where it was zero, the Marines being wary of the whole concept and inclined to believe that the entire Corps was a Special Operations Force.

Then, at the lowest ebb of the fortunes of the special operators – the debacle in the Iranian desert – came a revival of special ops. This was not initiated from within the Defense Department but from newly elected President Ronald Reagan. The Reagan administration announced its willingness to engage communist revolutionary insurgencies around the world, and sought to reverse their gains with a zeal not seen since the Kennedy era.

The new administration took a wide view of its national security responsibilities, as evidenced by the statement made by Caspar Weinberger, Secretary of Defense, during his senate confirmation hearings. Weinberger stated that his concept of the national security responsibility ran from 'acts of terrorism and violence against our diplomats and citizens up to and including possible attacks on the nation itself' (US Congress, Senate, 1981, 7).

But unlike Kennedy, the Regan zealots found unlikely allies, the United States Congress. This is not to say that the armed forces were oblivious to the variety of threats in the world, just that the focus remained firmly on large-scale conventional warfare with specific emphasis on the USSR as the probable enemy. The US military force structure followed this focus with little attention paid to other kinds of possible military engagements. All other threats were covered in a single, slim manual, FM-100-20 *Low Intensity Conflict*, issued in 1981 to replace the earlier guerrilla warfare and counterinsurgency manuals. This lumped all threats other than mid-to-large-scale conventional war into a single category called 'Low-Intensity Conflict' or just 'LIC'. While the Army and DOD may have failed to adapt to the changing international environment of 1980s, members of the Congress were more than willing to do through legislation what the Defense Department had not done for itself. Unsurprisingly, this initiative was not welcomed across the Potomac in the Pentagon. This chapter follows the attempts of the law-makers to force an unconventional response to the new conflict environment.

THE 1980S

If you believed the policy pronouncements of the 1980s, US soldiers were unlikely to fight for any reason short of a Russian landing in Florida. The idea that US military forces should not be committed to combat except under very specialized circumstances was an article of belief for successive administrations after the US involvement in the Vietnam War. The strongest expression of this policy was the so-called 'Weinberger Doctrine', named after Reagan's Secretary of Defense.

In 1984, the SecDef (Secretary of Defense) articulated a doctrine of 'six major tests' to be met before US combat forces were used abroad. These 'tests' seem to announce a policy in opposition to his own assessment of the low-intensity threat in his 1985 budget report that year. They were:

1. The engagement in question must be vital to US or allied national interests.
2. Any commitment must be wholehearted and with 'the clear intention of winning'.
3. Political and military objectives must be clearly defined.
4. Military forces should be appropriate to the need in 'size, composition and disposition'. This should be reassessed and adjusted as required.
5. There must be 'some reasonable assurance' of public and Congressional support.
6. The use of armed forces in combat 'should be a last resort'. (Excerpted text of Weinberger address, *New York Times*, 29 November 1984, A4)

This list was apparently intended as broad national strategic policy. While appropriate to large or even mid-scale conventional combat it lacks application to 'low-intensity' conflict unless the intent is to avoid it completely. The Weinberger list was endorsed (if not actively inspired) by the JCS, apparently to avoid anything but overt, conventional war.

However, Weinberger not withstanding, between 1981 and 1991 the US government chose to intervene militarily with ground forces on four major occasions (Grenada, Panama, Lebanon and the Persian Gulf), and to provide noncombat counterinsurgency assistance of important proportions in Honduras and El Salvador. Every one of these interventions had a prominent role for Special Operations Forces.

In addition to the major interventions cited above, the Reagan administration resorted to the use of military means in several other instances, ranging from the bombing of Tripoli in Libya by US air forces to the use of Navy aircraft to intercept a civilian aircraft carrying suspected terrorists. Through the CIA, with some SOF assistance, the administration provided clandestine and more-or-less covert support to irregular and insurgent forces such as the anti-Sandinista rebels in Nicaragua, the Mujahadeen in Afghanistan, and the antigovernment resistance movements in Angola and Cambodia.

US armed forces were repeatedly committed, often to provide advice, transportation, logistic support and physical security, and to 'contingency' situations that involved intermittent combat (Beirut 1983 and the Persian Gulf 1985–88). But US forces also saw sporadic combat (the Gulf of Sidra in 1981 and 1986, air action against Syrian positions in Lebanon in 1983, the Grenada invasion of 1983 and the Libya bombings of 1986). The Bush administration rounded out the decade with the Panama invasion of 1989 and Operation Desert Shield in 1990. The year 1991, of course, brought Desert Storm, the largest US combat operation since World War II.

THE REAGAN DOCTRINE

The closest approximation of a national policy for unconventional conflict in the 1980s was the Reagan Doctrine. However, as will be shown below, the so-called Reagan Doctrine represented no more than an ambition to 'rollback' the gains of international communism and was hardly coherent enough to constitute either national strategy or security policy.

The primary focus of national-security policy remained as it had been for nearly forty years, blatantly anti-Soviet and directed against the 'Evil Empire' of Russian communism (US President, 1988, 5; Huntington, 1983, 82–113; US Secretary of Defense, 1981, 991–2).

But a new variation emerged during the first years of the Reagan government that came to be called the 'Reagan Doctrine'. In general, this was a policy of security assistance not too dissimilar to the Nixon/Guam Doctrine. The important difference, however, was that this doctrine was active rather than passive and reactive. In its strongest form, the doctrine provided that the USA would give support (chiefly in the form of arms and other supplies) to anti-Marxist insurgencies (G. Schultz, 1985, 1986) around the world. This doctrine gradually became one of the major elements of the Reagan administration's foreign policy (Rosenfeld, 1986, 698; Copson and Cronin, 1987, 41).[1]

The genesis of the doctrine lay in a particular understanding of international events since the Vietnam War. Just as John F. Kennedy had been a generation earlier, policymakers were worried about Soviet advances in the Third World. As explained by Fred Ikle, Reagan's Undersecretary of Defense for Policy, the Soviet Union was both the inspiration and the guiding hand behind most of the terrorist and insurgent movements in the world:

> There is a driving organization behind it all: here it stirs up and feeds an insurgency, there it exploits a coup d'etat, here it instigates terrorism to weaken a democratic government. ... Two steps forward, one step back it diligently, relentlessly expands its dominance throughout the world.

> We in the West thought that the Atlantic Alliance had checkmated Soviet expansion of the Cold War period. But ... the Cold War was followed by insurgency warfare and other small-scale warfare in many regions. (Ikle, 1986)

Still, there was a brighter side to this analysis. It could, by the early 1980s, be argued that containment had succeeded as a policy. The Soviet Union had been unable to expand its perimeter either in Europe or in Asia. What successes the USSR had seen were in the Third World and of dubious value. However, like Kennedy in 1961, Reagan officials and sympathizers wanted a new, active policy of rollback to reverse Soviet gains. This policy had its roots in the foreign-policy defeats of the Carter administration, in particular the hostage crisis of 1979–80 and the 1979 Soviet invasion of Afghanistan. The threat posed by these reverses was a central concern of the newly elected President. To a large extent, the Republican victory in 1980 was seen as both a product of these foreign-policy defeats and a mandate for a more active foreign policy (Podheretz, 1981, 29, 34; Kegley and Wittkopf, 1982).

This interpretation of events was reinforced by another trend some commentators saw developing during the 1980s, the 'democratic revolution'. This was the belief that a resurgence of faith in Western-style democracy was becoming widespread in the Third World with a consequent rejection of Marxism. This in turn suggested that the time was right for a rollback of Soviet gains in the developing countries (Ledeen, 1985; G. Schultz, 1985; Silber, 1984). The question of aid to anti-Marxist insurgencies was a heavily debated issue.

Arguing in favor of support, former United Nations Ambassador Jeane J. Kirkpatrick explicitly identified the locations of these insurgencies (Cambodia, Mozambique, Angola, Ethiopia, Nicaragua and Afghanistan) and typed them as 'recent acquisitions' (post-1975) to the 'Soviet orbit' (Kirkpatrick, 1985, 555). The policy aimed at aiding existing insurgent movements, not at creating them. Kirkpatrick also specified that the policy would mean 'arms, training and transport' but not the use of US troops (ibid., 556). The implication was that the USA would 'break faith' and abandon a failing insurgency rather than support it through direct, armed intervention. As would be seen, however, it was precisely this need to keep faith with failing US-supported insurgency which was invoked to continue aid to the democratic resistance ('Contra') forces in Nicaragua two years later (US Congress, Joint Session, 1987, 191–4; also Felton, 1988, 3189).

By the beginning of President Reagan's second term, 'rollback', described as support for anti-communist insurgencies, was a major theme in foreign policy rhetoric. In the President's second inaugural address only one other foreign policy theme was mentioned, the Strategic Defense Initiative (SDI). The 1985 State of the Union address was even more explicit: 'we must not break faith with those who are risking their lives – on every continent, from Afghanistan to Nicaragua – to defy Soviet-sponsored aggression and secure rights which have been ours from birth' (US President, 1985).

Although support for anti-communist insurgencies was only one element of military low-intensity conflict doctrine, during the Reagan years it was certainly the most emphasized. It was also the most controversial aspect, since it clearly implied that the USA would seek the overthrow of sovereign governments. Previously, this kind of activity had been very limited and attempted (as in Iran and Guatemala) by the CIA through selective support of elite rivals to the faction in power, 'coups d'etat' if you will.

The kind of revolutionary support being contemplated by the Reagan government was pretty much absent from military doctrine and no one at the Pentagon was exactly sure of how to go about it. The whole notion of clandestine and/or covert warfare was far from the Napoleonic tradition or the principles of Karl von Clausewitz taught in military schools and colleges. Even within the special-operations community, this form of insurgency support was quite different from the traditional, OSS, World War II-bred notion of supporting partisans against an occupying power.

Rhetoric aside, Reagan policymakers were cautious to the point of outright reluctance in actually providing support to Third World anti-Marxist insurgencies. Of the four such movements consistently supported during this period, only the Nicaraguan Democratic Resistance ('Contras') was strongly backed by the administration. The policy of covert aid to the Afghan Mujahadeen was authored by the Carter government and extended by the Congress without executive initiative under Reagan. Congressional conservatives in both houses pressured the administration for support to the National Union for Total Independence of Angola for three years before assistance finally began in early 1986. Congressman Stephen Solarz (D-NY) was the prime mover in gaining aid for the non-communist insurgents in Cambodia (Ottaway, 1987, 4).

Among national-security scholars and military specialists the general critique of special operations and low-intensity conflict continued but was much muted from the level of the 1970s. Most criticism was based on the belief that unconventional involvements contributed little to US national security (Prados, 1986). But among some scholars and defense-establishment intellectuals there was a growing enthusiasm for Special Operations Forces as an instrument of national policy (Shackley, 1983; Kupperman and Taylor, 1985; Sarkesian, 1986a). However, much of this enthusiasm was principally for corps d'elite on the Ranger model (Thomas, 1985; Sarkesian, 1986b; Vlahos, 1987), including one book by a former Colonel of the 5th SFG, Charles Simpson (1983).

In January 1986, the Secretary of Defense, Caspar Weinberger, sponsored a Low-Intensity Warfare Conference (US Department of Defense 1986). This meeting called together both civilian and military specialists in the field including Sarkesian and Kupperman. The participants ignored insurgent support almost entirely and focused heavily on two other aspects of LIC, counterinsurgency and counterterrorism. Here, Secretary Weinberger implied that the US armed forces were the central actors in US counterinsurgency, explicitly naming 'Army special forces' as the primary operating element because of their role as trainers (ibid., 7). The conference was remarkable in that nothing offered there was a significant advance on the unconventional warfare proposals of the 1960s. Indeed, one primary speaker, Sir Robert Thompson, essentially repeated the same advice he had offered 20 years earlier while advising US officials in Vietnam (ibid., 74–88).

The Army showed few signs that it shared the administration's enthusiasm for these types of conflict.

ARMY DOCTRINE AND FORCES FOR LOW-INTENSITY CONFLICT
IN THE 1980S

In a 1980 White Paper, Army Chief of Staff Edward C. Meyer wrote that: 'The most demanding challenge confronting the US military in the 1980s is to develop and demonstrate the capability to success-fully meet threats to vital US interests outside Europe, without compromising the decisive theater in Central Europe' (Meyer, 1980, 1). Despite this challenge, the early 1980s doctrine for non-European threats, conventional or unconventional, was virtually stagnant, unchanged since the counterinsurgency era of the 1960s. Army FM 100-20, *Low Intensity Conflict*, was the first military manual dedicated to the subject. However, most of the new manual was no more than a combination of two Vietnam-era manuals, the 1967 *Counterguerrilla Operations* (DA FM 31-16, 1967) and 1972's *Stability Operations* (DA FM 31-23, 1972). It carried forward the Vietnam-era collapse of LIC into counterinsurgency and the accom-panying collapse of counterinsurgency into conventional light-infantry operations with the cosmetic addition of 'Civil Affairs'. That is, LIC was recategorized as counterinsurgency, which was reduced to counterguerrilla warfare, which in turn was characterized as con-ventional light-infantry operations. The manual emphasized 'such offensive tactics as reconnaissance-in-force, raids, movement to contact, hasty or deliberate attacks, and exploitation and pursuit' (DA FM 100-20, 1981, 81), all standard, conventional infantry tactics. Despite the failure of 'sweep-and-clear'/'search-and-destroy' methods in Vietnam fourteen years earlier, special stress was placed on the 'strike campaign' – 'a series of major combat operations targeted against insurgent tactical forces in contested or insurgent controlled zones' (ibid., 204) and 'cordon and search' operations (ibid., 180–9).[2]

At the US Army Command and General Staff College in 1981, LIC 'barely kept its foot in the door' with an eight-hour 'familiari-zation' block, of which one hour was devoted to counterinsurgency and two to counterterrorism. The remainder dealt with small scale conventional warfare (Pearlman, 1990).

THE LIGHT INFANTRY DIVISION

The first US military unit to be created with a specific capability in 'low-intensity conflict' (labeled as such) was not a special operations unit at all. Instead, it was a thoroughly conventional organization, the Army's Light Infantry Division. Nevertheless, it is another illustration of the same phenomena that saw World War II and Korea ranger-style units and later special operations units metamorphize into more or less standard, conventional units.[3]

In order to support AirLand Battle doctrine during the early 1980s, the Army reorganized its fighting components under the Division '86 concept ('Force Modernization 86/90', 1982). The world-wide reorganization was not hindered in the least by the fact that AirLand Battle was designed specifically for a single enemy in a single environment – the USSR and the Warsaw Pact in Europe. The reorganization called for the addition of armored vehicles and artillery to existing divisions to enable them to meet the mobility and firepower demands of AirLand doctrine.

The spirit of Creighton Abrams was evident in these new formations. In essence, armored divisions (those consisting primarily of tanks) received more tanks, artillery and mechanized infantry, while infantry divisions became mechanized infantry divisions through the addition of more tanks, new armored personnel carriers, and more artillery. The only substantial difference between the new armor and mechanized infantry divisions was the mix of forces: an armor division contained six tank battalions and four mechanized infantry battalions; a mechanized infantry division contained five tank battalions and five mechanized infantry battalions (Wickham 1984, 307).

The principal exceptions were three 'standard' infantry divisions and two special purpose divisions. The two special purpose divisions were the 82nd Airborne Division at Fort Bragg, North Carolina, a parachute infantry unit, and the 101st Airborne Division (Air Assault) at Fort Campbell, Kentucky, the Army's high-tech helicopter-borne infantry unit. 'Special purpose', however, meant 'special' within the context of AirLand Battle Doctrine. In fact, according to DA FM 90-4, *Air Assault Operations*, the value of such a special purpose unit was that it could 'dramatically extend a commander's area of operation, enabling him to execute AirLand Battle Doctrine' beyond the battlefield reach of other forces (DA FM 90-4, 1987, 1–4).

Recognizing that this created a very uniform fighting force, specialized for mid-to-high intensity, conventional warfare in Central Europe, the Army, on 21 October 1983, approved the concept for a new 10,000-man Light Infantry Division (LID) (Wickham, 1983). Unlike the issue of unconventional warfare, which had remained at a continual if ineffective simmer in the professional literature, there had been no special concern with the standard, conventional division structure. There certainly had been no grass-roots call within the Army to organize new, lighter units. In fact, a review of the most widely read professional publications, *Army* and *Military Review*, from 1980 through 1983 reveals no article on the subject.

A standard infantry division of the period had a strength of about 18,000 men, 84 percent of whom were in supporting roles. Only 16 percent actually conducted direct combat (US Congress, House, 1984, 348). Unlike the Division '86 units, the LID was conceived as a 'hard-hitting, light infantry force' of 10,000 soldiers with a 32 percent fighting strength (ibid., 306, 348). This was to be achieved by removing much of the unit's combat power (armor and artillery), and most of its transport capability (trucks, armored personnel carriers and aircraft). During the period 1985–86, one existing infantry division (the 7th Infantry at Fort Ord, California) was to become a LID, while another new LID (the 10th Division at Fort Drum, New York) was to be organized with personnel taken from existing units (US Congress, House, 1984, 307, 348–9, 403). A third LID was later created by redesignating the 172nd Infantry Brigade in Alaska as the 6th Infantry Division.

The newly designed divisions encountered problems from the very first. What emerged was an uneasy coexistence of roles (low-intensity versus mid-to-high intensity) with a distinct trend toward mid-intensity. As originally conceived, the LIDs would not be sent to high-threat areas. Although a convenient notion, this restriction could not be met in practice. The tactical environment in which the LID was to function simply did not exist in the modern world. There were no lightly armed, largely immobile enemies which the USA could reasonably expect to meet in conventional battle. Even major Third World armies such as North Korea's could field stronger, faster moving units than the LID. As one senior Army officer put it, 'There is hardly a contingency demanding LIC anymore. The forces [armies of probable adversaries] out there are just too big' (Barry and Thomas, 1989, 26).

However, given the generally Eurocentric focus of Army thinking, it was not surprising that their possible use in high-intensity Central European scenarios became an early consideration. This consideration drove further changes in structure and organization (US Congress, House, 1984, 392, 403). An initial decision was made that the 7th Division, although converted to a light division, would retain its tank and mechanized infantry battalions 'as nondivisional units that would be available to reinforce light divisions deploying to high-threat areas' (US DOD, 1984, 119). The 9th Division at Fort Lewis, Washington, was also to be considered a light division but, like the 7th, retained its heavy elements. Furthermore, the 9th was designated a 'High Technology Test Bed' to 'examine additional ways to improve the deployability and capability of our light forces' (ibid., 120). In practice, this meant discovering ways for the LIDs to survive on the mid-to-high-intensity battlefields of the real world.

By the time the LID concept was formally presented to Congress (US Congress, House, 1984) and to the Army (Wickham, 1984) the rationale for the light divisions had undergone significant change. Now their suitability for low-intensity conflict was a side issue. Instead the chief selling-point was their potential for rapid strategic deployability. The new LID could be deployed overseas entirely by air in four days with 478 sorties, as opposed to 11 days and 1,273 sorties required for the pre-LID infantry division (US Congress, House, 1984, 349). By contrast, the Division '86 armor divisions would require at least 30 days for overseas deployment, and use both air and sealift for their heavier equipment.[4]

The problem was that the new units really were far more readily deployable than other conventional formations. This was not lost on Army planners, who saw this rapid deployability as a strategic asset for the European, conventional-war scenarios that were the heart of the Army's mission (Petraeus, 1984, 36; Killebrew, 1985, 15). The fact that this would toss the light divisions into exactly the environment they were emphatically not designed for was not a consideration.

The Army Field Circular (FC) issued on Light Infantry Division Operations did not concern itself with the LIC environment, but instead stressed the capability to support heavier conventional formations (FC 71-101, 1984). At planning conferences, operations officers and logisticians began to complain that the new units would be unable to support themselves administratively or logistically, placing a further drain on already strained support from higher-echelon organizations. These problems and the possibility of combat in Europe required expansion of the LIDs, adding an air-defense capability and additional administrative and logistic support ('Light Division Gains Weight', 1984, 8).

By 1985 the LIDs had lost much of their identity, not merely as low-intensity forces, but even, to some degree, as light infantry. This tendency was not lost on the Army. Concern was raised privately among officers and publicly in the professional press but without any noticeable impact on the trend of events (Olson, 1985; Huddleston, 1985; Kafkalas, 1986). At the same time, some writers advocated further enlarging the LIDs to 14,000 troops with additional ground transport, aircraft and artillery (for example, Menser 1987, 53). This would have come close to restoring the old 'straight-leg' conventional infantry division.

In retrospect, it is somewhat amazing that any professional concern was raised by the apparent loss of focus on the LIC mission. The LID was created, not for a strategic requirement or a specific mission, but rather for a very narrow and restrictive capability – rapid strategic deployability. By the time the initiative was formally presented, the LIC capability had already become an afterthought, and was never officially presented as the principal rationale for the new units. Although official publications dealing with light divisions almost invariably listed LIC as one use of the unit's capabilities, strategic deployability in advance of or in support of heavier conventional units was always presented as their featured role.

By 1988, budget cuts had come into force. As explained by Secretary of Defense Frank C. Carlucci: 'Our force structure reductions have been carefully focused. Reductions have not been made in our heavy armored or mechanized forces, those that would bear the brunt of any conflict with the Warsaw pact or a comparably equipped opponent. We have instead made reductions in light infantry formations' (US Secretary of Defense, 1988, 183).

In April 1989, it was announced that the 9th Division would be reorganized again, this time as a Division '86-style mechanized unit. Budget constraints dictated that the 6th Division remain at brigade strength, although with a division-sized headquarters (Adelsberger, 1989, 15), In 1992 the 7th Infantry Division was eliminated. This left the 10th Mountain at Fort Drum, New York, a two-brigade 'roundout' division, as the Army's single remaining light division.

The brief history of the Light Infantry Division seemed to have ended; but the 10th would find itself busy indeed.

THE SPECIAL OPERATIONS REVIVAL

1980–84

The events of 1980–81, especially the highly critical Holloway report on the Iran hostage crisis, convinced Army Chief of Staff Gen. Edward C. ['Shy'] Meyer that the Central European focus of the

Army's doctrine and operational planning was too narrow. Like Maxwell Taylor in the late 1950s, he believed that there was need for a more flexible Army capable of a greater range of responses (Meyer, 1980). To develop this increased range of response would require a much greater special-operations capability than existed at that time. Col. Rod Paschall was Chief of Combat Developments at the Special Warfare Center from 1982 through 1984, when these issues were being raised. As related by Paschall, Meyer and the Special Forces officers with whom he consulted (including Paschall) made a deliberate decision not to repeat the mistake of 1960s; they wanted to ensure that Special Forces was 'really a part of the Army' (Paschall, 1989).

Their response was conditioned by two factors: the focus of the Army was on the conventional battlefield, especially the European/ NATO battlefield, and the anticipated short duration of such a war meant that there would be little opportunity for the development of unconventional warfare (UW) in the form of guerrilla operations (Paschall, 1989; Simpson, 1983, 223). The logical outcome was that being a part of the Army meant to do what the Army does: wage conventional warfare. For Special Forces to prosper as an organization and a capability it had to make itself useful within AirLand Battle Doctrine.

Although terrorism was the focus of much of President Reagan's rhetoric, little substantial was done, beyond the continued development of Special Forces Operational Detachment (SFOD)-Delta as a counterterrorist, essentially counterhijacking, unit. Delta also began to lose its character as a Special Forces unit to become a special purpose one-of-a-kind organization. During 1980 and 1981, Colonel Paschall, then Delta's commander, also took specific steps to divest Delta of any domestic counterterrorist role by working with the FBI to train bureau agents in counterterrorist tactics and techniques (Paschall, 1989).

The Reagan Doctrine seemed to hold real promise for the development of special ops since Special Operations Forces were seen as the logical military instrument in the administration's effort to achieve a 'roll back', through military or paramilitary means – insurgency, counterinsurgency and counterterrorism, all forms of unconventional warfare as defined in this book (US Congress, House, 1983, 2, 25 [HR2287]). The principal Special Operations Force remained the Army's Special Forces. However, by this point the USA's unconventional warfare capability had 'dwindled to almost nothing' (US Congress, House, 1985, 3 [HR2287]). As described by Colonel Simpson (*c.* 1982):

... the vast majority of officers and NCOs with SF experience and know-how have fled into retirement or the conventional Army. There is a pervading dearth of maturity and experience ... The A Detachments consist primarily of E-3s [privates first class] and E-4s [corporals], some commanded by second lieutenants. There are some experienced NCOs in the A Detachments, though too little detachment training to compensate for inexperience takes place. When there is a mission, they scrape together what experienced personnel there are and send them off, thus wearing out the old hands and leaving the newer soldiers still not fully trained or experienced. (1983, 219)

The preferred solution to these problems within Special Forces was to expand the organization and gather more resources rather than make the kinds of quality upgrades Simpson's analysis seemed to call for (see, for example, testimony in US Congress, House, 1983, 1–76 [HR2287]). Despite the 'reemphasis' of LIC and Special Operations, by 1983 the entire US Army active-duty Special Forces still numbered only 3,900 personnel (US Congress, House, 1985, 4, [HR2287]), an increase of about 900 since the all-time low point in 1974. Nevertheless, major increases were hard to justify in view of the missions then potentially available to special forces. Even in the extraordinarily unlikely event that unconventional operations were launched in all of the available areas (Cambodia, Afghanistan, Nicaragua, El Salvador, Peru, Angola, the Philippines and Lebanon), that, plus Delta's counterterrorist mission, still would not justify the increase of 6,200 men sought by the Army in 1985 (Defense Monitor, 1985, 5). Increases of this magnitude were, however, necessary if SF was to become an active player on the conventional AirLand battlefield.

In 1983 testimony, Maj. Gen. Robert L. Schweitzer, the Army's senior strategist and planner, was very critical of the state of SOF, especially Army Special Forces. He maintained that SF organization and doctrine suffered from '... seeming lack of focus, lowered resource priorities, lack of national and congressional support and resulting losses in overall Special Forces capability.' Schweitzer attributed this to a 'preoccupation with high-intensity war scenarios' at the Army planning level (US Congress, House, 1983, 31 [HR2287]).[5]

There was also overall indifference within the armed services. The military services, especially the Army and Air Force, retained their traditional close focus on the Soviet conventional threat in Europe (US Congress, House, 1983, testimony by Starry, 1815–28). The Navy, never an important player in the unconventional-warfare and special-operations arena, maintained a handful of SEALS, but concentrated its organizational attention on the goal of a 600-ship conventional fleet (US Congress, House, 1984, 488).

To comply with the SOF-revitalization policies the 1st Special Operations Command (SOCOM) was created as a provisional unit within the US Army on 1 October 1982. SOCOM was not an operational headquarters in the sense of commanding units in the field. Rather it was charged with the responsibility of developing means to respond to various military threats and challenges. This was a training and support mission. SOCOM's mission was to prepare, provide and sustain Army Special Operations Forces as they conducted foreign internal defense, unconventional warfare, strategic intelligence, psychological operations, Ranger operations, strike operations, and other special operations as designated by national command authority. However, the actual operational control of the SOF units lay with the theater CINCs, those regional Commanders-in-Chief in whose theater the SOF would operate. The organizational components of SOCOM were: three Special Forces Groups, two Ranger battalions, a Psychological Operations Group (POG), and a Civil Affairs Battalion.[6]

A glimpse of the new command's mind-set was gained by two puzzling initiatives: (1) the attempt to rid itself of the Psyops and Civil Affairs units, and (2) the inclusion of the conventionally trained and organized but highly regarded Ranger battalions as special-operations units.

Psyops, rather than being a primary role for special-operations officers, was designated as a secondary skill, not necessarily related to the core missions of special-operations units (Howard, 1988, 18). In general, Psyops had not enjoyed a high priority in either conventional or unconventional operations, despite increased emphasis under the Reagan government. Application of these methods was usually an afterthought and often slighted (Paddock, 1984, 231–51; McEwen, 1986, 59–67; Stillwell, 1987, 5–6). Within the special operations community it was felt that: 'PsyOps and CA [Civil Affairs] have long been incorrectly associated with special operations because of the existing command relationship that places PsyOps and CA units under the ... Special Operations Command at Fort Bragg, North Carolina. Although ... PsyOps, CA, and Special Operations are often mutually supportive, it is also true that PsyOps and CA missions ... are supportive of a vast array of national policy objectives and military operations' (Howard, 1988, 6). It might also be suspected that the non-commando parts of special operations – Psyops and Civil Affairs – looked too much like combat-support functions to be part of the 'real' special operations community. The Rangers, on the other hand, were a highly prestigious organization, respected throughout the Army as the best US fighting organization. In addition, they were devoid of the suspect 'covert' and unconventional associations which hurt Special Forces units in the eyes of the Army hierarchy. However, their training, equipment, organization and doctrine was thoroughly conventional with little hint of any special or unconventional capability. The Rangers, as a general purpose raiding and reconnaissance force, also fit neatly into the AirLand Battle Doctrine. In fact, the Ranger operation manual stressed the use of AirLand Battle Doctrine and the importance of Ranger units as an asset on the AirLand Battlefield (DA FM 7-85, 1987, 1–3).[7]

Early in 1983, Noel Koch, the Principal Deputy Undersecretary of Defense for International Security Affairs (the chief civilian official responsible for special operations and counterterrorism), briefed the Secretary of Defense on problems in national-policy level command and control arrangements for special operations. The Secretary asked Koch to brief the Joint Chiefs of Staff, formulate a unified plan of action, and return to him for implementation. In March 1983 Koch began his attempt to schedule such a briefing. According to Koch, his office contacted the Office of the Joint Chiefs of Staff (OJCS) weekly through March and April.

In April, the US Embassy in Beirut was destroyed by a terrorist bomb, underscoring the urgency of the problem. Finally, in August, the OJCS responded that, while they agreed on the critical nature of the briefing, there had been personnel changes including a new Director of the Joint Staff. Therefore it would be necessary to brief them first, before briefing the Chiefs themselves. Convinced that the Joint Chiefs were stonewalling, Koch began a separate initiative to establish a Joint Special Operations Agency within the Department Of Defense (Koch, 1986).

In April 1983, Congress began to take an active, overt role in the special operations issue when the House Armed Services Committee held hearings on the decline of special operations capability (US Congress, House, 1983 [HR2287]). Based on the results of those hearings, Congress initiated its program for the revitalization of US special-operations capability. The services quickly countered by initiating a number of impressive but superficial organizational changes. At the joint service, Defense Department level, the Joint Special Operations Command (JSOC) was established and given specific responsibility for low-intensity conflict, with special emphasis on terrorism. JSOC was a purely administrative and 'coordinating' organization; it had no forces assigned, no command authority, and no input to DOD's budget process.

The response of the services to Congress's attention remained sluggish at best, especially in funding special-operations units. Because the funding for these units was dispersed through numerous appropriations accounts throughout the budgets of the military services and defense agencies, the House Committee on Appropriations directed in 1983 that a separate 'special operations' budget estimate be prepared by DOD. That estimate, called Program 11, was to consolidate the funding and program descriptions of all DOD special-operations activities (US Congress, House, 1983, 786).

The Army slowly continued to 'revitalize' its SOF, largely by creating headquarters and redesignating existing units. The 1st Special Operations Command lost its provisional status and became a permanent organization. The school at Fort Bragg underwent yet another name change, from the US Army Institute for Military Assistance to the John F. Kennedy Special Warfare Center and School. A fourth, reduced strength, Special Forces Group was created at Fort Lewis, Washington by drawing from existing SF units. The 160th Aviation Battalion of the 101st Airborne Division (Air Assault) at Fort Campbell, Kentucky was redesignated Task Force 160, a special-operations aviation asset but remaining part of the conventional division. The announced (1983) goal for Army Special Forces was a total of 5,000 active duty personnel by 1990 (US Congress, House, 1983, 12 [HR 2287]). For its part, the Air Force established the 23rd Air Force. Similar in concept to the Army's SOCOM, it took responsibility for all US Air Force special-operations aviation and, oddly, all Air Force combat-rescue units.[8]

On 3 October 1983 the Office of the Secretary of Defense (OSD) issued a memorandum to the service secretaries, the JCS, and the directors of the defense agencies directing that special-operations revitalization be pursued as 'a matter of national urgency'. The memorandum directed four basic revitalization steps:

1. Force structure expansion, command and control enhancements and improvements in personnel policy should be 'implemented as rapidly as possible' and no later than the end of fiscal 1990.
2. Support activities should be enhanced to provide 'fully effective support'.
3. SOF and 'related activities' should be assigned 'sufficient resource allocation priority'.

4. Neither OSD nor Service staffs were to change or reduce 'current or programmed' 'resource decisions' unless approved by the Secretary of Defense (OSD, 1983).

On 19 October 1983 the JCS notified the Secretary of Defense that they had directed the establishment of a Joint Special Operations Agency (JSOA) at the national command level (i.e. JCS level). This was to be established by 1 January 1984 and 'fully manned and operational' by the end of fiscal 1984 (Rice, 1984, 799). It would be responsible for the coordination of multi-service special-operations doctrine and training but have no forces assigned, no administrative control of SOF units, no command authority, and no role in the DOD budget process (Surveys and Investigations Staff, 1986, 73). The new agency was established on schedule with this mission statement:

> advise the Joint Chiefs of Staff in all matters pertaining to special operations ... including national strategy, planning, programming, budgeting, resource development and allocation, joint doctrinal guidance, exercise and readiness evaluation and employment of forces. (JSOA, 1983)

It was at about this time that a note was passed from a Joint Staff Lieutenant General to a Colonel who had been particularly active in promoting special-operations revitalization initiatives. 'If you keep on with this', the note read, 'your next billet will be in a Dempsey Dumpster.' This was not a threat, simply well-meant advice. As a measure of JCS's attitude toward JSOA, it should be noted that the first director was a Marine Corps general officer, despite the fact that the Marines had no special-operations forces.

On 23 October another 'low-intensity' disaster occurred, this time in Lebanon. Two hundred and forty-one US Marines died when a terrorist drove a truckload of explosives into their Beirut barracks. The Marines had been in Lebanon as part of a US-sponsored international peacekeeping mission. The Long Commission, established to investigate the Beirut bombing, came to the general conclusion that the military is 'inadequately prepared to deal with this threat' (i.e. state-supported terrorism).

Koch still had not given his briefing to the Joint Chiefs. He states that, when approached on the topic, the Director of the Joint Staff replied, 'Well, you know, terrorism is an easy thing to ignore.' In regards to the SOF initiative, Koch quotes the Director as saying, 'You guys think you can tell people what to do, but if they don't want to do it, they're not going to do it' (US Congress, Committee on Armed Services 1988, 1987). Finally Koch resigned in protest.

The Defense Department's new Assistant Secretary of Defense for International Security Affairs (ASD–ISA), Richard Armitage, took charge of the DOD's SF-revitalization effort. Rather than implementing the expressed desire of Congress, his office began a declaratory policy supporting SOF improvement and change while at the same time promoting a *de facto* policy blocking any substantive change (Kief, 1987, 552).

The invasion of Grenada

Later the same month, US forces landed on the Caribbean island of Grenada as part of Operation 'Urgent Fury', characterized as an 'LIC-oriented operation' (Crouch, 1988, 20). The first units ashore were SOF, including Navy SEALs and Delta operators, while Army Rangers seized the island's major airfield. Gen. John A. Wickham Jr, Army Chief of Staff reported that 'Urgent Fury was an unqualified success' and 'Army doctrine is sound' (Wickham, 1984, 1).

However, the 'unqualified success' soon came under Congressional scrutiny. During planning for the operation, JSOC had argued that SOF, including Air Force special ops C-130 gunships and Army Rangers, should spearhead the invasion (J. Adams, 1987, 231). In the actual planning, SOF were given seven missions:

1. SEAL Team 6 would recon the Port Salinas Airfield.
2. SEAL Team 4 would recon landing beaches for the Marines.
3. Elements of the 1st and 2nd Ranger Battalions would parachute in to seize and hold the airfield.
4. Fire support would be provided by AC-130 gunships from the Air Force 16th Squadron of the 1st Special Operations Wing at Hurlburt Field, Florida.

Simultaneously:

5. A special composite SEAL platoon would rescue the British Governor General, Sir Paul Scoon, being held at his official residence by Grenadan soldiers.
6. A team of sixteen SEALs were to attack and disable the Grenadan government radio transmitter without destroying it.
7. A squadron from Delta would assault the Richmond Hill prison in order to free political prisoners held there. They would be

supported by four UH60 helicopters flown by Task Force 160
and a detachment of Rangers.

(Center for Military History, 1984, 90–5; USAWC, 1993, 32–3.) There
were immediate problems when the first element of SEAL Team 6
parachuted into high winds and heavy seas from a C-141 jet
transport at about 2 a.m. They vanished and were never found. The
second element started for shore in their rubber raiding craft but
were swept out to sea when high waves drowned the boat's outboard
motor. They were rescued without having reached their objective.
This left JSOC blind, without current information on the condition
of the airfield and, most importantly, on the state of its defenses. The
Air Force 1st Special Operations Wing was able to make a dangerous
pre-dawn run over the Port Salinas airport, using a Combat Talon
C-130 with low-light TV, to find that the runways had been blocked.

The only special operation that went off on schedule was the
SEAL beach reconnaissance. Approaching from the water, the team
was able to warn the waiting Marines of dangerous surf conditions
and observe the Grenadans preparing beach defenses. The other
missions suffered a series of delays, owing in part to the time required
to ready the Task Force 160 helicopters at Grantley Adams Airport
on Barbados. The cumulative effect of the delays was to rob the
special-ops forces of all tactical surprise and most of the cover of
darkness.

The lead aircraft for the Ranger airdrop experienced instrument
problems, delaying its arrival at the island (USAWC, 1993, 40). The
Rangers were already airborne, prepared to airland, rather than
deploy by parachute. The news of the blocked runway forced them
to re-rig in mid-flight for a parachute assault, further delaying their
landing time. The lack of good reconnaissance became painful when
the MC-130s carrying the Rangers of 1st Battalion, 75th Infantry
began their jump run over the airfield. The Cuban and Grenadan
troops surprised them with a hail of antiaircraft fire, causing the first
aircraft to abort its drop. Only one of the aircraft carrying the Rangers
was able to make its drop on the first pass (USAWC, 1993, 21–2).

By great good luck the anti-aircraft guns were poorly sited and
could not depress to hit targets below 500 feet altitude. The Rangers
made the dangerous decision to jump from 500 feet rather than the
usual 1,200, placing the planes beneath the heaviest enemy fire
(Bolger, 1988, 305–6; AWC, 1993, 22). The need for a second pass
caused confusion and some disorder on the ground when the aircraft
carrying the 1st Battalion became mixed with those carrying the 2nd
Battalion, 75th Infantry (USAWC, 1993, 22).

The SEAL raid against the government radio station went fairly well at first. Landing in their rubber raiding craft, the SEALs were able to take the transmitter off the air but not before an initial warning had been broadcast alerting the island and calling out the Grenadan militia (O'Shaughantesy, 1984, 202). The alerted militia arrived and succeeded in driving the tiny SEAL force from the radio station. Finally, an AC-130 gunship had to finish the job by destroying the site (USAWC, 1993, 41).

The other two raids had even less good luck. The Delta assault on the Richmond Prison went very badly, arriving late, about 6.15 a.m. against a fully alert opposition. The attackers caught heavy fire as their helicopters approached and several operators were pinned down after they rappeled to the ground. Delta suffered 'heavy casualties' and the attack was repulsed. At least one transport helicopter was knocked from the sky and by some accounts two attack helicopters also went down (AWC, 1993, 40).

Two SEAL teams managed to reach Governor General Scoon's residence and secure the building but they were quickly trapped inside by the arrival of a mixed unit of Cubans and Grenadans with a BTR-60 armored personnel carrier. The SEALs were supported by conventional attack helicopters for several hours until the arrival of Marine ground units saved the situation.

By 27 October, one of the Rangers' initial objectives, Calvigny barracks, still had not been taken and a helicopter-borne attack was undertaken by the 2nd Battalion and reinforced by C Company of the 1st Battalion. The planned Landing Zone turned out to be too small and alternates were hurriedly selected. All four UH-60s landed safely near the camp, but then enemy rifle fire wounded one pilot and damaged his helicopter's rotor system. The machine spun into the ground, smashing into a second helicopter and the nearby Rangers. The crew in the following Black Hawk veered their aircraft hard right, landing in a ditch and damaging the machine's tail rotor. Apparently not realizing that the helicopter's rotor was damaged, the pilot attempted to move the Black Hawk, which rose sharply, seemed to spin forward, and slowly crashed to the ground. In twenty seconds three machines were down. Debris and rotor blades flew through the air, killing three Rangers, severely wounding four and injuring a dozen others. These were the only deaths in the 2nd Battalion. When the soldiers swept through the barracks they found them deserted. 'Given the confused, tragic initial helicopter insertion, the Rangers were fortunate there was no real resistance' (Bolger, 1988, 342–3).

Civil Affairs in Grenada

The conflict lasted eight days, however, that was not the end of the operation. The post-conflict restoration continued for another 18 months. This was the department of Civil Affairs units but there were problems there as well. On 28 October the first elements of the only active Civil Affairs battalion, the 96th, arrived in Grenada and were immediately confronted with property control problems, dislocated persons and the problems of restoring public utilities.

This was a big operation and the tiny active duty CA structure simply could not support a civil military-action program of this size. Accordingly a reserve organization, the 42nd Civil Affairs Company from Fort Gordon, Georgia, was called to active duty and arrived during the second month of the deployment. Organized along functional teams, the Civil Affairs units had mixed success. While the CA provided outstanding staff guidance and planning, it lacked the assets to carry out what it had planned. Combat soldiers had to be used (USSOCOM, 1996, 6).

Aftermath

Although the massive conventional airborne and amphibious assault quickly carried the island, the role of Special Operations Forces left something to be desired. Although the exact figures remain classified, estimates of casualties are that a small number of special operators were killed, perhaps six or eight, and 20 to 30 were wounded. Most casualties occurred in the Richmond Hill prison mission and the attempt to take the government radio station (Marquis, 1997, 105). Only the Rangers, executing a conventional assault with parachute and airlanded troops, accomplished their task in good time. None of the missions went well. There was too much confusion and delay and too many changes of plan. The Ranger leadership was chagrined when a significant number of their heavily laden soldiers went down from dehydration in the tropical heat; this was precisely the sort of thing that rigorous Ranger training and leadership were supposed to prevent (McConnell, 1991, 42).

Most of the testimony remains classified, but what became known publicly from the post-Grenada hearings of the House and Senate Armed Services was disturbing at the very least. The SEAL team casualties were publicized along with the slowness in accomplishing the stated purpose of the invasion, to rescue US citizens held on the island. Overall, it took the various US units involved two days to locate many of the US medical students whom the operation was intended to rescue.

As reported by one Senate staffer, the testimony 'revealed that the Grenada operation was badly mismanaged and may have involved unnecessary loss of life' (Mellon, 1989). Here again, the critics focused on issues of organization, equipment and military technique. As in the case of the Desert One failure, excess secrecy and poor interservice cooperation were identified as primary causes of the invasion's problems. These would have been much more serious in a longer campaign against a more sophisticated enemy (Duffy, 1985, 12; see also 'Grenada Invasion Units Listed', 1983).

For their part, the special operators were not inclined to accept all the blame for problems with their portion of the mission.

> Contrary to sound military judgment, the island was divided between Army and Marine forces, and the chain of command was altered to accommodate the Marine presence. The ensuing command and control problems led to disproportionate special operations' casualties, including four SEALs lost at sea [who were attempting to fill intelligence gaps the CIA could not provide] and seven, out of nine, special operations helicopters were badly damaged. Targets had been shifted to accommodate a growing number of conventional forces, and none had the opportunity to rehearse because of time constraints. (USSOCOM, 2socorg, 1996, 3)

In December 1983 one of the reforms suggested by the Holloway Commission Report was implemented by OSD in the form of the Special Operations Policy Advisory Group (SOPAG). A number of retired flag-rank officers (generals and admirals) were approached and several, including General Yarborough, agreed to serve as an advisory element. The intention was that this semi-formal group would provide 'a high level forum for advice on critical national policy issues focusing on special operations'. The group met on an 'irregular basis' throughout the 1980s but their deliberations remain classified (Mabry, 1990). The hidden agenda was that, by involving respected senior military officers in special-operations policy-making, service resistance to these units and operations would be mitigated (Koch, 1989, 57).

In his annual budget report to Congress for 1984, Secretary of Defense Caspar W. Weinberger alleged that the DOD had given a high priority to SOF revitalization which: 'reflects our recognition that low-level conflict – for which SOF's are uniquely suited – will pose the threat we are most likely to encounter throughout the end of the century' (US Secretary of Defense, 1984, 276). In November

1984, Weinberger promulgated his six tests for US military involvement abroad. As noted earlier, these 'tests' seem to announce a policy
in opposition to his own assessment of the low-intensity threat in
his 1985 budget report.

   This is important, since, as demonstrated, policymakers explicitly
characterized 'low-intensity' involvements as the most common and
likely ones. Furthermore, the 'six rules' implied that there was some
wide national understanding of what constituted 'vital interests'. A
dubious proposition at best. More important, it implied that if
political and military objectives could not be clearly defined there
would be no involvement. This provision alone might eliminate, or
at least severely constrain, US involvement in long-term or
ambiguous conflicts, allegedly the most common sort. The conflicts
loosely subsumed under 'low-intensity' conflict tend to feature
both of those characteristics. Also, the often covert and clandestine
nature of these involvements made it impossible to determine the
nature of US public sympathy on any particular involvement. These
rules specified a set of circumstances which were very unlikely to
occur simultaneously and, if they did occur, were even less likely to
be evident in time to allow for prompt, decisive action. As stated,
these 'rules' effectively eliminated any possibility of employing US
forces in LIC, especially unconventional warfare. The 'rules', then,
were either inapplicable or irrelevant.

   Meanwhile, on 3 October 1984 a third Ranger battalion, the
3rd of the 75th, was added to the Army's roster at Fort Benning,
Georgia.

1985–88

Between 1981 and 1985 SOF funding increased from $441 million
to $1.2 billion, while the number of active duty SOF personnel in
all services rose from 11,600 to 14,900 over the same period (Budahn,
19 August 1986). This funding and personnel augmentation did not,
however, translate into increased effectiveness. A study conducted
by the Army–Air Force Joint Low-Intensity Conflict Project in July
1985 called for a coherent strategy for 'low-intensity wars'. The
project concluded that an interservice effort was required, but 'that
partnership currently is detracted by inter- and intra-departmental
rivalry ... the battle for budgets and the differing military views of
what are the appropriate missions' (Joint LIC Report, 1985; also
Budahn, 3 October 1986, 12). Just as they had for the previous forty
years, events of the following years repeated that pattern. As a
measure of its commitment to SOF, the Air Force offered to cut 40

percent from its FY 85 SOF budget as part of its response to DOD's request for a 5 percent service-wide budget reduction (Logan, 1986, 17). For the same fiscal year the Military Airlift Command placed SOF airlift fifty-ninth on its list of priorities (US Congress, Senate, Congressional Record, 1986, 3). In January 1986, *Time* magazine reported that less than half the US SOF units (all services combined) had earned a DOD readiness rating of better than C3 (marginally ready) ('A Warrior Elite', 13 January 1986, 24).

As the largest SOF element, Army Special Forces became the centerpiece of the national special-operations effort (US Department of Defense, 1986, 6; US Congress, House, 1983, 25, HR2287). In 1985, a Ranger Regimental Headquarters was activated at Fort Benning, Georgia, and assigned to SOCOM apparently as an attempt to satisfy demands for SOF enhancement. Rangers were, after all, general-purpose troops on the conventional model who, nevertheless could still be accepted by most observers as 'special operations' units. Task Force 160 was transferred from the 101st Airborne Division to 1st SOCOM although the unit remained based at Fort Campbell, Kentucky.

Under SOCOM, the special-operations role was still conceived in terms of conventional military operations. Not surprisingly, 'military operations' in this context became operationalized as small-scale war or as counterinsurgency. Counterinsurgency once again was interpreted as counterguerrilla operations. In the words of Maj. Gen. Robert L. Schweitzer, Director of the Army's Strategic Plans and Policy Directorate, 'it is nonsense to say that there won't be a winner in a guerrilla war, [that] you cannot win a war against guerrillas. You can. But it takes training. The training has to come from people who are trained in how to organize guerrillas, because they can then best train how to counter guerrilla action' (ibid., 26). Here again was the Kennedy era counterinsurgency rationale. As with the 'offensive guerrilla warfare' operations of the Vietnam War Delta units, the essence of the 1980s approach was to take the war 'away from the guerrilla' by attacking them in their base camps 'away from the population centers', while at the same time pursuing a policy of civic action for village-level economic development (ibid., 26). This approach includes no explicit recognition that some political rationale (a 'cause' or at least a consensus) including political mobilization and organization must underlie these actions.

But, despite even this limited rhetorical position there was no concerted effort to field an integrated counterinsurgency effort incorporating civic action, Psyops, and foreign internal-defense efforts. No integrated counterinsurgency effort was proposed from within the services and none was demanded from the national-command level. No structure similar to Kennedy's Special Group, Counterinsurgency, was created to coordinate the various agencies involved and provide a focus for national-command authority-level interest in low-intensity conflict.

Instead, counterinsurgency was seen as essentially a matter of training the host nation's military establishment in counterguerrilla tactics (US Congress, House, 1983, 25–7 [HR2287]). However, as experience in Vietnam, Guatemala and El Salvador showed, the ability to defeat guerrillas in the field was not sufficient for successful counterinsurgency. The direct lesson was seldom articulated: that to defeat guerrillas is not to defeat an insurgency. The implied lesson, however, that successful counterinsurgency required a coordinated, interagency effort, had been taught over and over again. Despite this widespread recognition of the need, there was no success in implementing the lesson.

Special Forces training of the 1980s provoked a real sense of *déjà vu* as troopers at Fort Bragg continued to replicate World War II France in the pine woods of North Carolina. Training remained clearly centered on the OSS model of guerrilla partisan rather than revolutionary insurgent, counterterrorist, or counterinsurgent activities. During a 1986 interview, Maj. Alan Freiberg, officer in charge of basic skills training for Special Forces soldiers, stated, 'Unconventional guerrilla warfare is what we stress. Our men are taught to go into a small town or village, arm the civilians, train them and lead them on missions.' The 'missions' referred to were then described as 'guerrilla raids' (Schad, 1986, 14). The final training exercise, as described, was directly on the preferred model of unconventional warfare, where US SOF leads local-national guerrillas against occupying 'aggressors'. In fact, the US-led guerrillas were even described as 'partisans' (ibid., 16). Once again unconventional warfare was conceived of as simply an adjunct to conventional warfare. The implication running through doctrinal literature was that 'unconventional' meant little more than to operate without all the elaborate technology and supporting elements of the mainstream Army divisions.[9]

By 1985 it seemed as if none of the various name changes and new headquarters had added anything substantial to SOF capabilities. The *Wall Street Journal* reported that, during the 1985 *Achille Lauro* hijacking, US SOF were literally unable to get off the ground: 'The Air Force plane assigned to carry them wasn't in shape to leave the country. After trying three planes, the SEALs finally took off, but they arrived after the terrorists had left the hijacked cruise ship, ending the hostage rescue drama' (14 October 1985, 14). That same year, in January, the Army/Air Force Center for Low Intensity Conflict (CLIC) was activated at Langley Air Force Base, Virginia as a joint initiative of the two services. This small (27-person) program was charged with the vague mission to 'improve the Army/Air Force posture for engaging in low-intensity conflict' and 'elevate awareness ... of the role of the military power in low-intensity conflict' (Activation Plan, 1986, A-1). The organization's chief function was to develop and distribute a series of 'CLIC Papers' throughout the two services 'dedicated to the advancement of the art and science of the application of the military instrument of national power in the low intensity conflict environment' (CLIC, 1987). The organization came under fire from Army staffers almost at once and CLIC labored in obscurity until it was quietly disbanded in 1996.

In the 1986 version of their manual, JP 1-02, Unified Action Armed Forces, the Joint Chiefs of Staff tasked the military departments to prepare for 'the effective prosecution of war and military operations short of war', but failed to give any indication of how this might be done. Army doctrine for these 'environments' took a faltering step forward in 1986 when Congressional pressure spurred the Army's Training and Doctrine Command (TRADOC) to host a Joint Low-Intensity Conflict Project for the armed forces and several government agencies. The Project's final report concluded: 'As a nation we do not understand low-intensity conflict; we respond without unity of effort; we execute our activities poorly; and we lack the ability to sustain operations' (Hunt, 1996, 4).

TRADOC also produced a pamphlet titled 'US Army Operational Concept for Low-Intensity Conflict' that was all but ignored.

Congress, especially factions led by Sens. William Cohen (R-ME), Barry Goldwater (R-AZ), and Rep. Dan Daniels (D-VA), was also dissatisfied with these efforts and accordingly initiated a series of hearings in 1986. According to testimony before the Senate Committee on Armed Services, neither SOCOM nor JSOA had been able to achieve an effective integration of the various service elements or to reconcile their doctrine (US Congress, Senate, Congressional Record, 1986, 3).

In a letter to the Secretary of Defense in January 1986, Senators Goldwater and Sam Nunn (D-GA) set forth part of their findings: 'We are particularly concerned that six years after the tragedy at Desert One, we appear to have made few significant improvements in this [special operations] capability ... It is especially discouraging to note that today we have exactly the same number of MC-130

Combat Talon [special operations] aircraft ... as we had at Desert One, and two fewer HH-53 Pave Low [special operations] helicopters than we had in 1980 [seven today, compared with nine in 1980]' (Russell, April 1986, 41). Again, as with General Schwietzer and the Army command-level planners, the issue is framed in terms of numbers, amount of resources, as though these were an indicator of effectiveness. The deeper, more essential, and more difficult issues of leadership, planning, training and national strategy were not addressed in any useful or consistent manner.

The 1986 House Appropriations Committee report on Special Operations stated flatly that, after a five-year effort at revitalization, Special Operations Forces were still seriously hampered by poor readiness, inadequate equipment, fragmented command structures, and a lack of joint doctrine (Russell, August 1986, 16). These were the same criticisms which had prompted the 1980 'revitalization' of US special-operations capabilities in the first place (US DOD, 1980; US JCS, 1980; Congressional Research Service, 1981).

Congress enacts the 'Special Forces' bill

Congress's patience was now at an end. Determined to act, lawmakers introduced two major proposals: HR 5109, sponsored by Representative Daniels, and S2453, co-sponsored by Senator William S. Cohen (R-ME) and the chairman of the Senate Armed Services Committee, Sam Nunn (D-GA). Daniels's bill, the most radical, would have broken with the Pentagon completely and created a National Special Operations Agency under a civilian director (US Congress, Senate, Congressional Record, 1986). Although falling short of Daniels's preferred solution (the creation of a new armed service), the House measure would have established a chain of command which bypassed the JCS and interposed a civilian between the military special-operations elements and the Secretary of Defense. The Senate bill contained four important elements: (1) a unified special-operations command; (2) an Assistant Secretary of Defense for Special Operations and Low-Intensity Conflict; (3) a Coordinating Board within the National Security Council for Low-Intensity Conflict; and (4) a four-star-rank military commander. This last was important because for the first time SOF would have a military advocate of senior rank with direct access to the JCS and the Secretary of Defense. Although milder than the House version, the Senate bill was the first attempt by Congress to create by law a military command. It also told the President how, in part, to organize his personal staff, since it mandated a coordinating board within the NSC.

Speaking for the Cohen–Nunn bill on the floor of the Senate, Senator Nunn remarked:

> For about three years we have been waiting on the five year defense plan to reflect the needs of the special operations forces ... We had the Iranian hostage rescue mission and a woeful inadequacy of transportation ... at that stage. Senator Goldwater and I had written letters, done everything we could ... the regular forces were not interested. So we mandated in the bill that they include transportation for special operations forces in the 5-year defense plan. And we held up certain aircraft programs until they did.
>
> Guess what happened? They finally decided they needed the aircraft.
>
> What happened then? They came back and now they have taken those special operations aircraft out of the plan ...
>
> This is a sad commentary ... This is what has happened over and over again with the forces [SOF]. I think most people in the United States would say, for goodness sake, these are the ones we are going to use. Why not give them priority? A perfectly logical question. But it never happens. (Motley, 1986, 18)

Both bills were strongly opposed by the Joint Chiefs of Staff and senior command elements throughout the services (Crowe, 1989; also 1986, 3). In January 1986, Gen. [ret.] Paul F. Gorman (former ASD for Counterinsurgency) addressed Secretary Weinberger and others at a DOD conference on low-intensity conflict. The general, in effect, invited the Secretary (and, by implication, Congress) to butt out:

> I am not in sympathy with the proposal to place SOF under a DOD agency. Their difficulty with service identity would be compounded, and their relationships with the unified and specified commands would be even more troubled than they are under the present arrangement. No, these are matters that the Secretary should instruct the JCS to work out, for only the Chiefs and the CINCs can set it all right. (US Department of Defense, 1986, 13)

The Defense Department quickly rallied against the onslaught and counterproposed a milder form of the Cohen–Nunn bill with the backing of the JCS. The major difference was a crucial one: the

DOD proposal would have placed a unified SOF command under a three-star rather than a four-star general, leaving it without an advocate in the civilian defense bureaucracy. It would also have left SOF without any budgetary role by leaving funding in the hands of the various services. SOF would have remained largely in the control of the individual services, failing to meet the congressional objective of institutionalizing special-operations capabilities. In the words of Representative Daniels, '[Congress] wants the Pentagon's renewed commitment to special forces "tied down by chains in law"' (Budahn, 28 July 1986).

Within the OSD, opposition to the congressional proposals was led by Richard Armitage, Assistant Secretary of Defense (ASD) for ISA. As the principal OSD officer responsible for SO and LIC he continued to resist any loss of those responsibilities. During the July 1986 House Armed Services Committee (HASC) hearings on the proposed legislation, Armitage objected that it would duplicate his duties as ASD (ISA). He identified the ISA as the 'focal point for interagency policy coordination', including 'coordination between the State Department, CIA and NSC', and rejected any specific control over SO or LIC activities, leaving that to the various services as preferred by the JCS. In testimony before the HASC he opposed the statutory integration of SOF responsibilities in a single DOD office: 'while I have overall SOF responsibility, my staff does not have the expertise to deal with ... acquisition programs ... or [provide] military advice for the JCS', averring that the existing diffused system of special-ops responsibility and control 'ensures several strong voices for SOF'.

At the same hearings Armitage further contended that he had already taken steps to incorporate Program 11 into the Planning, Programming and Budgeting System. He added that his office was still 'establishing' the national SOF command (JSOA) – even though it had been in existence for four years. In addition, he refused to recommend that Naval Special Warfare Units (NSWU, i.e. SEALs) be added to forces under national SOF command, despite the statutory requirement that they be so included.

In September, Noel Koch wrote a letter to members of both the House and Senate Armed Services Committee. In it, he detailed his unsuccessful 1983 efforts to bring terrorism and low-intensity conflict-related issues to the attention of the JCS and the Joint Staff. His description of the disinterest which greeted his initiatives was 'disturbing' to the committees (Mellon, 1989).

On 1 October, as the conferees of the House and Senate Armed Service Committees were conducting final negotiations on the remaining differences between their bills, National Security Advisor John Poindexter sent a letter to the conferees. The letter took a reassuring tone, stating:

> you should not conclude that the management and oversight of sensitive operations have been neglected in the past. I can assure you that this is not the case, and that personnel and coordinating groups within the National Security Council have supported the President's participation in such matters on a continuing basis ... I urge you to reconsider the need for restrictive detailed legislation on this sensitive issue. (Mellon, 1988)

As the Iran–Contra hearings were to show, less than a year later, the 'management and oversight of sensitive operations' was considerably less effective than Poindexter implied (US Congress, Joint Session, SR100-216/HR100-433, 1987). In a less conciliatory tone, Poindexter's letter concluded: 'If the conference agreement contains mandatory language it would present potential constitutional problems because it would impermissibly limit the President's authority as Commander-in-Chief' (Mellon, 1988).

The conferees were not persuaded and on the following day, 2 October, the final bill left the conference committee. On 18 October 1986, Congress acted on its own, against the wishes of both the JCS and the Defense Secretary, enacting S2453 as United States Public Law 99-661, Section 1311 S 167(f), commonly known as the 'Special Forces' bill. This legislation, an addition to the National Defense Authorization Bill for FY 87, created the United States Special Operations Command (USSOCOM). The law mandated the creation of an interservice special-operations command with overall responsibility for doctrine, training and equipment, which would be common to all US special operations forces. The command was also to be responsible for special operations planning and to ensure the interoperability of the various service elements involved. Since the Army was the major SOF component, this was seen by the other services as an Army victory over the interests of other services and another step in strengthening the Army grip on the special-operations arena.

In the Joint Explanatory Statement accompanying the legislation, the conference committee indicated that it considered the establishment of this command to be an extraordinary action:

> Although several elements of this provision [special operations reorganization] are more specific than may normally be expected in this legislation, the conferees determined that the seriousness of the problems and the inability or unwillingness of the Defense

Department to solve them left no alternative. The action of the conference committee is fully consistent with the power provided in the Constitution for the Congress to 'provide for the common Defense'. The conferees determined that the failure to act forcefully in this area and at this time would be inconsistent with the responsibilities of the Congress to the American people. (PL 99-661, 1986)

On 27 October 1986, Armitage requested and received authority from the Deputy Secretary of Defense to co-chair a Special Operations Reorganization Working Group which would oversee implementation of the law. The other chair was the Director, Joint Chief of Staff (JCS). In order to implement that reorganization a charter was required which would define the specific responsibilities, relationships, functions and authorities of the ASD(SO/LIC). In other words, the charter (as with all agencies in the federal bureaucracy) would operationalize the law in specific organizational terms. It would be an official directive of the Secretary of Defense, having the force of law within the DOD. Without such a document it is difficult, if not impossible, for such an office to function effectively in a highly competitive bureaucratic environment. The Working Group was to produce the ASD (SO/LIC) Charter by January 1987 (Kief, 1987, 553).

In November, Armitage proposed that the new ASD (SO/LIC) report through the ASD (ISA) for SOF and counterterrorism deployment-related activities (Kief, 1987, 553). In effect, this proposal would have made the new Assistant Secretary subordinate to Armitage. This was never acted upon. But in February, the Secretary of Defense's Report to the Congress on SOF Reorganization stated that, pending the actual establishment of the ASD (SO/LIC), the 'direction and development of this new DOD entity' would be under the 'cognizance and direction of the PD ASD (ISA)', that is, under control of Armitage's Principal Deputy, Lawrence Ropka. The report was authored by Armitage. At the same time, both the Army and Air Force continued to balk at funding any further special operations build-up (US Air Force, 1986, 1).

Perhaps the most important aspect of the new law was that it established two bureaucratic positions to coordinate, oversee and support these efforts at the national-executive level. The most significant was an Assistant Secretary of Defense for Special Operations and Low-Intensity Conflict. The second position, that of USSOCOMs military commander, parallel to but not under the control of the Assistant Secretary, was to be a four-star general. This placed the position on a par with the most important major military commands.

These changes were important for two reasons. First, they presumably placed SOF and LIC advocates in the upper levels of the defense bureaucracy; but secondly, and even more significantly, it formalized the longstanding view that SOF was the most appropriate service element to prosecute 'low-intensity conflict'. The battle, however, was by no means over. The next step, filling the positions, proved to be surprisingly difficult. The selection process for candidates for the ASD (SO/LIC) position was in the hands of Armitage and Ropka.

The reaction of the Defense Department bureaucracy, especially within the OSD and the JCS, remained consistent – declaratory acceptance and support, coupled with little substantive action. In particular, efforts on the charter had yet to produce a useful result. In January 1987, a Vietnam SF and MACV-SOG veteran, attorney Nelson R. Kief, was brought on active duty as a reserve Army officer for service with the ASD (ISA). Kief, an experienced special operations officer, was assigned to the ASD (ISA's) Special Planning Directorate Staff to assist with implementation of Public Law 99-661. His experience there is instructive. Prior to the enactment of PL 99-661, the ASD (ISA) had primary cognizance for SO/LIC; that is, Armitage was the OSD member with principal responsibility. Kief's responsibility was to draft the now overdue charter for the new ASD (SO/LIC) and manage the staff process of actually producing such a charter. His first observation was that, not only was the Planning Directorate Staff small, but only one member (a reserve lieutenant colonel without OSD experience or significant SOF experience), was assigned to the task of implementing the new law. That officer left soon after Kief arrived. Kief also observed in his Senate testimony that the initial DOD candidate for the ASD (SO/LIC), Lt. Gen. Edward Tixier, had no special operations experience but was formerly a deputy to the ASD (ISA). General Tixier's candidacy was rejected by the Office of the Director of Presidential Personnel (which passes on the qualifications of candidates for major appointed offices) (Kief, 1987, 554).

Although there were several other proposed candidates, none was generally considered well qualified and all failed to gain either or both DOD and Presidential Personnel approval. Finally, in December 1987, one candidate emerged, Kenneth P. Bergquist, at that time a Justice Department attorney. Bergquist was recommended to the White House by the Secretary of Defense and approved to go before the Senate (the first candidate to reach the stage of Senate confirmation). Bergquist's candidacy was especially curious for two reasons. First, although assigned to an SF reserve unit, he had little special operations training and no actual experience; and secondly, he had opposed not only the legislation which created the ASD(SO/LIC), the job he was now seeking, but apparently also the philosophy behind it (Bergquist, 1988, 492–7). Finally, for reasons of ASD (ISA) bureaucratic advantage having little to do with the purposes of the law, Bergquist apparently had agreed with, and may have participated in, ASD (ISA) decisions to 'slow roll' (i.e. halt or delay) both Program 11 and the ASD (SO/LIC) charter (Kief, 1987, 555). By the date of these hearings, 10 December 1987, the charter had not been forwarded to the Secretary of Defense. After numerous delays, Program 11 had been submitted in truncated form in September.[10] When testimony before the Senate Armed Services Committee raised these and other questions about his qualifications and his dedication to the position, Bergquist withdrew his nomination.[11]

On 12 July 1988 Ambassador Charles S. Whitehouse was confirmed as Assistant Secretary of Defense for Special Operations and LIC (US Congress, Senate, 1988). Whitehouse, a long-time State Department professional, had no special background in either special operations or LIC.[12]

USSOCOM was actually established per Presidential message on 23 April 1987 at MacDill Air Force Base near Tampa, Florida (US President, 1987). JSOA was dissolved without ever having really existed and its functions absorbed by USSOCOM. JSOC remained in existence as a separate component of USSOCOM (Sheffield interview, 1990). It is important to recall that this establishment did not occur through service initiatives but rather as a matter of law, passed by Congress over the sometimes bitter opposition of the OSD and the JCS. The Florida location, far from the centers of power and influence in Washington, DC, was chosen by the service chiefs.

The Army component initially consisted of the 1st Special Operations Command at Fort Bragg, North Carolina, but without the Civil Affairs and Psychological Operations units. On 1 August 1987, USSOCOM assumed operational command of the multi-service, Fort Bragg-based Joint Special Operations Command. After initial resistance by the new command, on 1 November the Army's Civil Affairs and Psychological Operations units were assigned to USSOCOM by direct order of Secretary of Defense Weinberger (US Congress, House, 1987).[13]

The unchanged focus of Army Special Forces training was reflected in a pamphlet distributed throughout the Army in 1988 by the John F. Kennedy Special Warfare Center, the agency most directly responsible for overall training planning, and coordination for Army Special Forces. In fact, it had changed little since 1952, this publication stating that an SF detachment is 'capable of organizing, training, and equipping a guerrilla force' (JFKIMA, 1988, 1). In an aside, the document added that 'in some cases' the SF soldier may assist in foreign national development through 'Military Assistance and Civic Action Projects' (ibid., 2). Although an interested observer might have commented that it still seemed like preparation to free occupied France, Maj. Glenn Harned of 1st SOCOM stated afterward 'We have consciously rejected the OSS model' (interview, 1989).

At the same time, while more money was being appropriated for Special Operations Forces, the spending 'is not concentrated on LIC missions' (R. Schultz, 1989, 11). According to a study by Prof. Richard H. Schultz of Harvard's Fletcher School of Law and Diplomacy, 'SOF revitalization has been focused, to a significant degree, on force readiness and equipment to meet the regional CINCs ... responsibilities for conventional wartime preparation' (ibid.).

By no means was the question of special-operations' roles a settled matter. In August 1988, US Marine Corps commanders sought to establish a special-operations-like role for their seaborne forces as 'amphibious raiders', explicitly suitable for 'low-intensity conflict situations'. At the same time, more conventionally minded Army officers sought to portray the Army's newly formed light infantry divisions as conventional formations ideally suited for these same missions (Adelsberger, 1988, 12).

Structural problems continued in SOF through 1988. Despite considerable designation and redesignation of commands and subcommands during 1987 and 1988, there was still confusion as to the support and control of these forces. This was especially apparent in the case of Army Special Operations Forces. By December 1989, the Army's military leadership remained reluctant to relinquish any significant control of SOF elements to USSOCOM, whose planners once again planned to seek a legislative solution through Congress (Mountel, 1989). Through the end of December 1988, there was still confusion as to the command and control linkage between national command levels and the operational units.

Despite the often-expressed concern of the Congress with 'low-intensity conflict' and special operations, the 1986 legislation had failed to have the desired effect. On 17 January 1989, the senior members of the Senate Committee on Armed Services sent a joint letter to Lt. Gen. Brent Scowcroft (US Air Force, [ret.]), National Security Affairs Assistant to the newly elected President George Bush. In that letter, they specified four key provisions of the 1986 law which had not been implemented.

The legislation:
1. required the President to create within the National Security Council a Board for Low Intensity Conflict – the board has never met during the two years since its creation, and subordinate groups have been ineffective.
2. recommended that the President designate a Deputy Assistant to the President for National Security Affairs for Low-Intensity Conflict – President Reagan did not act on this recommendation.
3. required the President to submit to Congress a report on principal low-intensity conflict threats to US interests, deficiencies in US capabilities, and corrective actions being taken – the report, submitted in December 1987 discussed these issues in vague and abstract terms.
4. established the position of Assistant Secretary of Defense for Special Operations and Low Intensity Conflict – opposition within the Department of Defense resulted in substantial delays in filling this position and has greatly limited the ability of the Assistant Secretary to carry out assigned responsibilities.

The 1980s revitalization of SOF showed that some enduring themes were still in operation. Just as they had during the Kenendy emphasis on special ops, the conventional Army and elements of the Defense Department resisted the development of special operations forces. Not only did these elements oppose the establishment of the US Special Operations Command, but, when Congress took a hand by passing SOF legislation, they actively sought to avoid the requirements of the law. In the case of the SOF aircraft, Psyops and Civil Affairs units and the Navy SEALs, the services simply ignored the Congressional mandate.

With the creation of USSOCOM, special operators now had an institutional sponsor but their troubles were by no means over. (See figure on p. 207 for USSOCOM structure. *Source*: United States Special Operations Command, 1997–98 Calendar, United States Special Operations Command Public Affairs Office and Executive Services Command Graphics, MacDill Air Force Base, Tampa, FL, 1997.)

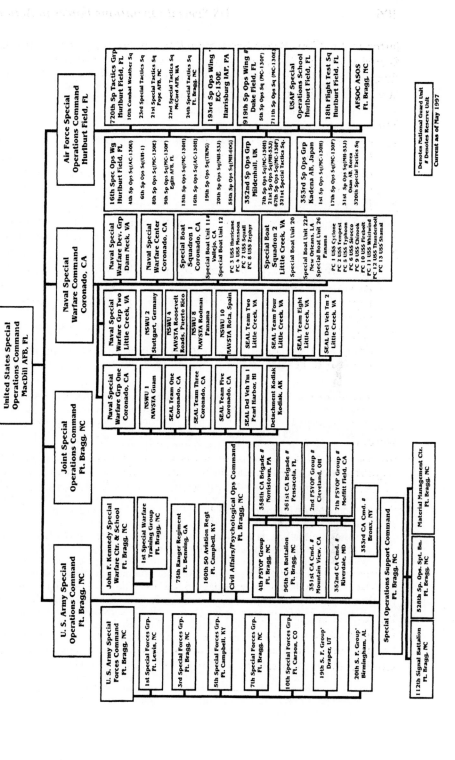

United States Special Operations Command
MacDill AFB, FL

U. S. Army Special Operations Command, Ft. Bragg, NC

- U. S. Army Special Forces Command, Ft. Bragg, NC
  - 1st Special Forces Grp. Ft. Lewis, NC
  - 3rd Special Forces Grp. Ft. Bragg, NC
  - 5th Special Forces Grp. Ft. Campbell, KY
  - 7th Special Forces Grp. Ft. Bragg, NC
  - 10th Special Forces Grp. Ft. Carson, CO
  - 19th S. F. Group* Draper, UT
  - 20th S. F. Group* Birmingham, AL

- John F. Kennedy Special Warfare Ctr. & School Ft. Bragg, NC
  - 1st Special Warfare Training Group Ft. Bragg, NC

- 75th Ranger Regiment Ft. Benning, GA
- 160th SO Aviation Regt Ft. Campbell, KY

- Civil Affairs/Psychological Ops Command Ft. Bragg, NC
  - 4th PSYOP Group Ft. Bragg, NC
  - 96th CA Battalion Ft. Bragg, NC
  - 351st CA Cmd. # Mountain View, CA
  - 352nd CA Cmd. # Riverdale, MD
  - 353rd CA Cmd. # Bronx, NY
  - 358th CA Brigade # Morristown, PA
  - 361st CA Brigade # Pensacola, FL
  - 2nd PSYOP Group Cleveland, OH
  - 7th PSYOP Group # Moffitt Field, CA

- Special Operations Support Command Ft. Bragg, NC
  - 112th Signal Battalion Ft. Bragg, NC
  - 528th Sp. Ops. Spt. Bn. Ft. Bragg, NC
  - Material Management Ctr. Ft. Bragg, NC

Joint Special Operations Command Ft. Bragg, NC

Naval Special Warfare Command Coronado, CA

- Naval Special Warfare Grp One Coronado, CA
  - NSWU 1 NAVSTA Guam
  - SEAL Team One Coronado, CA
  - SEAL Team Three Coronado, CA
  - SEAL Team Five Coronado, CA
  - SEAL Del Veh Tm 1 Pearl Harbor, HI
  - Detachment Kodiak Kodiak, AK

- Naval Special Warfare Grp Two Little Creek, VA
  - NSWU 2 Stuttgart, Germany
  - NSWU 4 NAVSTA Roosevelt Roads, Puerto Rico
  - NSWU 8 NAVSTA Rodman Panama
  - NSWU 10 NAVSTA Rota, Spain
  - SEAL Team Two Little Creek, VA
  - SEAL Team Four Little Creek, VA
  - SEAL Team Eight Little Creek, VA
  - SEAL Del Veh Tm 2 Little Creek, VA

- Naval Special Warfare Dev. Grp Dam Neck, VA

- Naval Special Warfare Center Coronado, CA

- Special Boat Squadron 1 Coronado, CA
  - Special Boat Unit 11 Vallejo, CA
  - Special Boat Unit 12
    - PC 3 USS Hurricane
    - PC 4 USS Monsoon
    - PC 7 USS Squall
    - PC 8 USS Zephyr

- Special Boat Squadron 2 Little Creek, VA
  - Special Boat Unit 20
  - Special Boat Unit 22 New Orleans, LA
  - Special Boat Unit 26 Panama
    - PC 1 USS Cyclone
    - PC 2 USS Tempest
    - PC 5 USS Typhoon
    - PC 6 USS Sirocco
    - PC 9 USS Chinook
    - PC 10 USS Firebolt
    - PC 11 USS Whirlwind
    - PC 12 USS Thunderbolt
    - PC 13 USS Shamal

Air Force Special Operations Command Hurlburt Field, FL

- 16th Spec Ops Wg Hurlburt Field, FL
  - 4th Sp Ops Sq(AC-130U)
  - 6th Sp Ops Sq(UH-1)
  - 8th Sp Ops Sq(MC-130E)
  - 9th Sp Ops Sq(MC-130H) Eglin AFB, FL
  - 15th Sp Ops Sq(AC-130H)
  - 16th Sp Ops Sq(AC-130H)
  - 19th Sp Ops Sq(TRNG)
  - 20th Sp Ops Sq(MH-53J)
  - 55th Sp Ops Sq(MH-60G)

- 720th Sp Tactics Grp Hurlburt Field, FL
  - 10th Combat Weather Sq
  - 23rd Special Tactics Sq
  - 21st Special Tactics Sq Pope AFB, NC
  - 22nd Special Tactics Sq McCord AFB, WA
  - 24th Special Tactics Sq Ft. Bragg, NC

- 352nd Sp Ops Grp Mildenhall, UK
  - 7th Sp Ops Sq(MC-130H)
  - 21st Sp Ops Sq(MH-53J)
  - 67th Sp Ops Sq(MC-130P)
  - 321st Special Tactics Sq.

- 193rd Sp Ops Wing # EC-130E Harrisburg IAP, PA

- 353rd Sp Ops Grp Kadena AB, Japan
  - 1st Sp Ops Sq(MC-130H)
  - 17th Sp Ops Sq(MH-53J) Osan AB, Korea
  - 320th Special Tactics Sq

- 919th Sp Ops Wing # Duke Field, FL
  - 5th Sp Ops Sq (MC-130P)
  - 711th Sp Ops Sq (MC-130E)

- USAF Special Operations School Hurlburt Field, FL

- 18th Flight Test Sq Hurlburt Field, FL

- AFSOC ASOS Ft. Bragg, NC

* Denotes National Guard Unit
# Denotes Reserve Unit

Current as of May 1997

NOTES

The official acronym for United States Special Operations Command is USSOCOM. 'USSOCOM's principal function is to prepare its forces to carry out their assigned missions under the operational command of the five geographic theater commanders' (US Secretary of Defense Report, 1988, 228).

Special Operations Expansion 1981 vs 1988

SOF Units	1981	1988
Army		
Special Forces Groups (1)	3	4(2)
Ranger Battalions	2	3
Psychological Opns Bns	3	4
Civil Affairs Bns	1	1
Navy		
SEAL Teams	2	5(3)
SEAL Delivery Vehicle Teams	0	2(3)
Air Force		
Special Operations Wings	1	1

(1) Does not include four reserve groups.
(2) Additional group formed at reduced strength using personnel and equipment from existing groups.
(3) Includes two Underwater Demolition Teams redesignated as SEALs in 1983.
(Data based on US Secretary of Defense Report, 1988, 295.)

1. It should be noted that, although used and popularized by former UN Ambassador Jeane Kirkpatrick and former White House Communications Director Patrick J. Buchanan among others (for example, Kirkpatrick's *The Reagan Doctrine and US Foreign Policy*, 1985), the term 'Reagan Doctrine' was apparently never used by the President or the White House (see Rosenfeld, 1986).
2. The parallels between the manuals are striking. A side-by-side comparison of FM 100-20 (1981) vs FM 31-16 (1967) reveals that large parts of the 1981 manual were copied nearly verbatim from the 1967 one. Sections on strike and consolidation operations were nearly identical in both versions, as were the sections on remote-area operations, urban-area operations and border operations (for example, 1981, 184; 1967, 113; 1981, 181; 1967, 111).
3. This was not the first incarnation of the Light Division concept. In 1944, the US Army tested a 8,984-man light-infantry division. This was like the 1984 version in two respects: it was designed to be air transportable and to be deployed to areas not suited to the heavier conventional divisions (in this case, Pacific islands). Like the 1984 light division, it was judged to have too little firepower and insufficient logistic support to sustain itself in battle (Kent R. Greenfield and Robert R. Palmer, *US Army in WWII: The Army Ground Forces: The Organization of Ground Combat Forces* (1947). For a comparison of structure between the 1944 and 1984 models, see Robert S. Rush (1st Sgt, US Army) 'Comparing Light Divisions' (1987).
4. The term 'sortie' means one flight by one aircraft. These figures are somewhat deceptive, since the 478/1273 sortie number is based on exclusive use of C5A aircraft, the largest transport in the USAF inventory. At that time (1984) there were only seventy-seven C5s in the US Air Force (US Secretary of Defense, Annual Report to Congress, 1984, 179). The 478 sortie/4-day figure presumes that all these aircraft

were flyable and dedicated to this single purpose. In reality, some use would
inevitably be made of smaller, more numerous aircraft, such as the C-130 and C-
141, raising the sortie rate and extending the deployment time.

5. General Schweitzer's title was Director, Strategic Plans and Policy Directorate, US
Army Chief of Staff.

6. A Special Forces Group of this period, by the official Table of Organization (TO),
consists of 776 soldiers organized into three battalions and a Group headquarters.
The Ranger TO called for three battalions, each with 660 soldiers.

7. 'In combat, the ranger regiment maneuvers to accomplish the mission in the manner
of other light infantry units. Ranger units make full use of published light infantry
doctrinal guidance' (DA FM 7-85, 1987, iv).

8. The inclusion of combat rescue (air-sea rescue of downed pilots) probably stems
from the notion of 'special operations' as conventional operations which are
'special' in the sense that they are unusual functions of regular forces in a
conventional environment. This is true of Air Force operations which are quite
similar in execution in both a conventional and an unconventional setting. This
distinction will be discussed further in Chapter 9.

9. Kief objects that the idea of US SOF leading guerrillas ('the military arm of a political
outgroup') in a revolution is 'absurd'. The leverage SOF operators have over
guerrillas is always questionable, especially if, as in the example of Allied support
to Tito's avowedly communist partisans in World War II, it is a marriage of con-
venience without basic political and ideological underpinnings.

10. The charter prepared by Bergquist and his staff at the Department of Justice was,
according to Kief 'a flat restatement of the law'. Bergquist allegedly defended the
charter's lack of specifics by stating that he would rely on 'the strength of his
personality to get things done' (Kief, 1987, 556). Commenting on this testimony,
Noel C. Koch characterized this as 'wanting to keep this thing [the ASD(SO/LIC
position] as vague as possible in order to make it easy to unravel' (ibid., 564). Kief
described Program 11 as submitted as 'lacking some substantial elements' prescribed
in the law. 'It has in effect left the status quo' (ibid., 567).

11. Bergquist was subsequently made the Assistant Secretary of State for Counterinsurgency. He was also appointed as J2 (intelligence chief) for Army Reserve special
operations forces (later abolished).

12. Ambassador Whitehouse's relevant background seems to have been confined to
State Department service as Ambassador to Laos during the Vietnam War.

13. In addition to the Army components mentioned earlier the operational components
now included the Army's 160th Special Operations Aviation unit at Fort Campbell,
Kentucky, the USAF 23rd Air Force at Hurlburt Field, Florida, and USN Naval
Special Warfare Groups One and Two. Three SOF training centers were also
assigned to USSOC: the Navy's Special Warfare Command at Coronada, California;
the Army's John F. Kennedy Special Warfare Center and School at Fort Bragg,
North Carolina; and the Air Force Special Operations School at Hurlburt Field,
Florida.

8 The SOF renaissance

Newly created and unwelcomed by virtually all parts of the military establishment, USSOCOM had a major piece of good luck. The actual establishment of USSOCOM remained a contentious issue, since there was no quick way to create a CINC-level four-star command. A solution to manning and basing a brand new unified command was to reflag an existing command.

Accordingly, Secretary Weinberger's February 1987 report to Congress on implementation of the SOF legislation provided that the US Readiness Command (USREDCOM) at MacDill Air Force Base in Tampa would be abolished, giving its staff and facilities to the new special operations command. The commander of REDCOM, General James J. Lindsay, would become the new commander of USSOCOM.

In March 1987, General Lindsay was named the Executive Agent for planning for USSOCOM's establishment. His first official task was to submit a draft charter, joint manpower program, an activation plan and a strategy for SOF by 27 March. DOD established a ceiling of 243 personnel assigned to USSOCOM, with seven additional billets for general/flag officers. The Department of Defense activated the US Special Operations Command on 16 April 1987, and nominated General Lindsay to command USSOCOM. The Senate accepted him without debate. Although officially activated on 16 April 1987, USSOCOM conducted its activation ceremony on 1 June 1987.

The command's mission was to prepare assigned forces to carry out special operations, Psychological Operations, and Civil Affairs missions as required, and if directed by the President or the Secretary of Defense, plan for and conduct special operations. Other responsibilities were:

1. Develop doctrine, tactics, techniques and procedures for Special Operations Forces.
2. Conduct specialized courses of instruction for all Special Operations Forces.

3. Train assigned forces and ensure interoperability of equipment and forces.
4. Monitor the preparedness of Special Operations Forces assigned to other unified commands.
5. Develop and acquire special operations unique equipment, materiel, supplies and services.
6. Consolidate and submit program and budget proposals for Major Force Program 11 (MFP-11).
7. Monitor the promotions, assignments, retention, training and professional development of all Special Operations Forces personnel.

Ironically, the principal speaker at the activation was Admiral William J. Crowe, Jr., Chairman of the Joint Chiefs of Staff, who had adamantly opposed the formation of the new Command. Crowe advised the new CINC:

> First, break down the wall that has more or less come between special operations forces and the other parts of our military, the wall that some people will try to build higher. Second, educate the rest of the military – spread a recognition and understanding of what you do, why you do it, and how important it is that you do it. Last, integrate your efforts into the full spectrum of our military capabilities. (USSOCOM, 1996, 5)

As it happened General Lindsay was a fortuitous choice. Widely known as one of the Army's most able general officers, he possessed two assets not common to successful generals. First, he had a talent for persuasion as well as command, and secondly, a background in both special ops and conventional forces. This made him more than acceptable to Congress. It also gave him a rare flexibility as well as wide experience. He would need both in the immediate future.

The services were not easily disposed to surrender any influence over their SOF assets and responded with a display of foot-dragging. But, according to section 1311 of the enabling legislation, 'Unless otherwise directed by the Secretary of Defense, all active and reserve special operations forces of all armed forces stationed in the United States shall be assigned to the Special Operations Command.'

Therefore, the Secretary of Defense assigned three components to the new command: the 23rd Air Force, headquartered at Hurlburt Field, Florida; the Naval Special Warfare Command, headquartered at Coronado, San Diego, California; and the 1st SOCOM, headquartered at Fort Bragg, North Carolina. On 6 May 1987 all of the Army's 1st SOCOM forces were assigned to the command including 1st, 5th, 7th and 10th SFGs, 75th Ranger Regiment; and Task Force 160, Special Operations Aviation but excluding the 96th Civil Affairs Battalion and the 4th Psychological Operations Group.

Instead, a plan was proposed by the Office of the SecDef to make Psyops into a separate subunified command. Like other SOF, the psychological operators had suffered severe cutbacks during the 1970s and 1980s and some proponents feared that Psyops would not have much better luck at USSOCOM. Lindsay wanted the CA and Psyops units and felt that a Directorate within USSOCOM would suffice. JCS approved the assignment of all Army and Air Force Psyops elements to USSOCOM on 15 October 1987. Nevertheless, Civil Affairs and Psychological Operations were not officially designated as Special Operations Forces until 3 March 1993.

On 8 October 1987, the Secretary of Defense directed that all CONUS-based Army Special Forces and Ranger units, Air Force Special Operations wings and squadrons, a Naval Component Headquarters, and the three Service Special Operations Schools be assigned to USSOCOM.

USSOCOM's Naval component had been established on 16 April 1987, but Naval Special Warfare Groups (NSWG) I and II were not assigned because the Navy felt that these organizations were 'Fleet' assets and should not be assigned to USSOCOM. USSOCOM maintained that the SEALs belonged to them along with all other special-operations units, on the grounds that the NSWGs' relationship to a fleet was the same as an SF Group's assignment to a particular theater. After a good deal of unproductive negotiation, Lindsay brought the matter directly before Defense Secretary Casper Weinberger.

Despite stiff opposition from the Navy, on 23 October 1987, Secretary Weinberger decided to assign the SEALs to USSOCOM. On 1 March 1988 the Naval Special Warfare Command assumed operational control of the Naval Special Warfare Groups from the Pacific and Atlantic and on 1 October 1988 also assumed administrative control. Shortly afterwards, Frank Carlucci replaced Weinberger as Secretary of Defense and the Navy tried for a reversal of Weinberger's decision. The new Secretary refused to change the previous decision and finally, on 1 April 1989, the Navy transferred budgeting authority for Naval Special Warfare Command to USSOCOM (USSOCOM, 1996, 30).

The 23rd Air Force, headquartered at Hurlburt Field, Florida presented a unique problem, since it incorporated two separate but related functions: first, as a numbered air force in the Military Airlift Command (MAC) with worldwide responsibilities, and secondly, as Air Force Special Operations Command with responsibility to provide special operations airlift to the Special Operations Forces of all services. Since USSOCOM expected all components to be major command equivalents, this arrangement created problems and later conflicts.

One of General Lindsay's first moves as commander was to initiate a JMA, a Joint Mission Analysis. It was his belief that the future of SOF lay in being able to deal with a wide variety of low-intensity but high-probability threats, while leaving the global-war requirements to the conventional armed forces. In the general's judgement, the place to begin was the US Southern Command, located in Panama and responsible for South and Central America. He believed that USSOCOM's real area of commitment should be the kind of regional conflicts then occurring throughout USSOUTHCOM from the guerrilla insurgency in El Salvador to the unstable government in Panama to the drug trafficking that flourished along the Andean Ridge.

The JMA was developed by USSOCOM's Joint Studies and Analysis Group (JSAG), along with a joint SOF master plan. General Lindsay felt that once the mission was analyzed and the threats were examined, then a joint SOF master plan could be developed. After examining the current state of SOF forces worldwide, JSAG developed a SOF master plan in April 1990. The master plan was an assessment of the status of all areas of special operations, Psyops, and CA in which USSOCOM had responsibilities. It was to be used as the central planning document within the command and was intended to be the primary reference document on command responsibilities and goals for the services, agencies and other government organizations. The plan also defined command responsibilities, provided command focus and direction, and served as the foundation for action. It supported resource-allocation decisions, provided background for the USSOCOM budget submissions to the POM, and projected command doctrine, organization and resource-related activities.

The first test for the new command was not long in coming. In Operation Earnest Will, a fairly small-scale special operation, special ops worked with conventional naval forces as part of a larger US–Allied response to Iranian operations against international oil tankers transiting the Persian Gulf. Army SOF helicopters from TF 160 teamed with SEALs and Special Boat personnel to capture an Iranian mine-laying ship. They carried out assaults on offshore oil platforms used by Iranians to harass international shipping, and Special Boat units performed escort, patrol and interdiction duties.

OPERATION EARNEST WILL

(Note: This account is derived from the USSOCOM report 'Special Operations Forces In Operation Earnest Will/Prime Chance I 1987–1989', courtesy of USSOCOM.)

Operation Earnest Will was designed to protect neutral oil tankers against Iranian attack. Iraq began attacking oil ships trading with Iran in 1981 during the 1980–88 Iran–Iraq War. Iran retaliated in 1984 by attacking oil tankers traveling to and from Kuwait, a major supporter of Iraq. Kuwait asked the US in December 1986 to register 11 Kuwaiti tankers as US ships and provide Navy protection. President Reagan agreed, hoping it would deter Iranian attacks on other ships.

    Since the Iranians used mines and small boats that were hard for conventional naval vessels to locate, the USA needed more than just surface combatant warships; it needed surveillance and patrol forces in the northern Persian Gulf and bases for these patrol forces. Special Operations Forces, including Army helicopter units and Navy SEALs and Special Boat Units, seemed ideally suited to monitor hostile activity, particularly at night when the Iranians conducted most of their missions. The Chairman of the Joint Chiefs of Staff, Admiral William Crowe initially asked Marine Corps Commandant General Alfred Gray about using Marine Corps AH-1T Cobra gunship helicopters. Gray recommended against using Cobras, because they lacked systems for target detection and engagement over water at night and their crews had no training for the mission.

    On the other hand, the Army's small special-operations helicopters were difficult to spot on radar and had relatively quiet engines, allowing them to get close to a target. Furthermore, the TF 160 helicopter crews trained extensively for night combat. Shallow-draft Naval Special Warfare patrol boats could patrol in waters that had not been swept for mines. They also had the endurance to monitor and track the Iranian patrol boats that were raising havoc in the Persian Gulf. In late July, the US Central Command (CENTCOM) asked for Navy Special Warfare assets. Six Mark III Patrol Boats (PBs), four Mark II PBRs (Patrol Boat Riverine), two Seafox patrol craft, two SEAL platoons, and an SBU detachment deployed in August.

The first PBs began their escort duties on 9 September. In early August, more special operations forces, including two MH-6 and four AH-6 Army special operations helicopters and 39 men, received orders to the region as Operation Prime Chance I.[1] On 8 August, the helicopters escorted the third Earnest Will convoy and looked for signs of Iranian mine laying. The first PBs began their escort duties on 9 September.

Planners, including special operations forces representatives, recommended two mobile sea bases (MSB) be constructed to avoid asking local nations to house the Special Operations Forces. Two civilian oil-servicing barges already in the Gulf, *Hercules* and *Wimbrown VII*, were chartered for six months as mobile sea bases. They provided Special Operations Forces with mobile forward platforms in the northern Persian Gulf capable of supporting operations to monitor and thwart clandestine Iranian mining and small boat attacks. Each base housed ten small boats, three helicopters, sufficient fuel, ammunition, equipment, and workshops to support their work, and more than 150 men. The mobile sea bases had to be prepared for this mission and would not operate forward until October.

Until that time, however, the Special Operations Forces operated from various surface vessels, including the command ship *Lasalle* (AGF-3) and the amphibious assault ship *Guadalcanal* (LPH-7). As the US strength increased, a new command structure was created, the Joint Task Force Middle East (JTFME). The JTFME assumed control of MEF and reported directly to USCINCENT. To support the Naval Special Warfare assets, four minesweeper boats and a marine radio reconnaissance and force reconnaissance platoon received orders to the Persian Gulf.

By early October, SEAL boat patrols and Army helicopters had determined the Iranian pattern of activity. The Iranians hid during the day near oil- and gas-separation platforms in Iranian waters, or on Farsi Island. At night they headed towards the Middle Shoals Buoy, a navigation aid in international waters which tankers had to pass.

Having determined the Iranian operating and attack pattern, Special Operations Forces made their plans accordingly, sending three helicopters and two patrol craft towing one Seafox toward the buoy on the night of 8 October. Arriving first, the helicopters found three Iranian boats, including two Boston Whalers, next to the buoy. As the helicopters closed in, the Iranians opened fire. The helicopters immediately returned fire, sinking all three. Following the helicopter assault, patrol boats moved in and picked up five Iranian survivors who were eventually repatriated.

The mobile sea bases entered service in early October in the northern Persian Gulf. Every few days they changed their location in the northern Gulf to frustrate Iranian targeting. With the bases in service, US patrol craft and helicopters had the base they required from which to monitor Iranian patrol craft and deter their attacks on merchant ships.

In November 1987, Special Operations Forces aviation assets grew, when two UH-60 Blackhawk helicopters arrived to provide a nighttime combat search-and-rescue capability.

Following these operations, Iranian attacks on neutral ships dropped drastically. The SEALs continued to plan contingency operations to seize an Iranian minelayer or oil platform, or attack an Iranian island if required. These plans never had to be put into action. On 18 July, Iran accepted a United Nations ceasefire; on 20 August 1988, the Iran–Iraq War ended.

Special Operations Forces began withdrawing in the wake of the ceasefire. On 16 July, the last AH-6 and MH-6 in theater departed. In October 1988, the US Navy began removing weapons and equipment from *Wimbrown VII*. Its Army OH-58 detachment and SEALs returned to the USA, while its patrol boats replaced those aboard the *Hercules*.

The final Earnest Will convoy was run in December 1988. The US Navy had escorted 259 ships in 127 convoys since June 1987. The Middle East Force wanted to retain Special Operations Forces to help monitor the situation, but its ships lacked space to house SOF units. The remaining SEALs, patrol boats and helicopters returned to the USA during summer 1989.

Special Operations Forces had provided the skills necessary to help US naval forces gain control of the northern Persian Gulf and counter Iran's small boats and minelayers. Their ability to work at night proved vital, since Iranian units often used darkness to cover their tracks. SEALs provided boarding teams to seize targets, PBs cruised the mined waters of the Persian Gulf, SEABATs served as night reconnaissance and attack assets, and UH-60s conducted search-and-rescue missions and provided administrative support.

The mobile sea-base concept provided a unique solution to the problem of hosting special operations forces when regional governments did not want a large US presence on shore.

The relatively small size of special ops units proved to be a handicap, although by no means insurmountable. Tours for many personnel were kept to 45–90 days to prevent wearing them out. This meant that the same personnel rotated back to the Persian Gulf for second or even third tours. Aircraft support exceeded expectations, and the MH/AH-6s and UH-60s performed well above expectations. Patrol craft fared worse, with only the large patrol boats having the size to cope with storms and heavy seas in the Gulf. Even the patrol boats found themselves taxed during five-day convoy operations. Eighteen months of strenuous duty had left the boats in poor condition, requiring extensive repairs.

By all measures, Earnest Will was a success as was the SOF participation in it. However, the new command's first major test would be in the Southern Command, in support of a conventional contingency operation of the kind that had proven so troublesome in Grenada.

OPERATION JUST CAUSE: THE GOOD NEWS AND THE BAD NEWS

By the time of the 1989 invasion of Panama, the SOF community had digested the mistakes of Grenada and conducted their missions with much more success and far fewer problems. The bad news was that, with two significant exceptions, their operations were almost entirely conventional. The conversion of SOF to a conventional asset was nearly complete. The good news was that the operation provided at least two examples of the unique potential of SOF to conduct operations that would have been impossible for conventional forces. On the night of 20 December 1989, the skies over Panama were the scene of an amazing display. Flying completely without lights, over 144 military aircraft maneuvered within a tight 20-mile circle over the capital, Panama City. Unlit transport planes and helicopters delivered thousands of Rangers, paratroopers and special operations soldiers in the dead of night while blacked-out fighters and armed helicopters darted in and out to attack targets in support of the invasion. On the ground about 20,000 soldiers already in Panama moved out to secure objectives throughout the isthmus (Paschall, 1996, 88; McConnell, 1991, 36–7).

Special Operations Forces played a major role in Operation Just Cause. More than 4,150 soldiers and 77 aircraft from USSOCOM took part in the invasion and the subsequent reconstruction efforts. (Testimony of General James J. Lindsay, Senate Armed Services Committee, February 8, 1990.) Determined to learn from the Grenada operation, SOF enjoyed considerable combat success but also found there were limits to what could be accomplished by light forces whose operations depended on skill and surprise. Remembering the problem with dehydration in the heat of Grenada, every soldier in the Ranger units had made it a point to drink as much as they could hold (McConnell, 1991, 87).

The major special-operations missions for the invasion were straightforward and mostly combat-related:

1. SEALs and Army SF, apprehend the Panamanian dictator, General Manuel Antonio Noriega and deliver him to US custody for trial on drug-trafficking charges.
2. Army Ranger's 2nd and 3rd Battalion (reinforced) parachute assault against the PDF base at Rio Hato west of Panama City.
3. 1st Ranger Battalion (reinforced) parachute assault to seize the Torrijos-Tocumen International Airport and PDF airbase complex.
4. Army SF from A Co, 3rd Battalion, 7th SFG capture and hold the Pacora River Bridge east of Panama City.
5. SEAL Team Four occupy positions to control the airfield at Punta Paitilla in Panama City where Noriega kept his personal jet. Their function was to block the runway and make sure that Noriega's plane could not leave.
6. SEALs and SBUs disable Noriega's personal yacht and two PDF gunboats in Balboa Harbor, seize PDF positions on Flamingo Island.
7. SFOD-Delta assault El Modelo prison in Panama City to rescue CIA operative, Kurt Muse.
8. A special-operations team was to deliver two 1109th Signal Brigade technicians to disable the Panamanian national TV station at Cerro Azul.
9. USAF 1st SOW, the Army 160th SOAR and 617th Special Operations Aviation Detachment provide transport, fire support and aerial surveillance for all of these missions and selected conventional operations.
10. Navy Special Boat Squadron control the Atlantic entrance to the canal.

The second, third, fourth and fifth missions were all designed to prevent Noriega's best forces, the Macho de Monte elite infantry at Rio Hato and the Battalion 2000 mechanized unit at Fort Cimarron, from ever reaching the main force battle in Panama City. The participation of Psychological Operations soldiers was limited to providing a few small Spanish-speaking teams to accompany the combat and forces and deliver surrender demands by loudspeaker. Soldiers from the 96th Civil Affairs Battalion also jumped in with the Rangers.

The build-up

Preceding the invasion, several special operators and units were secretly moved to Panama City from the US and concealed at various installations including Albrook Air Station and Howard Air Force Base. Included were modified UH-160 aircraft and a team of Delta commandos with supporting 'little birds' (highly modified Hughes 500 helicopters).

The most spectacular contingency mission for these operators was to capture the Panamanian strongman, General Noriega. The effort to apprehend Noriega had been an off-again-on-again special operations project since late in the Reagan administration, when it became obvious that the situation in Panama was not likely to resolve itself without intervention. Despite the best efforts of numerous operators, it was the most public and least successful special-ops effort of the entire intervention.

Allegedly, Secretary of State George Schultz and others evolved a scheme for Special Forces teams to 'kidnap Noriega and bring him back to the United States to stand trial on drug trafficking charges' (George Wilson, 'US to Add 1,300 Troops In Panama; "Instability" Cited', *The Washington Post*, 2 April 1988, A1). Noriega, who was apparently aware of the possibility from published reports in the US press, took great pains to conceal his location and movements, even using a double dressed in the General's uniform. US intelligence assets in Panama were unable to consistently track Noriega and nothing came of the plan.

By 1989, Noriega had become a considerable thorn in the side of the US administration. Relations between the Panamanian government and the US had become steadily worse since Noriega took office, reaching an all time low point late that year. President George Bush and his advisors were convinced that Noriega was the source of the USA's problems on the isthmus and had considered a variety of solutions short of invasion. The preferred method was to support the legitimate political opposition to Noriega and hope that he could be ousted through an election. But, when Noriega formed unemployed Panamanians into so-called 'Dignity Battalions' and sent them into the streets to attack the political opposition, stoning and beating candidates and their supporters, the possibility of legitimate opposition effectively died.

As reported by the *Washington Post*, two Army Special Forces teams had been readied in September 1989 to abduct Colombian drug cartel leader Pablo Escobar after US intelligence learned that Escobar was planning to visit Panama. A pair of 1989 Justice Department decisions supported the possibility. The first Justice Department decision, in June, allowed the US military to apprehend suspected criminals overseas for trial in the USA provided the soldiers were accompanied by DEA (Drug Enforcement Agency) or FBI officials. The second decision, in November, relieved this restriction and allowed military forces to operate alone but only in execution of a Federal warrant. The Escobar project faded away, but efforts to track the Panamanian leader were intensified. It still proved impossible to ensure that any special-ops snatch team would be able to pinpoint the general's location at the required time. The arrest of Noriega was then incorporated into Operation Plan Blue Spoon, the plan for military intervention in Panama.

Special Operations Forces move in

US military intelligence assets in Panama continued the hunt for Noriega up through the evening of the invasion with Army Special Forces and SEAL teams on standby. The SEALs had reason to put extra effort into the search for Noriega. One of several incidents that precipitated the invasion was the seizure of a Navy special operator and his wife by Panamanian Defense Forces (PDF) troops on 16 December. The couple were taken from their car in Panama City and interrogated by the PDF for several hours. No real military information was sought. The PDF apparently thought this was just an opportunity to terrify and belittle a gringo couple. What made the incident particularly galling was the sexual nature of the couple's treatment, during which the lieutenant was repeatedly kicked in the groin while PF interrogators fondled his wife and threatened to rape her. The pair were released to the US Military Police and their captors never realized that the lieutenant was part of a special-operations unit (McConnell, 1991, 18). At the same time, USSOCOM was holding a full-scale rehearsal, simulating all of the major missions at various locations in Florida and the southeastern USA.

As the level of tension rose in the days prior to the invasion Noriega had adopted a policy of constant movement among his numerous 'safe houses' and various mistresses in Panama City. At least four locations, including a Dairy Queen near the exclusive Paittilla district where the General was eventually located, were visited by the snatch team on the night of the invasion but without finding Noriega. As reported by the *Washington Post*, 'Navy SEALs burst into a seaside villa but found only smoking cigarette butts and women's purses'. Unknown to the US commandos, Noriega's movements were impossible to anticipate that night. Panicked by the massive simultaneous arrival of US forces and in fear of his life, the dictator and his bodyguards were driving aimlessly around Panama City in a state of near-hysteria.

There was a problem for the special-ops forces, though. As in Grenada, tactical surprise had been lost, in this case by the alertness of Noriega's intelligence apparatus and early inadvertent contact between elements of the US force and the PDF. The ability to surprise and overwhelm larger enemy forces before they could react was a key part of special-ops combat doctrine; lacking surprise put all their operations in jeopardy.

Ranger missions

The Army Rangers had two crucial missions in the invasion: to seize the Torrijos International Airport and PDF's Tocumen Airbase complex east of Panama City and to capture the PDF elite-forces base and airfield at Rio Hato. Both objectives were defended by antiaircraft guns and would be attacked first by aircraft to reduce or eliminate the antiaircraft threat. Unfortunately, it also warned the enemy of the approach of US forces.

Targeted against Rio Hato were 2nd Ranger Battalion, the 3rd Ranger Battalion (less one company which was attached to 1st Battalion for its assault on Torrijos/Tocumen), elements from 4th Psyop Group, Civil Affairs assets, Air Force Combat Control Teams (CCTs), and Marine Corps Air/Naval Gunfire liaison troops. Aerial-fire support was provided by two F-117 Stealth fighters, two AH-64 and four AH-6 helicopters, and one AC-130. The lack of tactical surprise was evident as the C-130 transport planes approached Rio Hato and the fully alert PDF greeted them with fountains of red and green tracers. Unlike at Grenada, the C-130s continued to bore in on the drop zones and the 2nd Battalion made a low-level jump in good order, despite the hail of enemy fire. Moving aggressively across the airfield, they destroyed two attacking V-150 armored cars and caused a third, heavy V-300, to flee until it was destroyed by a 105mm round from a Spectre C-130. Rio Hato was occupied by the PDF's elite Macho de Monte unit and resistance was heavy. When the Panamanians ignored loudspeaker demands to surrender delivered by a team from the 4th Psychological Operations Group, the Rangers cleared the buildings with fire and maneuver. Four Rangers were killed and 44 wounded in the Rio Hato operation.

To accomplish the mission at Torrijos-Tocumen airport, 1st Battalion's three companies were reinforced with Company C, 3rd Battalion, 75th Ranger Regiment, gun jeeps, motorcycles, Psyop teams, a Civil Affairs team, two AH-6 attack helicopters and Air Force combat-control teams (CCTs). In addition, an AC-130 gunship would be in direct support of the battalion.

The PDF at the airport was slower to react allowing a degree of tactical surprise to be achieved. The descending Rangers were met only by ground fire from small arms. Despite some scattering on the drop, the weapon-laden soldiers jogged quickly to their assigned objectives with discipline and precision. Company B, reinforced with 12 gun jeeps and ten motorcycles, fanned out immediatly to clear both runways and establish blocking positions that prevented other PDF forces from interfering with the battalion's operations. Supported by the ubiquitous Spectre gunships, they overcame disorganized resistance from the Panamanian 2nd Rifle Company and secured the airport complex on time with few casualties. The Rangers then devoted themselves to the dangerous business of rooting out PDF stragglers and holdouts hiding in the terminal buildings (McConnell, 1991, 86–91; USARSO, 1990, 22; USSOUTH-COM, 1990, unpaged). Unbeknownst to them, the Rangers nearly stumbled across General Noriega who had been enjoying a tryst at a hotel near the airport and fled just ahead of the US soldiers. The Rangers suffered only one soldier killed and 23 injured of which 15 were jump injuries.

The SEALs at Balboa Harbor and Paitilla Airport

The SEAL mission to Flamingo Island and the demolition mission against Noriega's yachts and two PDF patrol boats went off on schedule with no problems. Not surprising, since the boats were moored not far from the Navy's Rodman base in the same harbor. But in addition, the SEALs had another, more difficult assignment – to seize and secure the airfield at Punta Paitilla in the heart of downtown Panama City.

The Paitilla airfield assault force, designated Task Unit Papa, had a 62-man ground force with three SEAL platoons, Air Force combat controllers to perform liaison with an AC-130H gunship, and a command, control, communications and mortar team. A 26-man support team included surveillance forces, a signals intelligence team, a Psychological Ops team, and boat crews. Most of the SEALs were familiar with the objective having been in the rehearsals or recently returned from Panama.

The assignment of this mission to the SEALs points up one of the problems with joint operations, including special operations. When a joint command undertakes a mission, all the components want a share in the action. By any reasonable calculation airfield seizure was a mission for either Army paratroopers or Rangers. Both units train for these missions and the Paitilla airfield was probably a company size objective for either the Rangers or the conventional paratroopers of the 82nd Airborne Division. In the original plan, the Rangers had been slated for this mission, and certainly there were ample Rangers available for the operation. However, the politics of the situation dictated that Navy special operators receive a significant mission during the invasion. The Navy was not about to be left out. For this reason a reinforced SEAL team was given the mission.[1]

Things began badly when a Panamanian fishing boat discovered the commandos moving into position during the night and illuminated them with a searchlight. Once at the airfield a SEAL platoon became delayed by a fist fight with night watchmen. The combined noise of the shouting watchmen and the commencement of the conventional invasion alerted the PDF guards. While a larger conventional force would have simply detached an element to subdue the watchmen without pausing in the mission, the small number of SEALs meant they became caught up in the fight. This both delayed the SEALs and alerted the PDF.

The result was a bloody firefight between the exposed SEALs advancing across the open airstrip and a large number of well-armed PDF concealed in and around Noriega's hangar supported by snipers in other airport buildings. The Spectre gunship overhead was unable to help because of the close quarters fight and the SEAL wounded in the open. The SEAL mission had never been to seize and hold the airstrip, but once the firefight began they seemed to have no other alternative.

Despite heavy casualties, the lightly armed SEALs lived up to their best traditions and managed to close with the enemy and secure the airfield after a bloody close-quarters fight. Nearly every one of the 44 SEALs involved had been wounded and several killed. A MEDEVAC helicopter had been requested when the first casualties were taken, but none came until 0205. One of wounded died after being evacuated.

The SEALs formed a smaller perimeter, expecting to be relieved by Army units at dawn. At 10:00 that day, the SEALS were informed that owing to heavy fighting, they would not be relieved soon. The SEALs hunkered down under intermittent fire that evening and waited. Finally, 15 SEALs arrived by helicopter at midnight, but it was not until 14:00 hours the next day that five CH-47 helicopters disgorged a Ranger company. Relieved, the SEALs left aboard the same helicopters. A planned 5-hour mission had turned into a 37-hour operation.

Special Forces at the Pacora River Bridge

Army Special Forces had been assigned another conventional operation, this one to block PDF armored vehicles from Noriega's Battalion 2000 which could be expected to attack the Ranger airdrop at the airport complex. A 24-man SF team had been assembled to seize and hold the Pacora River Bridge east of the airport, blocking any such attempt.

The defense of the bridge was originally planned as a reconnaissance mission by a four-man team infiltrated before H-hour. On the evening of 18 December, this changed to 'seize and deny use of' the bridge, the force was increased to 16 men to be transported by two MH-60 helicopters from the 617th Aviation Detachment. The force was later increased to 24 men when a UH-60 was substituted for one of the MH-60s. The mission was given to A Company of 3rd Bn 7 SFG, commanded by Maj. Kevin M. Higgins.

This had been a somewhat hasty change of mission. The SOF planners had intended to use a small force and timing was critical, since that force had to be in place before the armored vehicles crossed, but not so soon that they would have time to receive warning. In the event, the team was forced to leave early by reports that Battalion 2000 was on the move toward the bridge. The SF arrived at the bridge just as a PDF convoy was crossing and, after missing with the first shot, managed to deploy in time to destroy the lead vehicle with a well-placed rocket from an AT-4 (Light Anti-armor Weapon). While the SF soldiers fired rockets and rifles into the convoy, a Spectre racked it with 200mm gunfire, destroying the vehicles and killing or scattering the PDF inside.

What followed was a night of sporadic fighting as the PDF probed the American positions and tried to flank the small force. All of these efforts were detected in time and turned back with the help of Spectre fire support (USSOTHCOM, 1990, unpaged).

SFOD-Delta at El Modelo Prison

Delta's mission went very well at first. The prison guards were distracted by AC-130 gunships blasting holes in Noriega's nearby headquarters when a M113 armored personnel carrier provided by a conventional infantry unit suddenly deposited the commandos at the prison. The Delta operators quickly killed most of the guards and blew open Kurt Muse's cell, releasing him. Hauling the stunned Muse with them, the commandos ran to the prison roof where an MH-6 'Little Bird' from the 160th landed. Then, as the helicopter rose from the prison roof with Muse inside and the commandos clinging to the skids and handholds, a burst of gunfire smashed the engine housing, causing the machine to lose power. In a display of aviation virtuosity, the pilot managed to crash land and then hover-taxi through the gunfire into the prison parking lot. Three Delta troopers clinging to the outside of the small helicopter were severely injured in the crash. Taking shelter among parked vehicles, all were pinned down under fire in the parking lot until a Delta operator ran out and stood in the open to signal a 'Little Bird' that had been attacking the Commandancia. A short time later they were rescued by nearby infantry in armored personnel carriers.

Sealing the Atlantic End

A tiny Navy special-ops surface force, Task Unit Charlie, was assigned to secure the Caribbean side of the Panama Canal with eight SEALs, two riverine patrol boats, and two Army landing craft mechanized with 12 soldiers. Task Unit Charlie's first assignment was to block all ships entering the Canal from the Caribbean. The patrol boats broadcast a marine radio warning to all ships in the Canal area on 20 December. The patrol boats and the landing craft spent the night patrolling the shipping channel near the breakwater entrance, Limon Bay, and the ports of Colon and Cristobal against PDF attempts to commandeer boats and escape.

The unit prevented arms transfers to the PDF from a cargo vessel, halted looting in the pier area and exchanged fire on several occasions with PDF elements in the harbor area, all without sustaining serious casualties. The soldiers and sailors searched small craft in and around Colon and small cargo ships in Coco Solo. Search-and-seizure operations against 31 boats at the Panama Canal Yacht Club took place on 24 December. Task Unit Charlie continued patrol boat operations on 25 December, until 12:30, when its SEALs returned to their original units and the landing craft returned to the Army.

This use of special ops surface-warfare elements for seemingly routine operations was apparently mandated by the fact that the Navy's focus on 'blue water' missions and large vessels simply left it without other elements capable of performing these types of missions.

Summation and a counter-example

With the exception of the prison rescue, every special-ops mission in Operation Just Cause could have been carried out by conventional forces. In the case of the SEAL attack on Punta Paitilla it certainly should have been conducted by a conventional infantry force that could have overwhelmed the defense quickly. The lack of such a force was the principal cause of the SEAL deaths and injuries. As in Grenada, the Panama case illustrates how much the success of special operations depends on surprise and the ability to overwhelm the enemy at the point of contact before he can react. However, little noticed among the exploits of the commandos was a example of the truly unique abilities Special Forces can bring to bear. Operation 'Ma Bell' was the creation of Major Gilberto Perez, commander of A Company, 1st Battalion, 7th SFG. On 22 December, as the fighting was dying down around the major cities, Perez was told to prepare to assist the 2nd brigade of the 7th Infantry Division in pacifying four rural districts of Panama. His job was to obtain the surrender of the PDF *cuartels* (generic term for a military base) in these areas. Perez's plan was simple and effective. Rather than a military occupation force, he took a small SF element with him to the airfield nearest each cuartel. Since he or one of his officers had worked with and was personally acquainted with most of the commanders, he simply called them by telephone from the airfield and invited the commanders and their garrison to witness a display of firepower from a Spectre gunship. There was, he explained, no dishonor in surrender to superior force. The PDF was required to surrender their arms but left with their dignity by being invited to conduct joint 'law-and-order' patrols in the local towns with soldiers from the 7th Infantry Division. Finally, he conducted a flag-raising ceremony in which the Panamanian flag was raised while all present, American and Panamanian, saluted to show respect for Panama and to demonstrate the Americans had not come as conquerors. Most importantly, this was not just a gesture or a clever trick but a genuine demonstration of support for the legitimate civil authorities in the country.

The result was that, in five days, he was able to neutralize the PDF garrisons without bloodshed on either side, while obtaining the willing cooperation of the area population. Major Perez, backed up by elements of the 7th Infantry Division, pacified a large area while establishing a solid foundation for follow-on Civil Affairs operations. This action demonstrated the unique skills that Special Forces can provide the military based on language capability, area knowledge and appreciation for the nature of unconventional operations. (This account is based on material developed by CALL (Center for Army Lessons Learned), 1990, 16–17.)

Civil Affairs in Just Cause

The role of civil operations forces in Just Cause was limited, but the operation did provide at least a glimmer of the potential of an approach that combined the capabilities of Special Forces, Civil Affairs and Psychological Operations specialists with Army Engineers and military police in a manner reminiscent of the Vietnam-era Special Action Forces.

Civil Affairs missions were largely confined to post-conflict operations and these were neglected during the 22 months of planning that lead up to the invasion. The degree of emphasis can be judged by General Maxwell Thurman's statement that his concentration was almost wholly on the conventional military operational aspects of the invasion (Schultz, 1993, 16). General Thurman was the Commander in Chief of USSOUTHCOM, and thus overall commander of Operation Just Cause. To the degree that these issues were considered at all, they were regarded as a 'short-term proposition and not part of a broader political-military strategy' (Schultz, 1993, 17).

When the planned-for US civil-military structure simply collapsed under stress a makeshift organization was created that provided a hint of a combined special operations capability. The new Military Support Group (MSG) brought together Special Forces personnel, members of the 4th POG and civil affairs soldiers, both from the

96th CA at Fort Bragg and the 361st Civil Affairs Command, a reserve organization. Additional elements from the military police and Army engineers were later assigned, making it a multi-capable structure. Their task was described as the 'conduct of nation-building operations to insure that democracy, international standards of justice and professional public standards were established in Panama' (Fischel, 1995). The combination was effective but hard for the US Embassy to accept, especially the use of Psychological Operations.

Psychological Operations were clearly a necessary part of the mission, especially in promoting professionalism in the newly created Panamanian police force and helping restore the population's confidence in their government. However, US embassy officials (including the Ambassador) apparently thought this was not a military responsibility and not even an appropriate role for military forces. In April, the Psyoperators were ordered out of the country under pressure from the embassy. In December 1990 the entire MSG was closed down on the grounds that its work could be accomplished by the restored US embassy and its country team (Schultz, 1993, 57–8). As had been the case with the Special Action Forces during the Vietnam War period, a combined military approach to civil matters did not meet a warm welcome in the US interagency community and found no welcome at all from the State Department. The performance of Special Operations Forces in Panama impressed Congress, leading Senator John Warner to tell the Secretary of Defense and the Chairman of the Joint Chiefs, 'I wish that we had put more emphasis on the SOF. If there were any lingering doubts here in Congress about the ability of those forces, Panama ended that debate' (US Congress, Senate, 1990). SOF, especially Army SOF, underwent some important force structure changes. The US Army Special Operations Command (USASOC) was activated on 1 December 1989 as a major Army Command replacing and assuming the functions of the Army's former 1st Special Operations Command. The new USASOC was to be the Army component of the USSOCOM.

On 16 May 1990 Task Force 160 was reorganized, redesignated the 160th Special Operations Aviation Regiment (Airborne), and assigned to the US Army Special Operations Command. Its principal aircraft include modified OH-6 light observation helicopters, MH-60 utility helicopters and MH-47 medium-lift helicopters. The Regiment currently (1997) consists of three battalions. The 1st and 2nd Battalions are located at Fort Campbell, Kentucky, while the

3rd Battalion is located at Hunter Army Airfield, Georgia. On 20 June 1990 the 3rd Special Forces Group was activated at Fort Bragg, North Carolina.

SOCCOM enters the drug war

In 1990, President George Bush had directed more participation by the Department of Defense (DOD) in the National Drug Control Strategy. At the direction of the Secretary of Defense, General Lindsay began cautiously to move USSOCOM into the counterdrug arena early in 1990 by supporting other government agencies (mainly DEA, Customs, US Coast Guard and the Border Patrol), expanding Psyops and CA-training activities and using some SOF reserve assets. Like most of the military community, however, USSOCOM's approach to counterdrug missions was tentative and not marked by great eagerness.

Mindful of the difficulties with intelligence for SOF operations experienced in Grenada and the attempt to apprehend Noriega, General Lindsay tried to leverage the post-Just Cause good will into greater freedom for SOF to conduct independent 'advance force operations' (essentially intelligence and reconnaissance) in areas where SOF might expect to be committed; the specter of 'out of control' special operators operating on their own arose again (Starr, 1990, 231).

Remembering Iran–Contra and the Special Operations Division scandal of the 1980s, the Senate Armed Services Committee was very specific that it did not want to simplify or expedite procedures for approving any of SOF's covert operations.

In the mid-1980s, the Army's Special Operations Division in the Pentagon had set up a highly secret operation called 'Yellow Fruit' which in turn created a 'commercial cover' named Business Security International. The function of Yellow Fruit and its cover organization was to support SOF covert operations, especially intelligence missions connected with counterterrorism. Unfortunately Yellow Fruit became the very model of an out-of-control project. Funds were misspent or unaccounted for, documents were falsified and, worst of all in conventional military eyes, the operation became involved in several CIA activities that were themselves questionable. The fuss had barely died when the Navy's Delta Force equivalent, SEAL Team Six, became involved in similar charges.

All of this became the subject of embarrassing press disclosures and Congressional inquiries extending through 1988. The affair was also featured in at least two popular books: Steven Emerson's *Secret Warriors* (Putnam Books) in 1988 and Tim Weiner's *Blank Check: The Pentagon's Black Budget* (Warner Books) in 1990.

One policy analyst, Robert Kurz of the Brookings Institute, claimed that the USSOCOM initiative showed 'that despite the history of Iran–Contra, agencies of the US government still seek to act secretly, without coordinating with their fellow agencies or with congressional oversight' (quoted in Madison, 1990, 1801). Furthermore, Lindsay's proposal was widely viewed as part of the drive for SOF autonomy, as was the appointment of his successor as Commander, USSOCOM, General Carl Stiner.

NOTES

1. The original solution to the problem of Noriega's plane had been proposed by 7th SFG during planning for the operation. They had suggested placing a sniper with a heavy-caliber rifle some distance away and simply punching holes in the aircraft windshield, avionics and engines, making it unflyable.

9 Desert Storm, Provide Comfort and the drug war

Carl Stiner was a experienced officer who had great credibility, having commanded JTF South during the Panama invasion and JSOC as well as the conventional 82nd Airborne Division and its parent organization, the XVIII Airborne Corps. He was also an outspoken supporter of more independence for special ops. Stiner's opportunity to shape the course of US special operations was greatly affected by events in the Middle East.

SOF during Operations Desert Shield and Desert Storm

US Special Operations Command Central

Army	Navy
5th Special Forces Group	Naval Special Warfare Group One
3rd Special Forces Group (-)	
10th Special Forces Group (-)	SEAL Team One (2 platoons)
	SEAL Team Five (2 platoons)
TF 3-160 Special Operations Aviation Rgt	Swimmer Delivery Vehicle Team 1
4th Squadron, 17th Air Cavalry	(1 platoon)
528th Special Ops Support Bn	Special Boat Unit 12 (High Speed Boat
112th Special Ops Signal Bn(-)	Det and Rigid Inflatable Boat Det)
	Mobile Communications Team
	Naval Special warfare Development
	Group (High Speed Boat Det)

Air Force

7th Special Operations Wing
8th Special Operations Squadron (MC-130E)
9th Special Operations Squadron (HC-130)
20th Special Operations Squadron (MH-53J)
55th Special Operations Squadron (MC-60G)
71st Special Operations Squadron (HH-3)

Operations Desert Shield and Desert Storm were the largest military operations since World War II, eventually arraying several allied divisions, an air armada and a seaborne task force against Iraq. This force included SOF and special operations in what would become the largest SOF deployment to a single region in history. Nevertheless, although SOF had a useful role to play in the war, they were essentially marginal players. But the Iraq case is important because it illustrates the dangers and difficulties of employing Special Operations Forces on a conventional battlefield (USDOD, 1992, J-1).

At about 02:00 hours on 2 August 1990, two Iraqi divisions, the Hammurabi Armored Division and the Tawakalna Mechanized Division crossed the Iraq border into Kuwait, brushing aside a Kuwaiti brigade guarding the border. At the same time, heliborne Iraqi Special Forces attacked Kuwait City while Sea Commandos came in from the Persian Gulf to cut the coastal road south, the only paved road connecting Kuwait with Saudi Arabia. By 05:30 Iraqi Army units were in Kuwait City. By 14:00 the fighting was substantially over, and Kuwait was in Iraqi hands (Hutchinson, 1995, 2).

General Stiner was at CIA headquarters in Langley, Virginia, when he learned of the invasion. With members of his staff, he left immediately for his headquarters in Tampa, Florida, aboard a small USAF executive jet. Three of his primary units, SFOD-Delta, a battalion of Army Rangers and elements of the 160th Special Operations Aviation Regiment, were finishing an exercise along the Texas/New Mexico border and he ordered that they be recalled at once. General Wayne Downing, commander of the Joint Special Operations Command (JSOC), also began planning for a war in the Kuwait/Iraq area by meeting with Israeli officers on their established contingencies for war with Iraq (including plans to hunt for Iraqi Scud missiles in the desert) (Hutchinson, 1995, 2).

Immediately after President Bush announced that US forces would be sent to the Persian Gulf, Special Operations Forces were on the ground in Saudi Arabia. A Navy Special Warfare composite unit of SEALS, SBUs and SDUs arrived on 12 August. They were followed by an Air Force Combat Control team. Operating under the command of SOCCENT (Special Operations Command Central) members of the 10th Special Forces Group arrived in Saudi Arabia on 31 August. These were the first US SOF personnel to be deployed (DA, 1993, 123).

If the SF component of SOF was early on the scene, the Psyops and Civil Affairs components must be counted as late in arriving. First of all, these elements were not involved in planning for the

Gulf War until very late in the process. The reason for this, as the USASOC history notes, was 'the Army's unfounded belief that it would operate in an environment virtually free of civilians' (USASOC, 1994, 110).

The Bush administration in the meantime created a multinational military force called the 'Coalition' with the avowed purpose of ejecting Saddam Hussein's forces from Kuwait. In a diplomatic coup, the President succeeded in persuading several Arab states to join the Coalition, avoiding the appearance of an American/European crusade against an Arab state. Numerous diplomatic initiatives failed to resolve the situation, as did economic sanctions and the Coaliton prepared for war.

General Norman Schwartzkopf, commander of the US Central Command (CENTCOM) became the overall commander for the Persian Gulf campaign, including Coalition forces. General Schwartz-kopf was not a great believer in special operations and his staff made two critical decisions on SOF employment very early in the campaign. First of all, CA and Psyops, the SOF assets most directly useful to conventional commanders, were stripped away from SOCCENT, the theater special operations headquarters. Secondly, the special-ops units were forbidden from crossing into Iraq. In General Schwartzkopf's view, they would only get into trouble and he might have to 'divert forces from the real war to and bail them out. I did not want a hostage situation' (quoted in Gordon and Trainor, 1995, 243).

The Army Civil Affairs and Psychological Operations units were given low priority at first and consequently were slow to arrive. Upon arrival they were assigned to ARCENT, the conventional Army headquarters for Desert Storm. Likewise, the Air Force component, CENTAF, took control of the AC-130 gunships from the 16th and 919th Special Ops Squadrons as well as the EC-130 Psychological Operations aircraft from the 193rd Special Ops Group (Pennsylvania Air National Guard) (USDOD, 1992, J-3,4). As events proved, this did not significantly handicap SOCCENT, given the generally constrained nature of its operations throughout the war.

Bureaucratically, SOF operated at a disadvantage, since each of the services was represented at CENTCOM by a three-star general while the special-operations chief for the theater was a colonel. General Stiner, a four-star, made several attempts to have himself assigned to CENTCOM as commander of special operations but was rebuffed each time, finally by General Colin Powell, chairman of the Joint Chiefs of Staff (Gordon and Trainor, 1995, 242).

General Schwartzkopf wanted the special-ops players to fit into his conventional scheme of operations, not out on their own, and that is what happened. There would be no special-operations missions without his personal approval (Waller, 1994, 251).[1] For all of these reasons and because of the overwhelmingly conventional nature of the war, SOCCENT was restricted to five conventional (and largely secondary) missions throughout the desert conflict:

1. Coalition Warfare Support – position liaison teams with Coalition forces to ensure coordination of Coalition warfare activities. Provide training as required.
2. Special reconnaissance – of Iraqi forces within the Combined Special Operations Area (CSOA).
3. Coordinate CSOA forces passage of friendly lines with appropriate ground-force commanders.
4. Combat Search and Rescue (CSAR) in Iraq and Kuwait.
5. Provide training to reconstitute the Kuwaiti ground and naval forces from the remnants left after the Iraqi invasion.

Additionally, at the actual beginning of ground combat, a 14-man Navy SEAL platoon had part of the war's largest deception – to assist major fleet elements in simulating preparations for an amphibious landing on the Kuwaiti coast, thereby forcing the Iraqis to reposition their forces. SEALS and British Marines also boarded by force at least 11 merchant vessels in the Gulf as part of sanctions enforcement.

Most important, however, was an unanticipated seventh mission – hunting for the elusive Iraqi mobile short-range ballistic missiles called Scuds (derived from USDOD, 1992, J5, 6). Conceivably, this last might have been the most significant single operation of the war.

Civil Affairs and Psyops

Both Civil Affairs and Psyops seemed to receive their usual treatment as afterthoughts. This had very serious consequences in the case of CA, nearly all of which was in the reserve. To bring those forces on active duty and prepare them for the Kuwaiti theater meant that a lengthy 'call-up' process was required. As a result, very few CA elements arrived until 132 days after mobilization and were not present in any strength until the war actually began. The few on hand before that were put to work with the Kuwaiti government-in-exile and the US State Department's Kuwaiti Task Force to plan the rebuilding and post-war administration of Kuwait (USASOC, 1994, 111).

As CA units finally arrived they were formed into a Civil Affairs Task Force under ARCENT and given a variety of missions including attachments to all ground units including the Marine Corps. Their most important initial function was really a Psyops task, to defuse the Iraqi propaganda campaign that painted the US and European Coalition members as contemporary 'crusaders' and 'enemies of Islam'. CA soldiers informed troops and commanders of cultural sensitivities and, as the war began, helped commanders avoid damage to Iraq historical religious and cultural sites thus depriving Iraq of useful propaganda incidents.

With the liberation of Kuwait, they were able to help restore basic services and assist with civilian-related matters. An example of this occurred when CA soldiers intervened directly to prevent Kuwaiti abuse of Palestinian workers accused of supporting the Iraqi occupiers. As it developed, some of the Palestinians had actually taken part in the resistance to the occupation (USASOC, 1994, 112).

Psyops loudspeaker teams deployed with the 82nd Airborne Division in August and Psyops planners accompanied CENTCOM headquarters into the theater, but the organized Psyops campaign got off to a late start. It would have been even later had not a fully fed-up General Schwartzkopf sent a stinging message on the subject to Washington in December. The CENTCOM commander might have been a skeptic about special operations but Psyops made sense to him. The problem lay in the fact that the strategic Psyops campaign plan for Iraq, like all such plans, had to be approved at the presidential level.

This took months and left Baghdad with uncontested control of the propaganda stage. The Iraqis understood the importance of Psyops and the psychology of the Arab world. Their well-funded and carefully planned campaigns targeted specific clans and religious sects, with telling effect. Meanwhile, a ten-minute video produced by the 4th Psychological Operations Group took almost two months to receive approval; by then it was out of date and had to be re-edited, adding more time before distribution. It was November 1990 before 650 specialists from the 4th finally arrived from Fort Bragg, and December before they had approval for a Psyops campaign; leaflet drops finally began in January 1991 (Waller, 1994, 285, 291–3; USASOC, 1994, 113).

On the first day of the airwar, 17 January, the psyoperators began to hit their stride as their 'Voice of the Gulf' began broadcasting 18 hours a day, sending music and news interspersed with surrender appeals. 'Volant Solo', EC-130s from the Pennsylvania Air National

Guard's 193rd SOS flew over the Gulf, rebroadcasting the message throughout Iraq (USASOC, 1994, 114–15; DOD, 1992, J-21). Iraqi prisoners stated that this was the third most listened-to station, following the BBC and the long-established Radio Monte Carlo (USASOC, 1994, 114).

The Psyops coup of the war, however, originated with the CENTCOM commander. Schwartzkopf, remembering the psychological effect of the devastating B-52 raids in Vietnam, decided to simply warn Iraqi units 24 hours in advance that they would be bombed and advise them to leave the area. The bombing would occur on schedule and another set of leaflets would be dropped, assuring the stunned survivors that the same thing would happen again. The second strike always resulted in heavy desertions among the units targeted (USASOC, 1994, 115).

Looking for work

Since CENTCOM had barred Special Forces from crossing the border, there was only limited scope for special operations. This did not, however, prevent the special operators from looking for missions on their own.

Undiscouraged by the lack of success with the attempt to capture Noriega during Just Cause, the JSOC planners and intelligence staff devoted considerable energy to a plan to snatch or even assassinate the Iraqi dictator Saddam Hussein and another to grab high-ranking Iraqis in Kuwait City. Despite great efforts, it proved impossible to reliably target the dictator and the scheme was shelved. Both Schwartzkopf and Powell reportedly felt that any attack on the Iraqi leadership had a low chance of success and a high probability of provoking Baghdad to act before CENTCOM was ready (Gordon and Trainor, 1995, 242; Waller, 1994, 238–40).

Early in the build-up period of Desert Storm, JSOC also developed a plan called 'Pacific Wind', an operation to rescue the diplomats remaining at the US embassy in Kuwait City. This was a complex and chancy operation with only a bare chance of success. In any case, the diplomats were released by Iraq in December and the mixed force of Rangers and Delta commandos training back in the USA never had to execute the elaborate plan (Gordon and Trainor, 1995, 241–2; Waller, 1994, 244–6).

Conspicuously missing from the short list of special ops tasks were two obvious items for special operators, especially Army SF and Rangers. In fact there were no plans to even bring Ranger units into the theater. Army Rangers were an odd omission since these were the closest thing to an elite conventional force in the special-operations community. As events developed, USSOCOM made several proposals that would have involved the Rangers including a raid on an Iraqi terrorist training camp. To CENTCOM this looked a lot like SOCCOM making work for itself, and none of the plans was approved by Washington or CENTCOM.

There were no direct-action missions as in Panama and Grenada and no plan to create Guerrilla Warfare Operational Areas (GWOA) in the Iraqi rear. General Stiner proposed that GWOAs be opened in Iraq and Kuwait. There were rebellious Kurds in northern Iraq and a tiny, fragmented resistance movement inside occupied Kuwait. SF teams had trained extensively to develop resistance forces in enemy-held areas, and this seemed like a perfect opportunity to put it into practice. SEALs could lead raids and Delta commandos might strike at high-value targets or kidnap enemy officials. It was a chance to tie up the Iraqi Army in a guerrilla war.

No one else was enthused about the scheme, neither CENTCOM, nor the Joint Chiefs nor the White House. The CIA had little specific data on resistance movements in Kuwait, which in any case seemed too tiny and geographically restricted for real guerrilla warfare. Also, the SF guerrilla warfare capability was largely generic with no specific competency in Iraq. Furthermore, although the Kurdish population of Iraq was known for its willingness to rebel, there were strong political reasons not to encourage this by providing direct aid or advisors. Simply put, two of the Coalition partners, Syria and Turkey, had restive Kurd populations of their own. Those governments had a long history of animosity with their own Kurds and would strongly oppose any scheme to arm and support Kurdish populations in Iraq or anywhere else.

Finally, Schwartzkopf was planning a short war, four months at the maximum, so there would be little time or need to develop a resistance movement. He wanted nothing that might trigger an Iraqi attack before he was ready. That was a command-level decision and not for debate, but the lack of both unconventional and direct action missions rankled.

To make matters worse, in January Schwartzkopf was finally pressured into making an exception to his 'no cross border operations' rule and allowing British special operations troops from the Special Air Service (SAS) to conduct reconnaissance across the Iraq border. Like the US SOF, the British were anxious to place reconnaissance assets on the ground inside Iraq and senior British

officers kept returning to the issue with CENTCOM. Permission
was finally given, chiefly as a political decision, brought about by
the desire not to offend an important ally, but it rankled the US SOF.
In the end, it would have fortunate consequences when the Scud
Hunt began.

Coalition Warfare Support

Coalition Warfare Support turned out to be a booming business for
SOCCENT, which passed the mission on to Army Special Forces
and the Navy SEALs. But, except for a 20-man SEAL element and
Special Boat sailors, almost all of the burden fell on the Army SF.
By the end of the war, 109 SF Coordination and Training Teams had
been established and took up virtually all the available SF resources.
Initially, the training was confined to Saudi Arabian units but
eventually expanded to include forces from Egypt, Syria, Oman,
Morocco, Bahrain the United Arab Emirates and Qatar. Even France
requested and received an SF training team (USDOD, 1992, J-8, 9).
    The other half of Coalition Warfare Support, in addition to
training, was the liaison function. Reporting was a problem for
CENTCOM, especially from the Arab–Islamic units, which did not
report in English and whose methods and standards were very
different from those of the NATO-style US and European military.
Basic information about unit locations, status, capabilities and
current situation was often lacking and virtually unobtainable. The
solution was to use Army SF teams to link the Islamic units directly
to the CENTCOM maneuver planning staff. As events progressed,
these teams also provided coordination between adjacent Coalition
forces (USDOD, 1992, J-9). This successful application of SOF
created a standing requirement for such teams and Army SF
continued to provide Coalition Support Teams to the standing
brigades of the Kuwaiti military through 1997, fully six years after
the end of the war (Wakeman, 1997).

Reconstituting the Kuwaiti military

Although the Defense Department described this as a 'key SF
mission', the recovery of the Kuwaiti armed forces got off to a slow
start. The plan was to train a Kuwaiti Special Forces battalion and
a commando brigade from the remnants of the Kuwaiti ground
forces. The mission went to the 5th SFG which provided 6 SFODs
to conduct the training, a total of about 72 personnel. For their part,

however, the Kuwaitis initially provided only 60 personnel to be trained, about one under strength company. Initial training was conducted through September 1990 but then halted until December because of a lack of ammunition, equipment and Kuwaitis. By 22 February 1991, a total of 6,5357 Kuwaitis were trained, making up an SF battalion and four miniature infantry brigades; each roughly equivalent to a US battalion (USDOD, 1992, J-7).

At the same time, Naval Special Warfare Group Central undertook the training (actually the recreation) of the Kuwaiti Navy. By 17 January the SEALs and Special Boat Unit personnel had trained and equipped crews for three Kuwaiti ships that were used to support CSAR in the Gulf for the remainder of the war.

Strategic reconnaissance

The initial reconnaissance application of special-ops forces was along the Kuwait–Saudi–Iraq order and the Kuwaiti coast, where SEALs and Army SF had a border observation mission during the first months of Operations Desert Shield, the defensive phase of the Gulf War. CENTCOM had almost no information about the activities of Iraqi forces in the border and coastal areas. SOF were able to fill this void during August and September until other forces could enter the theater.

Beginning with the offensive phase of the war, Operation Desert Storm, in mid-January 1991, SOCCENT forces conducted 12 deep-recon missions hundreds of kilometers behind enemy lines. These missions were supposed to be the bread-and-butter of special-ops forces in a conventional war. However, as described by the Army's official history of the Gulf War, the first missions were less than wholly successful:

> The insertion of the teams went smoothly enough ... the 3/160th ... came in 20 feet off the desert floor at 140 knots in the dead of night. Problems arose at daylight when the teams attempted to hide in terrain absolutely void of folds or vegetation. Not a hill, a bush, not even a small depression was visible for miles. The ground was hard, usually with only a thin covering of sand. (DA, 1993, 198)

Whatever the difficulties, CENTCOM needed intelligence on Iraqi movements, especially around Highway 8, where elite Republican Guard armored units might begin to maneuver for a counterattack. So, on the night of 23 February, eight SF recon teams flew into Iraq:

Several, unable to find hide sites in the barren terrain, were extracted;
the Iraqis discovered others. Teams that chose softer cultivated areas
to dig in soon found themselves surrounded by inquisitive farmers.
(DA, 1993, 198)

One team, discovered by shepherds who summoned Iraqi soldiers,
was soon fighting for their lives. They became the object of an
elaborate and successful air-rescue operation that extracted them
safely while destroying any possibility of concealing the deep-recon
effort from the Iraqi high command. But, despite their brief stay,
the teams did confirm that no major reinforcements were on the
road.

It seemed like a meager reward for the effort and risk involved.
The 'snapshot' obtained by risky deep-recon missions could have
been obtained safer, cheaper and more easily by a variety of means
including aircraft reconnaissance and satellite imagery. One of the
important criticisms of these methods is that they provide only a
snapshot, capturing a single brief moment in time and do not serve
well in fluid situations or when the enemy is taking deliberate
deceptive measures such as hiding vehicles and equipment. The
advantage offered by SOF deep recon is that the teams can enter an
area, remain for extended periods and provide a continuing picture
of a fluid situation while penetrating enemy-deception methods that
might deceive other collection means. When the area is not suitable
for team to remain, as the pertinent areas of Iraq were not, the value
is greatly decreased.

Another part of the deep reconnaissance mission would soon
have an even more urgent purpose when Iraqi Scud missiles began
impacting on Israel and Saudi Arabia.

A Special Mission Unit in action: the Scud hunt

'Scud' is the NATO term for a Soviet-made missile modified in Iraq
and used for attacks on Coalition forces and Israel. The Scud model-B
is a 37-foot missile with a range of about 400 miles. This meant that
it could hit targets in both Israel and northern Saudi Arabia from
deep inside Iraq. The fact that it could be fired from mobile launchers
about the size of an ordinary semi-trailer truck made it a very difficult
target to find and hit. Iraq had about 1,200 of these missiles. After
the airwar against Iraq began on 17 January 1991, Scuds were fired
the following day against targets in Saudi Arabia and, most
significantly, against Israel, a nonbelligerent (Message, 1991, 1).

Precise information on the Scud-hunting activities of Special Operations Forces in the Gulf is hard to obtain. Much of the subsequent testimony and reporting is classified, and virtually all other sources are contradictory. For example, the Army's official history of the war specifically mentions that a number of Scuds were destroyed by special-ops-directed air strikes. Other analysts suggest that all Scud kills claimed by special ops were either ordinary semi-trailer trucks or decoys.[2] The USASOC official history devotes several pages to the Gulf War without mentioning the Scud hunt at all.

But, it is certain that by the second week of the airwar Scuds were a serious problem. Fifty-three of the missiles had been launched – 26 against Israel and 27 against Saudi Arabia. The original Soviet Scud was a fairly inaccurate weapon. The Iraqis had modified it to obtain longer range and in so doing degraded its accuracy even further. Of no real military importance and causing only minimal damage, its use was strictly as a terror weapon. Furthermore, the US Patriot missile proved capable of intercepting a number of incoming Scuds. But despite the Patriot batteries, some Iraqi missiles were still striking.

This made the attacks very important for two reasons. One was the real possibility that Saddam Hussein might chose to use chemical rather than conventional, explosive warheads, making them a more serious threat to both military and civilians throughout the target area. The other, even more important reason, was political.

It was obvious that the attacks on Israel were intended to provoke an Israeli military response and bring Tel Aviv into the war as a *de facto* co-belligerent with the Coalition. The effect of this on the Arab members of the anti-Iraq Coalition would be tremendous and all of them allegedly informed the US and CENTCOM that it would become politically impossible for them to remain in the alliance if this occurred. The general population of the Arab states simply would not abide their armed forces fighting on the same side as Israel against a fellow Arab nation. Even though Israel had received two batteries of Patriot missiles for self-defense, the Patriot was not perfect and Tel Aviv could not be expected to stand idly by while Iraqi missiles continued to fall. Despite their negligible military significance, this made the Scuds a political threat of the highest magnitude.

Fortunately, most of Iraq's advanced warplanes had fled to Iran, where they were interned for the duration of the war. This left a number of Coalition strike aircraft free for missions against the Scud launchers. The brand-new USAF F-15E, 'Strike Eagle', so new it was technically still in testing, was the aircraft of choice. Eventually three squadrons of Coalition aircraft, chiefly F15Es, would be dedicated to the hunt. The problem, however, was finding the missiles. The MAZ-543 mobile launchers could be set up and fired from pre-surveyed positions in the open desert. Then, in less than ten minutes they could be gone, escaping before fighter planes could respond to the infrared signature of the firing. Furthermore, the area of possible firing locations was huge, covering thousands of square miles of western Iraq. Since Iraq was apparently not using any of its known fixed launching sites, finding the elusive mobile launchers became a problem for special operations.

The SAS had been operating inside Iraq producing useful intelligence, but their low-tech approach of using foot patrols and ground vehicles kept them close to the Saudi border, allowing only a limited series of commando raids and no Scuds. The effort needed the advanced helicopters and specialized tools of the US SOF including the sophisticated Global Positioning System (GPS) navigation equipment to make pinpoint strikes possible in the uniform desert terrain.

To counter the missile threat, USSOCOM created a special 877-man Joint Special Operations Task Force (JSOTF) for the specific purpose of finding and killing Scuds. With first elements arriving on 31 January, the force eventually consisted of two squadrons of Delta operators, Army SF, and the 20th Special Operations Squadron of the 1st SOW. To no one's surprise the new 'Black SOF', was placed directly under CENTCOM, rather than under SOCCENT (US DA, 1993, 182–3; Waller, 1994, 341–2).

The attempts to snatch the political prisoners on Grenada, Noriega in Panama and the proposed capture of Saddam Hussein were all more-or-less within Delta's mission parameters; but Delta was not trained, equipped or configured for Scud hunting or anything like it. Why use the expensive, irreplaceable one-of-kind counterterrorist unit for a deep-recon mission in the desert?

One answer was that almost every available Special Forces soldier was committed. Because of the low initial priority CENTCOM had assigned to the Scuds, the entire 5th SFG and parts of the 3rd were tied up in the training missions listed earlier or liaison duties with the various Arab military forces. Large portions of the 10th SFG were occupied in the CSAR operation being run out of Turkey. There was no other comparable unit available. Unfortunately this does not account for the Army Ranger units, who had not been employed at all in the war to this point and were trained for 'behind the lines' reconnaissance and raids. The answer to that was that the Israelis were increasingly restive under the steady drizzle of Scuds and only the introduction of the premier US commando element would satisfy them.

Working with the by now experienced SAS, the force was quickly readied under intense scrutiny from Washington and Tel Aviv. On 7 February the first mission launched, inserting Delta teams and their vehicles at night. By 4 a.m. General Downing was showing Schwartzkopf a videotape of Scuds being blown up 120 miles inside western Iraq. There was initial rejoicing at CENTCOM but later intelligence analysis revealed that the Scuds were decoys (Gordon and Trainor, 1995, 245).

The hunt continued, with Humvee and Land Rover equipped teams inserted by helicopter, hiding by day and hunting Scuds by night. Delta and SAS teams accompanied by USAF combat air controllers would locate a target and guide in airstrikes. Some teams stayed in the desert as long as three weeks. Despite several firefights with Iraqi patrols, no one died, although several operators were wounded. Other targets were also added to the list including communications sites, convoys and command posts (Waller, 1994, 344–5). The Scud hunters were fortunate in that the area they were searching, especially the more northern parts, were less inhabited than the regions closer to the Euphrates River where the strategic recon teams found so much difficulty.

The expanded target list finally allowed scope for a Ranger combat mission, the only one of the war. So, Bravo Company, 1st Battalion reinforced by the 1st platoon and weapons platoon of Alpha company, deployed on 12 February 1991 to Saudi Arabia. USAF F-15E Strike Eagles were to attack nearby antiaircraft batteries and the helicopters of the ever-reliable 160th SOAR would deposit the Rangers at an Iraqi communications site near the Jordanian border. CENTCOM planners had objected that the F-15s could just as easily bomb the communications site and eliminate the need for the raid entirely. SOCCOM countered that the Rangers would be able to capture secret documents and take Iraqi prisoners. But, as at Rio Hato in Panama, the attack on the antiaircraft batteries provided warning, this time allowing the Iraqis to escape. Although a technical success, no prisoners were taken and no significant documents retrieved (Gordon and Trainor, 1995, 246).

Despite all the effort, the number of actual Scuds destroyed was very low, by some accounts, zero. Even the major success of the Scud hunt, an air strike that took out about 20 missiles and their launchers, seems to have occurred by luck and without special-ops targeting.

A postwar Air Force study concluded that no mobile Scuds had been hit by commandos and that most of the reported successes by aircraft or commandos were actually decoys, gas tanks, flat bed trucks and oil tankers, all of which could look a great deal like missiles or their carriers. Joint Special Operations Command members insist that what they struck were real Scuds (Waller, 1994, 349–50).

Nonetheless, it seems reasonable to believe that the presence of the commandos and the rapid response of strike aircraft made life very difficult for the Scud-launching crews, forcing them to launch hastily, from unsurveyed sites and in bad weather. For some observers the reduction in effectiveness is suggested by the steadily decreasing number of missiles launched and their increasing lack of accuracy, all of which may attest to the difficulties posed by the presence of the SAS and Delta Scud hunters and the supporting fighter-bombers (Waller, 1995, 350). In the end, the basic purpose of the hunt was accomplished – it kept Israel out of the war and in all probability saved the Coalition by so doing. This is the kind of strategic-level political outcome that might be expected from a national command asset like Delta, but it was still not very satisfying to those players hungry for a high count of Delta-destroyed Scud launchers.

By virtue of skill, training and great good luck, only 21 special-operations members died in combat or from combat-related causes: 3 Delta operators, 4 men of the 160th SOAR, and 14 Air Force crewmen from the SOW, killed when their AC-130 gunship was downed by an Iraqi missile over Khafji. Additionally, an Army SF soldier was killed in a weapons-testing accident.

In the last analysis, however, the Army SF were not always well trained for their missions. During the 1980s the SF Groups had concentrated on foreign internal-defense (FID) missions and strategic reconnaissance. As it developed, the 5th Group found that it was unequipped and unprepared for any mission other than FID. They preformed very well in this role, especially in the CSTs (Boyatt, 1993, 26). However, there was little time to provide the training required for deep recon and most of those missions were unsuccessful.

Operation Provide Comfort: rescuing the Kurds

In March 1991, the Kurdish population of northern Iraq, encouraged by Coalition propaganda during the just-concluded Gulf War, rose in rebellion against the regime of dictator Saddam Hussein. In the aftermath of the uprising, US SOF, principally Army Special

Forces and Air Force assets, conducted a humanitarian assistance operation that provided an example of how a blend of Special Operations Forces, SF, CA and Psyops working together with appropriate support can provide a unique capability.

Task Force Alpha
  10th Special Forces Group (-)
  40 Commando, Royal Marines (Britain)
  Infantry Platoon (Luxembourg)
  Elements, 4th Psychological Operations Group
  39th Special Operations Wing, USAF

Civil Affairs Command
  353rd Civil Affairs Command
  354th Civil Affairs Brigade
  432d Civil Affairs Company
  Elements, 96th Civil Affairs Battalion

Although weakened by the US-led Coalition during the war, Saddam's forces were able quickly and ruthlessly to crush the Kurdish rebellion. The defeated Kurds fled into the mountains along the Iraq–Iran–Turkey border relentlessly pursued by Iraqi Mi-24 helicopter gunships. The rebels took their families and whole village populations with them as Iraqi troops began laying waste to the Kurdish areas (Bolger, 1995, 232).

Neither Turkey nor Iran, with volatile Kurd populations of their own, was anxious to permit the entry of a massive, armed migration of rebel Kurds. The migration stalled in the mountainous border region along the Iraq–Turkey–Iran frontier. By early April nearly a million Kurds were scattered through the bitterly cold high mountain passes with no sanitation, no medical aid, very little food or water and only the most makeshift shelters. For the most part, these were town-dwellers, unprepared for life on the harsh mountain slopes. Soon, between 500 and 1,000 of them were dying daily from starvation, dehydration, dysentery and exposure. On 5 April, President George Bush ordered US forces to begin airdrops of food and water to the refugees. The 10th Special Forces Group was alerted the next day for operations in Iraq.

During the war, personnel from the 10th Group, supported by MC-130 transports and MH53 helicopters from the USAF 39th Special Operations Wing, had infiltrated northern Iraq to recover downed Coalition airmen. Now, on 9 April, a handful of teams from 1st Battalion, 10th SFG entered the area in order to coordinate airdrops from the 39th's aircraft, supervise food distribution and provide what help they could with medical care and sanitation. None of these were Kurdish or Arab-speaking and had only minimal support from an Arabic-speaking CA officer. This was a real handicap, but the teams dealt with this on the ground by locating English-speakers within the Kurdish camps and using them as translator/interpreters (Wakeman, 1996).

Some of the refugee camps were utterly without outside help, in others they found that nongovernmental organizations (NGOs) such as Médecins sans Frontières (Doctors Without Borders), the Red Crescent and the International Red Cross were providing help with medical care, food relief and water purification. But despite the best efforts of the special operators and the NGO community, it was quickly apparent that this was not enough (USAJFK, 1991, 81; Bolger, 1995, 233, 235, 237; Seiple, 1996, 21, 32). There were two problems with the drops. First of all hundreds of thousands of scattered, displaced Kurds could not be supported indefinitely with airdrops. Secondly, there were several incidents in which Kurds were injured or killed when they crowded underneath the parachute-dropped pallets as they landed. Airdrops were not the solution; it was necessary to get them out of the mountains.

On 16 April, Bush supported the formation of a combined British/French/US Task Force called Provide Comfort, headquartered at NATO's Incirlik Airbase near Adana, Turkey. Its principal components were two subordinate task forces (Alpha and Bravo), a Civil Affairs Command, a Combined Air Forces command plus support units. When completely manned, this would become the largest US-led humanitarian effort since the Berlin Airlift. The initial entry force was Joint Task Force Alpha, commanded by General Richard Potter. It was organized around Potter's composite unit composed of the 10th Special Forces Group and the 39th Special Operations Wing, which was already operating among the refugee Kurds in the border areas. Alpha's basic mission was to stop the dying and stabilize the situation, then begin moving the Kurds to an internationally protected site near the city of Zakho, Iraq (USAJFK, 1991, 76-9).

Potter, a long-time SF veteran, had overall command of US Special Operations Forces in Europe (SOCEUR) and had commanded the earlier pilot recovery force. Even though Provide Comfort was a hurried, *ad hoc* operation, Potter's special operators had three great advantages often denied forces in contingency missions – they had worked together, they were designed to be deployable and had practiced numerous deployments and finally they were familiar with the area of operations. These advantages would stand them in good stead in bringing order out the chaos.

Joint Task Force Bravo, was commanded by a US Army Major General and consisted of the US Marine Corps' 24th Marine Expeditionary Unit, a number of NATO infantry battalions and supporting elements. JTF Bravo had the mission of creating three huge refugee camps near Zakho for the expected massive influx of displaced Kurds. The camps were to be operated by the Task Forces's Civil Affairs Command, formed around the 254th CA Brigade, reservists still on duty from the Gulf War and the only CA Brigade on active service. In addition to the camps, a security zone was declared inside Iraq, surrounding Zakho and the other Kurdish camps and enforced by strong combat-air patrols backed up by the ground-combat elements of Task Force Bravo (USAJFK, 1991, 54–7).

The military agenda was quite simple, to return the Kurds safe and sound to Iraq, where they would be supported by various humanitarian relief agencies, allowing the military to depart. Because of excessive delays in moving Civil Affairs units from Saudi Arabia to southern Turkey and northern Iraq, the commander did not have any Civil Affairs units or assets until 19 days into the operation. Furthermore, US and international civilian agencies were not immediately prepared to undertake aid missions of the scope and volume required, especially in such remote locations. The answer was Army Special Forces, deployed in their basic 'A' Teams.

SF was an appropriate unit, since, despite the humanitarian nature of the operation, it was not without risk, especially the risk of armed conflict. This was a humanitarian mission, but it occurred in a heavily armed environment: there were three separate armed factions of Kurds and three different classes of Iraqi military and paramilitary forces to contend with. As an 'umbrella' organization the Pesha Merga had only moderate influence over the three chief Kurdish factions. All of the Kurdish and Iraqi groups had shown themselves very willing to resort to violence and would do so again.

The Kurds themselves were a source of anxiety given their bellicose record. Each of the three distinct Kurd factions had ties to various sponsors in the region including Syria, Iran and occasionally even Iraq. All of the factions were too willing to fall back into armed squabbling among themselves once their survival needs were cared for. Furthermore, it was not beyond them to foment trouble deliberately, in an attempt to manipulate the situation to their advantage. The Task Force reported 11 incidents of violence by Kurds during the operation, most but not all, involving rioting or mob action against Iraqi officials. As an example, the Iraqi police chief in Dihok was attacked by a mob on 25 May and two days later Kurds abducted Iraqi policemen in Mangesh (Garner, 1993, unpaged).

The Iraqi military had what amounted to three factions of their own: paramilitary Special Police, the elite Republican Guards and the regular armed forces. All three hated the Kurds, were resentful of the Task Force and cooperated only under the direct threat of air and ground action by the Coalition. In the weeks following the close of the Gulf War it was not clear that any of these were under firm central direction. The various Iraqi military units were responsible for 12 violent incidents during May and June. Not only were Task Force aircraft fired on, but attacks were made on Kurd civilians resulting in at least 11 deaths (Garner, 1993, unpaged). The Iraqis had also planted mines throughout the region resulting in numerous deaths and serious injuries among the Kurds and injury to several Task Force soldiers including two Americans (Rudd, 1993, 12).

At the camp level these difficulties fell squarely on the SF 'A' teams. For the most part it was handled by working through the Pesha Merga, an umbrella organization temporarily uniting the principal armed guerrilla factions of the Kurds. Several brigades of these Kurdish guerrillas were active in the camps and provided both leadership and security. These elements were used by the SF to identify the principal extended-family groups in the camps and use them to distribute food and relief supplies.[3]

The situation was made even more difficult by the wide assortment of non-military organizations involved, all with widely varying purposes, interests and objectives. These were an incredible muddle of governmental, nongovernmental and official international agencies, not to mention a full complement of international press representatives. To a large degree, all these non-military players were the business of the JTF Civil Affairs Command.

Civil Affairs operations

From the Civil Affairs Command viewpoint, the most important non-military actor was probably the US Agency for International Development's DART (Disaster Assistance Response Team) which provided funding and helped coordinate the other agencies, including the assortment of UN groups: the World Food Program, the High Commissioner for Refugees and the World Health Organization.

However, the key groups in terms of immediate assistance were the various volunteer nongovernmental, humanitarian relief organizations. These handled more-or-less specific elements of the refugee's needs. CARE International, for example, supplied basic foods while Médecins sans Frontières (MSF) provided medical care.

Finally, the various other nations involved, notably Turkey, had their own national priorities to pursue. In the Turkish case it was to remove the Iraqi Kurds from Turkish territory while doing nothing to encourage unrest among their domestic Kurdish minority. In practice this meant they were cooperative, but not very supportive (USAJFK, 1991, 74).

All of these agendas elbowing each other while trying to focus on the Kurdish refugee issue made for an uncomfortable situation indeed. In order to accomplish their mission, the SOF troopers had to gain Kurdish trust, keep them alive and help them to the camps at Zakho while protecting them along the way. And all of this had to be accomplished without involving the Task Force in what was, after all, an Iraqi civil war. Unfortunately, nearly all of the Psychological Operations capacity and Civil Affairs expertise was concentrated at the Task Force command level. Little or no support was provided at ground level for the SF teams (Wakeman, 1996).

In the mountains, relief workers from nongovernmental organizations (NGOs) were impressed with the cultural awareness of the SF troopers, including such fine points as having tea with clan leaders before talking business (Seiple, 1996, 40–1). This was a complicated business, since it required the various SF operators (chiefly noncommissioned officers) to deal with various Kurdish factions, handle tribal matters and generally to immerse themselves in Kurdish cultural and tribal environments while retaining their individuality and their identity as a US soldier.

A key SF ability that emerged was their ability to produce assessment of the state of the population in terms of health, welfare, morale and medical needs. At the same time the SF provided immediate life-saving help as in the camp at Cucuka. There the SF medics found 250 infants that the local doctors had triaged as hopeless, beyond saving. The medics saved all but three of the children.

The reports provided a comprehensive estimate of the situation as it progressed and could be combined with NGO reports to determine the needs in various locations. This led to a loose prioritization in which NGOs acting according to need, expertise, preference and location would take up the tasks required. As Seiple points out, this illustrates a basic tenet of cooperative operations:

something must be exchanged. NGOs and others will not cooperate in most cases unless they gain something from it, in this instance information and logistical support (Seiple, 1996, 41).

The ability to provide transport was another, and perhaps more important, reason for NGO/military cooperation. Beginning with SF UH-60 Blackhawks and Air Force C-130 cargo planes, supplemented by Navy helicopters and later trucks from the allies, the special-operations teams could deliver relief supplies with unmatched speed and efficiency. The result was a net gain for all concerned. The NGOs gained immediate credibility with both sponsors and aid recipients by using military transport to deliver large amounts of needed aid quickly and where required. In return for this service the NGOs accepted *de facto* the military coordination of the effort, which facilitated the military desire to stabilize the situation and end their mission successfully (Seiple, 1996, 43). The major point here, perhaps, is that Task Force Alpha was willing to take a secondary, cooperative role of facilitating the NGO relief activities rather than trying to be in charge.

Lieutenant Colonel Nick Petrella, the Civil Affairs officer in charge of NGO coordination, explained it this way, 'never create the impression that you're in charge ... in essence, we are, but you can never give that impression' (Seiple, 1996, 43). There was also the question of interaction within the special-operations units. Petrella had, for example, to be careful to maintain a good relationship with the special-ops Blackhawk pilots, who were not always enthusiastic about working with the NGOs. Despite some 'initial ambivalence' the pilots finally accepted the idea that helping the NGOs was the fastest way to wind up the mission and cooperated (Seiple, 1996, 44).

Finally, the skill of the individual troopers was essential. Here the professional skills of the Special Forces soldier came into play. The doctors and medical technicians of MSF (Doctors Without Borders) were distinctly anti-military at first and very reluctant to work with the SF medics or share facilities with them. But the level of professionalism of the highly trained medics and their obvious concern for their refugee patients soon broke down these barriers. Ironically, however, in some of the mountain camps the same MSF personnel refused to remain without Army SF teams to provide security (Wakeman, 1996).

In the same way, the capability of other SF team members to assist with construction and public measures went a long way toward building an atmosphere of mutual respect between Task Force Alpha and the nongovernmental relief agencies.

Psychological Operations

Psychological Operations are treated as an afterthought in most accounts of the operation, when they are mentioned at all. This is neither just nor justifiable. Like Civil Affairs, Psychological Operations are key and essential to the successful conduct of unconventional operations. In the case of Provide Comfort, a 78 man Psychological Operations Task Force (POTF) was established at CJTF headquarters in Incirlik, Turkey. A number of these were assigned as direct support to the various elements of the Combined Task Force, including Task Force Alpha (4th POG, 1994, 2).

As described by General Potter, there were four parallel campaigns at the highest level. One targeted the fractious Kurds with the message that the Task Force was not concerned with internal Kurdish strife but was there to help all Kurds and needed their cooperation to do so. Another was simply instructional, aimed at instructing the refugees themselves in obtaining and using relief supplies and returning to their homes. A third was aimed at the Iraqi forces in the area, making sure they understood the safety and exclusion zones and out-of-bounds areas established by the Task Forces. The final campaign was more general in its targeting and sought to inform the international community in the operation of the rules, conduct and prohibitions that applied to their activities.

The critical role of Psyops is not always easy to appreciate, but they are the link to the population. In situations where military commanders and civilian relief workers must communicate with nearly a million people in many scattered locations, Psyops services are impossible to live without. A handful of SF 'A' Teams and relief workers could not reach, let alone provide instruction to, any significant fraction of the refugees.

At the survival level, the 4th POG helped stop the dying by creating leaflets in Kurdish, explaining the airdrops, how to prepare the military rations, identifying and explaining the special infant food dropped as well as providing simple instructions on sanitation in a survival situation. In the initial stages of the operation the Psyoperators also prepared loudspeaker messages, radio broadcasts and leaflets explaining how to reach the refugee camps and how to avoid the thousands of mines spread indiscriminately by the Iraqis.

Once the Kurds had been assembled in the camps, the loudspeaker teams were used for crowd control, peacekeeping and information functions such as safety messages. As in the mountains, their language ability and regional expertise made the Psyoperators an invaluable link between the helping organizations and the population they were attempting to serve (4th POG, 1994, 3).

Most official accounts of Operation Provide Comfort describe the operations of the conventional Task Force elements in some detail. Likewise, the Special Forces teams involved receive at least a nod. The Civil Affairs and Psychological Operations units involved, however, are barely mentioned. Arguably, Civil Affairs operations were the lynchpin of the entire mission. Without skilled specialists able to contact, coordinate and influence the dozens of non-military organizations involved it would have been impossible for the military forces alone to succeed.

By the same token, the Psychological Operations teams provided more than the traditional surrender demands. Their ability to communicate with large numbers of people through basic mass communications – loudspeakers and leaflets – was essential to the success of the mission. Without units like the 4th Psyops Group, it is simply impossible for the various elements of the military force to provide information, instructions or even basic advice to tens of thousands of persons.

All of the special operators – SF, CA and Psyops – demonstrated their ability to survive, operate and succeed in an austere environment.

Most accounts place great emphasis on the regional expertise, language ability and cross-cultural training of the special operators. But interviews suggest that this was largely confined to those few SF teams who had been part of the aircrew-recovery mission during the Gulf War and did not even apply to all of those. More important was the willingness of all the special-ops personnel to accept the idea that cultural questions were central to success, not merely side issues.

The unconventional warfare training (meaning working with guerrillas) emphasized in SF training proved to be important by providing a model of 'how to proceed' in an unfamiliar situation.

> There was nothing specific in my training to prepare for a situation like this. I used the basic steps of UW organization – contact methods/ training procedures and confidence-building measures – as the basis for what I did in the camps. We just never did combat operations. (Wakeman, 1996)

The fact the all the 'A' teams had at least some degree of cross-training gave them a capacity for flexible organization that enabled commanders to task organize to meet demands that were unforeseen in conventional or special operations organization tables. Cross-training enabled other team members to assist the medics or the team engineers or in air operations as the situation required.

In the dismal mountain refugee sites, the SF set about using available materials to improve sanitation, dispose of waste and train the refugees in proper sanitation. In the words of one observer: 'this could never be taught in a block of instruction ... it came from the quick wit, flexibility and ingenuity of the well-trained SF soldier' (USAJFK, 1991, 53).

Much of the advantage of the special operators came from their capacity for dirty, unglamourous tasks well removed from ordinary military skills. For example, SF and Civil Affairs specialists quickly determined that military rations were not the best food for the refugees. In addition, they found that much of the other food relief delivered was wasted, since these items, such as snack foods and a huge shipment of cranberry sauce, were often nutritionally doubtful and culturally unacceptable to the Kurds. What they wanted and could use were the bulk foods to which they were accustomed – tea, rice, flour, tomato paste and the like. These could be efficiently delivered in quantity and procured locally in Turkey.[4]

The equally unglamourous SF and Civil Affairs ability to conduct public-health assessments and provide instruction and assistance with sanitation was one of the keys to survival of the refugees, but is often overlooked in accounts of the mission. Medical assistance alone, no matter how dramatic or professional, could not break the cycle of poor sanitation, pollution and disease. The military credibility of the SF troopers helped them influence the Kurds properly to intern dead bodies, dig latrines and clean up refuse, while soldiers and Kurds worked together at the dirty but necessary business of burying garbage and dead animals (USAJFK, 1991, 82).

This flexibility combined with the maturity and problem solving ability of the SOF to result in an uncanny ability to solve problems with available resources and within existing limitations. This. together with UW training, enabled them to overcome the language problem by using Kurdish English-speakers. This is not so simple as it might seem, since all of the English speakers were members (and often important ones) of various factions within the Kurdish independence movement and required delicate handling as well as an awareness of their agendas.

The special operators were also unique in their ability to function with minimal support in the harsh mountain environment of the refugee camps. Both NGOs and conventional military units usually possessed more personnel, better specialized equipment and had professional skills such as medicine that the special ops teams could not match. The special operators, however, were disciplined, self-contained and could support themselves while assisting the refugees. As one observer said, 'Any other unit would have spent more time trying to survive than helping the DCs [displaced civilians]. The SFODAs require very little to operate – a mission, their organic equipment, MREs and a little patch of dirt to call home' (USAJFK, 1991, 80).

Although General Potter's staff had the advantage of having worked together during the Gulf War, most of the other SOF elements had not. Given the emergency nature of the mission, with virtually no planning or preparation, the flexibility of SOF was at a premium.

While the military status of the SF soldiers may have initially put off some of the NGOs, it was an important asset in working among the warlike Kurds who respected the armed soldiers and welcomed their protection. As already noted, the active cooperation of the Pesha Merga guerrilla organizations was essential. The SF identity as soldiers gave them status among the tribespeople that enabled them to develop an infrastructure within each camp. This was vital, since an 83-man SF Company could not control distribution of food, bottled water, clothing and other supplies (USAJFK, 1991, 81).

By mid-July 1991 virtually all coalition forces from both Task Force Alpha and Bravo were withdrawn from Northern Iraq and the relief responsibilities assumed by the United Nations and various NGOs (USASOC, 1994, 118).[5]

This was not a humanitarian operation that could have been mounted or maintained by other than a military force. This reality was brought home by a sadly ironic counterpoint when the relief effort in northern Iraq collapsed in September and October of 1996 following an Iraqi military strike and fighting between two factions of the Kurds. In September about 2,000 Kurds who were employed by the remaining nongovernmental relief organizations were evacuated from Iraq by a US-led rescue effort and taken to the island of Guam, a US territory. An additional 4,500 were similarly evacuated to Guam between November 1996 and January 1997 (*Washington Post*, 'US Flies Iraqis to Guam', 7 December 1996, 1).

USSOCOM continues the drug war

By 1991, USSOCOM had made considerable progress in accomplishing its basic purpose, standardization among the various Special Operations Forces. Equipment, terminology, training, weapons and even communications equipment and frequencies were far more standard than ever before and the separate service components trained together on a regular basis.

In 1991, under some pressure from Congress and DOD, the new USCINCSOC, tasked his operations staff to find out what more could be done by SOF to advance the national counterdrug effort. Shortly afterwards, USSOCOM increased its training program with US law-enforcement agencies (LEAs) and began supporting counterdrug operations throughout the US Southern Command area of responsibility (AOR) and along the US–Mexico border. SOF Mobile Training Teams (MTTs) were deployed on a short-term basis to the principal cocaine-producing countries (Colombia, Peru and Bolivia) in support of the Andean Ridge Drug Strategy. They trained host-nation armed forces assigned to counternarcotics duties, primarily through exercises and mobile training teams.

Along the US southwest border, SOF conducted special reconnaissance missions and military skills training for law-enforcement agencies. SOF engaged in some limited operational assistance and Psychological Ooperations support to host nations. Army Special Forces provided light infantry training to host-nation counterdrug police and military forces. Special Boat Unit personnel and SEALs provided riverine training and instruction in coastal ship interdiction operations. SOF aviators also conducted foreign internal defense training of host nation air force units. In addition to these activities, CA personnel provided assistance and psychological operations personnel furnished military information support teams (MIST) to assist US embassies.

By late 1991, SOF accounted for 30 percent of all Joint Task Force Six (JTF-6) counterdrug (CD) operations along the US southwest border in support of LEAs. At the same time in the SOUTHCOM AOR, SOF participation in CD deployments for training (DFT) and mobile training teams (MTT) increased by 200 percent over previous years.

Under Stiner's successor, General Wayne Downing, the new USCINSOC, the scope of SOF counterdrug activities widened. In particular, Army Special Forces increased their support of US law-enforcement agencies. SOF deployed on training operations in South America and MTTs throughout the world to train host-nation military and paramilitary forces. Special Forces, SEALs, and Air Force special operations command foreign internal-defense units traveled overseas to conduct small unit tactical training of foreign military and law-enforcement personnel, and provide operational planning assistance, to enable them to carry out drug-interdiction activities within their own countries.

In the southwestern USA, Army Special Forces units manned a Rapid Support Unit (RSU) to support short-notice requests by the US Border Patrol and other law enforcement agencies for special reconnaissance and listening posts/observation posts (LP/OP). These units conducted clandestine surveillance of suspected illegal trafficking sites and assisted law-enforcement interdiction activities.

Not all SF commanders and personnel were pleased about the diversion of effort into what one derisively referred to as the 'pillow-fight against drugs'. One SF Group commander complained that the use of his teams was not so bad, but the manner of use was a real problem. The tendency, he said, was for a law enforcement agency or military unit to ask for special skills such as medics or radio/electronic communications; since his Group did not have 'spare docs or radio operators', filling these requirements meant that he needed to take the radio operators from his teams. The result was that those teams, now lacking critical personnel, could not be deployed for other purposes and were effectively lost to him until the missing soldiers returned.

Nevertheless, counterdrug missions continued. By 1997, USSOCOM coordinated and oversaw an average of 250 SOF counterdrug missions each year executed by Army, Navy and Air Force components within the USA and deployed to numerous host nations around the world. SOF conducted overseas missions, primarily to cocaine and heroin-source nations, by providing foreign internal-defense (FID) and unconventional training (USSOCOM, 'USSOCOM Counterdrug Efforts', USSOCOM History Office, 1997, 6).

NOTES

1. Trainor suggests that Schwartzkopf's feelings about SOF were a result of his experience with them during the invasion of Grenada. Personal correspondence with the author, January 1997.
2. General Trainor cites 'CIA/DIA sources' for this conclusion. Personal correspondence with the author, January 1997.
3. Many of these problems were felt at the camp level, where SF captains and majors often found themselves dealing with factional feuding among the Kurds, Iraqi military remaining in the area, and Iraqi military and intelligence attempts to infiltrate the camps. In many cases the infiltrators were apprehended by the Pesha Merga, creating still more problems. In one case, a US Marine Corp unit was used to release captured Iraqi infiltrators being held for execution at a Pesha Merga headquarters outside Zakho.

4. Wakeman notes that this was also true of what Europeans would regard as staple foods – corn and lima beans, for example. 'Piles of this kind of food were discarded by the Kurds. The problem was that we couldn't turn off the supply of these items.' On the other hand some non-European food items were popular, such as sunflower oil, since the Kurds used the oil both for cooking and for weapons maintenance (Wakeman, 1996).
5. General Potter felt strongly that the key to the success of the operation at the strategic level was the leadership of General Shalikashivili as overall commander of Operation Provide Comfort. His major contribution, in addition to the planning and overall control of the mission, was his ability to orchestrate the various entities involved to provide unity of command while keeping 'national reps at arms' length from his operational commanders' in order to minimize external influences (Potter, interview, 22 January 1997, Carlisle Barracks, PA).

10 Somalia and Haiti

In the fall of 1993 US SOF became involved in a mission that re-illustrated several uncomfortable truths about special operations. As noted in USSOCOM's 'Publication 1' (1996), special ops 'are focused on strategic or operational objectives'. The clearest example of this is the hope for a single decisive action that will end hostilities, a bold stroke that can only be accomplished by SOF. In Panama and Somalia this 'bold stroke' was the tantalizing prospect offered by the possibility of kidnapping a single critical leader. SOF's capacity for these high-risk, high-reward missions gives them a potential impact far beyond that of similar-sized or trained conventional units. This is equally true when an operation goes wrong.

In the summer of 1993, a United Nations civil-military operation called UNOSOM II (United Nations Operation in Somalia) was underway in the violence-racked East African nation of Somalia. This was a 'failed-state' situation in which the national government had literally collapsed and anarchy ensued. UNOSOM II was a follow-on to an earlier US-sponsored and led hybrid mission that combined humanitarian relief with security functions. The US-led mission, UNITAF (United Task Force) succeeded in bringing a degree of stability to the country and handed over its job to UNOSOM II.

Special Forces personnel from the 5th SFG had been present in the country under both UNITAF and UNOSOM II, performing a variety of low-profile functions but chiefly working with the local clans in the countryside to restore a measure of self-sufficiency. These were unconventional warfare missions, carried on far from the capital, Mogadishu, and attracted little notice. Conversely, another SOF mission, this time a direct-action effort by SFOD-Delta and the Rangers, would have enormous impact across the USA, reverberating in the White House with significant consequences for US foreign policy.

Although ordinary Somalis greeted the UN force as saviors from starvation, violence and disease, the warlords contending for power in the chaotic state saw the UN intervention as an impediment in their competition for control of the country. Controlling these violent armed factions was one of the important missions of the UN military contingent. Prominent among the leaders of these factions was 'General' Mohammed Farah Aideed, who led a powerful clan-based faction called the Somali National Alliance (SNA) (Butler, 1996).

On 5 June a group of soldiers from the Pakistani contingent of the UN force conducted a scheduled inspection of a weapons storage site belonging to the SNA in Mogadishu, the Somali capital. Despite hostile crowds of SNA supporters, the inspection went off without incident. But as the Pakistanis were returning to their base, they were ambushed and ferociously attacked with grenades and automatic weapons by members of the SNA. A US-manned Quick Reaction Force (QRF) and elements of the Italian military contingent went to the aid of the embattled Pakistanis but not before 24 Pakistanis were killed and 50 wounded. To make matters worse, the 24 dead were mutilated by the SNA. Major General Thomas Montgomery, deputy commander of UNOSOM II described them this way: 'I mean disembowelled, throats slit, eyes punched out, terrible things done to them' (Rosegrant, 1996, 6). When considered together with other attacks on UN forces, it was clear the ambush was pre-planned as part of a general offensive against the UN force.

According to General Montgomery, the SNA attackers 'used heavy weapons, they used machineguns and a rocket propelled grenade, and they covered the ambush site with women and children, making the whole scene look very innocent. It was not just a bunch of guys in flip-flops who were out there' (ibid.).

Acting at the behest of the Pakistani Ambassador, the UN Security Council immediately passed Resolution 837 confirming UNOSOM's authority to 'take all necessary measures against all those responsible' for the ambush, and targeting specifically the SNA. As related by Montgomery, 'The United Nations Security Council met over the night and gave us a new mission ... to find and arrest the people who were responsible for the massacre. There wasn't any doubt in anyone's mind in Mogadishu who that was' (ibid.). The obvious target was self-proclaimed 'General' Mohammed Farah Aideed, leader of the SNA.

Acting through UN Secretary-General Boutros Boutros-Ghali, the head of UNOSOM II, Special Representative Admiral Jonathan Howe, requested a variety of additional military support from the USA including Special Operations Forces. Howe felt that special operators would be useful both in hunting for Aideed and in the event of Aideed trying to retaliate by seizing any of the numerous UN civilians in and around Mogadishu. Washington dispatched equipment including extra AC-130 gunships but withheld further Special Operations Forces. However, the Pentagon did place Army Special Forces Detachment Delta on alert and told them to prepare for a possible mission in Somalia (Rick Atkinson, 'The Raid That Went Wrong', *Washington Post*, 30 January 1994, 1).

Beginning on 12 June, UNOSOM undertook operations to cripple Aideed's power and capture the warlord. The AC-130s and Cobra armed helicopters destroyed the SNA's radio station and five of its weapons storage sites. On 17 June, Aideed's command headquarters was attacked and destroyed by a coordinated air–ground assault. None of this was sufficient to bring Aideed under control or even to convince him to open negotiations with the UN. Accordingly, on the same day, Howe identified Aideed as personally responsible for the massacre of the Pakistanis and called for the warlord's arrest.

This was easier said than done. Mogadishu was a maze of alleys, choked streets and byways where the 'General' could vanish at will. It was almost impossible for an armed force to move through the crowded streets without Aideed and his supporters becoming instantly aware of the fact. Furthermore, UNOSOM II had only a handful of military intelligence analysts to meet the needs of the force, without adding the mission of tracking Aideed. Faced with these difficulties, Howe and Montgomery, supported by the US State department, once again asked for Special Operations Forces to assist in the hunt. Recalling the poor results of the hunt for Noriega in Panama, both Joint Chiefs Chairman Colin Powell and CENTCOM Commander Joseph Hoar reportedly opposed any SOF deployment because they feared further military entanglement and because the chances of success seemed very low (Butler, 1996).

Receiving no support for the request from the Pentagon, Montgomery gave the task of finding and arresting Aideed to the US Quick Reaction Force. Army SF elements already in Somalia provided training for the mission but the assignment was received with skepticism within the QRF, since it was primarily a conventional light-infantry battalion without the equipment or extended training for such a mission. 'The report we gave back to Washington ourselves is that UNOSOM II ... just did not have the capability to go out and hunt for this guy. So we weren't going to spend a lot of energy doing it' (Rosegrant, 1996, 8).

According to a member of Montgomery's staff, 'Everybody knew we didn't have the capability.' The staff then set two conditions designed to 'set conditions for success' by mandating that any such attempt to snatch Aideed would: (1) take place in an open, non-congested area to reduce the risk to both the force and local civilians, and (2) would take place only in an area where ground vehicles could be assured of reaching the force in the event of trouble (Butler, 1996).

In July the UN distributed a 'wanted' poster on Aideed and reward leaflets offering $25,000 for information leading to the General's apprehension. The initial response was a counteroffer by Aideed of $1 million for Admiral Howe's head.

Intense efforts by the tiny UNOSOM intelligence element finally paid off on 12 July when the QRF was able to successfully assault a meeting of the SNA's senior leadership. In contrast to the careful restraint of previous QRF strikes, this was a violent attack by ground forces and helicopter gunships which stormed the meeting site killing a number of SNA members, estimated at between 20 and 73.

Although it was a military success, the aggressive unilateral US operation created friction inside the UN mission. This was exacerbated when periodic clashes between peacekeepers and SNA militiamen resulted in UN, SNA and civilian casualties, creating the impression that a supposedly peaceful humanitarian mission had developed into something close to a war. Despite the clear fact that the US operation had come after a series of Aideed attacks, many still considered the latter to be SNA retaliation for the US raid. As a result of these pressures, an already shaky UN coalition began to show signs of unravelling.

UN officials argued that UNOSOM was responding to an altered situation. They pointed out that Aideed's forces had gone on the offensive with the Pakistani ambush and continued afterwards with attacks on the Italian, Nigerian and Moroccan UN contingents. Various negotiation options were considered but after four US military policemen were killed by a command detonated mine on 8 August, the USA agreed to dispatch the Special Forces requested earlier by Boutros-Ghali. The response took the form of a special mission unit or SMU. Later that month, Task Force Ranger, a combined force of about 450, made up of JSOC's deployable headquarters, C Troop of the Delta commandos, support personnel and Army Rangers from B Company, 3rd Battalion departed Fort Bragg. At the same time, 1st Battalion, 160th SOAR dispatched a group of more than a dozen helicopters, MH-60 Blackhawks, plus MH-6 and AH6J 'little birds', the transport and attack versions (Bolger, 1995, 307).

Task Force Ranger was not, however, to be under the control of the United Nations or UNOSOM. Instead, it was under unilateral US command, with control exercised by a newly created joint special-operations command for this mission under Major General William F. Garrison and reporting directly to General Hoar at Central Command (CENTCOM), the regional Commander in Chief for US forces.[1]

Even though the arrival of the new force was appreciated, it was not greeted with great optimism. James Woods, US Deputy Secretary of Defense for African Affairs, was quoted as saying, 'From the beginning, it was recognized that the operation probably would not succeed. That was made very, very clear to the people in charge. Snatching Aideed safely out of the midst of his neighborhood was a very unlikely proposition' (Rosegrant, 1996, 11). Nevertheless, grabbing Aideed from the midst of his guards and clansmen deep in the most hostile part of Mogadishu was not too different from a hostage rescue. Perhaps it could be done.

Task Force Ranger began operations while at the same time Howe sought to negotiate Aideed's voluntary abdication, possibly into foreign exile. This was sometimes referred to as the 'two-fisted' approach, and at first it seemed to be working. After an embarrassing first mission in which the Delta snatch teams descended on a UN compound by mistake, the Rangers and Delta staged six missions in pursuit of Mohammed Aideed and his top aides.[2] By early September, Aideed's lieutenants were in contact with the UN in Mogadishu as the Task Force kept up the pressure. Meanwhile Delta and the Rangers were succeeding nicely in upsetting Aideed's command arrangements and in arresting a number of his top aides, all without suffering a major casualty.

The 'Ranger raid'

Then, on the afternoon of 3 October, elements of B company Rangers and members of Special Forces Operational Detachment-Delta set out to raid the Olympic Hotel, an ambitious operation deep inside the SNA-controlled part of the city where Aideed was believed to be meeting with his senior lieutenants and supporters. Dropping out of their MH-6 'little birds' and specially modified Blackhawk helicopters, the Delta troopers caught the meeting by surprise while about 60 Rangers took up blocking positions at intersections around the building. When the soldiers burst into the hotel they did not find Aideed, but did succeed in capturing 24 senior members of his clan and two of the 'General's' personal aides (UNOSOM II, 1993, 1).

The team assigned to grab Aideed's followers called for extraction within 20 minutes of the first assault. Waiting Humvees and trucks driven by more of B Company set out through the city streets to pick up the prisoners and the assault force. Movement was slow through the crowded streets and stealth was impossible. The convoy was further slowed by an ambush that took one truck out of action.

Meanwhile Aideed's supporters, summoned by the commotion, rallied in the streets near the hotel and began firing automatic weapons and volleys of dozens of rocket-propelled grenades (RPGs) at the Task Force and its supporting helicopters. Special operations depend greatly on speed, being able to strike and depart before the enemy can rally and react. But once again, that kind of quick, clean operation was proving difficult to bring off. After forcing their way through the ambush, the trucks and Humvees reached the Olympic Hotel and began loading the prisoners and wounded. So far all was according to plan, or close enough.

Then a UH-60 Black Hawk was shot down by a RPG, crashing into the street just northeast of the hotel. A 14-man combat search and rescue (CSAR) team fast-roped into the crash site and secured the area but the opposition was fierce. When a platoon of 28 Rangers moved toward the crash scene, 25 were wounded before reaching the downed chopper (Spitzer, 1993, 2; USASOC, 1996, 1). The Somalis continued to have luck hitting the helicopters. RPGs damaged three more within a few minutes of each other while a mob of unarmed civilians protected the gunmen from counterfire. The second and fourth helicopters hit managed to limp back to friendly areas but the third, call sign 'Super 64', crash landed in a densely populated area.

Since the CSAR team was already committed and the helicopters spread thin covering the convoy and the first crash site, the situation was grim as gunmen within the mob began shooting at the downed Super 64. Two Delta snipers, Master Sergeant Gary Gordon and Sergeant First Class Randall Shughart, were covering the mission from an MH-6 and saw injured moving inside the wreckage of the downed aircraft. The pair tried to go to their aid but the tremendous volume of small-arms fire thwarted their first attempt. On the second try they managed to reach the wreck.

Back at the hotel the Rangers and Delta operators remained under heavy fire from automatic weapons, hand grenades and RPGs as they consolidated around the first crash site. They managed to group together and establish a perimeter inside buildings where they could try to keep their wounded alive and fight off the swarming gunmen. As the sun set, they finally gained an advantage. Using their night-vision goggles, they were able to spot the gunmen in the darkness without themselves being seen. Blackhawks from the 160th SOAR came through the withering fire to drop water and ammunition while other choppers gave fire support. Small groups of Somalis kept probing the US positions as the troopers kept shooting and waited for extraction. They would wait for ten hours.

A hastily assembled relief column, composed of the remainder of B Company, including cooks, clerks and all other Rangers, set out in six Humvees. But the streets were fully aroused by now and it was impossible. Although joined by the Quick Reaction Force from the conventional infantry, the lightly armed soldiers were pinned down by heavy fire and only broke contact with the aid of another infantry unit and helicopter gunships.

At the crash of Super 64, Shughart and Gordon managed to render first aid to the injured crew and move them to shelter despite a continuous hail of gunfire. Several times women and children ran forward to point out the sergeants as targets for the Somali gunmen. The two sergeants held back the surging mob until their ammunition ran out and they were killed along with three of the wounded crewmen. One of the wounded, a pilot, was beaten badly but taken alive as a prisoner.

Finally, at about 2 a.m. the next morning, an armored relief column composed of the remaining Rangers reinforced with elements of the 10th Mountain and led by Pakistani tanks and Malaysian armored vehicles managed to force their way through streets full of continuous gunfire and RPGs to reach the site of the siege and make a successful evacuation.

By the time the mission was finally over, 19 US soldiers were dead or missing, 17 from TF Ranger. Eighty-four US soldiers were wounded, 60 from TF Ranger. One Malaysian from the relief column had died, and four were wounded. The captured helicopter pilot was released 11 days later. Estimates of the number of Somali casualties ranged from about 300 killed and perhaps 800 wounded (Bolger, 1995, 327), to more than three times those figures (Boyatt, 1997).

Given the fact that the raid succeeded and that the Rangers and Delta had held out for over ten hours against overwhelming odds before withdrawing in good order, it had to be counted as a victory. But the political repercussions were immediate and negative. When international television showed the mutilated body of one of the Super 64's crewmen dragged through the streets by cheering Somalis the effect was enormous.

US domestic opposition to the presence in Somalia seemed to crystallize at once, and the Clinton administration was scourged in editorial columns across the country. Hearings were demanded in Washington as an outraged Congress called for immediate withdrawal. National Security Advisor Anthony Lake offered his resignation, which the President refused. Defense Secretary Les Aspin resigned later as he came under increasing criticism for his role in what was now perceived as a disastrously failed policy. The only question for the Clinton administration was whether the USA should pull out precipitously or over a period of time.

Ironically, US military leaders in Somalia were planning a major campaign against the SNA, whose faction had been severely weakened and demoralized by the large losses taken in the 3 October raid and the subsequent firefight with Delta and the Rangers. By some estimates as many as one-third of the SNA's total number of fighters had been killed or wounded in the battle. All of this came to a halt on 6 October when word came from Washington that the military campaign against Aideed would cease at once and preparations be made for a phased withdrawal of US forces. In the words of General Montgomery, UNOSOM's deputy commander, 'It's obvious that, if there was no political will in the United States to hang in there and see it through, we had to come out' (Rosegrant, 1996, 15).

Nor did the repercussions end there. The word 'Somalia' for a time became shorthand for opposition to several varieties of US foreign involvement including humanitarian missions, involvement in Africa, situations of 'failed states', or military involvement in such missions.

In a development far too reminiscent of Tet 1968, a resounding US military victory had turned sour. By any objective standard the siege at the Olympic Hotel should have been seen as a US triumph, but by the alchemy of press and policy it had been turned into an incredible political defeat.

This provided a graphic demonstration of the uncomfortable truth that 'strategic or operational objectives' carry high risks along with the possibility of great rewards. It also illustrated again that the success of this type of operation depends on speed, surprise and skill, and that even a superabundance of the last two may not make up for the lack of the first. As soon as the streets of Mogadishu began to approach the firepower levels of a conventional battlefield the special operators were hard pressed to hold their own.[3]

VOODOO WARRIORS: UNCONVENTIONAL WARFARE IN HAITI

Like Somalia, Haiti is an example of the gray area created when national governments collapse. This was a chaotic situation characterized by violence and a humanitarian emergency. The Haiti case is worth exploring as an example of SOF, especially Army SF, functioning in an unconventional role, a role for which they are uniquely suited, rather than as adjuncts to conventional forces. It also points up the limits of military intervention.

When Special Operations Forces were dispatched to Haiti in 1994, Army SF, CA and Psyops found themselves with the lion's share of the work. First they were assigned a variety of tasks during the long period of sanctions and negotiations that preceded the intervention. Then, after the actual intervention, the conventional forces virtually ceded the countryside to Army SOF while concentrating on the two principal cities, Port-au-Prince and Cap Haitien. This was an opportunity for the Army SF to show what their unconventional warfare capacity could do in action.

SOF operations in Haiti called for a variety of capabilities almost tailor-made for Army Special Forces including regional orientation, language capabilities, cross-cultural communication, Civil Affairs, Psychological Operations, and, importantly, the ability to present a military image that would prevent violence by intimidating any opposition.

Background to intervention

Occupying the western third of the island of Hispaniola, which it shares with the Dominican Republic, Haiti is by all measures the poorest country in the Caribbean. Ironically, the Haitian intervention was indirectly caused by what looked like a triumph for democracy in that desperately poor nation. In December 1990, Jean-Bertrand Aristide, a politically active Catholic priest, won a surprising electoral victory by mobilizing support among the poverty-stricken masses against the tiny elite that had historically controlled the island. For a brief period it seemed as if real reform might come to Haiti.

But, in September 1991, a violent military coup toppled Aristide's government and the president fled into exile in the USA. In the aftermath of the coup, USAID estimated that 3,000 Aristide supporters were slain outright (USAID, 1994). The increasingly desperate conditions led thousands of Haitians to seek asylum in the USA, leaving the island in rickety boats that too often failed to make the journey. When possible, US Coast Guard vessels intercepted the Haitians at sea, returning them to Haiti, then, when increasing numbers fled, to the US base at Guantánamo, Cuba.

Opposed by both the Organization of American States and the United Nations, the new government had no genuine legitimacy, internally or externally. The coup was followed by two years of violence against domestic opponents and political maneuvering to avoid international sanctions. In October 1993, when the junta reneged on a UN-brokered deal to return Aristide to power, international economic sanctions were reimposed and conditions on the island continued to worsen as the junta became ever more violent, corrupt and abusive in its rule. The Forces Armée de Haiti (FAd'H) combined both military and police functions, giving them an absolute monopoly of coercive power. In support of the *de facto* government, they carried out a massive and systematic series of human rights abuses. At the same time, the civil infrastructure (such as roads, ports, utilities, water, sewerage and hospitals) had been devastated by decades of neglect and deteriorated even further.

It was increasingly obvious that the situation was not going to resolve itself and the USA began to make military plans while pressing the UN for action. On 5 May 1994 the UN Security Council again called for the resignation of the military government and imposed even more stringent sanctions. The US XVIII Airborne Corps and Special Ops began planning for military action in Haiti. One lesson from Panama and Desert Storm was the need for early Psyops and Civil Affairs planning, and the accompanying realization that effective CA and Psyops on any large-scale meant reservists were needed. USSOCOM pressed for and received an early Presidential Reserve Call-up. The early call-up was critical, because it allowed USSOCOM to tailor a mix of Active and Reserve SOF specialties to mission requirements. Over 400 Reservists including the Air Force Special Operation Command's (AFSOC) AC-130A and EC-130 crews, and selected USASOC Civil Affairs and Psychological Operations units were called into active duty.

SOF pre-intervention missions in Haiti

Pre-intervention missions were:

1. Special Boat Units and SEALs conduct maritime interdiction in conjunction with conventional Naval elements.
2. 4th POG and 193rd Special Operations Squadron (Air National Guard) conduct Psychological Operations to prepare the populace for Aristide's return and the possibility of intervention.
3. 96th CA (augmented by reservists) and 4th POG assist in the operation of Haitian refugee camps at Guantánamo Bay, Cuba; and a Cuban refugee camp at Howard Air Force Base, Panama.[4]

These pre-intervention efforts all went well, with no serious problems.

From 24 May–25 October 1994, two Cyclone Class Coastal Patrol Craft (PC) from Navy Special Warfare Command (NAVSPEC-WARCOM) conducted continuous maritime interdiction near the Haitian–Dominican Republic border. Each PC was supported by an eight-man SEAL squad with a 40-foot Rigid Inflatable Boat.

Since the planners expected a 'forced entry' (SOF jargon for an invasion), Army and Air Force psyoperators conducted operations to prepare the Haitian people. Thanks to the year-long build-up for the operation and the inclusion of Psyops planners in early planning, the 4th POG was active and ready even before the incursion actually occurred. Air Force Special Operations Command (AFSOC) EC-130 'Commando Solo' aircraft flew along the coast of Haiti broadcasting taped messages from President Jean-Bertrand Aristide via radio and television.

Beginning in early July, Radio Democracy began AM and FM broadcasting from a Commando Solo Psyops C-130 flying off the coast of Haiti. Radio Democracy and a sister station, Radio AM 940, sent Creole-language messages devised to encourage reconciliation among Haitians, discourage migration and promote acceptance of Aristide's return. In August, Television Democracy went on the air. The radio and TV broadcasts began preparing the Haitian population for a US-led intervention to depose the ruling junta.

Between April and July of 1994 the refugee situation worsened as more than 23,000 Haitians were picked up at sea and transferred to the refugee camps (David Bentley, 'Operation Sea Signal', National Defense University, 1996, 2). In the camps at Guantánamo Bay, Army Civil Affairs and Psyops provided radio broadcasts, camp newspapers, social work/aid, construction, training and education, as well as critical cross-cultural skills to assist migrants in camp administration.

By mid-1994, nearly all possible sanctions short of war had been imposed, including a ban on international airline travel. Despite these measures the *de facto* military government steadfastly refused to allow the return of the elected president. In July 1994 the junta expelled the last United Nations human-rights monitors from Haiti and the Security Council finally passed resolution 940, mandating international military action to restore the legitimate government of Haiti.

By 13 September military action seemed inevitable and a US Navy Task Force sailing under the UN mandate steamed for Haiti. On the night of 14 September, more than 8,400,000 leaflets prepared by Army Psychological Operations units announcing President Aristide's imminent return were dropped over Haitian towns by AFSOC aircraft. The first drop managed to miss Port-au-Prince and a second run was made to hit the Haitian capital.[5] Even this had no effect on the ruling junta's determination to remain in power.

Accordingly, on the night of 18 September 1994, as the naval task force lay off Haiti, more than 3,000 combat-loaded Army paratroopers boarded Air Force C-141 transports bound for the island. Then, at literally the last moment, the invasion became a 'peaceful intervention'. When the coup leaders learned of the approaching invasion force they quickly made an agreement with a high-level US negotiating team headed by former President Jimmy Carter and accepted the United Nations mandate. The ruling junta, led by Haitian Lieutenant General Raoul Cedras, allowed the multinational intervention force peacefully ashore and agreed to relinquish power to the country's deposed leader, President Jean-Bertrand Aristide.

Within minutes the planned invasion turned into something else, a permissive intervention. Military forces, including SOF, had been poised for a combat operation to seize ports and airfields while 'surgically' striking FAd'H strongholds. Now they suddenly were forced to change plans and cooperate with the same FAd'H they had been prepared to kill. The day after the Cedras regime agreed to surrender power, psyoperators from the 4th POG were over Port-au-Prince in loudspeaker-bearing helicopters, preparing the population for the arrival of US troops.

Although further negotiations occurred between US Ambassador William Swing, LTG Hugh Shelton (commander of the US troops on the ground) and General Cedras, 'the discussions were one sided'. All together 20,000 US and Caribbean soldiers were on the ground within two weeks and Shelton 'made it quite clear that he was willing to use them' if the Haitian leadership proved uncooperative (Vane, 1996). The threat of military force successfully 'took' Haiti without bloodshed. Now, it remained to be seen what military force could do with it.

The original intervention force, consisting mainly of the Army's XVIII Airborne Corps and a Navy carrier task force never came ashore. Instead the Army's 10th Mountain Division, Marine Corps units and Special Operations units including elements of the 3rd Special Forces Group, entered the island. Largely for public-relations purposes, the intervention force also included small elements from various Caribbean states and was officially known as the Multi-National Force or simply 'the MNF'. Among Haitians the MNF was clearly identified as a US force and the presence of other foreign troops seen as some sort of odd American quirk.

The United States Special Operations Command (USSOCOM) deployed approximately 6,500 Active and Reserve Special Operations Forces to Haiti and the contiguous waters as part of Operation 'Support Democracy' and the follow-on mission, 'Maintain Democracy'. The Joint Special Operations Task Force, an element of the MNF, was commanded by Brigadier General Richard A. Potter.

The basic mission of the MNF, per the UN mandate, was to create a 'safe and secure environment' in Haiti, so that the entire operation could be handed over to a UN follow-on force. Crime and violence were pervasive in Haiti and a problem of the first order for any attempt to create the 'safe and secure environment' envisioned by the UN mandate. Grinding poverty and pervasive corruption combined with an atmosphere of general distrust and insecurity resulted in chronic violence throughout Haiti. Force was often the first resort for those who had the means to apply it (Schultz, 1996, 3). The issue of armed civil violence was a long-term social and economic problem that neither SOF nor the MNF could reasonably be expected to solve; but they were faced with it just the same.

Initial SOF deployments (September 1994)

Army
3rd SFG
4th POG (-)
96th CA Bn (-)
Company-size Ranger elements*
160th SOAR (-)
112th SO Signal Bn (-)
528th SO Support Bn (-)

*Not part of the initial intervention. During the MNF phase of operations various companies of the 75th Ranger Regiment acted as Quick Reaction Forces.

Reservists from:
358th CA Bde
360th CA Bde
361st CA Cmd
422nd CA Bn
450th CA Bn
15th Psyops Bn
305th Psyops Bn

Navy
SBU
SEAL Team
Support elements

Air Force
16th SOW
193rd Special Operations Squadron (Psyops)

SOF missions under the Multi-National Force

1. 3rd SF Group, supported by Psyops and CA elements, provide assistance to local governments throughout Haiti during the return to democratic rule.
2. 3rd SF Group confiscate weapons and ammunition from the FAd'H's Heavy Weapons Company at Camp d'Application.
3. 3rd SF Group with CA augmentation, provide Coalition Support Teams as required.
4. 4th POG and CA units develop and implement Psyops and CA programs to support MNF.
5. 16th SOW AC-130s provide general fire support.
6. Bn of 75th Rangers, act as Quick Reaction Force.
7. 3rd SF Group act as combat search and rescue (CSAR) element for initial intervention.

The last mission, CSAR, was never 'real' and quickly developed into a make-shift Quick Reaction Force, which was ineffective because it lacked dedicated aircraft. Finally, it evolved into a VIP escort service, tying up valuable assets in what was generally viewed as a waste of time.

Civil Affairs in Haiti

Civil Affairs activities fell into two general categories: helping to restore government functions at all levels, and facilitating the assortment of humanitarian organizations providing relief to the general population.

The generally impoverished condition of the population and lack of basic services was an immediate, serious problem. The mission had been planned to hand over quickly the humanitarian assistance aspects of the operation to international nongovernmental relief organizations (NGOs). However, the expected, immediate, massive nation-building effort by NGOs simply did not occur. Instead there was a more gradual build-up by relief organizations, with the result that the military had to fill the gaps as best it could for more than two months. Finally, by December 1994, there were over 400 NGOs of all sizes and descriptions providing humanitarian assistance in Haiti. They operated without central direction and little coordination, and varied in size and function from a single unfunded volunteer veterinarian to large international organizations such as CARE and Catholic Relief Services providing a range of relief and development assistance programs.

In an effort to coordinate the relief efforts of the various NGOs, the Civil Affairs officers of the MNF established a pair of Civil Military Coordination Centers (CMOCs), one in Port-au-Prince and the other in Cap Haitien. This was the work of CA generalists, company-grade officers and noncomissioned officers whose experience and training were primarily military. These were purely military operations, so in order to accommodate the civilian relief organizations, more benign-looking Humanitarian Assistance Coordination Centers (HACC) were established nearby 'outside the wire', and operated in cooperation with USAID's Office of Foreign Disaster Assistance (OFDA). Among other services the HACCs provided a common meeting place for relief providers and daily situation briefings (USAID, 1994). This also proved cumbersome, since the HAAC was a 20-minute drive across Port-au-Prince away from the CMOC. Lacking radio communication or civilian telephones, the two communicated for several weeks by USAID's satellite-communications gear. In the words of a USAID memorandum, 'a very expensive way to talk across town' (DART, 1994).

CA and USAID negotiated to open Haitian ports to relief vessels and allow humanitarian flights into Port-au-Prince. They also devised a system whereby NGOs and the UN relief agencies could request military assistance, usually transportation or security. Requests were prioritized by the HACC and reviewed by the CMOC. Although convoy escort was not an original mission for either the MNF or the UN follow-on force, looting quickly became a serious problem for relief organizations and the CMOC had to coordinate military security for the movement of relief supplies.

At the national-government level, Haiti suffered from the fact that none of its institutions was effective, with the single exception of the FAd'H. Given the flight of many Cedras-appointed officials and the general incompetence of those who remained, restoring even a basic level of government function was a challenge for the entire array of agencies attempting various parts of the task.

The major CA contribution here was the arrival of 'ministerial advisory teams' (MATs). These consisted of reserve officers with specialized civilian skills such as banking, economics, education and law enforcement, who helped the newly formed government of President Aristide establish, or re-establish, itself. Working in civilian clothes, they used their skills in governmental administration and related fields to help Aristide's new cabinet ministers establish their ministries (Jeffrey A. Jacobs, 1996, 65–7).

One important example of help on the most general governmental level was assistance to Haiti's paralyzed and utterly dysfunctional justice system. Suspects were commonly incarcerated for months before even being charged with a crime. As one 3rd SF report put it, there was no such thing as 'due process as we know it'. A big part of the reason was that judges were often unqualified, treated their jobs as a sinecure, and simply did not show up for court. Under State Department sponsorship, CA provided a 17-man Ministerial Advisory Team Judicial, made up almost entirely of Army reservists and attached to the US Embassy. Working with the Haiti Ministry of Justice, the reservists exposed judges who were corrupt, illiterate, poorly trained or simply lazy while mentoring and assisting others. Out in the countryside, the SF Teams did their best to reconstitute the courts and force the judges to do their jobs (3d SFG, 1994).

Post-intervention Psyops

According to Stephen D. Brown, an intelligence analyst for the 4th Psychological Operations Group (POG), 'Haiti's information- and rumor-saturated environment epitomized the post-Cold War challenge'. Psyops were a 'nonlethal, life-saving force multiplier' (Brown, 1996, 57).

Immediately upon arrival in Haiti, Colonel Jeffery B. Jones, 4th POG commander, established an Information Coordination Committee, chaired by the US Embassy Public Affairs Officer and consisting of representatives of the 4th POG, the JTF (Joint Task Force), USAID and the Department of Justice. The job of the Committee was to devise a coherent information strategy for the campaign.

Once in Haiti, the principal mission of the psyoperators was to gain popular support, to enhance the legitimacy of the operation in the eyes of the Haitian population and the international community. That is, to promote public acceptance of the restored Aristide government and the intervention force; and to encourage co-operation with both.

Because the majority of Haitians are illiterate, Psyops dissemination concentrated on loudspeaker teams, pictograph handbills and radio broadcasts (Brown, 1996, 57). This was especially important in support not only of national objectives such as reconciliation and the return of democracy, but also of more mundane issues such as local administration. Army SF teams in the countryside used local radio to keep people informed. Several even had regular 'talk shows' exploring local issues and, in areas where telephones still worked, answered questions from callers.

A major campaign and an example of 4th POG's 'coherent information strategy' undertaken by the Psyops personnel was the need to 'recast a Haitian police system long known for its brutality and corruption'. Police reform was the business of the US Department of Justice and the Haitian ministries, who together identified FAd'H police who were acceptable for an Interim Public Security Force (IPSF) while a new National Police Force was being trained. Not all FAd'H were utterly hopeless and the SF in the field undertook to identify the FAd'H members who were respected by the local people and showed some ability in their job. The Aristide government, however, generally ignored these recommendations in favor of police and 'supervisors' who were politically loyal but often corrupt and incompetent (Boyatt, 1997). Working with the Ministry of Information, Psyops specialists tried to promote acceptance of the new police by the public and an attitude of public service on the part of the IPSF and later the HNP (Brown, 1996, 71).

The problem with such a campaign is that it cannot be divorced from reality. While skillful Psyops can correct an erroneous perception, the fact was that most of Haiti's police really were not worthy of respect, a situation that remained until the new National Police Force was fielded.

Governing the countryside

The first elements of the 3rd SFG arrived on 20 September and quickly began 'hub and spoke' operations, placing ODBs or 'B' detachments (SF headquarters) in principal towns and then fanning out 'A' teams from there. For the most part, the Haitian Army created no problems and surrendered without violence. In Belladre, near the border with the Dominican Republic, two MH-60 helicopters dropped off Chief Warrant Officer Danny Averitt and his team of 15 SF in front of the yellow fortress-like headquarters of the local garrison. The 100 or so FAd'H inside surrendered promptly, without even being asked.

Nationwide, a number of the worst offenders among the FAd'H were identified, arrested and sent off to a military detention center near Port-au-Prince by the 3rd Group soldiers. The arrests were deliberately conducted as visibly as possible to provide maximum impact.

The popular reaction was immediate and enthusiastic. Teams were met by massive joyous crowds who, unfortunately, believed that the Americans had come to kill the FAd'H and replace the local government. The crowds also believed that government and other facilities could be looted and FAd'H attacked with impunity. Consequently, there were widespread cases of looting of stores and warehouses, and numerous cases where the SF teams found themselves protecting FAd'H members from vigilantes and even mobs. It took numerous arrests over a period of days before order could be restored. The concept of police accountability being unknown in Haiti, these arrests and detentions were carefully monitored by the SF. But since it placed the SF in cooperation with the FAd'H, this led to the perception that the Americans were protecting and even supporting the hated FAd'H (3rd SFG, 1994).

By mid-October, the SF had spread out across Haiti and visited every one of the 500 significant villages and towns, sometimes using motorcycles, horses and mules to reach isolated mountain areas. They left tiny 12- to 15-man A Teams in about 30 of the principal population centers to assist local government and monitor conditions in the countryside. About 1,300 SF troopers were devoted to the effort, most of them from the 3rd SF Group, later supplemented by reservists from the Army National Guard SF Groups.

The 3rd Group men in the countryside had a delicate balancing act to perform. Under the terms of the agreement by which the MNF entered the country, local Haitian authorities appointed by the military junta temporarily stayed in charge until they could be replaced through a process of elections. But things were not so simple. First of all, many of the local officials were hated by the populace. Secondly, many mayors, judges and city councils were defunct and those appointed by the Cedras government often fled, deserting their positions. Finally, others who did remain were too often untrained, corrupt and incompetent as well as given to violent abuses. Most had taken the positions as a source of personal wealth, and had little idea of how to carry out their ostensible functions and even less interest in learning.

This widespread collapse of civil authority in the countryside left a vacuum that was filled by the Army Special Forces teams. In effect, the ODBs and their A Teams were the *de facto* government. Little in the experience of these teams and nothing in their training had prepared the Special Forces or their Civil Affairs and Psyops augmentees to midwife village politics in a Third World nation, but nonetheless, the responsibility fell on them in the absence of other actors.[6]

Equipped chiefly with common sense and a problem-solving approach, the trio of SF, CA and Psyops went at the task. Working with local leaders, both official and unofficial, the teams appointed city councils, formed neighborhood watches, organized road crews, organized care of prisoners and cleaning of jails, and assisted in restoration of school buildings as well as distribution of UN-provided school supplies. Since the teams were not actually in the government business, much emphasis was placed on the creation of local self-government through the creation of town councils whose legitimacy and authority were supported by the SF presence.

With USAID, the SF teams organized the repair of utilities including water, electrical and sewage systems, placing the emphasis on community self-help. Since the FAd'H was disarmed, discredited and actively hated, the teams also often became *de facto* police, creating local volunteer police, acting as policemen, detectives and, in a few instances, even SWAT (Special Weapons and Training) teams. Along the border with the Dominican Republic they also took up duties as an interim border patrol to control crowds at crossing sites and monitor for weapons traffic. Several A Teams even boarded US Coast Guard cutters to conduct checks of coastal towns (3rd SFG, 1994).

Most of the crime problems were low-level ones – politically motivated assault, petty theft and domestic abuse. According to one SF sergeant assigned to the small port city of Miragone, 'We don't have any rules or training to be cops. We don't know the Haitian law. All we know is that if you explain to people why it is not right, they accept it: "No, you can't beat up this lady because her husband was in a paramilitary group"' (Rogers Worthington, 'Haiti Turns US Soldiers into Cops', *Chicago Tribune*, 30 October 1994, 21). The

SF's basic source of law was the Haitian constitution, a document they studied assiduously. The teams also distributed copies to local governments throughout the island. It was the first time most of these officials had ever seen the document.

Part of the problem in creating the 'stable and secure environment' sought by UN resolution 940 was the ubiquitous presence of former FAd'H, their paramilitaries (*attachés*) and ordinary criminals throughout Haiti. Like the elites in Port-au-Prince, they had benefitted from the old regime and viewed the prospect of democracy and the rule of law as a threat. In the town of Les Cayes, for example, the local FAd'H commander was found to be keeping 46 prisoners, who were suffering from malnutrition and severe emaciation. When the SF Team could find no record of charges against the prisoners, they were fed, medically treated and released. When the SF attempted to have him relieved, the FAd'H commander responded with a series of threats and attempts to intimidate the townspeople.

Then, on the night of 2 October, Special Forces interpreters picked up a message on the police radio ordering, 'Get your guns. We're going to kill the Americans.' Twenty minutes later, a SF sergeant on his way to an outdoor latrine was fired on and wounded by attackers scaling the compound wall. Returning fire, he drove the attackers away. Concerned that the incident might be the beginning of organized resistance, General Potter ordered Army Rangers into Les Cayes.

The presence of the Rangers in full battle dress with helmets and heavy weapons calmed the situation. The Rangers conducted patrols and a series of raids against the homes of FAd'H members believed to be involved in the shooting incident, seizing weapons and searching for those involved. Often operating in darkness with camouflage facepaint and night-vision devices, the Rangers quickly earned the sobriquet 'Voodoo Warriors'. 'The bad guys learned that armed confrontation was a losing proposition' (Potter, interview, 1996).

The SF tried to prevent this kind of problem through unilateral patrols, 'presence patrolling' in all of the principal villages, for the purpose of intimidating these elements. This included daytime patrols without helmets or flack vests and without accompanying FAd'H, to present a nonthreatening appearance and talk with local residents about the purposes of the military intervention and listen to their needs. But night patrols were also conducted on an unpredictable schedule with the specific purpose of intimidating the 'bad guys' and 'getting them off the streets'. In some locations curfews

were introduced with generally good results and support from the
population who reportedly felt safer (3rd SFG, 1994).

Efforts to extend the rule of law impartially exposed the SF to
the rough and tumble of grassroots politics. In Anse-e-Galets,
Captain James Dusenbury found himself not only trying to separate
fact from fiction in accusations of abuses and arms possession but
also accusations leveled by villagers that a 70-year-old blind woman
was in reality a werewolf. Then, the local magistrate appointed by
the military regime refused to hand over power, including the official
government seal, on the grounds that he had not been notified of
any change by Port-au-Prince. Persuasion and a ferry-ride to Port-
au-Prince changed his mind. Captain Dusenbury handled the
werewolf case by referring to what he called 'basic American
jurisprudence', an accusation without evidence is only that, an
accusation ('Are You Now or Have You Ever Been a Werewolf?',
Washington Post, 14 November 1994, p. 12).

Despite the application of 'basic American jurisprudence' there
were similar problems in many villages. The ordinary population
did not always seem grateful for these efforts. The chaotic nature
of village politics and the tradition of denouncing others for petty
revenge created difficulties for the arrest and detention program. It
meant that not all of the arrests were of the correct people and not
all the correct detentions were well received. The aggrieved parties
found a willing audience in the international media.

The US press reported that SF troops outraged Artibonite Valley
townspeople by siding with a local landlord and anti-Aristide leader
who seemed to have legal title to land that was also claimed by
Aristide supporters. Later, a near-riot was reported as occurring in
the city of Jeremie when Special Forces soldiers arrested a popular
Roman Catholic priest and Aristide supporter.

Others displeased with the SF included some prominent Aristide
supporters, who had expected *carte blanche* for revenge while
protected by US guns. They were not happy with the trooper's
attempt to apply an even handed brand of justice. Nor were they
hesitant to complain to the international press and make formal
complaints to the US Embassy. Unfortunately, not all embassy staffers
were experienced in the way grass-roots politics were carried out
in Haiti. They tended to take the most outrageous accusations of
SF abuse at face value and call for stern measures against the alleged
perpetrators.

Since the accusations were invariably followed by inquiries,
considerable bitterness was created among the SFers in the field.

Their feelings were reminiscent of Vietnam, when the troopers in the jungle often felt they were the target of criticism from civilians and 'rear-echelon m-f'ers' who did not understand the situation and seemed ready to believe any evil attributed to the SF.

Disarming the thugs

The question of disarming the vast array of criminals, former police, ex-military and ordinary thugs who had weapons was a thorny one. The issue of disarming was reportedly raised on several occasions in interagency working groups before the operation and among operational commanders, Haitian officials and the US Embassy after it began. However, it is impossible to point to a single discrete decision that no widespread disarmament of the population would be attempted. It was just something 'everybody knew' was probably impossible and almost certainly counterproductive (Potter, 1996).

The disarming of the major elements of the Haitian military was not a problem, especially in the case of units of the official FAd'H such as the elite Heavy Weapons Company at Camp d'Application. But the question of what to about the remainder of the vast number of weapons, mostly small arms, spread among the population was a difficult one. General Potter remarked, 'If we were going to reinstate the rule of law, we couldn't begin by kicking down doors all over Haiti' (Potter interview, 6 March 1996).

Special Forces teams did confiscate FAd'H weapons as part of the activity of the detachments spread throughout the country. Working on tips from informants, they also searched for weapons cached by the FAd'H and their associated paramilitaries. In Anse-e-Galets, the Mayor complained that more than 200 young men had been receiving paramilitary training there and that a crate of hand grenades had disappeared from the local military barracks just before the arrival of the Americans. The SF Team in the village found no more than 50. There were 'many dry holes' and 'unquestionably' the teams' efforts were 'used to settle old feuds', but each team reported locating at least one or two weapons caches. Most of the recovered weapons were rusted and unserviceable (Potter interview, 6 March 1996, also 3rd SFG, 1994).

As described by General Potter, 'All visible weapons were confiscated throughout Haiti. If anyone appeared on the streets with a weapon it was confiscated on the authority of the Task Force Commander.' In addition, stocks of FAd'H weapons taken under MNF control were, for the most part, destroyed (including crew-served and automatic weapons in police stations and a large cache discovered at Adm. Killick Naval base). The MNF rejected a widespread weapons-confiscation program in favor of a weapons amnesty and 'buy-back' program (16th MP Bde, 1995). In its evaluation of the countrywide MNF weapons-buy-back program the 3rd Special Forces Group (whose teams handled much of the program) termed it 'marginally successful'. The SF teams in the villages continued to run down leads on weapons caches and uncovered a few while disarming individuals known to have committed abuses under the military regime (3rd SFG, 1994; Potter, 1996).

The United Nations takes over

By February 1995, UN Officials were satisfied that a 'safe and secure' environment had been created in Haiti and that preparations for elections could get underway. The first step was to replace the MNF with a more international force under the blue banner of the United Nations.

UNMIH Force Deployments (after March 1995)

Zone I (Cap Haitien) – Pakistan Infantry Bn
Zone II (Gonaives) – Nepal Infantry Bn
Zone III (vic Jacmel) – Netherlands/Surinam Infantry Co
Zone IV (Les Cayes) – Caribbean Infantry Bn
Zone V (Port-au-Prince) – HQ UNMIH
Zone VI (Northern Port-au-Prince) – Bangladesh Infantry Bn
Quick Reaction Force (vic Port-au-Prince) – US Light Armored Bn

SOF Deployments (after March 1995)

Zone I (Cap Haitien) – ODB/ Five SF Tms
Zone II (Gonaives) – Fwd Operating Base/ODB/Five SF A Tms
Zone III (vic Jacmel) – ODB/Two SF Tms
Zone IV (Les Cayes) – Fwd Operating Base/ODB/Three SF Tms
Zone V (includes UN Zone VI) (Port-au-Prince) – 3rd SFG (Army SOTF Hq)/3 ODBs/Seven SF Teams/Military Information Support Team (MIST) and Civil Affairs. A Forward Operating Base was located at the Camp d'Application outside Port-au-Prince.

It is really too strong to say that the MNF simply took off their kevlar helmets and put on blue berets to become the UN force, but to some degree that is what happened at the troop level. Although under the command of USSOCOM, the ARSOTF (Army Special Operations Task Force) in Haiti was under the operational control of the Commander US Forces Haiti, who was also the UNMIH Force commander. After 1 April 1995, the presence of the UN Mission in Haiti (UNMIH) directed by a Special Representative of the Secretary General and with an American major general as force commander, made a difference in the organization and emphasis of the operation. While the focus of the MNF had been on providing a 'stable and secure environment', the central concern of UNMIH was to maintain that environment, hold local and national elections and transition to the newly elected government so that Haitians could once again take complete control of their own affairs. For the SOF it meant pretty much business as usual.

SOF missions under UNMIH

1. 3rd SF Group supported by Psyops and CA elements, continue to provide assistance to local governments throughout Haiti during the return to democratic rule.
2. MIST and CA develop and implement Psyops and CA programs to support UNMIH and the restored Haitian government.
3. 3rd SFG provide Coalition Support Teams (CSTs) to 'assist integration of UNMIH forces into their operational areas'.
(see UNMIH Operations Order 1-95)

UNMIH's operational concept was not too different from that of the MNF. The UN emphasized force presence in Port-au-Prince and Cape Haitien, rural patrolling to bolster the US Special Forces teams in the countryside and, after a rough start, an information campaign using Military Information Support Teams (MIST, a.k.a 'Psyops') to communicate with the population. The force also maintained a well-armed conventional quick reaction force (QRF). The nine legislative departments (or provinces) of Haiti were organized into six operational zones. Each of the UN Zone Commanders had responsibility for all forces and activities in his zone with additional support on call as needed.

The zone headquarters were deliberately placed in areas with a history of unrest, and the remainder of the force positioned to respond rapidly throughout its area of responsibility. The principal activity of these forces was to patrol their territory and provide stability through presence among the populace. Lastly, a full-time security element was organized to protect the President and ensure his safety as the visible symbol of Haitian sovereignty (UNMIH, AAR, 1996, 7). In the short term, these measures probably contributed to the legitimacy of the intervention force and certainly were helpful as support actions in ending conflict during the UN presence.

Psychological Operations under the UN: the name game

The inability of the Haitian government to communicate with its own constituents, the Haitian people, was a serious problem. The potential to further such communication lay with the US Army's Psychological Operations Forces (Psyops). The fact that the UN force commander was Major General Joseph Kinzer, a US Army officer and already a believer in Psyops helped. But, suspicion as to the nature and methods of Psyops as well as the capabilities and functions of these forces made UNMIH's civilian leadership reluctant to include them as part of the force. When it finally became clear that these elements were no more than militarized public-relations and media units the UN became more willing to take advantage of their capabilities. Since perception and labeling were very important to the UN officials, the psyoperators performed an internal mini-Psyops of their own by re-naming their units 'Military Information Support Teams' (MIST). This cosmetic change increased the comfort level of UN leaders in Haiti as well as at the Department of Peacekeeping Operations (DPKO) at UN New York.

The Psychological Operations Task Force, or POTF, thus became the UNMIH's MISTF (Military Information Support Task Force). Regardless of the name change, the unit developed and executed the UNMIH information campaign. In addition to developing information products (i.e. radio/loudspeaker messages, hand bills, posters and videos), it worked extensively with various government ministries and agencies, to assist them in improving their ability to communicate effectively with the population and prepare them to assume these tasks upon the departure of UNMIH.

Tactical dissemination teams (TDTs) were deployed throughout the AOR (Area of Responsibility), to provide general support to the zone commanders. They coordinated with local radio stations, used loudspeakers, and conducted face-to-face communication to disseminate information to the Haitian population. Surveys conducted by the TDTs were valuable in assessing the current attitude and perceptions of the Haitian people. Also, TDTs were extensively used throughout the country to disperse demonstrations and quell unrest (UNMIH, AAR, 1996, 9).

The Psyops efforts scored a success in changing public attitudes toward the police. An August 1995 survey by MISTF was cautiously optimistic, suggesting that public awareness of and confidence in the newly fielded Haitian National Police (HNP) was generally high.

Civil Affairs under UNMIH

The UN Mission was not familiar with the operations of military Civil Affairs and a period of education was required before the CA elements were fully accepted. The CMOCs and HACCs were continued under the UN Mission in Haiti (UNMIH). Obviously, these centers had no overt control over the various nongovernmental relief groups and depended largely on persuasion for their influence. Nevertheless, they were an important step forward in coordinating the development and assistance efforts of various players in Haiti. Ninety percent of the CMOC activities in Haiti involved facilitating this assistance. Assistance was also provided to governmental relief programs of the UN, the USA and the government of Haiti (UNMIH, AAR, 1996, 6, 9).

The ministerial advisory teams, a US unilateral project, were not continued under UNMIH. The continued use of these elements, however valuable, had begun to look too much like 'nation-building', for the taste of Washington policymakers, who were anxious to avoid any open-ended commitment in Haiti. The result was that this left most departments or ministries of the Haitian government with capable top leadership but almost none below the minster or deputy-minister level. There simply had not been time to build these competencies.

Back in the countryside

For the SF teams in the town and villages, the issue of weapons remained a headache under the UN Mission, as it had for the MNF. By the time of the turnover to UNMIH most of the paramilitaries had not been not disarmed and few of the weapons in the general population were seized. (Estimates are that about 30,000 of the estimated 175,000 small arms in circulation were confiscated;. Potter, 1996). UNMIH officers pointed out that disarmament was not specified in the UN mandate that empowered them, but that point was often lost in the cacophony of Haitian politics.

Aristide repeatedly accused the US forces under the UN of failing to disarm the former Haitian Army and their paramilitary allies. On 11 November, following the execution-style murder of Aristide's cousin, the Haitian President attacked the USA and the UN for this failure and called on his supporters to take the disarmament process into their own hands by seizing weapons. The result was two days of violent rioting and mob action in several areas of Haiti.

On 17 November 1995, the Haitian government formally charged that US forces had slowed down weapons searches and warned the targets of impending searches. In December 1995, President Aristide's Chief of Staff specifically accused the SF of having assisted the FAd'H and its paramilitary auxiliary in avoiding arrest and in hiding weapons. The *New York Times*, in an 8 December article ('Haiti Says US Troops May Have Helped Foes', 43) stated as a fact that 'Special Forces troops' 'viewed the FRAPH [Revolutionary Front for the Advancement and Progress of Haiti] as friends, not as the thugs and right abusers described by the State Department and human rights organizations'. This pronouncement was received with amazement and disgust among the SF teams in Haiti.

Under UNMIH, another weapons 'buy-back' program was instituted, but it also met with very limited success. It did, however, tempt numerous former FAd'H members who still had older weapons to turn these in for cash.

The neighborhood watch system, or 'vigilance brigades', formed with the backing of the Aristide government, came under citicism. Some groups had mutated from neighborhood watches, reporting to local police officials, to vigilante groups, dispensing popular justice rather than relying on the Haitian police and justice system (Brown, 1996, 72). This was a continuing problem, with 100 instances of vigilante justice in 1995 and probably about the same in 1996 (Schultz, 1996, 13).

With nation-wide local elections in June of 1995, followed by a presidential election in December, mayors and other town/village level officials gradually began to assume their responsibilities. Simultaneously, the new Haitian National Police Force began to replace the largely ineffective interim police. As the newly formed National Police came into being, the SF teams worked with them and gradually withdrew from the police role. This reduced the need for the SF Teams in the countryside, who were withdrawn in stages with the last units departing in early 1996.

Adding it up

The military intervention never set out to reform Haitian society; but that was what was really needed. The lack of a nation-building program was probably a mistake. But SOF, especially Army SOF, made a major contribution to the creation of the 'stable and secure environment' that was the mandated purpose of the intervention. The SF personnel understood this and, although it was never articulated as part of their mission, made a deliberate effort to demonstrate and encourage institutions, especially police, that were responsive and responsible to their communities. Between the activities of the CA and Psyops elements supporting the Haitian central government and the SF, who virtually controlled rural Haiti, it is not too strong to characterize the ARSOTF (Army Special Operations Task Force) mission as central to the overall success of the MNF and the UN operations.

The forces that were fielded benefitted greatly from the long planning time available and also from gradual development of SOF planning and command capabilities over the previous years. They used that experience well. When military planning for a US-led international intervention in Haiti began in mid-1993, a clear progression could be seen in the utilization of SOF, especially Army SF, CA and Psyops. Beginning with the hastily planned, poorly integrated, often ineffective SOF in Grenada, through the improvements of Operation Just Cause in Panama and the experience of Desert Storm, SOF had steadily improved.

Some old issues continued to surface, for example, dependence on reserves, especially for Psyops and Civil Affairs manning, continued to be a problem. The absence of more than token elements of these forces from the active structure meant that the personnel filling these responsibilities were temporary and often did not remain on active duty long enough to learn the situation on the ground and put that expertise into practice. Nevertheless, problems aside, the Psyops information programs and CA activities were effective and contributed directly to establishing and maintaining the secure and stable environment.

NOTES

1. Allegedly, both General Hoar and Joint Chiefs Chairman Powell were opposed to the deployment but were overruled by the National Security Council on the advice of Admiral Howe.
2. The embarrassment included the United Nations, when the raid uncovered a large black-market operation being run by members of the UN Mission.
3. Boyatt objects that, while this may be true as a general statement, in the Mogadishu case the Rangers and Delta more than held their own, suffering only one casualty after they managed to establish their perimeter.

4. The precise legal status of the persons in these camps was an object of contention, with the US government taking the position that these were 'migrants' and not 'refugees'.
5. When the leaflets came down, one woman in Port-au-Prince called police to complain that 'the Americans are dumping trash on my roof'.
6. Boyatt suggests that the previous experience of these teams as military trainers in Africa and the Caribbean gave them at least a basic understanding of the situation.

11 A brief excursion into the future

What we really need is probably a special forces – not commandos, but rather people who are thinking through the kind of environment they are going to fight in and who have enough intelligence information to do the proper things. We have enormous problems knowing the areas in which we are going to fight. (Rowan Scarborough, 'Pentagon Eyes Cuts', *Washington Times*, 13 December 1996, 1)

FIGURING OUT WHAT SOF OUGHT TO DO: DOCTRINE FOR THE TWENTY-FIRST CENTURY

If the conflict of the twenty-first century really requires a 'special force', one that can function in a wide variety of ambiguous conflict situations where violence is always possible, there is little in current doctrine that points the way to such a force. In fact, doctrine for the conduct of unconventional warfare did not advance markedly during the 1990s and most special-operations doctrine remained firmly fixed on conventional missions. USSOCOM illustrated this when it released its first formal doctrinal publication in 1996. Titled *Special Operations in Peace and War*, it offers the following definition:

> Special operations encompass the use of small units in direct or indirect military actions that are focused on strategic or operational objectives. They require units with combinations of specialized personnel, equipment, training or tactics that exceed the routine capabilities of conventional military forces. (USSOCOM, 1996, 1–2)

The manual then offers three historical examples of special operations, all from World War II and all largely conventional: the Doolittle bomber raid on Tokyo in 1942, the 1940 German night-glider assault on a Belgian fortress, and the reconnaissance missions conducted by the Sixth US Army Special Reconnaissance Unit (Alamo Scouts). The last two were thoroughly conventional missions. The first, although using conventional means, was conducted for psychological purposes. This uneasy mixture of conventional and unconventional reflects the general approach to SOF roles and functions that has been detailed throughout this book.

In the real world, SOF continued to accomplish a wide variety of roles and functions without much regard for doctrine. Unconventional missions during the 1990s were not limited to Somalia, Haiti and the drug war. A number of odd jobs also came their way:

SOF assisted relief efforts in several locations, notably Rwanda in 1994, Dade County Florida following Hurricane Andrew in 1992, and Bangladesh after Cyclone Martin in 1991. (Above list derived in part from Collins, 1994, 99,102.)

In 1993, a Special Mission Unit provided counterterrorism training, equipment and weapons to the security forces of the Republic of Georgia to protect President Edward Shevardnadze. A team of Georgian security specialists also received training at Fort Bragg.

Also in 1993, an SOF team of four doctors, three nurses and one corpsman inoculated 60,000 Cameroon citizens during a meningitis outbreak. The fact that a US pharmaceutical company donated the vaccine made the cost almost negligible.

In 1994, SOF from SOCEUR (Special Operations Command, Europe) began a continuing program to train game wardens in East Africa to protect their herds from poachers.

In 1995 Navy SEALs conducted a mid-winter hydrographic survey of the Sava River allowing NATO forces to cross into the former Yugoslavia.

In 1995 and 1996 Army Special Forces helped create a military observer force to police the newly created truce zone between Ecuador and Peru.

In 1996, SOF conducted a noncombatant evacuation operation to remove US citizens from Liberia in the midst of a civil war there. Army SF, Navy SEALs and Air Force SO Pilots also cooperated to locate and assist with the investigation of the crash of an Air Force flight carrying the US Commerce Secretary and provided personal protection for the commander of the international force in Bosnia.

What do SOF do? At least based on the list above, the answer is no clearer than ever.

Stepping into the unknown in an orderly manner

In 1993 the Army tried to deal with the new conflict environment when it issued the latest version of its basic or 'capstone' doctrine for military activities, FM 100-5 *Operations*. The volume utterly abandoned the AirLand Battle Doctrine that had been the centerpiece of US warfighting since 1986. The very term itself is absent from the book. Instead, the new volume seemed confused by the lack of a defined enemy, such as that offered by the now-defunct Soviet threat. Faced with an ambiguous environment, characterized by unclear threats from poorly defined enemies, it provides only a series of cautious prescriptions to avoid casualties and plan carefully. This is good advice but it does not add up to a plan of action. Since it is manifestly impossible to plan for everything, it is equally lacking as a guide to the future.

In 1996, John B. Hunt, a retired Army lieutenant colonel and veteran doctrine writer, summarized the state of military doctrine to deal with the kinds of 'gray area', not-quite-war situations that have been common since the 1980s. In Hunt's words, the concept of Military Operations Other Than War (MOOTW) 'has never reached maturity and remains confusing and unsettled' (Hunt, 1996, 3). Indeed, as Hunt points out, the Armed Forces have yet to settle on a name for these situations. Low-Intensity Conflict (LIC), stability operations, operations short of war, contingency operations and stability and support operations have all been used in various contexts.

The problem here is that what is being described is closer to a political situation or condition, than it is to a class of military operations. The lesson taught by the Vietnam War is that conventional military methods, however applied do not prevail in conflicts that are as much political as they are military.

However, to a large degree, the US military is slow and reluctant to recognize any form of warfare that is outside the conventional military tradition. It is even slower to make organizational adjustments for such conflicts, and when it does there are strong tendencies for those adjustments to drift back toward the conventional model.

Furthermore, doctrine, including mission categories, is not written in the pursuit of abstract truth or even consistency. Doctrine is usually written to serve some constituency – sometimes Congress; sometimes an individual commander, and sometimes a professional community. The constituencies change over time and so do mission priorities. This would be natural, expected and untroubling, except that there is no provision for comprehensive rewriting of doctrine for consistency. Even definitions may differ between the services and between service doctrine and joint doctrine.

THE US DOD'S VERSION OF THE FUTURE

High-technology conventional warfare

What does the US Department of Defense see as the form of future military conflict? In brief it sees it as conventional warfare, upgraded and improved by computer-driven information systems. Of course, guessing the future is a problematic business. The strategist Brian R. Sullivan, borrowing a page from the Greeks, compares it to walking backwards: all you can really see well is the immediate past; the distant past is too far away, the present is unfolding all around as you move backwards and, of course, the future is directly behind you and invisible. This has the ring of truth and, although Sullivan does not suggest this, it implies that the events that have the most effect on our decision-making are those in the immediate past (Sullivan, 1996, 2). For the US military that would be the experience of Desert Storm, a triumph of conventional arms interpreted as a result of coalition, especially US technical superiority. Indeed that seems to be the case.

Current high-level US planning for future military conflict is rooted in the conventional model and the experience of the Gulf War. Most future plans are based on the so-called 'two MRC [major regional contingency]' scenario which postulates open hostilities with a regional power requiring the commitment of US forces. Another regional power such as Iraq might well choose that opportunity to pursue its own ends through military means. This would mean that the USA needs the capacity to fight two separate middle-sized conventional wars simultaneously. This scenario drives the current strength of the armed services – 10 Army divisions, 18 Air Force wings, and a Navy of 350 ships. No one necessarily believes the 'two MRC' scenario is the most likely one, but military planning is not only based on the most likely contingency; it also must consider dangerous, if less likely, possibilities.

Since the collapse of the USSR, the US armed forces have gone through a series of three separate re-evaluations of its force structure in light of current world realities (1992, 1993 and 1997). The first two reviews resulted in adjustments and reductions but no fundamental changes in either the forces or the way they will be utilized. The current (1997) review added no more than minor adjustments and reductions. The two-MRC scenario is driven by political realities and the strategic planners will have to provide suffi-cient forces despite whatever reductions are required for domestic political reasons. This might be done by giving the reserve components a greater role or by planning for greater contributions by partners and allies. The idea of a high-tech military future is based on the belief that the USA will continue to fight this kind of more-or-less conventional war. If you believe this, the high-tech approach makes sense and a number of important people believe it.

The National Defense University's 1996 future study, called '2015: Power and Progress' (see Cronin, 1996), also sees the future in terms of high technology as competitor states attempt to achieve more and more capability from technological advances. 'Power and Progress' depicts the real challenge as a stealth contest between 'hiders' and 'seekers', in which military forces try to find and target the enemy force while successfully concealing their own.

This was followed, in the fall of 1996, by a document produced by General John M. Shalikashvili, Chairman of the Joint Chiefs of Staff and the Joint Staff, entitled 'Joint Vision 2010' in which the Chairman set forth his view of the future of the US armed forces. This document did not attempt to anticipate the future in any substantial way, but it did recognize the existence of a 'a broad range of deterrent, conflict prevention and peacetime activities' (p. 4). The comment is followed throughout the document by references to 'full spectrum dominance'. But 'Vision 2010' concerns itself with a vision that has little to do with ambiguous threats. What it sets forth is a vision of information-enhanced conventional warfighting with emphasis on technological superiority on nearly every page as the decisive element. In the techno-jargon of 'Joint Vision 2010' the various components of technological superiority come together as 'precision engagement', 'a system of systems' that allows US forces to locate and react to 'the objective or target ... generate the desired effect' and 're-engage ... when required' (p. 21).

Having propounded this vision, the Chairman remarks on page 1 that 'it must become a benchmark for Service and United Command visions'. Having received their marching orders, the services fell in, producing a series of reports as each of them fought to stake out a position for itself as essential to the envisioned high-tech battlefield. Although the Navy took the expected stance that its role of maritime dominance was basically unchanged, the Air Force took an extreme position when it published 'Global Engagement: A Vision for 21st Century Air Power' in November 1996. This document took the position that, contrary to long-held military doctrine, ground forces were not always essential to win wars. Allegedly, air forces, using the kind of high-technology, precision-strike methods seen in the

Gulf War, could eliminate the need for large-scale heavy ground forces (for example, the US Army). Asserting Air Force primacy as the combat force of the future, Air Force Chief of Staff General Ronald Fogleman was quoted as saying 'those who assert that only ground forces can be decisive are clearly wrong' (Diamond, 1996, 12).

The Army version

The Army could be expected to stake out a position in this high-tech future for itself and so it did. In a memo distributed to the Army on 6 October 1996, Army Chief of Staff General Dennis J. Reimer warned against what he saw as the 'potential infatuation with precision engagement. Too many people are looking for the silver bullet which makes war nice and clean and surgical. History shows that it doesn't exist'. But, in fact, the Army's position was different from the Air Force's, chiefly in that it gave the dominant battlefield role to the Army.

The Army counterpart to 'Joint Vision 2010' is 'Army Vision 2010', in large an attempt to out-tech the other services with concepts including 'battle space dominance' and 'precision strike' emphasis on pin-point attacks with artillery and missiles. Like the Joint Chief's 'Vision' statement, 'Army Vision' at least makes a nod toward the idea of something other than conventional warfighting as important. It clearly identifies for the first time an explicit Army responsibility to conduct Military Operations Other Than War (MOOTW) as secondary only to the responsibility to 'fight and win the nation's wars'. It is the only service to do so.

'Land force', it goes on, 'is also the force of choice to respond to natural disasters, assist communities during civil disturbances and perform civic action/nation-building projects as required.' This may seem a small concession, but potentially at least it could be more than that. For the first time, there has been a clear statement at the highest Army level that MOOTW is not incidental to the real job of war-fighting but an important responsibility in its own right. Some commentators point to this as a revolution in Army thinking and an embracing of MOOTW (for example, Patrick Preston, 'Future Seizes Operations Other Than War', *Army Times*, 25 November 96, p. 8). However, having said that MOOTW are important, it fails to follow through.

THE ROLE OF SOF IN THE DOD FUTURE

'Joint Vision 2010' manages to discuss the military future for 35 pages, including several mentions of 'land, sea and maritime' and even 'space forces', without ever mentioning Special Operations

Forces. Its central theme of 'dominant maneuver' used to control 'battle space' may have application to something other than conventional warfighting, but this is not discussed. If SOF have a role in this scheme, then by implication it is as an element of the conventional forces.

'Army Vision', on the other hand, makes explicit mention of SOF, at least Army SOF. 'Army Vision 2010' identifies seven mission 'categories' including a total of 19 specific missions. Except for five that are identified as 'technical' missions, all include SOF. Among other things, this illustrates that the SOF have succeeded in becoming thoroughly accepted as part of the Army and are treated very much as are the conventional forces.

Missions	Required Army Capabilities
– Defending or Liberating Territory	
MRC	HVY/LT/SOF
LRC	HVY/LT/SOF
– Punitive Intrusion	
Counter Drug	LT/SOF/TECH
Counter Terrorism	LT/SOF
Counter Proliferation	SOF
– Conflict Containment	
MOOTW	HVY/LT/SOF
– Leverage	
TMD	TECH
Space Applications	TECH
C4I Systems Integration	TECH
Battlefield Awareness	TECH
– Reassurance	
Presence	HVY/LT/SOF
– Core Security	
NMD	TECH
Counter Drug	HVY/LT/SOF
Illegal Immigration	LT/SOF
Crime in the Streets	LT/SOF
– Humanitarian	
Disaster Relief	LT/SOF
Population Evacuation	HVY/LT/SOF
Refugee Protection	HVY/LT/SOF
Cooperation, Exchanges & Trng	HVY/LT/SOF

(taken from DA, 'Army Vision 2010', 8)

This chart has some interesting implications for special ops. The first is the lack of SOF exclusive missions: except for counter-proliferation, SOF has no missions that belong to them. The chart treats them as a part of the conventional Army along with heavy and light forces. A suspicious observer might draw from this an inference that there is no huge difference between SOF and other forces after all. Another inference stems from the number of mission categories identified for 'light' units. As of 1997 there are ten active-duty Army divisions. Of these, the Army has only four that can reasonably be described as 'light': the 101st Airborne (Air Assault), the 82nd Airborne Division, the 25th Infantry and the 10th Infantry (Mountain). The first is essentially a light-infantry division but is tied to the brigade of helicopters that give it the 'Air Assault' capability that is its *raison d'être*. The long lead time to move the helicopters and their heavy-support requirements make the 101st a poor candidate for most 'light' missions. Likewise, the 82nd Airborne is considered a 'signature' division, used in contingencies such as Desert Storm to demonstrate US resolve by quickly placing ground forces in a conflict area. As such it is not available for most 'light' missions. This leaves the 25th and the 10th Mountain as the only usable, readily deployable light units. Both of these are small, two-brigade divisions. Because of this, both have been stretched thin, employed whenever contingencies arise, for example, Somalia and in Haiti, natural disasters along the Pacific Rim, etc.

One obvious conclusion is that the overlap between light and SOF missions will very quickly lead to the use of SOF to fill in for the absent or very over-stressed light forces, that is, the badly overworked 25th Infantry and the 10th Mountain. This in turn might give credence to the old notion that SOF is no more than light infantry with air and naval support. If the Army loses a light division, as seems possible given anticipated force reductions, the situation will only become worse. Since it is unlikely that Navy SEALs or Air Force combat controllers will be able to help with the abundant large and small-scale light infantry missions, this leaves the Army's numbered SF groups as the only candidates. Using SOF in this manner can only advance their 'conventionalization'.

A SLIGHTLY DIFFERENT LOOK AT THE FUTURE

Not everyone agrees with the official DOD view of the future. Nor is everyone convinced that 'precision strike' lived up to its billing in Desert Storm. It certainly was of no help in Haiti or Somalia and is unlikely be useful in hurricane relief. Early in 1997, strategists at the US Army War College made an informal assessment of the near-term future. The resulting vision of the future of military conflict is not too dissimilar in principle to the official DOD one, but with an important difference in emphasis. First of all, it is an attempt to assess the probable state of the world, the larger international environment. Secondly, it argues that, in the absence of the conventional enemy force pictured by 'Joint Vision', other capabilities will be needed. Thirdly, and most importantly, it is not driven by the need to adapt operations to technology.

Some of the major points of the assessment are:

* No major competitors will engage the USA militarily. Presumably, potential enemies have learned lessons from the Gulf War too. Operations other than war are certain to occur and, in some cases, will be essential to enhancing stability in regions important to US interests.
* The international environment will continue to be chaotic struggle on several levels, subnational, national and international. It will be characterized by ethnic conflict, breakdown of states, quest for strategic resources/materials, increasing influence of subnational actors, increasing strains between developing and developed world over economic and environmental issues. The weakening of classical sovereignty will continue (thanks to flow of capital, information technology, satellites and global news, increased influence of international corporations and other organizations, changing norms over intervention, emergence of 'international civil society', etc.).
* The USA will face many challenges in dealing with the consequences of this erosion of the Westphalian state system, including maintenance of access to markets and materials, support of key friends and allies, promotion of free markets and democratic ideals, encouraging internal development, and not least maintaining the security of its own borders.
* Rapid technological development in precision weapons, command, control, communication and intelligence collection is not confined to the USA. It will also empower weak states and subnational actors. The USA's own reliance on this technology can leave it vulnerable to offensive information warfare or facing low-tech opponents to whom high technology is simply irrelevant.

What does this imply for the way the US Armed Forces are structured
and employed? Again, according to the War College strategists:

- Future conflicts may not be suitable to the employment of the
  most expensive parts of the US arsenal. Bomber and fighter
  aircraft, attack submarines, aircraft carriers and main battle tanks
  are examples of very expensive systems that may not be useful
  in most conflicts. Lower-tech solutions may work just as well or
  better. Ironically, the best argument for the high-tech systems
  may be the old one that their very existence makes conventional
  war less likely.

- Investment in human capital (regional studies, language training
  and other forms of support to operations other than war) will
  be extremely important to the conduct of the type of operations
  most common in the future.

- Sufficient conventional Army force structure will be required to
  provide both a conventional defense and to participate in
  operations other than war.

- More skills (such as CA, Psyops, MP, etc) that exist primarily in
  the Reserve Components need to be brought into the active force
  to provide a ready and sustainable capability to deal, on short
  notice, with the kinds of protracted operations envisioned.

- Service claims, to the contrary, by mission, tradition and current
  capability the US Army is the only full-service land force.

  Its CA, Psyops, foreign-area specialists, MP, SF and Combat
  Support units have capabilities that can not be duplicated by any
  other existing organization, military or not.

  The Army logistics system, signals, engineers, and its wide
  range of combat capability, both conventional and unconventional, is unique.

  USMC is a great expeditionary force but can only sustain itself
  for short periods within a relatively few miles from littoral areas.
  They also do not have the range/depth/variety of skills that the
  Army has.

  The Air Force, Navy or Marine Corps do not possess and have
  never sought to develop an Unconventional Warfare capacity
  even remotely comparable to that of Army SOF. Even the SEALs
  are primarily a raiding force.

  US Air Force and Navy air superiority and precision-strike
  capability is important – but not solely sufficient for any likely
  form of warfare.

Another credible voice came to similar conclusions. General Lewis McKenzie, a Canadian officer and veteran of the war-but-not-war conflict in Bosnia, stated that well-trained and disciplined soldiers are still the 'key' ingredient but that, in his experience, the new environment called for some 'extras' – negotiating skills, public relations, Civil Affairs and what he called 'the humanitarian assistance extras, the hearts and minds piece of the effort'. Furthermore, these skills need to be available down to the lowest level, so that junior officers and noncomissioned officers, and not just task-force commanders, develop these abilities (McKenzie, remarks at the US Army Peacekeeping Institute, Carlisle Barracks, PA, 5 June 1996). All these sound very much like SF, Civil Affairs and Psychological Operations skills.

What comes out of this analysis, simply, is that international competition and threats from other actors will continue to require military responses from the USA. Although conventional war threats will not disappear, they are likely to be less important. In any case it is unlikely that any enemy will appear who has a military capacity equal to that of the USA. In short, there is less need for high-technology systems, especially weapons systems. There is however, more need for a force that can be placed in harm's way when the nature of that harm is unclear, and even the source of it may not be obvious.

There is much potential work out there for a UW force, and there will continue to be a wide variety of unconventional challenges. Indeed, the number and degree of possible involvements is limited only by resources and national-policy considerations. But meeting those challenges requires a capability to conduct those poorly defined forms of engagement here termed UW, or unconventional warfare. However, this capacity does not come cheaply, and it may mean heavy expense in areas where the Pentagon prefers not to spend its money, training personnel in non-military skills.

BACK TO THE 'BOOM AND BUST' MENTALITY?

As the examples of World War II and Vietnam show, Special Operations Forces from all the services have been subjected to a repeating pattern of build-up followed by severe diminishment. Treatment of the SOF capacity recently does not provoke optimism on this score. Army SOF received less than one page (out of 97 pages total) in the United States Army Posture Statement for Fiscal Year

1997 (DA, 1996, 25). Since this is the Army's formal presentation to the committees and subcommittees of the US Congress, it suggests that these units are not considered critically important.

The problem of institutional sponsorship for SOF has been mitigated by the 1986 legislation requiring the creation of USSOCOM and associated elements. However, this is legislation that could all too easily be changed. In the past special operations has suffered when it lost its senior executive-branch proponents, notably Presidents Roosevelt and Kennedy. It is far too easy to envision the Joint Chiefs, at some not too distant point, declaring that SOF are now fully integrated into all aspects of the armed forces and there is no need for an extensive separate command. The more that SOF become simply an elite conventional force, the easier this argument is to make. Because of the association with 'unconventional warfare' in the past, SOF were often marginalized. By posturing themselves as part of the team, making themselves useful to the conventional forces, SOF have largely changed this perception; but in so doing they also diminish the rationale for having a separate command, and especially separate funding. Given a compliant Congress, the services would be only too pleased to pick up the resources now being dedicated to special ops forces.

Nor is such a move without precedent. When the Army/Air Force Center for Low-Intensity Conflict was dissolved in 1995–6, the reason given was that, allegedly, Low-Intensity Conflict doctrine was so thoroughly integrated into Army and Air Force training and operations that a special purpose center was no longer required.

The indirect approach: DAMPL

During late 1995, Department of the Army staffers quietly floated a proposal that would have deactivated one of the SF Groups. For reasons that are unclear, the issue quickly died. But, having failed in that initiative, in early 1996, the Army set out to achieve the same goal by different means. It proposed reducing the priority of all but two Special Forces Groups for support.

The Department of the Army Master Priority List (DAMPL) establishes each Army unit's priority for equipment, personnel, training, manning and modernization. In short, everything that unit requires to remain capable. The 1996 proposal would retain the 1st SFG (targeted for the Pacific theater) and the 5th SFG (targeted for the Middle East) as Category I units, while reducing the remaining three active duty groups to Category II and both National Guard Groups to Category III. The rationale for this was based on the current US national military strategy, which required that the Army be prepared to fight two major regional contingencies (MRCs).

The plan was especially hurtful in regard to the National Guard units, which gained increasing importance during the 1990s. It is not too strong to say that the Haiti mission and perhaps the Bosnia mission would have been impossible without the participation of reserve Special Forces soldiers and other special operations troops, especially in the area of Psyops and Civil Affairs.

This raised the distinct suspicion in some quarters that the Army was returning to the 'boom or bust' approach to SOF resources, repeating the experience of the 1970s and the 1980s in which special-ops forces were cut in favor of conventional Army forces ('Advisory Board Report, Summer 1996', Special Forces Association, Fayetteville, NC). The difference this time was that this was exactly the sort of move that the 'Special Forces Bill' of 1986 had been created to prevent.

Deactivating the SF reserve

Summer 1996 also saw a puzzling initiative in which the United States Special Operations Command sought to deactivate the two last remaining battalions of Army Special Forces from the National Guard and three Civil Affairs brigades from the Army Reserve. The move immediately provoked Congressional ire because, apparently, it had not been coordinated with the Department of the Army but was 'a strictly budget driven decision between Special Operations Command and the OSD'. Even the units to be deactivated were not asked for their 'input or opinions' (Rep. Gillespie V. Montgomery, letter to Hon. Togo D. West Jr, Secretary of the Army, 10 July 1996). Furthermore, according to Rep. Nick J. Rahall, 'this reduction of forces is in direct contradiction to the department-wide Bottom Up review that was conducted in 1991 and the Off-Site Agreement in 1993. Further, the plan ... contradicts the USSOCOM's Program Objective Memorandum for Fiscal year 1992' (Rep. Nick J. Rahall II, letter to Hon. Togo D. West Jr, Secretary of the Army, 11 July 1996).

This proposed reduction was especially irksome to members of

Congress because the earlier 1993 Off-Site Agreement had already resulted in the loss of 50 percent of the reserve Special Forces units (the 11th and 12th SF Groups from the Army Reserve), leaving only the two Army National Guard SF Groups, the 19th and 20th. Neither reservists nor Congressmen could be blamed if they suspected this was another move to eliminate all or most Special Operations Forces from the reserve components.

In the words of Congressman Montgomery: 'Has the world changed so radically since the Offsite as to merit reducing these essential assets? If this is the case, why are they constantly being called upon to perform missions in Haiti, Bosnia and other regions of the world. In fact, half of the Special Forces personnel utilized in Haiti were from the National Guard' (Montgomery, letter to Hon. Togo D. West Jr, 10 July 1996).

Senator Trent Lott, Senate Majority Leader and a long-time supporter of SOF, also expressed his concern and received the following reply from General Henry H. Shelton, Commander of USSOCOM. 'United States Special Operations Command plans no new Army National Guard or Army Reserve force structure reductions in fiscal year 1997' (General Henry H. Shelton, letter to Hon. Trent Lott, 15 July 1996).

Reducing the SF rank structure

Because it consists entirely of experienced soldiers with longer and more extensive training than other organizations, SOF in general and Army SF in particular tend to be rank heavy. There are no privates or second lieutenants in special operations. Just about every squad-size element in special operations is led by a commissioned officer and consists entirely of upper-grade noncommissioned officers. Each Army SF company has a sergeant major as its senior noncommissioned officer. Conventional units have only one sergeant major per battalion. Likewise, the senior noncommissioned officer in a 12-man A-team is a master sergeant. In conventional formations there is usually only one master sergeant per 100 soldiers, not for every 12. The Army SF rank structure came under attack in 1997 when it was proposed to reduce these ranks as part of an Army-wide reduction, bringing the structure more into line with similar-sized conventional units. The need for SOF to attract, reward and retain high-performing soldiers was not a consideration.

In fact, the moves to reduce SOF make sense if you look at special operations as part of the conventional armed forces that should be

A brief excursion into the future 301

reduced along with other such forces in a time of shrinking budgets. The suspicious might also regard it as part of an attempt to make Special Forces more like the rest of the Army.

This book regards all the above moves as counterproductive and wrongheaded at best, and at worse as actively dangerous to national security and military capability. SOF is relatively inexpensive in comparison with ordinary conventional units. In Fiscal 1997, the total SOF budget for all services is about 1 percent of the total Defense budget. But worse, these initiatives suggest that the vast array of unconventional, 'gray area' engagements are still considered of marginal importance. The idea that other-than-war threats will continue to threaten US interests always receives a mention and a nod from conventional planners; but they often go on to argue that these are tasks that can be done by any well-trained soldier. It is odd to believe that the best choices to prosecute these conflicts are an 18-year-old high-school graduate with basic combat training and a military specialist course, commanded by a 23-year-old officer who has completed a basic officer course and generalist training in some military field. There is a better way and that way is with unconventional warfare forces, specifically Army Special Forces, CA and Psyops as the core element, supported by other SOF and conventional units as required.

Unlike some analyses, this book does not argue that conventional forces are irrelevant to future warfighting or that conventional military power will cease to be important. The threats that theorists characterize as central to the New World Order, chiefly revolutionary warfare, complex emergencies and large-scale organized crime, are not all that new. Furthermore, conventional, 'Clausewitzian' war is an incredibly powerful tool that is to a large degree responsible for the rise of the nation-state as the dominant system of political organization in the world. Hailing the demise of the nation-state is not new either, it is virtually a cottage industry among social theorists. Although it is certainly true that new means of power are emerging, and that non-state actors have increased importance, none of this necessarily means that nation states will become obsolete nor that the direct application of military force will become useless or even unimportant. High-tech systems and information networks remain susceptible to physical destruction. Conventional units, capable of 'putting steel on target', will be an important component of power for the foreseeable future.

Nevertheless, there is, and always has been, a field of military activity that can be called 'unconventional warfare'. That is, warfare that does not fit the conventional model and is not best prosecuted by force organized, train, equipped, etc. for conventional warfare. But, by the same token, current SOF missions and units do not always lend themselves to this role.

FROM SOF TO UNCONVENTIONAL OPERATIONS FORCES

Based on the historical examples examined in this book, the military organization most capable of conducting UW, and the only organization with a record of success in UW, is US Army Special Forces, especially in combination with Civil Affairs and Psyops assets. In order to maximize the ability of the SF/CA/Psyops team to act as an Unconventional Operations Force, it is necessary to disentangle the current mix of SOF missions and separate out those which are conventional from those which are unconventional. As explained in Chapter 1, Special Operations Forces currently have nine principal missions and seven collateral activities.

Missions

Direct Action (DA)
Special Reconnaissance (SR)
Foreign Internal Defense (FID)
Unconventional Warfare (UW)
Combatting Terrorism (CT)
Counterproliferation (CP)
Civil Affairs (CA)
Psychological Operations (Psyops)
Information Warfare (IW)

Collateral Activities

Coalition Support
Combat Search and Rescue (CSAR)
Counterdrug Activities (CD)
Countermine Activities (CM)
Humanitarian Assistance (HA)
Security Assistance (SA)
Special Activities

(taken from USSOCOM 1996, fact sheet, undated, provided courtesy of USSOCOM, December 1996)

This list is a hodge-podge of conventional, unconventional and just plain odd missions, some of which are actually subsets of others. The list results in part from a general willingness at the command levels of the SOF community to accept almost any mission as one in which SOF can succeed. There is an idea that, by accepting many missions, SOF demonstrates its fitness and remains competitive with other organizations in the struggle for a share of the diminishing military budget. This leads to the inclusion of things like demining, which clearly is and ought to be a conventional military-engineer mission. SOF, in particular Army SF, became involved because most demining activity in this context means instructing foreign military personnel in land mine and booby-trap removal. The problem with things like demining is that they require significant amounts of training time to prepare the instructors and significant amounts of deployment time to conduct the training in what is essentially a duplication of an existing engineer capability.

Other missions, such as counterterrorism and special activities, are so specialized or rare that realistically they can be accomplished by the small specialized units of the Joint Special Operations Command and really should not concern the greater SOF community at all. Their inclusion as SOF missions serves only to lengthen the list.

At least as explained in unclassified publications, counter-proliferation is too vague to really allow anyone to focus resources on it (see, for example, USSOCOM 1996, *Special Operations Forces Posture Statement*, 31). Its inclusion in the list seems to be intended to make a political-policy point that the US government opposes proliferation of weapons of mass destruction and will use 'military power' to do so, when and if appropriate.

Still other missions, in which SOF has played a major role, are not mentioned at all – for example Noncombatant Evacuation Operations in which threatened US civilians and selected foreign nationals are removed from harm's way in situations such as the 1996 evacuation of Liberia.

Unscrewing the inscrutable

Because, as noted earlier, the current mission list is a result of diverse influences (congressional legislation, bureaucratic fiefdoms, historical accidents, initiatives by the special-operations community and so forth) and because some of those missions are vaguely defined, it is difficult to reorder them in a way that makes sense. What follows is an attempt to break down the two chief types of missions that make SOF special and which result in much mission confusion.

Unconventional warfare missions are those which include 'special' activities that are not part of conventional warfighting. This is what makes them 'special'. The other group of missions are those which are more-or-less conventional activities but which are 'special' because they are done at a very high level of proficiency and often in very difficult circumstances.

In the first case, unconventional warfare, it is the missions which are special. In the second case, the missions are essentially ordinary conventional warfare activities, but it is the units that are 'special' because of their unique equipment and high proficiency.

Therefore, which missions are really special in the sense of different and which are those best carried out by a highly-trained conventional military force?

Re-ordered Missions and Units*
1. Unconventional Warfare (UW)** – Army SF/CA/Psyop
   – Peace Operations (PO)
   – Support to Insurgency (SI)
   – Foreign Internal Defense (FID)
      – Security Assistance (SA)
      – Counterdrug (CD)
      – Humanitarian Assistance (HA)
2. Direct Action (DA) – Rangers, SEALs, SMUs, Conv Forces
   – Counter Terrorism (CT)
   – Personnel Recovery Missions
   – Countermine (CM)
3. Special Reconnaissance (SR) – Rangers, SEALs, SMUs, Conv Forces

Collateral Activities
1. Special Activities – Rangers, SEALs, SMUs
2. Combat Search and Rescue – USAF Special Ops
3. Coalition Support – Conventional Forces

General Support
1. Civil Affairs
2. Psychological Operations
3. Special Operations Aviation
4. USAF Special Operations
5. Navy Special Boat Units
6. Swimmer Delivery Vehicle Teams

* Information Warfare and Counterproliferation fall out as too poorly defined. Combat Search and Rescue would become an Air Force Special Ops mission with assistance as appropriate by other SOF. For example, in areas where Army Special Forces were conducting UW, the SF would assist with downed-pilot or sensitive-equipment recovery.
** Navy and Air Force SOF would provide some specialist training to their counterpart services in foreign nations as part of UW.

In the beginning, this book defined unconventional warfare simply as warfare outside the conventional warfare, that is, warfare that is not conventional. Following the usage originated by Colonel Mark D. Boyatt, it introduces the term Unconventional Operations Forces (UOF) meaning those elements of US SOF most suited to perform unconventional warfare, namely Army SOF (Boyatt, 1993, 7). These are Army SF, Psyops and Civil Affairs, supported by appropriate other elements. The long-standing practice of SF soldiers has been to regard Civil Affairs and Psychological Operations units as outside the 'core' group of Special Operations Forces. Perhaps in some sense they are, but they are very important for most forms of unconventional warfare and therefore are 'core' forces for Unconventional Operations Forces.

As Boyatt points out, the unconventional role consists in large part of assisting the indigenous military and paramilitary forces in the conduct of a large slice of what are now considered SOF missions and collateral activities: foreign internal defense, guerrilla warfare, humanitarian assistance, nation-building and counterdrug missions. UOF then, are forces that 'accomplish their mission through counterpart relationships. The only SOF specifically trained, organized and equipped to conduct these missions in this manner are the numbered Army Special Forces Groups' (Boyatt, 1993, 7).

Additionally, however, three of these roles, nation-building, guerrilla warfare and humanitarian assistance, have a strong requirement for Psyops and CA skills. Large-scale foreign internal-defense missions would certainly benefit from CA and Psyops participation, and even counterdrug operations would find these capabilities useful.

Training time

In many respects, the question of what SOF does or ought to do comes down to training time. To expect a single organization, no matter how talented, to undertake missions as diverse and complex as those assigned to Army Special Forces is to expect the impossible.

Missions like CT, DA and SR are interesting and widely respected, and therefore receive an undue amount of attention, to the detriment of the time and resources needed for other missions – especially something as complex and convoluted as what this book terms 'unconventional warfare'. Language training and maintenance alone is time-consuming enough.

There is a tendency, especially among those who like to call themselves common-sense thinkers, to say that all the flailing about and confusion over definitions and mission categories is wasted energy. SOF, they might say, will continue to do whatever needs to be done. But, as usual, life is not so easy.

Lack of appropriate training arose as an issue in Desert Storm, Provide Comfort (northern Iraq) and Uphold Democracy (Haiti), and it is one of the reasons for the sense of frustration some SOF members feel about unconventional warfare missions. Elementary psychology tells us that groups and individuals function better if they have a sense of mastery of their task(s); that mastery stems from some combination of native ability, training and experience. Since ability is hard to select for in this case (since we do not have a good definition of what we are looking for), the variable we can control to produce mastery with the most certainty is training.

But, it is hard to decide exactly of what that training ought to consist. Should it be training in communications, marketing, psychology or languages and light-weapons handling? This very difficultly probably accounts in large part for the tendency of SOF to gravitate back towards the well-understood conventional model and the traditional military tasks associated with it. By the same token, area-specific training is very important for UW, but which areas should we anticipate and prepare for? Which languages should be emphasized?

The current military intelligence system simply is not set up to provide this kind of detailed information, especially not on short notice. Intelligence officers and special operators both complain about the difficulty in obtaining even basic information about many countries in the world where sudden contingencies arise. The cure is to give the numbered SF Groups a real, carefully considered regional orientation and force commanders at all levels to stick to it in planning and deployments. But it also means they will not be available for the current, full range of SOF missions as defined in current doctrine.

The difficulty of defining appropriate UW training goes back in turn to the lack of definition that bedevils the whole area of UW.

No wonder it is easier to devote training time to weapons rather than, for example, negotiation skills. Although this type of alternative training has been available to the SOF community for more than two years and some interest has been expressed, there have been few takers.

DEVELOPING AN UNCONVENTIONAL WARFARE FORCE

Why does SF not embrace UW as its principal mission? In part for the reasons given above, because it is very hard to define and prepare for. But there are cultural reasons as well. Since the Vietnam War, part of the problem is the attractiveness of DA, CT and SR as missions. Such missions, and the resulting image of deadly resourceful fighters, are the principal reasons soldiers undergo the extraordinary hardships of special-operations training and duty. These commando-like activities are close to the conventional model of warfighting and have great appeal, and thus tend to consume a disproportionate amount of the unit's attention and training time. 'They are high visibility, immediate gratification missions, well within the comfort zone and easily identified with by most people.' But the same missions can be performed by other SOF and some general-purpose forces.

Some special-ops units, such as Delta and the Ranger Battalions, Marine Corps Reconnaissance, SEALs and some conventional units are better trained, organized and equipped for these missions than Army SF. This is duplication that is hard to justify in a shrinking military. Furthermore, UW and its associated missions are sufficiently difficult and complex to require all the training time and resources available.

Finally, the game of 'anything you can do, I can do better' in conventional warfare is too competitive and results in duplication of capabilities, accompanied by endless fruitless arguments as to which of the similar capabilities is really superior. For example, the US Marine Corps is a primary competitor with the Army's Ranger Regiment for a variety of contingency missions. The USMC is already upgrading its demanding initial entry training program ('boot camp') by adding an additional five days called 'Crucible Week', making it more similar to Army Ranger training (*US News and World Report*, 'The Few, the Pround, the Smart, the Moral', 16 December 1996, 33).

Despite success in the 'social work' side of the SOF business, it is not always popular with the operators who do virtually all this work, Army Special Forces. In November and December 1994, a series of interviews were conducted among US forces in Haiti by researchers from the Army's Walter Reed Research Institute. These psychologists asked soldiers from all specialties and all ranks from captain and below how they felt about their work in Operation Uphold Democracy. Of the 3,205 soldiers interviewed, 147 were Army SF. Forty percent of the SF interviewed did not feel this was appropriate or important, compared with 22 percent of military police and 23 percent of intelligence personnel who felt similarly.

Not surprisingly, the SF soldiers feelings were most strongly duplicated in the other combat arms (infantry, artillery and aviation) in Haiti. If nearly half of the SF soldiers involved in a typical UW mission like Haiti did not feel that it was an appropriate SF mission, clearly there is considerable disagreement among operators as to what Army SOF, in particular SF, ought to do.

From SOF to UOF

Unconventional Operations Forces can allow the USA to compete in the area of not-quite-war that this book terms 'unconventional warfare'. In most applications it will have the added advantage in a media-soaked political environment of being conducted routinely enough, in a sufficiently low-profile manner to attract little press coverage.

The SOF community in general and SF in particular have a tendency to spread themselves too thin. In an admirable display of 'can-do' spirit, SOF units tend to disparage what they call 'hand-wringing' and boast they can do 'anything, anywhere, anytime'. To some degree this is even true. However, the fact that a unit can manage to accomplish a task does not mean that it is the best suited unit or that training for peripheral tasks is the best use of its time.

The Vietnam War heritage, with its emphasis on conventional offensive warfare, direct action and strategic reconnaissance, has played SF false. Despite the appeal of DA and SR, the fact is that these missions seldom occur and, when they do, they are for the most part the province of SMUs. Historically, we have seen that while SF can perform these missions, they are not its forte. In Panama, Somalia and the Gulf War these missions tended to be given to SMUs, who in turn produced the most successful record of accomplishment.

The same historical record of success at unconventional-warfare functions shows that SF has a solid base of accomplishment. In the Gulf, in northern Iraq, Somalia, Panama and Haiti they performed missions and scored successes that no other type of organization, military or civilian, matched or could match. SF is the only type of organization, SOF or conventional, with the training, equipment and organization to conduct UW missions.

To take maximum advantage of this capability will require a real change in thinking, at the national-policy level and within the SOF community and in the Department of Defense to allow SF to make the changes required for the warfare of the twenty-first century. At the highest levels, it will require a change in strategic thinking and policymaking to accept UW and 'gray area' conflict as an important arena, not peripheral to national interests but one that can have serious, far-reaching effects on the USA and its partners and allies. Changes will be needed in the way national agencies process and disseminate intelligence so that information needed for UW decisions is timely and available.

For the Defense Department, it means a serious, long-range investment in personal training and education at a time when technology and hardware solutions are far more popular. It means rank and salary scales as well as challenging missions to retain trained personnel. Technology can no longer be allowed to drive strategy as it has in the development of 'battlefield dominance' concepts and 'precision engagement'. This means that any changes will likely be made without the support of the major industrial suppliers who stand to profit from high-tech approaches.

At the joint and service command level it means a difficult and time-consuming effort to develop systematic approaches to these conflicts, and translate those approaches into usable doctrine that will guide force development and training. It means a willingness to allocate scarce intelligence resources to the analysis of UW problems.

Within Special Forces it will mean a willingness to place much less emphasis on the image and skills of the commando and much more on the ability to apply military, civil and psychological capabilities at the tactical and operational levels.

Most importantly, for all of these groups and organizations it means a shift in expectations. For the most part, UW is devoid of clean solutions and clear victories. Nor is it usually rapid. This means a willingness to accept lengthy commitments and incremental progress. None of these adjustments will be easy. But all of them are necessary and important if the USA is to survive and prosper in the complex and dangerous environment of the twenty-first century.

NOTE

Much attention is being devoted in military circles to theories of, 'fourth-generation' warfare, sometimes referred to as non-Clausewitzian warfare. These theorists begin where the conventional thinkers' 'information revolution' ends and run with the idea. They suggest that this revolution is so profound that the military systems developed for the conventional battlefield are largely irrelevant to coming forms of conflict. The most extreme theorists take this to the limit and argue that conventional battle is a vanishing phenomena to be replaced by other forms of conflict.

The basic notion of 'fourth-generation' warfare is that there have been four distinct stages or generations of military development, each characterized by a new development that came to dominate warfare. The first three generations were: the smoothbore musket *c.* 1648; the adaption of the industrial revolution to combat *c.* 1850; and the rise of maneuver warfare *c.* 1918 (Lind *et al.*, 1989). The newest, fourth generation, rests on a pair of intertwined ideas. The first idea is that the rise of pervasive computer-based information and communication systems will create a media-drenched environment similar to that characterized by the Tofflers in their influential book *War and Anti-War* (1993). The second ingredient is the anticipated demise, or at least serious loss of influence, by the nation-state brought about the rise of non-state competitors (corporations, revolutionary groups, special interests, etc) similar to the 1970s-era 'Polyarchy' concept proposed by Seyom Brown and mentioned in Chapter 1.

An example of this 'fourth-generation' dynamic in action might be the demise of the USSR, said to have been brought about by the inability of the totalitarian state to subdue the separatist ambitions of its component entities, desires that were actualized by the use of information systems that were outside state control. Despite a great deal of ink being spilled in this debate, those who believe that state-centered, conventional warfare will continue to be predominant clearly have the upper hand for at least the time being.

Bibliography

NOTE ON SOURCES

Material taken from the Military Reference Branch, Main Branch, National Archives, Washington, DC is designated by the letters MBNA.

The Washington National Records Center, National Archives, Suitland, MD, is a major depository for official US military records including those of the Vietnam War. The Vietnam records are incomplete, largely uncataloged, and unindexed. Furthermore, as reported by Archivist R. Boylan, most pre-1966 records of the 5th SFG were destroyed in Vietnam (*c.* 1965) because of storage problems. According to the Archivist Supervisor there, numerous records remain classified while many others have been removed by various governmental agencies and are unavailable for research. For reference purposes, records are identified by location (i.e. WNR for Washington National Records Center) and VN for Vietnam followed by the unit designation, i.e. '5th SFG'. Microfiche records are identified MF followed by the records group number, catalog number, file-box number, or other identification.

The Center for Military History, Pulaski Building, Washington, DC is abbreviated CMH with HRB representing 'Military History Branch' and SEAB 'South East Asia Branch', both subdivisions of the CMH.

The US Army Military History Institute at Carlisle Barracks, Pennsylvania, is abbreviated MHI. Material from the Senior Officer Oral History Program is designated OHP and the name of the interviewee. On 16 February 1972, MACV's Data Management Agency produced a massive eight-volume Historical Document Listing of over 4,700 pages. Microfilm copies of many of these documents are located at MHI. Items from this file are designated HIMS (Historical Information Management System) with the roll number and date of the document, when available. In most cases, there are no frame numbers on these microfilms.

The Washington National Records Center, National Archives

retains approximately 30,000 feet of records relating to Special Forces activities conducted on behalf of or in cooperation with the CIA. These records remain classified and unavailable for public reference.

Material taken from Gareth Porter's *Vietnam: The Definitive Documentation of Human Decisions* (1979) is referenced as VDD, following the title and date of the document.

1st SFG (Special Forces Group). *Special Action Force* (Okinawa: Special Forces Group, 1971).

3rd SFG (Special Forces Group). Haiti Unconventional Operations Briefing, Port-au-Prince, Haiti; 11 December, 1994.

4th POG (Psychological Operations Group). 'Psychological Operations in Support of Operation Provide Comfort' (Fort Bragg, NC: USAJFKSWC, 1994).

5th SFG (Special Forces Group). Operations Report, November 1970, Records Group 472, Box 3, 5th SFG, USA (VN) WNR.

5th SFG (Special Forces Group). Organizational History File. Document 'CIDG Conversion', dated 1 October 1962; File K, Box 4 WNR VN 5TH SFG.

16th MP Bde (Military Police Brigade (Airborne)) briefing, undated but provided to the author *c.* Jan. 1995. Courtesy of MNF/JTF 190, Port-au-Prince, Haiti.

75th Infantry Regiment. 'Unit History' (Special Operations website, Dec. 1996).

'A' Detachment Handbook. Issued by HQ, 5th SFG, Nha Trang, RVN, undated but signed by Col. Francis J. Kelly. Handbook is mentioned in microfiche AD 500-859 as published in the fall of 1966, Records Group 472, Box 3, 5th SFG, US Army (VN), WNR.

Abrams, Creighton (Gen., US Army COMUSMACV). Message to subordinate commanders, subject: 'Accelerated Redeployment', dated 7 July 1971; Abrams Papers, message file for 1971, MHI.

— Memorandum to US Amb. Samuel Berger, RVN, undated but found in message file for 1968, Abrams Papers, MHI.

Activation Plan. Army/Air Force Center for Low Intensity Conflict (CLIC) 26 January 1986, published by Headquarters Department of the Army, Deputy Chief of Staff/Operations and Plans and Headquarters Department of the Air Force, Deputy Chief of Staff/Plans and Operations; courtesy of CLIC.

Adams, James. *Secret Armies: Inside the American, Soviet and*

European Special Forces (New York: The Atlantic Monthly Press, 1987).

Adams, Thomas K. 'Organizing for Counterterrorism', *Syracuse Scholar* 8, 1 (Spring 1987): 90–106.

Adelman, Robert H. and Walton, George (Col., US Army [ret.]). *The Devil's Brigade* (Philadelphia, PA: Chilton Books, 1966).

Adelsberger, Bernard J. 'Built on a Doctrine of Small-unit Actions', *Army Times* (13 June 1988): 12–13, 16, 18, 55.

— 'Motorized Burnout', *Army Times* (10 April 1989): 14–15.

AFIF 123 (Armed Forces Information Film). 'The Third Challenge – Unconventional Warfare' (USMA AVIT Collection, 1962).

Ahmad, Eqbal. 'Revolutionary War and Counterinsurgency', in David S. Sullivan and Martin J. Sattler, eds., *Revolutionary War*, (New York: Columbia University Press, 1971), pp. 1–47.

Anderson, Kent. *Sympathy for the Devil* (Garden City, NY: Doubleday, 1987).

Army Field Forces. 'Training Bulletin Number 8' (Fort Monroe, VA: Office of the Chief of Army Field Forces, 16 November 1951).

Army Ground Forces, Intelligence Section, Fort Monroe, VA. Memorandum from individual named 'Farris' to Lieutenant Colonel Gleszer, War Department General Staff, Record Group 319, Army Intelligence Files 1941–1948, 373.14, Box 874, MBNA.

Army Times, 'Grenada Invasion Units Listed'. *Army Times* 44, 12 (31 October 1983): 23. (Official DOD list of units involved in the Grenada invasion, including SFOD-Delta.)

Asprey, Robert. *War In the Shadows: Guerrillas in History*, 2 vols. (Garden City, NY: Doubleday & Co., 1975).

Attitude Report, Weekly PsyOps Field Program, III CTZ, Civil Operations and Revolutionary Support, dated 28 December 1967, HIMS, MHI.

Ball, Harry P. (Col. US Army [ret.]). *Of Responsible Command* (Carlisle, PA: Association of the US Army War College, 1983).

Bank, Aaron (Col., US Army Special Forces, [ret.]). Commander, First Army Special Forces unit to be organized, 1952). *From OSS to Green Berets* (New York: Pocket Books, 1986).

— Personal communication with author, 10 April 1989.

Barkley, Katherine and Banning, Garrett. *Two, Three ... Many Vietnams* (San Francisco, CA: Cornfield Press, 1971).

Barry, John and Evan Thomas. 'Getting Ready for Future Wars', *Newsweek* (22 January 1990): 24–6, 28.

Barton, Fred H. *Salient Operational Aspects of Paramilitary Warfare in Three Asian Areas* (Chevy Chase, MD: Operations Research Office, 1954).

Beaumont, Roger A. *Military Elites* (New York: Bobbs-Merrill, 1974).

— 'Military Elite Forces', *Parameters* 9, 1 (March 1979): 17–29.

— *Special Operations and Elite Units* (New York: Greenwood Press, 1988).

Beckman, Robert L. (Asst. Prof. of Political Science, US Naval Academy). 'Ethical Existentialism: Phoenix and the Iran/Contra Affair'. Unpublished paper presented at the National Defense University, 11 January 1989.

Beckwith, Charlie A. *Delta Force* (New York: Dell, 1983).

Bentley, David. 'Operation Sea Signal', *Strategic Forum* (May 1996): 2.

Bergquist, Kenneth P. (Candidate for ASD (SO/LIC) 1987). Testimony in Senate Hearing, 1988.

Bibliography of Intelligence Literature, no author listed (Washington, DC: Defense Intelligence College, 1981).

Bishop, Richard D. (Maj., US Army, Special Forces, [ret.]). Bishop was an instructor at 1st SFG's Counterinsurgency School, Okinawa, 1961–63. Interview with author 18 July 1989, Fayetteville, NC.

Blackburn, Donald B. (Gen., US Army [ret]). Blackburn papers, Oral History Interview transcript, 1983. OHP, MHI.

Blackjack, Operation OCONEE (Blackjack 12), Company C, 5th SFG, April 1967; this file includes accounts of other Blackjack Operations through July 1967. Microfiche AD 387-325, Box 3, Records Group 472, 5th SFG, WNR.

Blackstock, Paul W. 'The United States Intelligence Community and Military Intervention', Ellen Stern, ed., in *The Limits of Military Intervention* (Beverly Hills, CA: Sage, 1977), pp. 1257–79.

Blaufarb, Douglas. *The Counterinsurgency Era: US Doctrine and Performance, 1950 to the Present* (New York: Free Press, 1977).

Bloomfield, Lincoln P. and Leiss, Amelia C. *Controlling Small Wars* (New York: Knopf, 1970).

Bolger, Daniel P. *Americans at War: 1975–1986 – An Era of Violent Peace* (Novato CA: Persidio Press 1988).

— *Savage Peace: The Americans at War in the 1990s* (Novato, CA: Persidio Press, 1995).

Boyatt, Mark D. (Col., US Army Special Forces). 'Unconventional Operations Force of Special Operations' (Student Research Project, US Army War College, Carlisle, PA, April 1993). Personal correspondence with the author, 25 January 1997.

Bradford, Zeb B., Jr (Lt Col., US Army). 'US Tactics in Vietnam', *Military Review* 52, 2 (February 1972): 63–76.

Bradford, Zeb B., Jr and Brown, Frederick J. (both Lt Cols., US Army). *The United States Army in Transition* (Beverly Hills, CA: Sage, 1973).

Bradley, Francis X. (Col.) 'The Fallacy of Dual Capability', *Army* (Oct. 1959), pp. 18–22.

Brauer, Richard F. 'Case Study: The Son Tay Raid' (Carlisle Barracks, PA: US Army War College).

Brodie, Bernard. *War and Politics* (New York: Macmillan, 1973).

Brown, Harold (former US Secretary of Defense). *Thinking About National Security* (Boulder, CO: Westview Press, 1983).

Brown, Seyom. *New Forces in World Politics* (Washington DC: Brookings Institute, 1974).

Brown, Stephen D. 'Psyop in Operation Uphold Democracy', *Military Review* (September–October 1996): 57-64

Bruckner, Herbert (OSS operator, France and Indochina/10th SF). Interview with author, Fayetteville, NC, 20 July 1989.

Budahn, P. J. 'Chief's Propose Special Operations Command', *Army Times* (28 July 1986).

— 'Senate Passes Plan for Reorganizing Special Operations', *Army Times* (19 August 1986): 4.

— 'Coherent Strategy Urged for Low-Intensity Wars', *Army Times* (3 October 1986): 12.

Burhans, Robert (Lt Col., US Army [ret.]). *The First Special Service Force* (Wilmington, DE: Infantry Journal Press, 1947).

Butler, Samuel J. (LTC, US Army). Interview, Carlisle Barracks, PA; 3 December 1996. LTC Butler was Director of Planning, for both Headquarters UNOSOM II and US Forces, Somalia April 1993–March 1994.

CALL (Center for Army Lessons Learned). 'Soldiers in Panama', pamphlet issued by the Center for Army Lessons Learned, Fort Leavenworth, KS, 1990, pp. 16-17.

Campbell, John C. *Defense of the Middle East: Problems of American Policy* (New York: Praeger Publishers, 1960).

Carhart, Tom. *The Offering* (New York: Warner Books, 1987).

Center for Military History, *Analysis of Operation Urgent Fury* (Military History Institute Archives: Carlisle Barracks, PA, 1984).

Chandler, Robert W. *War of Ideas* (Boulder, CO: Westview Press, 1981).

Chaney, James M. (Major General US Army). Letter to Commanding General US Army, Northern Ireland Force, subject 'Commando Organisation', 1 June 1942. WNR-WWII, INBN file, 72-37, roll 1, frames 4–6.

Chinh Anh (Commander, Viet Cong Company 10, Vinh Long Province, RVN). Letter containing death threat against a GVN agroville recruiter, 29 March 1960, in Zasloff, pp. 38–39.

Clarke, Jeffery. *Advise and Support The Final Years 1965–73* (Washington DC: Center of Military History, 1988).

Cleaver, F. W., *et al*. *UN Parisian Warfare in Korea 1951–1954* Operations Research Office, Chevy Chase, MD (Baltimore, MD: Johns Hopkins University Press, 1956).

CLIC (Center for Low-Intensity Conflict). 'Operational Considerations for Military Involvement in Low-Intensity Conflict' (CLIC: Army/Air Force Center for Low-Intensity Conflict, Langley Air Force Base, VA, June 1987).

Cochran, Alexander S., Jr 'American Planning for Ground Combat in Vietnam, 1952–1965', *Parameters* 14, 2 (1984): 63–9.

Cocklin, Robert F. (Col., US Army). 'Classrooms in the Jungle', *Army* 10, 11 (November 1959): 24–6.

Cohen, Eliot A. *Commandos and Politicians* (Cambridge, MA: Center for International Studies, Harvard University, 1978).

Colby, William E. (former Director, Central Intelligence Agency 1973–6). Personal correspondence of the author, 29 December 1988.

— Statement, notes prepared for opening statement before the Senate Foreign Relations Committee, 16 February 1970, HIMS, MHI.

— Confidential Statement of Ambassador Colby, 16 February 1970; prepared by MACVCORDS. These are the classified briefing notes used by Ambassador Colby in executive session hearings of the Senate Foreign Relations (Fulbright) Committee on Vietnam and Pacification, February 1970. MACV Historical Document Listing, pp. 1611–12. Declassified by USAMHI, 4 January 1989. MHI.

Colby, William E. with Forbath, Peter. *Honorable Men: My Life in the CIA* (New York: Simon & Schuster, 1978).

Colby, William E. with McCarger, James. *Lost Victory: A Firsthand Account of America's Sixteen Year Involvement in Vietnam* (Chicago, IL: Contemporary Books, 1989).

Coles, Harry and Wienberger, Albert. *Civil Affairs: Soldiers Become Governors*, Series: US Army in World War II (Washington, DC: GPO, 1964).

Collins, Arthur (Lt Gen., US Army [ret.]). 'Canal Defense in an Age of Terrorism', *Officer* 54, 1 (January 1978): 20–2.

Collins, John M. *Special Operations Forces: An Assessment*, Institute for Strategic Studies (Washington, DC: National Defense University Press 1994).

COMUSMACV. 'Role of RF/PF in Pacification'. Conference briefing, COMUSMACV, 23 October 1967. Roll No. 133, HIMS, MHI.

Congressional Research Service. Library of Congress. The Iran Hostage Crisis Report, DS-320 (Washington, DC: GPO, May 1981).

Cook, John L. (Capt., US Army). (MACV intelligence advisor to Phoenix Program in Bein Hoa Province 1968–69). *The Advisor* (New York: Bantam Books, 1987; first publication 1973).

Cook, Nancy. Public Affairs Officer. Personal interview with author, US Army Special Warfare Center, Fort Bragg, NC, 19 July 1989.

Cook, Steven E. 'Field Manual 100-25: Updating Army SOF Doctrine', *Special Warfare* 9, 3 (August 1996): 36–7.

Copson, Raymond W. and Cronin, Richard P. 'The Reagan Doctrine and its Prospects'. *Survival* 29, 1 (January/February 1987): 40–55.

CORDS. Messages from MACV Dep for CORDS to Province Senior Advisors:

— subject: 'Activation of Territorial Security Forces', 16 July 1968, F0032030 HIMS, MHI.

— subject: 'Territorial Security Forces', 24 December 1968, F0371534 HIMS, MHI.

— subject: 'Territorial Security Forces', 20 January 1969, F0640325 HIMS, MHI.

— subject: 'Territorial Security Forces', 15 June 1969, F0640348 HIMS, MHI.

— subject: 'Territorial Security Forces', 4 July 1969, F0640352 HIMS, MHI.

CQ. 'End the War Resolutions Debated', CQ Almanac 1972 (Washington, DC: Congressional Quarterly, 1972).

Cronin, Patrick M. (ed.) *2015: Power and Progress* (Washington, DC: National Defense University Press).

Crouch, Thomas. *Compilation of LIC References* (Langley Air Force Base, VA: CLIC, 1988).

Crowe, William Jr (Adm., USN and Chairman, JCS). *Army Times* (28 July 1986): 3.

— Personal interview with author, West Point, NY, 29 November 1989.

DA FM 7-85. *Ranger Operations* (Washington, DC: USGPO, 1987).

DA FM 31-15. *Operations Against Airborne Attack, Guerrilla Action and Infiltration.* Department of the Army (Washington, DC: GPO [Government Printing Office], 1953).

DA FM 31-16. *Counterguerrilla Operations* (Washington,DC: GPO, March 1967).

DA FM 31-20. *Low Intensity Conflict* (Washington, DC: GPO, 1981).

DA FM 31-23. *Stability Operations* (Washington, DC: GPO, 1972).

DA FM 31-20. *Operations Against Guerrilla Forces.* Department of the Army (Washington, DC: GPO, 1951).

— *Special Forces Operational Techniques* (Washington, DC: GPO, 1965).

DA FM 31-21. *Guerrilla Warfare.* Department of the Army (Washington, DC: GPO, 1955).

— *Guerrilla Warfare and Special Forces Operations.* Department of the Army (Washington, DC: GPO, 1958).

DA FM 90-4. *Air Assault Operations* (Washington, DC: GPO, 1987).

DA FM 100-5. *Operations.* Department of the Army (Washington, DC: GPO, 1982).

— *Operations.* Department of the Army (Washington, DC: GPO, 1976).

— *Operations* (Washington, DC: GPO, 1993).

DA FM 100-20. *Low-Intensity Conflict* (Draft). Depts of the Army and Air Force (Army-Air Force Center for Low Intensity Conflict, Langley Air Force Base, VA, 1987).

— *International Defense and Development* (Washington, DC: GPO, 1973).

— *Internal Defense and Development* (Washington, DC: GPO, 1974).

— *Low-Intensity Conflict* (Washington, DC: GPO, 1981).

— *Stability and Support Operations* (Draft) (Washington, DC: GPO, 1996).

DA FM 100-25. *Doctrine for Army Special Operations Forces* (Washington, DC: GPO, 1991).

— *Doctrine for Army Special Operations Forces* (Draft) (Washington DC: GPO, 1996).

DA (Department of the Army) Directive AGAO-322, 13 October 1960.

— *Dictionary of United States Army Terms* (Washington, DC: GPO, 1996).

— *Certain Victory: The United States Army in the Gulf War* (Washington, DC: GPO, 1993).

— US *Army Posture Statement for Fiscal Year 1997* (Washington, DC: GPO, 1996).

DA General Staff G-2. 'Summary of French Resistance, 6 June–31 August 1944', MHI.

DA. 'Guerrilla Resistance Movements in the Philippines', MI Section, General Staff, Headquarters, South Western Pacific Command, archives, Marquart Library, SWC, Fort Bragg, NC, 1946.

DA Office of the Chief of Information. *Special Warfare US Army* (Washington, DC: GPO, 1962).

— Letter to Department of the Army from President Kennedy, 11 April 1962.

DA OCPW (Office of the Chief of Psychological Warfare). Minutes of Staff meetings, 29 March and 19 July 1951. Records Group 319, Army-Chief of Special Warfare, TS Decimal Files, Box 2, MBNA.

DA Organization and Training Division. 'A Study of Special and Subversive Operations', 25 November 1947, G-3 Hot File, 091.412TS. 1949, box 10. MBNA.

DA Report R-185. *The American Experience with Pacification in Vietnam*, Vol. 3, *History of Pacification* (Arlington, VA: Institute for Defense Analysis, March 1972).

Daniels, Dan (Representative, US Congress). 'US Special Operations: The Case for a Sixth Service', *Armed Forces Journal International* 123, 3 (1985): 70–7.

Darragh, Shaun M. 'Rangers and Special Forces: Two Sides of the Same Dagger', *Army* 127, 12 (December 1977): 14–19.

DART (Disaster Assistance Response Team). USAID-Haiti, Memorandum for Record, 21 October 1994. Courtesy of USAID-Haiti.

Daughtery, William E. and Janowitz, Morris. *A Psychological Warfare Casebook* (Baltimore, MD: Johns Hopkins University Press, 1958).

Davidson, Philip B. (Lt Gen., US Army [ret.]). *Vietnam at War* (Novato, CA: Persidio Press, 1988). General Davidson was J2 (Intelligence Chief) MACV 1967–69.

Dawson, Joseph G., III. 'American Civil-Military Operations and Military Government', *Armed Forces and Society*, 22, 4 (1996): 555–72.

Day, James Sanders. 'Partisan Operations of the Korean War', unpublished Masters of Arts thesis, Department of History, University of Georgia, Athens, GA, 1989.

Decker, George H. (Gen., US Army). Speech, 'The Military Challenge of the Sixties' (1960). George Decker Papers, Box 3 , 1959–62, MHI.

Decree 044-SL/NV, 31 March 1969, File 31, USMACV HIMS, MHI.

Defense Monitor. 'America's Secret Soldiers: The Buildup of US Special Operations Forces' (Washington, DC: Center for Defense Information), *Defense Monitor* 14, 2 (1987): 12.

Department of Defense. JP1-02, *Dictionary of Military and Associated Terms*, 1994.

de Silva, Peer. *Sub Rosa – the CIA and the Uses of Intelligence* (New York: New York Times Books, 1978).

Diamond, John. 'Each Military Branch is Seeking to Promote its Future Importance', *Philadelphia Inquirer*, 23 November 1996: 12.

Dietchman, Seymour. *Limited War and American Defense Policy* (Cambridge, MA: MIT Press, 1964).

Documentary Recordings No. 560 'Special Forces', San Diego, CA, 1986.

DOD (Department of Defense). Intelligence Information Report, VC Morale and Activity IV, CTZ, 17 March 1970. HIMS MHI.

Donahue, James, G. *No Greater Love: A Day with the Mobile Guerrilla Force in Vietnam* (New York: Signet Books, New American Library, 1988).

Doughty, Robert A. 'The Evolution of US Army Doctrine 1946–1976'. Leavenworth Papers #1 (Fort Leavenworth, KS: Combat Studies Institute, 1979).

Doughty, Robert A. and Smith, Robert V. *The Command and General Staff College in Transition* (Fort Leavenworth, KS: US Army Command and General Staff College, 1976).

Drew, Dennis M. (Col., US Air Force). Insurgency and Counter-insurgency. Report No. AU-ARI-CP-88-1 (Maxwell Air Force Base, AL: Air University Press, March 1988).

DTIC (Defense Technical Information Center) report: 'Accommodation in South Vietnam' Cameron Station, Alexandria, VA, 1967; WNR VN DTIC.

— 'Insurgent Organization and Operations: A Case Study of the VC in the Delta'. Cameron Station, Alexandria, VA, 1968; MF AD AO32 420 WNR VN DTIC.

Duffy, Michael. 'Grenada: Rampant Confusion', *Military Logistics Forum* 2, 1 (July–August 1985).

Dulles, Allen W. 'Memorandum Respecting Section 202 (Central Intelligence Agency) of the Bill to Provide for a National Defense Establishment', 25 April 1947; to the Senate Committee on Armed Services, National Defense Establishment (Unification of the Armed Services) Hearings on S. 758. 80th Congress 1st Session (Washington DC: GPO, 1947), pp. 525–7.

Dulles, John Foster. 'Challenge and Response in United States Policy', *Foreign Affairs* (October 1957).

DuPuy, Trevor N. *Understanding War* (New York: Paragon House, 1987).

Dyer, Murrey. *The Weapon on the Wall: Rethinking Psychological Warfare* (Baltimore, MD: Johns Hopkins University Press).

Edwards, Britt Lynn. 'Reforming the Army'. Unpublished doctoral dissertation, University of California, Santa Barbara, CA, 1985.

Eisenhower, Dwight D. (US President, 1953–61). *Mandate For Change* (Garden City, NY: Doubleday, 1963).

Elliott, John D. (Maj., US Army). 'Action & Reaction', *Strategic Review* 4 (Winter 1976): 60–7.

Ewell, Julian J. (Lt Gen, US Army [ret.]) and Ira A. Hunt, Jr (Maj. Gen., US Army [ret.]). 'Sharpening the Combat Edge: The Use of Analysis to Reinforce Military Judgment' (Washington, DC: Department of the Army Vietnam Studies Series, 1974).

Fairbank, John K. *Chinabound* (New York: Harper & Row, 1982).

Fallaci, Oriana. *Interview With History*, trans. by John Shepley (Boston: Houghton Mifflin, 1976). The Giap interview, pp. 74–87.

Fawcett, Bill, ed. *Hunters and Shooters: An Oral History of the US Navy SEALs in Vietnam* (New York: William Morrow, 1995).

FC 71-101. *Light Infantry Division* (Washington, DC: GPO, 1984).

Felton, John. 'Contra Policy: Support Fades, Dilemma Lingers', *Congressional Quarterly* 46, 45 (5 November 1988): 3189–91.

Fialka, John. 'Vaught's Leadership Raises Some Questions on Hill', *Washington Star* (15 May 1980): A3.

Fine, Donald C. 'Rescue Helicopters Drawn from Fleet', *Aviation Week and Space Technology* (5 May 1980): 24–5.

Fischel, John T. (LTC, USA, ret.) Interview, 1 June 1995, Fort Leavenworth, KS. Colonel Fischel was a member of the Civil Affairs planning staff for Operation Promote Liberty and the Military Support Group.

Fitzgerald, Frances. *Fire in the Lake* (Boston, MA: Little, Brown, 1972).

Fitzsimons, Louise. *Counterinsurgency: The Fatal Illusion* (New York: Random House, 1972).

Flint, Roy K. (Brig. Gen., US Army). 'The United States Army on the Pacific Frontier'. Conference paper, Ninth Military History Symposium, Colorado Springs, CO, 3 October 1980; courtesy of General Flint.

'Force Modernization, Army 86/90.' *Commander's Call*, Department of Army, Washington, DC (January–February 1982): 2–40.

Ford, Corey. *Donovan of the OSS* (Boston, MA: Little, Brown, 1970).

Fulbright, J. William. *The Crippled Giant* (New York: Vintage Books, 1972).

Gabriel, Richard A. 'The US Rescue Mission into Iran, April 1980', *Canadian Defence Quarterly* (Winter 1980–81): 6–10.

Gaddis, John Lewis. *The United States and the Origins of the Cold War* (New York: Columbia University Press, 1972).

Garner, Jay M. Lieutenant General, Assistant Deputy Chief of Staff for Operations and Plans, Force Development 'Briefing on Provide Promise' in *Fouth Annual Strategy Conference Briefing*, US Army War College, Carlisle, PA, February 1993. Military History Institute Collection.

Garthoff, Raymond L. *Detente and Confrontation* (Washington, DC: Brookings Institute, 1985).

Gates, John M. *Schoolbooks and Krags: The United States Army in the Philippines, 1898–1902* (Westport, CT: Greenwood Press, 1973).

Giap, Vo Nguyen. *The Liberation War in South Vietnam in South Vietnam 1954–1965: Articles and Documents* (Xunhasaba: Hanoi, DRV, 1966), pp. 5–36.

Gillespie, Vernon (Maj., US Army). Interview with Vernon Gillespie by WGBH-TV. *Vietnam: A Television History*, vol. 3, episode 5 (Boston, MA: WGBH-TV, 1985).

Goodall, Harry A. (Lt Gen., US Army). Deputy Commander in Chief, USSOCOM). Remarks before Congress, Special Operations Panel, House Committee on Armed Services, February 1988. Copy provided by HQ USSOCOM, Tampa, FL.

Gordon, Michael R. and Trainor, General Bernard E. *The General's War* (New York: Little, Brown, 1995).

Graham, Warren and King, William L. *Military Advising in Vietnam 1969–1970*, HUMRRO Technical Report 73-24, Alexandria, VA, November 1973.

Green Book MACV/CORDS-PHX attached as Tab 1, to Internal Security in South Vietnam, dated 12 December 1970; apparently prepared by J2 (Joint Intelligence) MACV.

Greenfield, Kent R. and Palmer, Robert R. *US Army in WWII: The Army Ground Forces: The Organization of Ground Combat Forces* (Washington, DC: US Army Office of the Chief of Military History, 1947), pp. 339–48.

Grinter, Lawrence E. Telephone interview with author, 23 April 1990, confirmed quote and date.

Griswald, Terry and Giangreco, D. M. *Delta: America's Elite*

Counterrorist Force (Osceloa, WI: Motorbooks International, 1992).

Guerrilla TOE, November 1952. HQ Guerrilla Division Far East Command Liaison Detachment, 8240th Army Unit, Seibert Papers, MHI.

Hackworth, David H. (Col., US Army, ret.). *About Face* (New York: Simon & Schuster, 1989).

Hadley, M. A. (Maj., US Army). 'Special Operations and the AirLand Battle', *Military Review* (September 1985): 73–83.

Hall, Edward Y. (former Capt., US Army and MACV Advisor Team 100, Capitol Military District 1966–1967). Telephone interview 18 November 1988.

— Letter, personal correspondence of the author, dated 16 December 1988.

— *Valley of the Shadow* (Spartanburg, SC: Honoribus Press, 1986).

Halperin, Morton H. *Limited War* (Cambridge, MA: Cambridge Center for International Affairs, Harvard University, 1962).

Hanrahan, Gene F. *Japanese Operations Against Guerrilla Forces* (Chevy Chase, MD: Operations Research Office, 1954).

Harned, Glenn M. (Maj., US Army Special Operations). Chief of Doctrine Development, Army Special Warfare School. Telephone interview with author, February 1989.

Harriman, W. Averell, as quoted by *New York Times* (17 November 1983): A3.

Hattaway, Herman. 'Commentary', in John McCorkle, *Three Years with Quantrill* (Norman, OK: University of Oklahoma Press, 1992), p. 19. See also Michael Fellman, *Inside War: The Guerrilla Conflict in Missouri* (New York: Oxford University Press, 1989).

Haviland, H. Field, Jr, Fabian, Larry L., Mathiasen II, Karl, and Cox, Arthur M. *Vietnam after the War: Peacekeeping and Rehabilitation* (Washington, DC: Brookings Institute, September 1968).

Hawkins, Philip. *Blackburn's Headhunters* (New York: Norton, 1955).

Heintges, John A. (Lt Gen. US Army [ret.]) 1974. Folder 1, *Heintges Papers* (Military History Institute, Carlisle Barracks, PA, 2 vols., based on 1974 interview by MHI).

Henderson, William D. *Why the Viet Cong Fought: A Study in Motivation in a Modern Army in Combat* (Westport, CI: Greenwood Press, 1979).

Henry, Tom (Col., US Army, Special Forces [ret.]). 'Techniques From Trung Lap'. *Army* (April 1964): 35–43. In 1964, then-Major Henry was an advisor with the Army of the Republic of Vietnam.

— Letter, personal correspondence of the author, dated 6 September 1988.
— Letter, personal correspondence of the author, dated 9 March 1989.
Herman, Edward S. *Atrocities in Vietnam: Myths and Realities* (Philadelphia, PA: Pilgrim Press, 1970).
Herrington, Stuart (Colonel, US Army Intelligence). Interview, Carlisle Barracks, PA, 26 November 1996. Colonel Herrington served as a Phoenix Advisor from 1971 through 1972.
Hilsman, Roger (Assistant Secretary of State for far Eastern Affairs, 1963–64, former Director of US State Dept Bureau of Intelligence and Research). 'Must We Invade the North?', *Foreign Affairs* 46, 3 (April 1968): 419–30.
— *To Move a Nation: The Politics of Foreign Policy in the Administration of John F. Kennedy* (New York: Dell, 1967).
Hinsley, F. N. *British Intelligence in the Second World War*, 2 vols. (New York: Cambridge University Press, 1979).
History, 160th Special Operations Aviation Regiment, Fort Bragg NC, 1996. Courtesy of the 160th SOAR.
Howard, Russell D. (Maj., US Army Special Operations). 'Public Diplomacy and Psychological Operations: A Policy for Co-ordination', unpublished research paper, John F. Kennedy School of Government, Harvard University, 12 April 1988. Colonel Howard went on to become Commander of the First Special Forces Group at Fort Lewis Washington.
Howarth, Patrick. *Undercover* (London: Routledge & Kegan Paul, 1980).
Howell, Edgar M. DA Pamphlet 20-244. *The Soviet Partisan Movement* (Washington, DC: GPO, 1956).
HQ Guerrilla Division, Operations Reports, Far East Command, Liaison Detachment, 8240th Army Unit: 'Operation Leopard' (September 1952); Operations Order #4 (26 September 1952); Operations Order #6 (28 October 1952); Guerrilla Operations Outline dated 11 April 1952. Seibert Papers, MHI.
Huddleston, Louis D. (Maj., US Army, Infantry). 'Light Infantry Division: Azimuth Check', *Military Review* 65, 1 (September 1985): 4–13.
Hunt, Albert R. 'The Campaign and the Issues', in Austin Ranney, ed., *The American Elections of 1980* (Washington, DC: American Enterprise Institute, 1981).
Hunt, John B. (Lt Col., US Navy [retd.]). 'OOTW: A Concept in Flux', *Military Review* (Sept.–Oct. 1996): 3–9.

Huntington, Samuel P. 'The Defense Policy of the Reagan Administration: 1981–1982', in Fred I. Greenstein, ed., *The Reagan Presidency* (Baltimore, MD: Johns Hopkins University Press, 1983), pp. 82–113.
— *The Common Defense* (New York: Columbia University Press, 1961).
— *Strategic Imperative: New Policies for American Security* (New York: Ballinger, 1982).
Hutchinson, Kevin D. *Operation Desert Shield/Desert Storm* (Westport, CN: Greenwood Press, 1995).
Ikle, Fred C. Speech to the Inland Empire of Southern California, World Affairs Council, 30 January 1986. Courtesy of Dr Ikle.
Infantry School (US Army). 'Lessons From Korea', Fort Benning, GA, July 1954. MHI.
'Internal Security in South Vietnam, PHOENIX', USMACVCORDS for Amb. William E. Colby, 12 December 1970, microfilm 27, MACV HIMS, MHI.
Jacobs, Jeffrey A. (Major (Reserve), US Army Civil Affairs). 'Civil Afairs in the Assault', *Military Review* (Sept.–Oct. 1996): 65–7.
Janowitz, Morris. *The Professional Soldier* (New York: Free Press/Macmillan, 1960).
JCS (Joint Chiefs of Staff). Memorandum 1807/1. JCS to the Secretary of Defense, 17 August 1948 in Department of the Army, Plans and Operations Division, 'Study on Guerrilla Warfare', 1 March 1949, Records Group 319, Army Operations 1949–52, Box 10, National Archives.
— Letter from JCS to MACV, Adm. H. H. Epes, Jr Chief Far Eastern Division, JCS Plans and Policy Directorate to Maj. Gen. R. F. Schaefer (US Air Force). Assistant Chief of Staff (Plans) USMACV, 2 February 1970. HIMS MHI.
— Department of Defense. *Dictionary of Military and Associated Terms* (Washington, DC: GPO, 1 June 1987).
— Joint Pub 3-07. *Military Operations Other than War*. 1995.
— 'Joint Vision 2010', *Joint Forces Quarterly* (Summer 1996): 34–50.
JFKIMA (John F. Kennedy Institute for Military Assistance). SWC Special Forces, Fort Bragg, NC, 1988.
JIC (Joint Intelligence Center). Staff meeting of 4 August 1942 in US War Department History Project, vol. 2, Strategic Services Unit, *War Reports of the OSS* (Washington, DC: GPO, 1976), p. 4.
Johnson, Harold K. (Maj. Gen., US Army). Letter to Col. and Mrs George Chapman, Jr, 27 May 1963. Harold K. Johnson Papers,

Personal Correspondence File, 1962–63, MHI.
Joint Low-Intensity Conflict Project Final Report. Washington, DC, 1985. This is the unclassified, digest version of a classified report.
JSOA (Joint Special Operations Agency). Mission Statement, 3 December 1983.
Jureidini, Paul A., La Charite, Norman A., Cooper, Bert H., and Lybrand, William A. *Casebook on Insurgency and Revolutionary Warfare: 23 Summary Accounts* (Washington, DC: Special Operations Research Office, 1962).
Kafkalas, Peter N. (Maj., Infantry, US Army). 'The Light Divisions and Low Intensity Conflict: Are They Losing Sight of Each Other?', *Military Review* 66, 1 (January 1986): 18–28.
Kahin, George *Intervention: How America Became Involved in Vietnam* (New York: Alfred A. Knopf, 1986).
Kaplan, Refert. 'US Set to Help Evacuate Kurds', *Washington Times* (25 Nov. 1996): 1.
Karnow, Stanley. *Vietnam: A History* (New York: Viking, 1983).
— Telephone interview, 15 July 1989.
Kegley, Charles W., Jr and Eugene R. Wittkopf. 'The Reagan Administration's World View', *Orbis* 26, 1 (Spring 1982): 23–44.
Kelly, Francis J. (Col., US Army). *US Army Special Forces 1961–1971*. Department of the Army Vietnam Studies Series (Washington, DC: GPO, 1973).
— (Col., US Army [ret.], Cdr 5th SFG 1966–1967.) 'A Problem in Counterinsurgency', Unpublished PhD dissertation, Department of Political Science, University of Denver, 1980.
Kennan, George F. (writing as 'X'). 'The Sources of Soviet Conduct', *Foreign Affairs* (25 July 1947): 566–82.
Kennedy, John F. (US President 1961–63). *Public Papers of the Presidents of the United States* (Washington, DC: National Archives, 1961).
— 'Address to the Graduating Class of the US Military Academy', 6 June 1962; document collection, USMA Library, West Point, NY.
— Message, PRESUS to Command and General Staff College, Fort Bragg, N.C. Message number WH670-61, date illegible, document collection, SWC.
Kennedy, Robert M. DA Pamphlet 20-24. *German Anti-Guerrilla Operations in the Balkans (1942–1944)* (Washington, DC: GPO, 1954).
Khrushchev, Nikita S. 'For New Victories in the World Communist Movement', speech of 6 January 1961, *Current Digest of the Soviet Press* (16 February 1961): 16–19.

Kief, Nelson R. Special Planning Staff, Assistant Secretary of Defense for International. Security Affairs, OSD. US DOD statement in Senate Hearings, 1987.

— (Maj., US Army [ret]). Special Forces, MACV-SOG RVN. Personal correspondence of the author, 5 June 1989.

Killebrew, Robert B. (Lt. Col., US Army). 'NATO, Deterrence and Light Divisions', *Military Review* 65, 5 (May 1985): 2–15.

Kimball, Jeffery P. 'The Stab-in-the Back Legend and the Vietnam War', *Armed Forces and Society* 14, 3 (Spring 1988): 433–58.

King, Michael J. *Rangers: Selected Combat Operations During World War II,* Combat Studies Institute, US Army Command and General Staff College, Fort Leavenworth, KS (Washington, DC: GPO, 1985).

King, Wayne. 'Carte Redux', *New York Times Magazine* (10 December 1989): 38–41, 101, 103, 108.

Kinnard, Douglas. 'A Soldier in Camelot: Maxwell Taylor in the Kennedy White House', *Parameters* 17, 4 (December 1988): 13–24.

Kirkpatrick, Jeane J. (US Ambassador to the UN). 'Anti-Communist Insurgency and American Policy', *The National Interest* 1, 1 (Fall 1985).

— *The Reagan Doctrine and US Foreign Policy* (Washington, DC: Heritage Foundation, 1985).

Kissinger, Henry. *The White House Years* (Boston, MS: Little, Brown, 1979).

Kitson, Frank. *Low-Intensity Operations: Subversion, Insurgency, Peacekeeping* (London: Stackpole Books, 1971).

Koch, Noel C. (former Principal Deputy Asst. Secretary of Defense). Speech presented to the 23rd Air Force as reprinted in the Congressional Record, 1986.

— 'Objecting to Reality: The Efforts to Restore US Special Operations Forces', in Loren B. Thompson, ed., *Low-Intensity Conflict* (Lexington, MA: Lexington Books, 1989), pp. 52–76.

Komer, Robert W. Memorandum, 27 October 1968, from Komer to Abrams, no subject line.

— Message to Colby, AC of S CORDS, subject: Police and Military Coordination, dated 11 June 1968. HIMS, MHI.

— (MACV Deputy for CORDS). Message to Commanders US 1st, 3rd, and 25th Infantry Divisions (based in area around Saigon), dated 21 July 1968. HIMS, MHI.

Kousoulos, George. *Revolution and Defeat: The Story of the Greek Communist Party* (London: Oxford University Press, 1965).

Krepinevich, Andrew F. Jr. *The Army and Vietnam* (Baltimore, MD: Johns Hopkins University Press, 1984).

Kupperman, Robert and Taylor, Jr, William J. 'Special Supplement: Low-Intensity Conflict, the Strategic Challenge', in George E. Hudson and Joseph Kruzel, eds., *American Defense Annual* (Lexington, KY: DC Heath, 1985), pp. 207–22.

Lackey, Douglas P. *The Ethics of War and Peace* (Englewood Cliffs, NJ: Prentice Hall, 1989).

Ladd, James. *Commandos and Rangers of World War II* (New York: St Martin's Press, 1978).

Lansdale, Edward G. (Maj. Gen., US Air Force [ret.]). Letter, subject: 'Resources for Unconventional Warfare in Southeast Asia', to General Maxwell Taylor, copies to Secretary of Defense MacNamara, Secretary of State Rusk, DCIA Dulles, and their respective deputies, 1961, Office of the Secretary of Defense.

— *In the Midst of Wars* (New York: Harper & Row, 1972).

— Letter to Cecil B. Currey, 10 July 1984, courtesy of Cecil Currey.

Laqueur, Walter. *Guerrilla: A Historical and Critical Study* (Boston, MA: Little, Brown, 1976).

Leary, William M. *The Central Intelligence Agency: History and Documents* (University of AL: University of Alabama Press, 1984).

Ledeen, Michael. 'How to Support the Democratic Revolution', *Commentary* 74, 3 (Spring 1985): 43–6.

Leinbarger, Paul. *Psychological Warfare* (New York: Duell & Pearce, 1954).

Leppin, Frederick (WO1, US Army). 'Consider the Low Echelon Advisor', *Military Review* 56, 6 (February 1976): 18–20.

Lewy, Guenter. *America in Vietnam* (New York: Oxford University Press, 1978).

Lider, Julian. *On the Nature of War* (Farnborough, UK: Saxon House, 1977).

— *Military Theory* (New York: St Martin's Press, 1983).

'Light Division Gains Weight', *Army Times* 44, 25 (30 January 1984): 8.

Lind, William S. *et al*. 'The Changing Face of War: Unto the Fourth Generation', *Military Review* (October 1989): 2–11.

Logan, Patrick E. 'Special Operations – Lost in the Shuffle?', Individual Writing Requirement, Armed Forces Staff College, Norfolk, VA, October 1986.

London, Herbert J. *Military Doctrine and the American Character* (New Brunswick, NJ: Transaction Books, 1984).

Luttwak, Edward N. *On the Meaning of Victory* (New York: Simon & Schuster, 1986).

MAAG-V (Vietnam). 'MAAG-Vietnam Narrative Statement', dated 8 November 1959, MHI.

Mabry, Robert C., Jr. (Capt., US Navy). Acting Director for Requirements and Intelligence, Asst Secretary of Defense for Special Operations and Low-Intensity Conflict. Personal correspondence with the author, 8 March 1990.

MACCORDS-PHX. 'Fact Sheet, subject: PHUNG HOANG Advisor Training', signed by John H. Mason as Director, Phoenix; dated 1 December 1970, HIMS, MHI.

Macksey, Kenneth. *Commando* (New York: Stien & Day, 1987).

MACV Directive 381-46. 'Military Intelligence Screening of Detainees', Annex A, 1967, in 'Contemporary Practice of the United States Relating to International Law', *American Journal of International Law*, 62 (1968).

MACV Message. Abrams, to CORPS Commanders, no subject line. Message number CONFIDENTIAL 32161, dated 29 October 1968, DEPCORDS.

MACV, Report. 'Combat Experience', dated 5 January 1970, MACV Command History, Roll 97, HIMS, MHI.

— Message to COMUSMACV, dated 6 February 1970, subject: Captured Documents, Roll 145, Document 02-1195-70; see also Document 02-1135-75 dated 28 December 1969, HIMS, MHI. Both indicate continuing existence of VCI and ability to attack GVN local officials.

— Message from COMUSMACV to J271 (MACV Intelligence) Report number P0053, dated 2 February 1970. HIMS, MHI. Intensive attacks vic. Phuc Long.

— Message from 3rd Riverine Area (I CTZ) to J2-MACV, dated 27 March 1970, Roll 97, MACV Command History, HIMS, MHI.

MACV Working Paper. 'Improvement of Security Within SVN', HQ MACV, 2 April 1967, HIMS, MHI.

Madison, Christopher. 'Watching Over Covert Forces', *The National Journal* (July 1990): 1801.

Mahan, Francis (Lt Col. US Army SF [ret.]). Mahan served as a Major in the 10th SF during the organizational days in 1952–54. Personal interview with author, Fort Bragg, NC, 27 July 1989.

Malbin, Michael J. 'The Conventions: Platforms and Issue Activists', in Austin Ranney, ed., *The American Elections of 1980* (Washington, DC: American Enterprise Institute, 1981).

Mandell, Bill. 'The Ayatollah Had the Last Laugh', syndicated column, *San Francisco Examiner* (13 June 1989): A39.

Mantell, David. *True Americanism: Green Berets and War Resisters – A Study of Commitment* (New York: Teachers' College Press, 1974).

Marchetti, Victor and Marks, John D. *The CIA and the Cult of Intelligence* (New York: Victor Knopf, 1974).

Marquis, Susan L. *Unconventional Warfare* (Washington, DC: Brookings Institution, 1997).

Mattloff, Maurice, ed. *American Military History* (Washington, DC: GPO, 1985).

McClure, Robert (Brig. Gen., US Army). OCPW, Dept of the Army, Washington, DC. Letter to Lt Gen. Charles Bolt, Commander in Chief US Army Europe, 1953, no further date.

McCollum, James. 'The Airborne Mystique', *Military Review* 56, 11 (November 1976): 16–22.

McConnell, Malcom. *Just Cause* (New York: St Martin's Press, 1991).

McEwen, Michael T. 'Psychological Operations Against Terrorism: The Unused Weapon', *Military Review* (January 1986): 59–67.

McNamara, Robert S. Address to the American Bar Association, Chicago, III, 17 February 1962. Reprinted in *Army Information Digest*, 17, 4 (April 1962): inside front cover.

McRaven, William. *Theory of Special Operations* (Monterey, CA: Naval Post Graduate School).

Mellon, Christopher K. (Legislative assistant to Senator William S. Cohen (R-ME), principal assistant for legislation relating to special operations). 'The Low Frontier: Congress and Unconventional Warfare', remarks at the National War College, 11 January 1988. Courtesy of Christopher Mellon.

— Personal correspondence of the author, 23 January 1989.

Memorandum, ASD (Assistant Secretary of Defense). To: Mr Steadman, subject: Anti-Infrastructure and Civilian Security Suspects, unsigned but originating in the Office of the ASD, dated 20 September 1968. DEPCORDS.

Memorandum No. 3. 'Conclusions of the Cuba Study Group', 13 June 1961. SECRET, declassified in Operation Zappata. (Frederick, MD: University Publications of America, 1981). This is the text of the report and testimony of the Cuba Study Group with minor deletions for security purposes.

Memorandum No. 4. 'Recommendations of the Cuba Study Group', 13 June 1961. SECRET, declassified in Operation Zappata. (Frederick, MD: University Publications of America, 1981).

— Parker, Evan J. Director Phoenix Staff. To: DEPCORDS, subject: 'Phoenix Spot Report', dated 29 December 1968. DEPCORDS.

— Parker, Evan J. Director Phoenix Staff. To: For the Record, subject: 'PRU and PHUNG HOANG.' Details infighting between Vietnamese National Police and ARVN for control of the PRU, dated 13 January 1969. DEPCORDS.

— Komer, Robert. To COMUSMACV, subject: 'Presidential Decree on Phung Hoang Program', dated 22 July 1968, HIMS, MHI.

— Walker, William. For general distribution, subject: Guidelines for Declassification of MACV/MACTHAI/USARV Records, from William A. Walker, Acting Archivist of the Army, dated 5 January 1988.

Mendelssohn, John, ed. *OSS Jedburgh Teams* (2 vols.) (New York: Garland Publishing, 1987).

Menser, Michael W. (Maj., US Army). 'Light Infantry and Change', *Military Review* 67, 12 (December 1987): 53–7.

Message, COMUSMCV. To: Gen. Cao Van Vien, Chairman, RVNAF Joint General Staff, Saigon, dated 27 February 1968, HIMS, MHI.

Message, MAC Intelligence, Scott Air Force Base, IL. To: worldwide addresses including CENTCOM, ref: Saudi Arabia Situation Report 026-90 – Scud Attack, dated 0230 18 Jan 91.

Meyer, Edward C. (Gen., US Army, ret). Personal correspondence with the author, 7 February 1990.

— 'White Paper 1980: A Framework for Molding the Army of the 1980s Into a Disciplined, Well-Trained Fighting Force' (Washington, DC: GPO, 25 February 1980).

Miles, Milton (Adm., US Navy [ret.]) and Hawthorne, Daniel. *A Different Kind of War* (Garden City, NY: Doubleday, 1967).

Mills, Jim Pat. 'El Salvador: Lessons Learned the Hard Way', *Army Times* 49, 35 (10 April 1989): 34–50.

Morgenthau, Hans J. *Politics among Nations* (New York: Alfred J. Knopf, 1948; updated and revised by K. W. Thompson, 1985).

Morris, James. *War Story* (Boulder, CO: Paladin Enterprises, 1979).

Morton, George. (Colonel, US Army SF [ret.]). Interview, Riyadh, Saudi Arabia, January 1976.

Motley, James B. 'Washington's Big Tug of War Over Special Operations Forces', *Army* 36, 11 (November 1986): 17–24.

Mountel, Robert A. (Col., US Army [ret.]). Special Forces. Telephone interview with author 14 July 1989.

— Personal interview with author, Force Integration Office, Special Warfare Center, Fort Bragg, NC, 20 July 1989.

Muller, Bobby. 'An American Serviceman's View of the South Vietnamese Army', in Robert McMahon, ed., *Major Problems in the History of the Vietnam War* (Lexington, MA: DC Heath and Co., 1990), pp. 408–9.

Muradian, Vago. 'Defense Study Will Boost Army Funding, Top Officer Says', in *Defense Daily* (29 October 1996): 159.

National Security Action Memorandum No. 124. 'Establishment of the Special Group (Counterinsurgency)', 18 January 1962. Microfiche in Defense Declassified Documents System.

Ney, Virgil. *Guerrilla Warfare in the Philippines* (Washington, DC: Office of the Chief of Military History, 1953).

Nguyen, Thi Anh. NLF political officer. Interview, *Vietnam: A Television History* (Boston, MA: WGBH, 1987).

Nguyen, Vo and Le Tan Danh. 'The Liberated Zones of South Vietnam' in *South Vietnam 1954–1965: Articles and Documents* (Xunhasaba: Hanoi, DRV, 1966), pp. 156–79.

Nolan, Kieth W. *Into Laos* (Navato, CA: Persidio Press, 1986).

O'Ballance, Edgar. *The Greek Civil War 1944–1949* (London: Faber & Faber, 1966).

O'Dowd, Edward. (Lt 101st Airborne Div, Capt. 4th Infantry Div, US Army, RVN). Personal interview with author, West Point, NY, 28 March 1989.

Office of Secretary of Defense (OSD). Memorandum from Paul Thayer, Deputy Secretary of Defense to the Secretaries of the Military Departments, Chairman of the Joint Chiefs of Staff, Undersecretaries of Defense, Assistant Secretaries of Defense, Director (Program Analysis and Evaluation), Assistants to the Secretary of Defense, Directors of the Defense Agencies 3 October 1983; attachment to testimony of Noel Koch, Principal Deputy Undersecretary of Defense (International Security Affairs) in House Hearings 1983, 797–8.

Olson, William J. 'The Light Force Initiative', *Military Review* 65, 6 (June 1985): 2–17.

— *Low-Intensity Conflict and The Principles and Strategies of War* (Carlisle Barracks, PA: Strategic Studies Institute, US Army War College, 20 May 1986).

Operational Groups, Folder #987. Reports of operational groups deployed in France 1944, OSS Files, Marquart Library, Special Warfare Center, Fort Bragg, NC.

Operation Cedar Falls: Memorandum: Complaints of Gen. William DePuy on Handling of Refugees, dated 8 January 1967, HIMS MHI.

Operations Reports, 5th SFG. See for example 'Operations Report for Quarterly Period Ending 31 December, 1965', dated 15 January 1966; same title for 31 October 1966, dated 15 November, 1966, 31 October 1967, also 31 October 1968, dated 15 November 1968, and 31 January 1969, dated 15 February 1969; Records Group 472, Box 3, 5th SFG, USA (VN) WNR.

— Dated 14 November 1967, reproduced as DTIC publication AD390958, Defense Technical Information Center, Cameron Station, Alexandria, VA.

OSD (Office of the Secretary of Defense). *United States–Vietnam Relations 1945–1967*; otherwise known as the 'Pentagon Papers'. Compiled by a special task force for the Office of the Secretary of Defense (OSD) and the House Armed Service Committee. Published in twelve volumes (Washington, DC: GPO, 1971).

OSS. Operations reports from North Africa and Corsica, Folder #982, 1942–1944, Marquart Library, Special Warfare Center, Fort Bragg, NC.

— 'Aid to the French Resistance in World War II', Folder #980. Operations reports 1942–45, OSS Files, Marquart Library, Special Warfare Center, Fort Bragg, NC.

— 'Organizing Resistance in France', Folder #985, 1945 OSS Files, Marquart Library, Special Warfare Center, Fort Bragg, NC.

— 'Operation Plan for OSS Activities in Pacific Ocean Areas', 2 January 1945, Records of the JCS, Part I (1942–1945). Reel 8, Frame 0282, University Microfilms, Frederick, MD, 1981.

Ottaway, David B. 'Constraints on US Involvement in Third World Protracted Warfare', Paper presented at the 16th Annual Conference on Protracted Warfare – The Third World Arena, 22–4 April 1987. The Fletcher School of Law and Diplomacy, Medford, MA.

Paddock, Alfred H. 'Psychological Operations, Special Operations and US Strategy', in *Special Operations in US Strategy*. (Washington, DC: National Defense University Press, 1984), pp. 229–51.

— *US Army Special Warfare: Its Origins* (Washington, DC: National Defense University Press, 1982).

Palmer, Dave R. (Col., US Army [ret.]). *Summons of the Trumpet* (Novato, CA: Presidio Press, 1984).

— *Readings in Current Military History* (West Point, NY: Department of Military Art and Engineering, US Military Academy, 1969).

Paret, Peter. *Makers of Modern Strategy* (Princeton, NJ: Princeton University Press, 1986).

Parker, James E. *Codename Mule: Fighting the Secret War in Laos for the CIA* (Annapolis, MD: US Naval Institute Press, 1995).

Paschall,· Rod. (Col., US Army Special Forces). G3 SWC1962–3; aide to General Yarborough 1964, Cdr MACV-SOG. 'Night Attacks', *Military History Quarterly*, 8, 1 (Autumn 1995): 88–9.

— Interview with author, Carlisle, PA, 7 March 1989.

Patti, Archimedes L. *Why Vietnam?* (Berkeley, CA: University of Californian Press, 1980).

Payne, Chuck (Major, US Army Special Forces). This information was taken from the Special Operations Website maintained by Major Payne on the Internet, 1996.

Pearlman, Michael D. Personal interview with author, Combined Arms Center, USACGSC, Fort Leavenworth, Kansas, 5 February 1990.

Peers, William R. (Lt Col., US Army). Commander, OSS Detachment 101. 'Guerrilla Operations in Northern Burma', *Military Review* 28, 3 (June 1948): 10–16.

— 'Guerrilla Operations in Northern Burma', *Military Review* 28, 3 (June 1948): 10–16; part 2 (July 1948): 11–17.

Peers, William R. and Brelis, Dean. *Behind the Burma Road* (Boston, MA: Little, Brown, 1963).

Pentagon Papers, actual title is *United States Vietnam Relations, 1945–1967*, twelve volumes, prepared by the Department of Defense for the House Committee on Armed Services (Washington, DC: USGPO, 1971).

Perry, Mark. 'The Secret Life of An American Spy', *Regardies* 9, 6 (February 1989): 81–99.

Petraeus, David H. (Capt., US Army). 'Light Infantry in Europe: Strategic Flexibility and Conventional Deterrence', *Military Review* 64, 12 (December 1984): 35–55.

Pezzle, Roger M. 'Military Capabilities and Special Operations in the 1980s', in Frank R. Barnett, B. Hugh Tovar and Richard H. Shultz, eds., *Special Operations in US Strategy* (Washington, DC: National Defense University, 1984).

Pike, Douglas E. *Viet Cong* (Cambridge, MA: MIT Press, 1966).

PL 99-661. (Public Law) National Defense Authorization Act for Fiscal Year 1987 (Washington, DC: GPO, 14 November 1986).

Plaster, John L. (Maj., US Army [ret.]). SOG veteran. *SOG: The Secret Wars of America's Commandos in Vietnam* (New York: Simon and Schuster, 1997).

Podheretz, Norman. 'The Future Danger', *Commentary* 71, 4 (April 1981): 29–47.

Porter, Gareth, *Vietnam: The Definitive Documentation of Human Decisions* (Stanfordville, NY: Coleman Enterprises, 1979).
Potter, Richard A. (Brigadier General, SF, USA, ret). Interview, Carlisle Barracks, PA; 6 March 1996.
Prados, John. *President's Secret Wars* (New York: William Morrow, 1986).
Presidential Decree 280-4/TT/SL, dated 1 July 1968, MF Roll 31, HIMS, MHI.
Prouty, Leroy F. *The Secret Team* (Englewood Cliffs, NJ: Prentice-Hall, 1973).
Psychological Warfare Division, Supreme Headquarters, Allied Expeditionary Force. 'An Account of Its Operations in the Western European Campaign, 1944–45' (Bad Homburg, Germany, October 1945, MBNA).
Pye, Lucien. 'Armies in the Process of Political Modernization', in John J. Johnson, ed., *Role of the Military in Underdeveloped Countries* (Princeton, NJ: Princeton University Press, 1962).
Race, Jeffery. *War Comes to Long An* (Berkeley, CA: University of California Press, 1972).
Rainey, James W. (Lt Col., US Army). During 1972–73, Rainey served with MACV-J2 (combined intelligence) as an intelligence analyst and later the Joint Military Commission. Personal interview with author, West Point, NY, 23 January 1990.
Ranelagh, John. *The Agency: Rise and Decline of the CIA* (New York: Simon & Schuster, 1987).
Ranger Company (Tentative). (USAIS: Fort Benning, GA, November 1950). Document collection, MHI.
Rank, H. P. (Lt Col.). 'A United States Counter-Aggression Force', *Military Review* 30, 7 (July 1959).
Ransom, Harry R. *Central Intelligence and National Security* (Cambridge, MA: Harvard University Press, 1958).
Reagan, Ronald. 'Nomination Acceptance Address', 17 July 1981, in *A Time For Choosing: The Collected Speeches of Ronald Reagan, 1961–1982* (Chicago, IL: Regnery Gateway, 1983), pp. 221–39.
Research Reference Service, USAID. *Administrative History – Agency for International Development* (unpublished, courtesy of Research Reference Service, USAID, Washington, DC, 1969).
Rheault, Robert (Col., US Army [ret.]). Special Forces, commander 5th SFG, 1969. Personal papers and interview transcript, OHP, MHI.
— Telephone interview, 13 April 1989.

— Personal correspondence with the author, 2 May 1989.
Rice, Wesley (Maj. Gen., US Marine Corps). (Director, JSOA 1984).
   Statement before the House Appropriations Committee, in House
   Hearing, 1984).
Ridgeway, Matthew B. (Gen., US Army). *Army Chief of Staff: Soldier*
   (New York: Harper & Row, 1956).
— Letter to Commanding General, Army Field Forces, subject:
   Organization of the Army During the Period 1960–70. Army
   Chief of Staff Files, Chief of Staff 320, MBNA.
Rifkin, Herbert. 'From Rockets to Rifles: The President's Guerrilla
   Policy', *Policy Review* (May–June 1962): 1–12.
'Role of RF/PF in Pacification' Conference Briefing, COMUSMACV,
   dated 23 October 1967, Roll No. 133, HIMS, MHI.
Romjue, John L. 'From Active Defense to AirLand Battle: The Develop-
   ment of Army Doctrine, 1962 to 1973'. TRADOC Historical Mono-
   graph Series (Fort Monroe, TRADOC Historical Office, 1984).
Roosevelt, Kermit, ed. *War Report of the OSS* (2 vols.) (New York:
   Walker and Co, 1976). Originally compiled by the War Depart-
   ment, 1947.
Rosegrant, Susan. 'A Seamless Transition', Kennedy School of
   Government Case Program C09-96-1325, Harvard College,
   Cambridge, MA, 1996.
Rosenfeld, Stephen S. 'The Guns of July', *Foreign Affairs* 64, 4
   (Spring 1986): 698–715.
Rottman, Gordon L. *US Army Rangers and LRRP Units 1942–87*
   (London: Osprey Publishing, 1987).
Rudd, Gordin W. Lieutenant Colonel 'Operation Provide Comfort',
   briefing to *Fouth Annual Strategy Conference* (US Army War College,
   Carlisle, PA, February 1993. Military History Institute Collection).
Rush, Robert S. 'Comparing Light Divisions', *Military Review* 67,
   1 (Jan. 1987): 62–9.
Russell, James A. 'SOF: They Can't Get There From Here', *Military
   Logistics Forum* 2, 2 (April 1986): 41.
— 'House Report Says Pentagon Special Commando Units are Well
   Below Par', *Defense Week* (11 August 1986): 16–17.
Ryan, Paul B. (Capt., US Navy ret). *The Iranian Rescue Mission*
   (Annapolis, MD: Naval Institute Press, 1985).
Saal, Harve. *SOG*, 2 vols. (Ann Arbor, MI: Edwards Brothers, 1990).
Sarkesian, Sam C. 'Special Operations Forces in the 1980s', in
   Stephen J. Cimbala, ed., *The Reagan Defense Program: An Interim
   Assessment* (Wilmington, DE: Scholarly Resources, 1986a), pp.
   93–118.

— *The New Battlefield* (New York: Greenwood Press, 1986b).

Schad, Dave. 'Winning the Green Beret', *Soldiers* 41, 8 (August 1986): 13–17. (An official publication of the United States Army Office of Public Affairs.)

Schell, Johnathan. *The Military Half* (New York: Alfred A. Knopf, 1968).

Schemmer, Benjamin F. *The Raid* (New York: Harper & Row, 1976).

Schlachter, David C. (Maj., US Air Force) and Stubbs, Fred J. (Maj., US Army). 'Special Operations Forces: Not Applicable', *Military Review* 58, 2 (February 1978): 15–25.

Schlesinger, Arthur M., Jr. *A Thousand Days* (Boston, MA: Houghton Mifflin, 1965).

— 'Origins of the Cold War', *Foreign Affairs* (October 1967).

Schultz, G. (US Secretary of State). 'New Realities and New Ways of Thinking', *Foreign Affairs* (Spring 1985).

— 'Moral Principles and Strategic Interests: The Worldwide Movement Toward Democracy', speech on 14 April 1986 (*Dept. of State Bulletin*, June 1986).

Schultz, Richard H., Jr. 'Discriminate Deterrence and Low Intensity Conflict', Unpublished manuscript, School of Government, Harvard University, 1989. Courtesy of Richard Schultz.

— *In the Aftermath of War: US Support for Reconstruction and Nation-Building in Panama* (Maxwell Air Force Base, AL: Air University Press, 1993).

Scott, Alexander. 'The Lessons of the Iranian Raid for American Military Policy', *Armed Forces Journal International* (June 1980): 26–32, 73.

Seiple, Chris *The US Military/NGO Relationship in Humanitarian Intervention* (Carlisle, PA: US Army Peacekeeping Institute, 1996).

Selton, Robert. 'Communist Errors in the Anti-Bandit War', *Military Review* 46, (September 1965): 31–40.

Senior Officer Debriefing by Col. Harold Aaron (Commander, 5th SFG) dated June 1969 Microfiche AD500-359, Box 3, Records Group 472, WNR.

Shackley, Theodore (retired CIA operations officer). *The Third Option* (New York: McGraw-Hill, 1983).

Shawcross, William. *Sideshow* (New York: Simon & Schuster, 1979).

Sheehan, Kevin. 'Preparing for an Imaginary War? Examining Peacetime Functions and Changes of Army Doctrine', Unpublished doctoral thesis (Dept. of Government, Harvard University, Cambridge, MA, 1988).

Sheehan, Neil. 'Annals of War: An American Soldier in Vietnam', Part IV, *The New Yorker* 64, 21 (11 July 1988): 31–59.

— *The Pentagon Papers* (New York: New York Times, 1971), this is an extensively edited version of the twelve-volume official version, cited above as OSD (1971).

Sheffield, Richard B. (Lt Col., US Air Force). Public Affairs Officer, USOCOM. Telephone interview with author, Tampa, FL, 23 April 1990.

Silber, John R. 'The Kennedy Doctrine: Principles for a Settlement in Central America', *Strategic Review* 12, 1 (Fall 1984): 13–21.

Simmons, Clyde R. 'The Indian Wars and US Military Thought', *Parameters* 22, 1 (Spring 1992): 60–72.

Simpson, Charles M., III (Col., US Army Special Forces). *Inside the Green Berets: The First Thirty Years* (San Francisco, CA: Presidio Press, 1983).

Slim, William. *Defeat into Victory* (London: Cassell, 1956).

Smith, R. Harris. *OSS: Secret History of America's First Central Intelligence Agency* (Los Angeles, CA: University of California Press, 1972).

Sorenson, Theodore C. *Kennedy* (New York: Harper & Row, 1965).

Special Warfare Board Report (Fort Bragg, NC: Special Warfare Center, 1952).

Spector, Roland M. *Advice and Support: The Early Years* (Washington, DC: Center of Military History, US Army).

SPHINX – These are supplements to MACV J-2 Monthly Intelligence Summaries (DISUM) covering the period 1970–71, HIMS Roll 107, MHI.

Spitzer, Kirk. 'The Siege of Mogadishu', Gannett News Service, October, 1993.

Spore, John B. 'Toward A New National Strategy', *Army* 10, 1 (January 1960): 8–10.

Stanton, Shelby L. *Vietnam Order of Battle* (Washington, DC: US News Books, 1981).

— *The Rise and Fall of An American Army* (New York: Dell Publishing, 1985a).

— *Green Berets at War* (Novato, CA:Presidio Press, 1985b).

Starr, Barbara. 'JDW Interview: General James J. Lindsay', *Jane's Defense Weekly* 1(2 May 1990): 231.

Starry, Donn A. (Gen., US Army). Commander, US Army Training and Doctrine Command, 1981–83. 'A Tactical Evolution – FM 100-5', *Military Review* 58, 8 (August 1978): 2–11.

Steele, Dennis. 'A Force of Great Utility', *Army Magazine* (April 1992): 24–33.

Stein, Jeff. *A Murder in Wartime* (New York: St Martin's Press, 1992).

Stillwell, Richard (Gen., US Army [ret.]). 'Political /Psychological Dimensions of Counterinsurgency', Paper presented at the 16th Annual Conference on Protracted Warfare – The Third World Arena, 22–24 April 1987, The Fletcher School of Law and Diplomacy, Medford, MA.

— 'Report on Counter-Insurgency Operations Course and Related Matters' (6 October 1961), in USCONARC (US Continental Army Command), Summary of Major Events and Problems FY 1962, HQ USCONARC, 1962.

Sullivan, Brian R. 'The Future National Security Environment: Possible Consequences for SOF', *Special Warfare* (official publication of the US Army Special Warfare Center at Fort Bragg, NC) (August 1996): 2–12.

'Summary Report, Military Counterinsurgency Accomplishments Since January 1961', Memorandum for the Special Assistant to the President for National Security Affairs, CM-843-62, 21 July 1962.

Summers, Harry G. (Col., US Army [ret.]). *On Strategy: A Critical Analysis of the Vietnam War* (Novato, CA: Presidio, 1982).

Surveys and Investigations Staff. 'Special Operations Forces', Department of Defense House Appropriations Committee, US Congress (Washington, DC: GPO, February 1986).

SWC (Special Warfare Center). 'Multi-Purpose Force Study: US Army Special Forces'. Principal author Col. Robert A. Mountell, G3 (Operations Officer) USAJFKCENMA, dated 28 October 1976. This study remains TOP SECRET, citations are from unclassified paragraphs only.

Tanham, George K., Jenkins, Brian S., Wainsten, Eleanor,and Sullivan Gerard. 'United States Preparation for Future Low-level Conflict', *Conflict* 1, 1 (Winter 1978): 1–20.

Talbot, George (Maj. Gen., US Army). Commandant, US Army Infantry School, Fort Benning, GA. Message to Lieutenant General Stillwell, Office of the Chief of Staff of the Army, dated 23 March 1971, Stillwell Papers, MHI.

Taylor, Maxwell D. (Gen., US Army). Letter to Commander, Continental Army Command, subject: Reorganization of Current Infantry Divisions, Chief of Staff Files, Chief of Staff 320, MBNA.

— 'On Limiting War', *Army Information Digest* 13 (June 1958): 4–6.

— 'Improving Our Capabilities for Limited War', *Armor* 68 (January–February 1959a): 22–23.
— *The Uncertain Trumpet* (New York: Harper and Bros., 1959b).
— *Swords and Ploughshares* (New York: W. W. Norton, 1972).
Thayer, Charles W. *Guerrilla* (New York: Harper & Row, 1963).
Thomas, David. 'The Implications of Commando Operations in Modern Warfare: 1937–1982', *Journal of Contemporary History* 18, 4 (October 1985): 689–717.
Timmerman, Frederick L. (Col., US Army [ret.]). 'From the Editor', *Military Review* 66, 1 (Jan. 1988): 1.
TOE (Table of Organizational Elements) 1–66, 'CIDG Guerrilla Companies (Light)', 5th SFG, 20 April 1966. MF AD 391-694, Box 3, Records Group 472, WNR.
TRADOC (US Army Training and Doctrine Command). 'Operational Concept for the AirLand Battle and Corps Operation, 1986', Pamphlet 525-5. Fort Monroe, VA, 25 March 1981.
— 'AirLand Battle 2000'. Fort Monroe, VA, 10 August 1982.
Trinquier, Roger. *Modern Warfare* (London: Pall Mall Press, 1964).
Troung-Son. *A Bitter Dry Season for the Americans* (Foreign Languages Publishing House: Hanoi, 1966). This is an example of propaganda intended to play on the fears and frustrations of Americans in the United States rather than those of the soldiers.
Troy, Thomas F. *Donovan and the CIA: A History of the Establishment of the Central Intelligence Agency* (Frederick, MD: University Publications of America, 1981). [Note: this was originally published in classified form for internal CIA use by the CIA's Center for the Study of Intelligence.]
Truman, Harry S. 'Recommendations on Greece and Turkey', delivered before a joint session of Congress, subsequently published as Department of State Publication 2785 (Washington, DC: GPO, 1947).
Turner, Stansfield (Adm., US Navy [ret.]). DCI 1977–81. Personal Interview with author, 8 September 1989.
UNMIH AAR (United Nations Mission in Haiti). 'Success in Peacekeeping', UNMIH After Action Report (AAR), US Army Peacekeeping Institute, Carlisle Barracks, PA. This report was prepared by General Kinzer's staff in May and June of 1996.
UNOSOM II (United Nations Operation in Somalia). Statement of 4 October 1993, Office of the Deputy Force Commander, UNOSOM II and USCENTCOM.
USAID (US Agency for International Development). Bureau for Humanitarian Response, Haiti Emergency, Situation Report #2,

1 November 1994. Courtesy USAID.

USAJFK (US Army JFK Special Warfare Center and School). 'Operation Provide Comfort – Lessons Learned', US Army JFK Special Warfare Center and School, October 1991.

USAJFK SWC. *Special Forces.* Leaflet (Fort Bragg, NC: US Army Special Warfare Center, 1988).

— Mimeographed 'Fact Sheet' titled 'Lineage of Special Forces', n.d., located with 1960 documents in G-1 Archives, USJFKSWC, Fort Bragg, NC.

US Army. *Field Service Regulations* (Washington, DC: GPO, editions of 1905, 1908, 1910). USMA-SC.

— *Infantry Drill Regulations: 1911* (corrected to 6 May 1918) (New York: Sherwood Co., 1918). USMA-SC.

US Army Lessons Learned. 'US Army Lessons Learned From Operation Urgent Fury' (S/NF), 1984, quote from unclassified portion, p. 1.

US Army Special Warfare Board. *Special Forces* (Fort Bragg, NC: USJFKIMA, 1962).

US Army Special Warfare Center. SWC Staff Study Laos (HQ, SWC, Fort Bragg, NC, 16 February 1961, courtesy of Library and Archives, SWC Fort Bragg, NC).

US Army War College. *Counterinsurgency* (Carlislie Barracks, PA: US Army War College, 1962). MHI.

USARSO (US Army Southern Command). 'Operation Just Cause/Promote Liberty Supplement', in *Annual Command History for Fiscal 1990* (History Office, USARSO, Fort Clayton, Panama).

USASOC (United States Army Special Operations Command). *To Free From Oppression: A Concise History of US Army Special Forces, Civil Affairs, Psychological Operations and the John F. Kennedy Special Warfare Center and School* (Fort Bragg, NC: USASOC, Directorate of History and Museums, 1994).

— Untitled information sheet provided by USASOC Public Affairs Office on 18 November 1996.

USAWC (US Army War College). *Case Study: Operation Urgent Fury* (Department of Military Strategy, Planning and Operations, Carlisle Barracks, PA, 1993).

USCONARC (US Continental Army Command). 'Lessons Learned', CON PAM 350-30-1, Headquarters, Fort Monroe, VA, 18 October 1965, WNR VN CONARC.

— 'Report on the World Wide Combat Arms Conference II', Fort Leavenworth, KS, 25–29 June 1962. TAG Records File, No: 338-71A2332, Box 4, WNR.

— 'Master Copy Final Report', World Wide Combat Arms Conference, Fort Sill, OK, 7–11 December 1959. TAG Records File, No: 338-71A2332, Box 4, WNR.
— 'Counterinsurgency Conference Report', Fort Monroe, VA, 23–24 March 1962. Historical Branch, US Army Training and Doctrine Command, Fort Monroe, VA.
US Congress. House. Khruschev's Speech of 6 January 1961, A Summary and Interpretive Analysis. 87th Cong., 1st sess., 1961. S. Doc 14.
— Committee on the Judiciary. Terroristic Activity, International Terrorism: Hearings before the Committee on Judiciary. 94th Cong., 1st sess., 14 May 1975, part 4 (Washington, DC: GPO, 1975).
— Committee on Appropriations 1983. *Department of Defense Authorization of Appropriations For Fiscal Year 1984: Hearings before the Committee on Appropriations on HR 2287*. 98th Cong., 1st sess., part 6 (Washington, DC: GPO, 1983).
— Committee on Appropriations 1984. *Department of Defense Appropriations for Fiscal Year 1985: Hearings before the Committee on Appropriations*. 98th Cong., 2nd sess., part 2. Prepared by John F. Lehman, Jr, Secretary of the Navy (Washington, DC: GPO, 7 March 1984), pp. 485–759.
— Committee on Appropriations 1984. *Department of Defense Appropriations for Fiscal Year 1985: Hearings before the Committee on Appropriations*. 98th Cong., 2nd sess., part 2. Prepared by Gen. John A. Wickham, Army Chief of Staff (Washington, DC: GPO, 8 March 1984), pp. 231–483.
— Committee on Appropriations 1984. *Department of Defense Appropriations for Fiscal Year 1985: Hearings before the Committee on Appropriations*. 98th Cong., 2nd sess., part 8 (Washington, DC: GPO, 1984).
— Committee on Armed Services 1981. *Military Posture: Hearings before the Committee on Armed Services*. 97th Cong., 1st sess., part 1 (Washington, DC: GPO, 1981).
— Committee on Armed Services, 1983. *Department of Defense Authorization and Oversight Hearings before the Committee on Armed Services*. Testimony by Gen. Donn A. Starry, Commander, US Army Training and Doctrine Command. 98th Cong., 1st sess., part 3 (Washington, DC: GPO, 1983), pp. 1815–28.
— Committee on Armed Services, 1983. *Defense Department Authorization and Oversight Hearings on HR 2287* (HR 2969). 98th Cong., 1st sess., part 6, 1983. H.R. 2287, 1–76.

— Committee on Armed Services 1984. *Department of Defense Authorization and Oversight Hearings on H.R. 2287 (H.R. 2969): Hearings before the Committee on Armed Services.* 98th Cong., 1st sess., part 6 (Washington, DC: GPO, March, April 1984), pp. 1–76, HR2287.

— Committee on Armed Services 1987. Remarks before Special Operations Panel by Lt. Gen. Harry A. Goodall, Deputy Commander in Chief, USSOCOM, undated. Copy provided by HQ USSOCOM.

— Committee on Armed Services, 1988. *Hearings on Special Operations and LTC,* 100th Cong. 1st sess. (Washington, DC: GTP, Jan.–Dec. 1987, published 1988).

— Committee on Foreign Affairs, 1981. 'The Iran Hostage Crisis – A Chronology of Daily Developments', report prepared for the Committee on Foreign Affairs by the Foreign Affairs and National Defense Division. 97th Cong., 1st sess. Congressional Research Service, Library of Congress, March 1981.

— Committee on International Affairs, 1976. Comptroller General. Seizure of the Mayaguez. 94th Cong., 2nd sess., part 4. (Washington, DC: GPO, 4 October 1976).

US Congress. Joint Session. Hearings: Select Committee on the Iran Contra Investigation. Testimony by National Security Council Aide (Lt Col. Oliver North, US Marine Corps). 100th Cong., 1st sess., part 1, 7–10 July 1987.

— Senate Report 100-216/House Report 100-433. *Report of the Congressional Committees Investigating the Iran–Contra Affair with Supplemental, Minority and Additional Views* (Washington, DC: GPO, November 1987).

US Congress. Senate. Committee on Armed Services. *Bombing in Cambodia: Hearings before the Committee on Armed Services.* 93rd Cong., 1st sess. (Washington, DC: GPO, 1973).

— Committee on Armed Services 1981. *Nomination of Caspar Weinberger to be Secretary of Defense: Hearings before the Committee on Armed Services.* 97th Cong., 1st sess. (Washington, DC: GPO, 6 January 1981; published 1981).

— Committee on Armed Services 1988. *Nomination of Robert T. Herres, et al.: Hearings before the Committee on Armed Services.* Includes testimony concerning nomination of Kenneth P. Bergquist to be ASD for Special Operations and LIC. 100th Cong., 1st sess. (Washington, DC: GPO, January through December 1987; published 1988).

— Committee on Armed Services 1988. *Nomination of Charles S.*

    Whitehouse: Hearings before the Committee on Armed Services.
    Includes testimony concerning nomination of Ambassador Charles
    S. Whitehouse to be ASD for Special Operations and LIC. 100th
    Cong., 2nd sess. (Washington, DC: GPO, 12 July 1988).
— Armed Services Committee Hearing Transcript, Richard Chaney,
    Secretary of Defense and General Colin Powell, Chairman Joint
    Chiefs of Staff – FY 1991 Defense Budget, 1 February 1990. Legi-
    Slate transcript ID 560095.
— Committee on Governmental Affairs, 1978. *An Act to Combat
    International Terrorism: Hearing before the Committee on
    Governmental Affairs.* Testimony of David E. McGiffert.
    (Washington, DC: GPO, 1978, 192).
— Committee on the Judiciary, 1975. *Terroristic Activity, Inter-
    national Terrorism: Hearings before the Committee on the Judiciary.*
    94th Cong., 1st sess., part 4 (Washington, DC: GPO, 14 May 1975).
— Congressional Record 1986. 99th Cong., 2nd sess. (26 June
    1986), pp. 3–4, HR5109 and S.2403.
— Congressional Record 1988. 100th Cong., 2nd sess. (12 July
    1988), p. 16. S9439.
— Public Law 597, The Lodge Bill: An Act to Provide for the
    Enlistment of Aliens in the Regular Army. 81st Cong., 2nd sess.,
    30 June 1950. S. 2269.
US Department of the Army. Office of the Chief of Information,
    *The Development and Training of the South Vietnamese Army
    1950–1972.* Official DA study by Brig. Gen. James Lawton
    Collins, Jr. (Washington, DC: GPO, 1975).
US Department of Defense. Intelligence Information Report, VC
    Morale and Activity IV CTZ, 17 March 1970.
— 'Rescue Mission Report' (also known as the 'Holloway Report')
    (Washington, DC: GPO, 1980).
— *Annual Report Fiscal Year 1982* (Washington, DC: GPO, 29
    January 1981).
— *Conduct of the Persian Gulf War.* Final Report to Congress
    (Washington, DC: USDOD, April 1992).
US Department of State. NSC 68. 'United States Objectives and
    Programs for National Security', 14 April 1950, in *US Dept of
    State, Foreign Relations of the United States: 1950,* vol. 1, 240
    (Washington, DC: GPO, 1951).
US Joint Chiefs of Staff. *Rescue Mission Report* (Washington, DC:
    GPO, August 1980). Also known as the 'Holloway Report'.
USMACV. 'Command History, 1965' and Annex B, 'Command
    History, 1966', HRB, CMH.

US President. *Public Papers of the Presidents of the United States.*
'Special Message to the Congress on the Defense Budget', 28
March 1961 (Washington, DC: GPO, 1961).
— *Public Papers of the Presidents of the United States* (Washington,
DC: Office of the Federal Register. National Archives and
Records Service, 1974), Richard M. Nixon, 1968–1974.
— 1969. Item 195. 'Address to the Nation on Vietnam', 14 May
1969, 369–95.
— 1970. Item 373. Remarks in Ashville, NC, 20 October 1970,
373–7.
— 1971: Item 126. 'Address to the Nation on Progress Toward Peace
in Vietnam', 20 April 1970, 373–7.
— 1972: Item 134. 'Address to the Nation on the Situation in
Southeast Asia', 7 April 1971, 522–7.
— 'The War in Vietnam', *Vital Speeches of the Day*, 35, 12 (1 June
1969): 482–4.
— 'A Vietnam Plan', *Vital Speeches of the Day*, 36, 23 (15 November
1969): 67–9.
— *Public Papers of the Presidents of the United States* (Washington,
DC: Office of the Federal Register. National Archives and
Records Service, 1969–1972, Richard M. Nixon).
— 1969. 'Remarks on Arrival at Guam International Airport', 25
July 1969.
— 1972. 'A Redefinition of the United States Role in the World', 25
February 1971, United States Foreign Policy – 1971 (Washington,
DC: US Department of State, Richard M. Nixon, 1972).
— *Public Papers of the Presidents of the United States* (Washington,
DC: Office of the Federal Register). National Archives and
Records Service, 1961–1982, Ronald W. Reagan.
— State of the Union Address, 1985.
— 'Unified and Specified Commands; Message from the President',
23 April 1987. House Document 100-69, House of Repre-
sentatives, US Congress (Washington, DC: GPO, 1987).
— *National Security Strategy of the United States.* Executive Office
of the President (Washington, DC: GPO, January 1988).
US Secretary of Defense. Report of the Secretary of Defense to
Congress, 1952 (Washington, DC: GPO, 1952).
— *Rescue Mission Report* (also known as the 'Holloway Report')
(Washington, DC: Department of Defense, August 1980).
— *Annual Report to the Congress.* Caspar Weinberger, Secretary of
Defense (Washington, DC: GPO, 1981).
— *Annual Report to Congress on the Fiscal Year 1985 Budget, Fiscal*

Year 1986 Authorization Request, and Fiscal Year 1985–89 Defense Programs. Report by Caspar W. Weinberger, Secretary of Defense (Washington, DC: GPO, 1 February 1984).

— *Annual Report to Congress Fiscal Year 1988*, Caspar W. Weinberger, Secretary of Defense (Washington, DC: GPO, 12 January 1987).

— *Annual Report to Congress Fiscal Year 1989*, Frank C. Carlucci, Secretary of Defense (Washington, DC: GPO, 18 February 1988).

USSOCOM (US Special Operations Command), *Special Operations Forces in Operation Earnest Will/Prime Chance I 1987–1989* (USSOCOM History and Research Office, McDill Air Force Base, FL, Sept. 1995).

— Document '2socorg', 1996, provided by History Office, USSOCOM.

— 'USSOCOM Counterdrug Efforts' (USSOCOM History Office, McDill Air Force Base, FL, 1997).

— *Special Operations in Peace and War* (McDill Air Force Base, FL: USSOCOM, 1996).

— 'Special Operations Forces', factsheet provided by Public Affairs Office, USSOCOM, McDill Air Force Base, FL; undated, received by author December 1996.

— *United States Special Operations Forces 1996 Posture Statement* (McDill Air Force Base, FL: USSOCOM, 1996).

USSOUTHCOM (US Southern Command). 'Operation Just Cause', briefing dated 1990, unpaged. The account of the Ranger missions is in the section titled 'Torriojos' and the Pacora Bridge account in the section titled 'Holding the Pacora River Bridge'. Collection of the Military History Institute, Carlisle Barracks, PA.

US Strategic Operations Force Far East (Provisional). 'Position Paper On Unconventional Warfare', 1 February 1957, MHI.

US War Department. General Staff. G-2 unsigned letter from HQ Western Task Force, 26 November 1942, Research Group 319, G2 322.001 (1 October 1942), Box 576, MBNA.

— 'Report of the War Department Manpower Board', extracts in 'Minutes of the General Council', Office of the Chief of Staff, Department of the Army; 13 November 1945. MHI.

— General Staff. Military Intelligence Division. Memorandum from Col. M. A. Soloman, Asst. Executive Officer, Director of Intelligence, to: Director Organization and Training Division, subject: Airborne Reconnaissance Units, 6 March 1947. Record Group 319, Army Intelligence Files 1941–1948, 373.14, Box 874, MBNA.

— History Project, Strategic Services Unit. *War Reports of the OSS* (Washington, DC: GPO, 1976, 2 vols).

Utley, Robert M. *Frontier Regulars: The United States Army and the Indian* (New York: Macmillan, 1973).

Utley, Robert M. and Washburn, Wilcomb E. *Indian Wars* (New York: American Heritage, 1985).

Vagts, Alfred. *A History of Militarism* (New York: Alfred J. Knopf, 1937).

Valentine, Douglas. *The Phoenix Program* (New York: William Morrow and Company, 1990).

Vandegrift, A. A. (Gen., US Marine Corps [ret.]). (USMC Commandant during World War II who abolished Marine Raiders and reconstituted them as a regular regiment). *Once A Marine* (New York: W. W. Norton, 1964).

Vanderpool, Jay D. (Col., US Army/CIA [ret.]). Senior Officer's Oral History Program. Transcript of interview, 1983, MHI.

Vane Timothy, LTC, USA. Public Affairs Officer, XVIII Airborne Corps in Haiti, correspondence with the author dated 10 May 1996.

Vann, John P. Letter to Fred O'Niel, Refugee Coordinator, USOM Saigon, dated 25 September 1965.

— Memorandum, US Embassy, Saigon. Discussion with Ambassador Porter, 16 March 1966, Vann Papers, MHI.

Vaughn, Charles A. (Col., US Army). 'Progress Report on USA. Rangers' to HQ Special Service Brigade, US Army Northern Ireland Forces estimated date per location in file 1942, Microfilm INBN 72-37, roll 8, frames 84-85. WRC.

VDD *Vietnam: Definitive Documentation*. Gareth Porter, ed., Coleman Enterprises, Stanfordville, New York (1979). Vol. 2 includes trans. of several PRD/NLF documents esp. item 58 'Direction of the Revolution in the South' (1979, 119–20) and item 23, 'Study Document on Revolutionary Strategy in the South' (1979, 52).

Vlahos, Michael E. 'Responding to Locally Generated Contingencies', in John H. Mauer and Richard A. Porthin, eds., *Military Intervention in the Third World* (New York: Praeger, 1987), pp. 207–30.

Volckman, Russell W. *We Remained: Three Years Behind Enemy Lines in the Philippines* (New York: W. W. Norton, 1954).

Vought, Donald B. 'Preparing for the Wrong War', *Military Review* (May 1977): 16–34

Wakeman, Daniel, LTC, US Army Special Forces; telephone interview, 12 February 1997. LTC Wakeman was Commander, C Co, 1st

Bn 10th SFG, Operation Proven Force, Jan.–April 1991. He also served in Operation Provide Comfort in April and May of 1991.

Waller, Douglas C. *The Commandos: The Inside Story of America's Secret Soldiers* (New York: Simon & Schuster, 1994).

Walt, Lewis (Gen., US Marine Corps). *Strange War, Strange Strategy* (New York: Funk & Wagnalls, 1970).

Watson, Peter. *War on the Mind: The Military Uses and Abuses of Psychology* (New York: Basic Books, 1978).

Webbe, Stephen. 'Chorus of Retired Admirals and Generals: Make US Forces Battle Ready', *Christian Science Monitor* (31 December 1980): 6.

Weigley, Russell F. *History of the United States Army* (New York: Macmillan, 1967).

— *The American Way of War* (New York: Macmillan, 1973).

West, Francis J., Jr. (Capt., US Marine Corps). *Small Unit Action in Vietnam*, Historical Branch, G3 Division, Headquarters USMC, Washington, DC (New York: Arno Press, 1967).

Westmoreland, William C. 'Commanders Estimate of the Military Situation in South Vietnam (March 1965)', dated 26 March 1965.

— Report on the War in Vietnam. Part 2 'Report on Operations in South Vietnam (January 1964–June 1968)' (Washington, DC: GPO, n.d.). (Internal evidence indicates 1968. Adm. U. S. Grant Sharp (CINCPAC) is also listed as author, but this seems to be a courtesy to Westmoreland's nominal superior since the document appears to be a USMACV product.)

— Message to Harold K. Johnson (Army Chief of Staff), 28 May 1967, Westmoreland Papers, MHI, Carlisle Barracks, PA.

— *A Soldier Reports* (New York: Da Capo Press, 1989). This is a re-issue of Westmoreland's 1976 narrative of his command tenure in Vietnam (New York: Doubleday). New introductory material was added.

— Personal interview with author, West Point, NY, 25 April 1990.

Wickham, John A. (Gen., US Army, Army Chief of Staff). 'Wickham Says Time is Right to Create Light Divisions', *Army Times* 44, 12 (31 October 1983).

— 'White Paper', reprinted in *Army Times* 43, 30 (7 May 1984): 10–12.

Wienstein, Michael P. 'The Eisenhower Doctrine', Seminar Paper, University of Pennsylvania, 1985. Document collection, USMA Library, West Point, NY.

Woolard, R. W. 'Special Operations – A Perspective', Student monograph, US Army War College, Carlisle, PA, 1968.

Yarborough, William P. (Gen., US Army Special Forces, [ret.]). Yarborough Papers, OHP, MHI.

— Lt Gen., US Army [ret.]). 'Counterinsurgency: The US Role', Conference paper, Conference on Protracted Warfare, Fletcher School of Law and Diplomacy, Medford, MA, 22–24 April 1987.

Yergin, Daniel. *Shattered Peace: The Origins of the Cold War and the National Security State* (Boston, MA: Houghton Mifflin, 1977).

Zasloff, Joseph J. *Rural Resettlement in Vietnam*. Michigan State University Vietnam Advisory Group, USAID contract ICA c1126 (USAID:Saigon). Collection of the USMA Library, West Point, NY. Undated but internal evidence suggests *c.* 1963.

Index